CENGAGE
Learning™

INFOTRAC®
COLLEGE EDITION
The Online Library

Use the access code inside this card to activate your

FREE 4-Month
Subscription

Exclusively from
Cengage Learning

Here is your FREE access code to InfoTrac® College Edition
Only available with NEW copies of Cengage Learning textbooks

To open, detach at perforation

DO NOT DISCARD
Your Access Code to
Online Library Inside

academic.cengage.com/infotrac

InfoTrac® College Edition offers:

- More than 10 million articles from nearly 5,000 academic journals and other sources

- Daily newspapers and monthly magazines

- Online help with research papers

- Easy-to-use search features

Log On & Get Started

ISBN-13: 978-0-534-27494-8
ISBN-10: 0-534-27494-3

Beyond Policy Analysis

Public Issue Management in Turbulent Times

FOURTH EDITION

Beyond Policy Analysis

Public Issue Management in Turbulent Times

FOURTH EDITION

Leslie A. Pal
Carleton University

NELSON / EDUCATION

NELSON EDUCATION

Beyond Policy Analysis: Public Issue Management in Turbulent Times, Fourth Edition
by Leslie A. Pal

Associate Vice President, Editorial Director:
Evelyn Veitch

Editor-in-Chief, Higher Education:
Anne Williams

Publisher:
Cara Yarzab

Acquisitions Editor:
Bram Sepers

Marketing Manager:
Ann Byford

Developmental Editor:
Heather Parker

Permissions Coordinator:
Natalie Russell

Production Service:
Macmillan Publishing Solutions

Copy Editor:
Gail Marsden

Proofreader:
Dianne Fowlie

Indexer:
Maura Brown

Senior Production Coordinator:
Ferial Suleman

Design Director:
Ken Phipps

Managing Designer:
Franca Amore

Interior Design:
Nelson Gonzalez

Cover Design:
Peter Papayanakis

Cover Image:
"Lost at Sea" by Anthony Sepers

Compositor:
Macmillan Publishing Solutions

Printer:
Webcom

Library and Archives Canada Cataloguing in Publication Data

Pal, Leslie A. (Leslie Alexander), 1954–
    Beyond policy analysis : public issue management in turbulent times / Leslie A. Pal. — 4th ed.

Includes bibliographical references and index.

ISBN: 978-0-17-650102-0

    1. Policy sciences—Textbooks.
2. Political planning—Canada—Textbooks. I. Title.

H97.P343 2009   320.6
C2009-900076-8

ISBN-13: 978-0-17-650102-0
ISBN-10: 0-17-650102-9

Table of Contents

Preface

This book is entitled *Beyond Policy Analysis* not because I consider policy analysis to be unimportant, but because I consider it so important that we need to think carefully about the craft of policy analysis in the modern world. The first edition of the book (1997) argued that this world had changed so dramatically that it was important to go beyond conventional categories and tools of analysis. I identified three broad factors that were affecting both the theory and practice of policy analysis. The first was the changing nature of governance under the pressures of globalization, information technology, demands for more efficient and leaner government, and more deeply diverse societies and cultures. The second was the emerging demand for better and more effective government in the face of these challenges and forces. This was not simply about making government more business-like, though in the late 1990s and early 2000s, that was the high note in complaints about how modern governments organized themselves and worked. It was also about a renewed appreciation concerning the importance of government and good policy in dealing with a host of new challenges, from terrorism and security to climate change. The third factor was a fresh debate within the discipline of policy analysis about its intellectual foundations and practical accomplishments. Then, as now, it seemed to me that these factors force a reconsideration of what it is that we do when we engage in policy analysis.

None of these fundamentals has changed in any significant way. It remains impossible to discuss public policy in Canada, or elsewhere for that matter, without considering globalization, information technology, changing public values and cultural assumptions, citizen distrust, new public management techniques and practices, policy networks, consultation, or engagement. But there have been some changes in tone and emphasis since 2006, all of which are reflected and discussed in this new edition. There is, for example, a continued acute sense that globalization is having tremendous effects on all domestic governments. However, if anything, our appreciation of the impact of global competition (e.g., China, India), global value chains, and global threats to security is even greater now than it was then. The sense of interdependency around issues like climate change and security has increased, and been intensified by the global financial crisis, leading to a G-20 meeting in Washington in November, 2008 to discuss a coordinated, global response. As a significant immigrant receiving country, Canada has also experienced globalization through flows of human populations and the integration of newcomers to our society and economy. Those newcomers are essential for economic growth and a vibrant labour force, but also pose challenges of social cohesion and accommodation. Since 2006, Europe has experienced riots and disruption around integration and accommodation of Muslim populations, especially in Denmark (the Danish cartoon incident) and France. In the United States there has been serious discussion of fencing off the border with Mexico and making English the official language. Canada has mercifully been spared these extremes, but tensions in Quebec led to a commission on "reasonable accommodation" that raised fundamental (and healthy) questions about citizenship and social cohesion.

On questions of governance, the previous edition spent some time considering the impact of a broad movement in the 1990s entitled "new public management" (NPM). There were several variants of NPM (for example, in Scandinavian countries versus Anglo-Saxon democracies), but all boiled down to attempts to make government more business-like, smaller and more efficient, and more focused on policy than on delivery of services (which could be either outsourced or devolved onto different types of agencies). Canada was not immune to the allure of NPM, and indeed echoed many of its main tenets in various government reform projects between 1985 and 2005. As I noted in the previous edition, however, a post-9/11 world meant that at a minimum, government could not abandon its security responsibilities, and indeed that these responsibilities in many ways called for larger and more robust government machinery. It was also clear by 2005, whatever one's political inclinations, that government was a necessary and vital tool in addressing some key challenges facing the country, such as health care, epidemics, and competitiveness in the new, global knowledge economy.

This edition argues that NPM continues to have a powerful effect in many areas of governance, but has been overtaken by several new perspectives, some unique to Canada and some more general. One of the more general perspectives, seen reflected in OECD documents and reports, is an even more intense appreciation of the importance of governance for a well-functioning society and economy. In little over a decade, leading international institutions such as the OECD, the World Bank, and the donor community (including international financial institutions), have collectively come to the conclusion that good governance is the foundation for economic and social development. As Chapter 9 shows, this is not merely rhetoric—there has been an explosion in governance measures and indicators, all based on core assumptions about what constitutes good governance, whether it is the quality of the bureaucracy or financial management systems. Two other factors are specific to Canada. One is the continued emphasis on fiscal probity. The last edition was somewhat agnostic on whether the phobia over deficit spending would continue past the mid-2000s, given the constant temptation for governments to spend their way to political popularity. What could not have been anticipated at the time was the continued boom in the Canadian economy (slowing in mid-2008 in the face of the US recession), rising resource and commodity prices, and the consequent tax haul that most Canadian governments enjoyed in the last three years. The federal government has been in the happy situation of being able to increase its spending, cut taxes, and still run surpluses (though of decreasing size). All provincial budgets have been in surplus as well. It seems that public and political disapproval of deficits has stayed firm, though the financial crisis in the fall of 2008 forced unprecedented bail-outs to ward off a deep recession, and Ontario projected a deficit for 2009 as the federal government reluctantly admitted that deficits might once again be in its future as well. This sentiment has policy consequences for how governments raise their revenues and how they frame their spending initiatives.

The second factor peculiar to Canada (though not exclusively) has been the emphasis on values, ethics, and accountability in the last three years. The federal Conservatives won the 2006 election in large part due to the sponsorship scandal and the Gomery Inquiry that afflicted their Liberal predecessors. Once in office, their first piece of legislation was the Federal Accountability Act, which introduced sweeping changes across the federal system in terms of oversight and reporting. Indeed, those changes were so extensive that within a year of passing the legislation there was serious discussion about the federal public sector being tied down and paralyzed by a "web of rules." This concern formed the backdrop to yet another effort at public service renewal—an effort that this time would not be guided by an NPM emphasis on downsizing government, but rather by a sense that the public sector was crucial to Canada's success as a country, and that a reinvigorated public service would somehow have to combine service, efficiency, ethics, and accountability.

This fourth edition has been thoroughly revised and updated to take account of these shifts, as well as numerous other developments in Canada and internationally since 2006. As with previous editions, each chapter is roughly divided in two: the first half reviews the current literature in the field on the chapter's subject, and the second half goes beyond and looks at contemporary changes and challenges. Chapter 9 concludes the book with a discussion of what distinguishes good policy and good governance. Each chapter closes with a list of key concepts, which are printed in bold in the text, along with suggestions for further readings. Weblinks relevant to each chapter may be found at the book's website, www.policyanalysis.nelson.com

I am grateful for the advice and comments of several colleagues: Cheryl Collier, Rianne Mahon, Lisa Mills, Ellen Russell, and Glen Toner, all from the School of Public Policy and Administration at Carleton University. Students in my undergraduate course at Carleton's Kroeger College, and in my graduate policy seminar at the School, contributed several valuable ideas and insights that flowed into the revisions for this edition. My thanks as well to Ha Nguyen, whose outstanding research assistance made this project a much more enjoyable and efficient enterprise than it might otherwise have been.

The team at Nelson Education Ltd. was, once again, both professional and supportive: Bram Sepers, Cara Yarzab, Heather Parker, Susan Calvert, Gunjan Chandola and freelance editor, Gail Marsden.

My deepest thanks go to my family: Mary, my wife, Matthew and Michael, my two sons, and Meredith, my daughter. Their support and love during this project and others over these past years has moved me deeply, and I will strive always, however imperfectly, to be worthy of them.

1

Policy Analysis:
Concepts and Practice

Public policies are an essential element in modern democracies in that they provide both guidance for government officials and accountability links to citizens. Governments may do things for a wide variety of reasons—patronage, political competition, reflex, tradition—but when their actions are grounded in policy, they presumably are taking a course of action that has been thought through in terms of the nature of the problem they are addressing and the circumstances they face. Insofar as these policies are visible and measurable to the public, they become key tests of the government's record at election time. Thus, organizing policy work in government and developing a public conversation about policy is central to healthy democratic politics. Despite general misgivings about the specific analytical techniques used by policymakers to achieve their objectives, the importance of policy to democratic governance has enjoyed a resurgence in recent years. Indeed, there has been growing domestic and international interest in developing policy capacity. This chapter introduces the key concepts of public policy and policy analysis and explores some of their characteristics. It then reviews some prominent Canadian and international examples of the global policy "movement" that has developed recently in the face of new governance challenges. These challenges are taken up in detail in Chapter 2.

What Is Public Policy?

Citizens expect many things from their governments, but at the very least they expect intelligent decisionmaking. Perhaps even more importantly, however, they expect those decisions to flow from some general position or vision. Unfortunately, governments can be very decisive without being terribly intelligent. Intelligent decisions come from operating within some consistent framework, however general. We will return to this issue of consistency below, but for the moment it should be clear that the very nature of intelligent and accountable **governance** in a democracy demands more than mere decisions—it demands decisionmaking guided by a framework. In short, we demand that our governments have policies.

For the purpose of this book, **public policy** will be defined as a course of action or inaction chosen by public authorities to address a given problem or interrelated set of problems. Several aspects of this definition bear emphasis. First, note that it refers to a course of action. This picks up on the idea of frameworks or patterns—policies are guides to a range of related actions in a given field (Anderson, 2006). A "policymaker" is someone who develops these guides, a "policy-taker" is someone who operates within that **policy framework**, applying it to new situations. Immigration policy, for example, is a broad framework that structures the actions of a host of different organizations, from our foreign embassies to refugee boards at home. When political parties differ over their immigration policies, we know that they differ over first principles (e.g., open versus closed immigration, admission based on family considerations or economic contributions). When a policy is changed, the actions that take place within its framework are reconfigured to yield different results.

Another aspect of the definition is that it refers to action as well as inaction, as long as it has been chosen by public authorities (Kraft and Furlong, 2007: 5). As Howlett and Ramesh put it, "Public policy is, at its simplest, a choice made by government to undertake some course of action" (2003, p. 5). Consider the issue of recognizing same-sex marriages. Until a few years ago, it never would have entered the minds of most policymakers that this was a policy issue to be addressed, and so the absence of action on this front cannot be seen as a policy decision. On the other hand, once the Supreme Court decided in May 1999 in *M. v. H.* that existing federal and provincial legislation discriminated against gay and lesbian couples, and once litigation around the issue occurred in British Columbia, Ontario, and Quebec, government inaction could properly be defined as a policy choice. In 2005, in the face of these court rulings, Parliament passed legislation to legalize same-sex marriage. In the 2006 federal election, the Conservatives promised to hold a free vote on the issue, did so, and were defeated 175–123 on December 7, 2006. Prime Minister Stephen Harper then stated that he considered the matter closed—the government's policy was not to act again on the issue. Not everything that governments do is policy driven, of course. Indeed, in a "crisis situation" governments have little option but to react. As deLeon (1988) points out, a crisis is a surprise, it is "unpredictable and unavoidable" (p. 116). Rochefort and Cobb (1994) note that decisionmaking in crisis situations is synonymous with an emergency mentality that enables "quick responses but also tended to produce temporary Band-Aid solutions" to major public problems (p. 21). As well, some actions taken by government agencies are so far down the chain of implementation that they are properly seen as reflections of organizational routine rather than policy per se. The municipal bus driver's route is a function of policy; changes in routes due to road construction or seasonal weather are just administrative decisions.

Finally, note that the definition refers to problems and interrelated sets of problems. Public policy, whatever its symbolic dimensions, is seen by policymakers and citizens as a means of dealing with problems or sometimes with opportunities. In this sense, policies are largely "instrumental"— that is, they are not ends in themselves, or even good in themselves, but are instruments or tools to tackle issues of concern to the political community. But the instrumental character of public policy does not remove it from the realm of values. For one thing, problems and opportunities are defined as such only in relation to goals or things we value. For another, means and ends are not so easily separated—in public policymaking, to use the "right tool" means both using the tool best suited (in an instrumental sense) to the task as well as the tool that is consistent with a morally acceptable range of government behaviour. The appropriate balance of technical or instrumental analysis and values in policy work is a perennial debate in the field. The rationalist roots of policy analysis in the 1960s held out the hope that with enough data and analysis, policy problems could be solved largely in technical terms, without too much contamination by values. A more recent trend in the literature has argued that almost everything in policy analysis is affected by values and that consequently the challenge is to develop techniques and processes of tackling public problems that encourage exchanges and ultimately consensus-building among citizens, politicians, and experts (Stone, 2001; Fischer and Forester, 1993; Fischer, 1993; Fischer, 2003). As we will note below, the contemporary practice among policy analysts seems to have settled on working conscientiously within policy "visions" articulated by democratically elected governments but being sensitive to the way in which both analysts' and citizens' values will affect each phase of the analytical process as well as **policy development**, implementation, and evaluation.

The most important overarching value in public policy is the public interest. It is the touchstone or benchmark for all that democratic governments do. The Values and Ethics Code for the Public Service, for example, notes that the "democratic mission of the Public Service is to assist Ministers, under law, to serve the public interest." It states that "public servants, in fulfilling their official duties and responsibilities, shall make decisions in the public interest." The Tait Report (*A Strong Foundation*, 2000) noted that a "fundamental value of public service is loyalty to the public interest or the public good" and argued that devotion to the public interest was the defining characteristic of the public service as a profession. Moreover, the concept is more than purely philosophical—it is commonly referred to in regulatory decisions, and in one estimate, is mentioned 224 times in 84 federal statutes (MacNair, 2006). There is no single definition of the public interest, but there are some basic orientations that stress some balance of the majority's views, common interests within the political community (e.g., clean water and safe streets), and binding values (e.g., respect for minorities) (Pal and Maxwell, 2004). Different political actors will define the public interest in different ways, but will typically justify their policy recommendations by that standard.

This mix of values and technical analysis can be illustrated with reference to a policy field that at first blush seems almost completely technical—taxation. At its most basic level, tax policy is about generating revenue for government. Taxes can also be used, however, as instruments that encourage or discourage certain kinds of behaviour: lower business taxes, for example, might encourage investment, while higher "sin" taxes on alcohol and cigarettes might discourage drinking and smoking (Bird and Stoney, 2006). Both of these dimensions entail technical considerations: what is the ideal or best level and incidence of taxation to both produce revenues and have the desired policy outcomes? Overly high levels of taxation will encourage tax evasion, thus lowering yields. Then there are questions of the progressivity of tax rates, the number of income brackets, and so on. But the actual policy debate around taxes in Canada and in other countries is also strongly affected by values. The Conservatives promised to lower the GST from 7 percent to 5 percent, and did so through two consecutive budgets in 2006 and 2007. Virtually every economist in the country disagreed with the move, arguing that technically it made more sense to keep consumption taxes high and lower income taxes, thus lowering disincentives to work. The Tories ignored the advice, partly for political reasons, but also because they believed in the value of lower taxes overall—they reduced both the GST and income taxes in those two budgets. The same value debate can be seen over flat taxes (Alberta has had a flat income tax for years). While there are important technical issues over the efficacy of flat versus progressive taxes, a good part of the debate is between alternative visions of the public interest.

Policies rarely tackle single problems; rather, they deal with clusters of entangled problems that may have contradictory solutions. Many policy problems are complex "because of their size and breadth; they comprise *sets* of other, perhaps smaller problems whose very interconnectedness makes them difficult to comprehend, and whose boundaries are difficult to define across issues and over time" (Desveaux, Lindquist, and Toner, 1994, p. 497). Policy design therefore becomes a process of balancing different solutions that address different aspects of a cluster of problems. In

2002, for example, the House of Commons ratified the Kyoto Protocol, and since then has found itself working "to resolve the inherent contradiction between two of its stated policy goals: first, the extraction and sale of fossil fuel in order to contribute to economic development, and second, reductions in fossil fuel consumption" (Vannijnatten and MacDonald, 2003, p. 72). The federal Conservative government openly attacked the Protocol, claiming repeatedly that Canada could not meet its 2012 targets without inflicting severe economic damage. Indeed, at the UN Climate Change Conference in Bali in December 2007, the government initially resisted the targets recommended by the Intergovernmental Panel on Climate Change, proposing its own emissions plan with significantly lower targets. At the eleventh hour, facing strong international pressure and the possibility of being isolated from world opinion, the government reversed itself and agreed to enter into negotiations for a protocol that would replace Kyoto. There are severe complications in dealing with this policy problem. First, there is the question of how to meet these more stringent targets—through instruments like a carbon tax or hard caps on emissions. Second, there is the regional character of the Canadian economy—Western provinces, in particular Alberta with its tar sands, are most exposed if the federal government moves seriously to curtail emissions. But the effects could be quite different in the Ontario industrial heartland. Finally, this is not a policy issue that can be resolved within one country's borders. It will require several more years of international negotiation, bringing in train a host of complicated foreign policy considerations. Unsurprisingly, given the technical, regional, and international dimensions of this policy issue, Ottawa has grappled for consistency and coherence without much luck.

The general character of a public policy therefore is that it is a guide to action, a plan, a framework, a course of action or inaction designed to deal with problems. This fits with the classic definitions of public policy in the field. Thomas Dye simply defined policy as "whatever governments choose to do or not to do" (1984, p. 1), and Harold Lasswell, arguably the originator of the modern policy sciences, defined it as "the most important choices" (1951, p. 5). Colebatch uses the term "coherence" to describe the same thing: "the assumption that all the bits of the action fit together, that they form part of an organized whole, a single system, and policy has to do with how this system is (or should be) steered" (Colebatch, 1998, p. 3). All of these definitions are grounded in a **rational model** of what it means to make decisions and respond to problems: "policy or strategy is formulated consciously, preferably analytically, and made explicit and then implemented formally" (Mintzberg and Jørgensen, 1987, p. 216). The intentional aspect, as we noted above, is important in this classic approach to defining policy. Another approach is to de-emphasize intention in favour of action: organizations can engage in consistent patterns of behaviour that emerge or form rather than being planned. Mintzberg and Jørgensen refer to this as **emergent strategies** that bubble up from all corners of an organization. In this perspective, policy is what governments actually do, not what they say or intend (Burt, 1995). As they point out, however, this concept is at most a corrective, since no organization could survive through the "hothouse" generation of uncoordinated strategies.

The definitional exercise does not end there, however. Of what does this guide or framework consist? If someone asked you to search out the government's policy on X and summarize it, what would you look for and where? Let's begin with the "where" since it takes us to yet another aspect of the definition that seems so natural that it is easily overlooked. Policies emanate from public authorities, but that is not to say that every public servant has the power to articulate policy. Since policy is a guide, it has a normative or coercive dimension: if the policy says you must do X, then you must (should) do X. Of course, not everyone is empowered to make these sorts of statements. Policies get made in organizations all the time, and typically they are made by "management." When we speak of public policy, we are referring to policies that deal with public problems, not organizational routines or structure. Policy, to put it simply, comes from those who have the legitimate authority to impose normative guidelines for action. In a democracy, policy is made by elected officials in concert with advisors from the higher levels of the administration. In strongly hierarchical systems of government like Canada's, public servants often ruefully joke that policy is whatever the minister says it is. The hard truth behind the humour is that since the minister is the elected official at the apex of the government department, only he or she has the right to enunciate policy. If the written documents say one thing, and the minister says something else, then that "something else" (at least temporarily) is the policy. Of course, once a policy has been authoritatively announced, nonelected officials can—and usually are required to—re-articulate and fine-tune policy. They also have an obligation to implement policy through programs. As well, the judiciary can get into the policy game by rendering judgments as to whether legislation is constitutional. Progress toward the legalization of same-sex marriages in Canada and in the United States has come about completely as a result of courts striking down existing marriage laws as contravening human rights.

Not everyone, therefore, is empowered to articulate policy. But for those who are, what is it that they are saying in a **policy statement**? Every policy has three key elements. The first is the definition of the problem, the second is the goals that are to be achieved, and the third is the instruments or means whereby the problem is to be addressed and the goals achieved.

Problem definition will be considered the central element of a policy statement. If there is no perceived problem, or a problem seems insoluble, one would hardly expect a public policy to solve it (though policies are sometimes framed as efforts to capitalize on an opportunity). In Chapter 3 we will consider the nature of problem definition more closely, but several points should be noted here. First, problems have to be recognized and defined. Recognition might be nothing more than a sense that "something is wrong" or that some new situation is looming. This often happens as a result of changes in some fairly systematic indicator that suggest a problem: "Such indicators abound in the political world because both governmental and non-governmental agencies routinely monitor various activities and events: highway deaths, disease rates, immunization rates, consumer prices, commuter and inter-city ridership, costs of entitlement programs, infant mortality rates, and many others" (Kingdon, 1995, p. 90). Second, the process of problem definition can either be exhaustive or casual. The Royal Commission on Aboriginal Peoples, for example, spent five years and over $50 million dealing with a two-page mandate calling for it to "investigate the evolution of the relationship among aboriginal peoples (Indian, Inuit and Métis), the Canadian government, and Canadian society as a whole" (P. C., 1995; 1997). On the other hand, the editorial pages overflow with instant experts on every conceivable public problem, and the policy positions of many groups are quite predictable since they base those positions less on analysis than on ideology. Third, as noted above, problems usually come in clusters, and so problem definitions typically operate across a range of dimensions. For example, trying to enhance innovation in the Canadian economy embraces tax policy, R&D in both the private and public sectors, and financial institutions and their lending practices. Fourth, problems can sometimes appear in the guise of a substantially changed context or situation, more like new realities or opportunities to which we have to adapt. The most arresting example of this aspect comes from our foreign policy. The impact of 9/11 and the destruction of the World Trade Center on Canada's security posture, our relations with the United States, our immigration and refugee policies, and our defence policy have been profound. Dealing with the global financial crisis may result in equally profound changes. Fifth, all problem definitions have a causal character: they indicate what the problem or issue is, and bundle that with some indication of the factors that led to it in the first place. Without this causal connection, it would be difficult to determine what to do about the problem.

The irony of problem definition is that while it is central to understanding public policy, it is rarely articulated in great detail in a policy statement itself. Interest groups and the media spend a great deal of time debating problem definitions and causal factors, and governments cannot avoid rooting their policy reactions in the often exhaustive analyses undertaken by their departments or other agencies. However, the policy statement in itself will rarely reflect this level of detail. As the definitions of public policy cited earlier suggest, policy is about action or deliberate inaction. It is the framework or guide, and while problem definition is crucial to understanding the rationale for policy, it is not in itself crucial to the statement of what that guide is to be. From a purely practical point of view as well, the rationale for an action is often considerably more complex than the action (or statement of what that action will be). The importance of this is simply that doing policy analysis—trying to make sense of a policy statement—involves a fair amount of detective work in tracking down both the policy statement and the supporting rationale in terms of problem definition.

Problem definitions are inextricably bound to **policy goals.** A key distinction, however, is between **general goals** and **policy-specific goals.** Health care policy, for example, has as its most general goal the maintenance and improvement of health among the Canadian population. At this level, almost no one disagrees about goals—the same is true of general goals in foreign policy, education policy, social policy, and so on. As policies get more specific, however, so do their goals. Those goals are still related to the broader ones, but they are contributory rather than final. A provincial health care policy to improve services for at-risk youth will have goals that are directly tied or related to those youth (e.g., safer pregnancies, reduced substance abuse). If achieved, those goals will contribute to the larger goals in the health care field.

As with problem definitions, intermediate policy goals sometimes have to be inferred since they are not always clearly stated. Occasionally, policymakers do articulate clear objectives and measurable intermediate goals. The Kyoto Protocol, for example, would have had Canada reduce its greenhouse gas emissions by 2012 to 6 percent below what they were in 1990. The agreement signed in Bali established a range of 25 to 40 percent reductions in the next decade. Another example was the 2007 federal–provincial agreement on Patient Wait Time Guarantees for certain medical procedures such as hip and knee replacements. In both of these examples, the goals are clear and numerical, and so make it easier to hold government to account. However, most policy goals are fuzzy: in these cases, the mere fact that the problem is not getting worse is sometimes used as a claim that the policy goals are being met. Another problem, of course, is that the real goals of the policy might be quite different from the stated goals. Politicians may decide that they want to "send a message" rather than solve a specific problem; the promise by the federal Conservative party to scrap the national gun registry is a case in point. The gun registry was introduced in 1995, but took until 2003 to be fully implemented. Originally estimated at a net cost of roughly $80 million, it was tagged by the Auditor General of Canada as approaching $1 billion. The registry became a lightning rod for public anger over waste, and became a fine symbol to attack. Another example is legislation introduced in 2008 (originally in 2007) to deal with violent crime. Provisions call for a Safer Communities strategy to deal with the connection between drugs, youth, and property crime, toughening the Youth Criminal Justice Act to make young offenders more accountable to victims, and new police powers under the National Anti-Drug Strategy. These measures are all defensible in policy terms, but they are also bundled with the government's desire to "send a message" that it is tough on crime (while the opposition is not).

The third key component of a public policy statement is some indication of the nature of the **policy instruments** or means whereby the problem is to be addressed and the goals achieved. Defining a policy problem and determining a solution are frequently overshadowed in the policymaking process by the question of "how." The choice of instruments is also entangled with a choice of the means of implementing those instruments. A government might choose, for example, to dissuade substance abuse through advertising. But who will do the advertising, and how? The first is an instrument choice issue, the second is an implementation issue. In principle, governments have a wide range of instruments from which to choose to tackle a policy problem and achieve their goals. They can rely on information (the advertising example), they can spend or tax, they can regulate, or in some instances they can set up agencies that combine these instruments under public auspices and address the problem directly. Linder and Peters (1989, p. 56) list as many as twenty-three types of instruments (see Chapter 4).

The theoretically wide range of choices over instruments is actually quite constrained in the real world. For one thing, even as policies change from time to time, governments take for granted the instruments to achieve their goals. Canadian broadcasting policy, for example, has evolved substantially since the 1960s, but the key instruments of achieving its policy goals—the Canadian Radio-Television and Telecommunications Commission and the Canadian Broadcasting Corporation—have remained. Health policy has changed marginally from time to time, and yet the key delivery mechanisms of hospitals, health care professions, and public expenditures have been quite stable since the 1960s (though information technology is being used in more sophisticated ways to enhance medical services). Sometimes, of course, policy changes so radically in terms of problem definition and goals that instruments get reconfigured quite dramatically as well. The federal government, for example, decided some years ago that innovation and research were keys to a productive, high-tech economy, and that universities in turn were the keys to fostering research and innovation. Over the last five years, Ottawa has become a major funder of university research through a host of new policy instruments such as Canada Research Chairs and the Millennium Foundation (discontinued in the February 2008 federal budget, but replaced with the Canada Student Grant Program), and its 2007 policy entitled *Mobilizing Science and Technology* which promised to spend an additional $1.9 billion.

Instrument choice can also be significantly constrained by perceptions of legitimacy. In only rare cases, for example, are Canadians prepared to accept government coercion over matters of sexual behaviour. Therefore, government action to deal with problems like sexually transmitted diseases has had to rely primarily on informational instruments. Legitimacy is elastic, and will change with circumstances (e.g., an epidemic of sexually transmitted diseases could lead to acceptance of stronger government action, just as the SARS crisis in 2003 gave public health and border officials legitimacy to impose stringent controls), and it is also culturally contingent. The Vancouver Health Authority, for example, since 2003 has been operating a safe injection site for heroin addicts, where they can come and get clean needles and shoot up under some degree of supervision. As a "harm reduction" strategy, this may make sense in the local context, but the practice has been widely criticized both in Canada and by the United States, and in mid-2008 Health Canada was re-evaluating the exemption that it provides so that the site can operate legally.

Finally, instrument choice can be limited by legal restrictions—a constitutional division of powers or international agreements that prohibit the use of some policy tools—or by practical constraints. Both are important. In the Canadian case, federalism divides sovereignty between two levels of government, so that the provinces, for example, have control over health and education whereas Ottawa has exclusive powers over employment insurance and banking. Governments can still use some instruments to effect policy changes in fields outside their jurisdiction—the classic Canadian case is Ottawa's use of its spending power in the health care and postsecondary education fields. The North American Free Trade Agreement is a good example of an international agreement that limits the trade policy instruments governments can use. Canada, the United States, and Mexico, for example, cannot give preferential treatment to their own national firms in contrast to those from the other two countries. Consequently, a host of traditional economic policy tools to pump up one's own companies against their competitors are simply not available by agreement—though this should not be taken to mean that governments will give up trying to find a way around the rules. Human rights conventions do much the same thing in fields as diverse as language and the treatment of children. These legal constraints can be joined by more practical ones. Examples include limits on spending programs due to high deficit levels or limits to taxation and regulatory policies in a global environment where investors and capital are increasingly mobile and can go

Figure 1.1   Elements of Policy Content

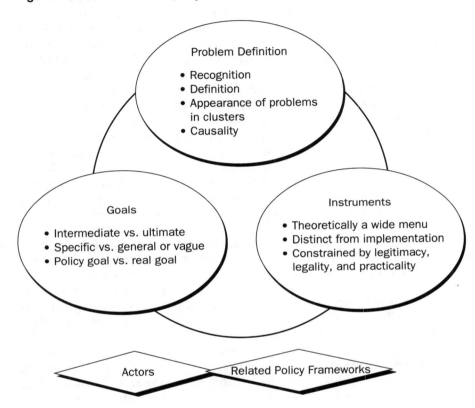

anywhere they please. Also, instrument choice is often constrained by organizational routines and preferences: regulatory departments reach first for regulatory instruments; finance departments reach first for fiscal instruments; and so on.

Figure 1.1 summarizes the preceding discussion of policy content. If one were asked to find out the government's policy on X, one would (1) seek an authoritative source for the policy statement, and (2) search relevant documents for clues on problem definition, goals, and instruments. All of these concepts and some of their nuances will be explored in greater detail in subsequent chapters. Note that Figure 1.1 connects these elements in a loop. While problem definition is central to an understanding of policy in a logical sense, in reality the three elements are inextricably entwined. Policymakers' goals orient them toward certain problems they think need solving; expertise with a set of policy tools encourages one to seek out problems and goals that are consistent with what is achievable with the tools. Moreover, it is virtually impossible to understand any one of these elements without considering the others. In this sense, policy analysis is usually iterative: it moves through the loop several times, refining an understanding of any one element in light of the others. The two diamonds at the bottom of the figure refer to actors and related policy frameworks. These are not directly "elements of policy content" but they are important contextual factors that enrich one's understanding of a given policy. For example, it would certainly be true that a basic summary of Canada's Afghanistan mission would require knowing: the problem definition (international terrorism, with a strong base in that country), the goals (defeat the Taliban and rebuild the country), and the instruments (military, aid, and diplomacy). But that understanding would be even deeper if one had a scan of who the key players/actors are with respect to our policy—from military, to key government departments, to the Prime Minister, opposition parties, and civil society groups. And as well, knowing the related policy frameworks—our foreign policy, our international development strategy—situates the Afghanistan mission much more clearly. It sometimes helps to think about a given policy as existing within a wider "**policy space**" that is populated by other actors/organizations and other policies and programs that tackle different elements of a wider set of problems. For example, in 2008 the federal government was working hard on renewing the public service and developing a sophisticated human resource strategy. The lead agency was the Canada Public Service Agency, but other players included the Public Service Commission, the Treasury Board, the Privy Council Office, among others, each of which is responsible for a different element of human resource management.

The loop also suggests that there will be consistency between the different elements. A definition of a problem should "fit" somehow with the instruments and goals. Policy consistency is an important concept to appreciate, since it underpins both what we do as policy analysts and how we perceive public policies as citizens. Policies are expected to be consistent in several interrelated ways (see Figure 1.2 on page 13). First, as noted above, we expect policies to have an **internal consistency** among the three elements of problem definition, goals, and instruments. Second, we expect a policy to be **vertically consistent** in the sense that the programs and activities that are undertaken in its name are logically related to it. This is in part the nub of implementation. Policy statements are normally fairly abstract and general. They must be actualized through an implementation process that elaborates programs and activities to give the policy effect. A municipal policy to maintain the liveability of the downtown core assumes programs and initiatives that support business and residential developments in that area. If the municipality simultaneously

Figure 1.2 Policy Consistency

had programs to disproportionately encourage suburban development, these would on their face appear inconsistent with the larger policy framework.

A third type of consistency is **horizontal consistency,** or consistency within the wider policy space and across policy fields, not just within them. This is an expectation that what governments do in one field will not contradict what they do in another. A fiscal policy of restraint coupled with high spending in a wide variety of areas makes no sense. An open trade policy would be inconsistent with an industrial policy to encourage domestic producers and limit competition. This type of consistency is important in democratic politics, since it implies that there is an underlying philosophy of government that cuts across all policy fields. From a policy perspective, when people vote, they often vote less for specific policies than for the "whole package." It is a way of ensuring a degree of accountability, since every part of the government is expected to follow a broadly consistent line of policy. Horizontal consistency varies considerably in the real world, both because of the sheer sprawl of government and the existence of multiple jurisdictions. There are so many actors with some influence over the policy process, and so many agencies with relatively autonomous control of their policy fields, that it is not unusual to have quite widely disparate policy frameworks operating at the same time, even within the same policy space. In systems like Canada's, where the executive has greater control over the policy agenda and is internally more coherent due to the role of the Prime Minister and the governing party, there is a higher degree of policy consistency. Even here however, where strong ministers can control their own departments, horizontal consistency is never perfect. Nonetheless, the concept (if not the term) seems to be gaining favour. There have been examples at both the federal and provincial level of governments/parties putting coherent and detailed proposals before the electorate (though this varies by election and by party), and there has been growing emphasis in administrative circles on "horizontality." It is tempting to speculate that budgets recently have become and may continue to be the great engines of horizontal policy consistency for many governments. In the old days, when fiscal constraints did not matter or were ignored, the budget was little more than a compendium of spending initiatives undertaken by departments. Now that money is tight (or our attitudes have changed toward deficits), everything gets measured against the bottom line, which in turn becomes a compelling reference point for all departments (more on this in later chapters).

In reflecting on the nature of public policy, we also have to realize what it is not. It is not the implemented program, the behaviours of public servants who put it into effect, or indeed the reactions of citizens affected by it. If we take the definition developed above, we are forced to realize that public policy—as a course of action—is not the action itself, in the same way that a map is different from travelling. Policies are mental constructs, strings of phrases, and ideas. The text of a policy statement and the programs and actions that follow it are simply evidence for the mental construct. Analyzing policy is akin to trying to figure out which maps people used by studying the paths they took on their journey. The fact that there was a journey and a destination is not proof that maps were in fact used, as anyone who's taken a pleasant ramble in the woods can attest. But we presume that our governments are doing more than rambling, that they have a plan, that their journeys and their destinations are guided by policy. This presumption will often be proven wrong—government actions may be the result of accident, instinct, or habit, rather than of policy. Once we understand this, we understand the challenge of doing policy analysis—it is nothing less than an attempt to grasp an underlying structure of ideas that supposedly guides action.

What Is Public Policy Analysis?

In this book, **policy analysis** will be defined as the disciplined application of intellect to public problems. This is similar to Dunn's definition: "policy analysis is a process of multidisciplinary inquiry designed to create, critically assess, and communicate information that is useful in understanding and improving policies" (Dunn, 2008, p. 1). Apropos of the last point in the previous section, policy analysis is a cognitive activity—a thinking game, if you will—a large part of which focuses on public policy outputs in terms of their problem definition, goals, and instruments. As Wildavsky (1979) pointed out, it is not exclusively a matter of "cogitation" but of "interaction" as well—of letting problems get solved through experimentation, bargaining, and exchange, rather than exclusively through planning—but the reflective, cognitive aspect is central (p. 11). Ours is a broad definition and is complemented by a thicket of other conceptual terms such as **"policy studies,"** "policy science," and "policy evaluation." The central distinction to keep in mind is between a style of policy analysis that is more explanatory and descriptive and a style that is more applied or prescriptive or between what Harold Lasswell (1970) called "knowledge of the policy process" and "knowledge in the policy process" (p. 3). Dobuzinskis et al. make a similar point in their definition of policy analysis: it "refers to applied social and scientific research—but also involves more implicit forms of practical knowledge—pursued by government officials and non-governmental organizations usually directed at designing, implementing and evaluating existing policies, programmes and other courses of action adopted by states" (2007, 3–4). The distinctions among these terms are less important than what they have in common:

> Obviously, the conceptual distinction between these terms is rather indistinct. It would appear that, when the word policy appears as a prefix to the words science, studies, and analysis, we are talking about activity that investigates some form of government problem or output. This includes studies that examine the policy-making process to determine how it affects the output of that process. (McCool, 1995, p. 10)

Or, as George Graham (1988) argues: "The policy orientation provides a means for dealing with human purposes in the best scientific framework possible to aid those who will make social choices. The instrumental end is better intelligence" (p. 152; quoted in McCool, 1995, p. 10).

All these definitions stress the degree to which this reflection is more than just casual observation—the idea that analysis is disciplined implies that it is both grounded in some method and that it is systematic and multidisciplinary. Dunn (2008, p. 3) stresses the multidisciplinary nature of policy analysis in that it draws on a range of social and behavioural sciences, ethics and other branches of social and political philosophy, normative economics, and decision analysis. Indeed, the formal dictionary definition of "analysis" is that it is the process of breaking something complex down to its various simple elements—in our sense, into problem definition, goals, and instruments, but possibly even further with respect to each one of those three key dimensions, and in addition to thinking about actors and related policy frameworks. The methodological basis can vary from a generic (and usually multidisciplinary) approach to one that is solidly grounded in either natural or social sciences. Policy analysis of environmental issues, for example, will be informed by several natural sciences, but this is not to say that only natural scientists can analyze environmental policy. Economics offers an intellectual apparatus that is broadly applicable to a wide range of policy issues, but once again the central concerns of the policy analyst have less to do with the disciplines that seem to be "naturally" aligned to the policy issue than with the larger issues discussed in the previous section: how well is the problem defined, what are its characteristics, what goals are being pursued, and are the instruments adequate and likely to produce results? In fact, as we will see in a moment, there is a host of supplementary issues that also are well within the scope of policy analysis per se, rather than separate disciplines. The other aspect of policy analysis is that it is systematic—it proceeds logically through a series of clearly defined stages to come to its conclusions. It should be possible, in other words, to see how someone arrived at his or her conclusions.

All this may seem self-evident, but it holds three implications of great importance to the way that we view contemporary policy analysis. The first is that, at least insofar as policy analysis seems to be allied with scientific disciplines, not just anyone can do it properly. Ordinary citizens have opinions about public policy, but their views may be determined by prejudice or what happened to be on that morning's front page. Sometimes people have extraordinarily strong views about policy that they cannot explain. Once again, this would seem to fall short of policy analysis. The issue this raises of course is the division between citizens and experts. Can policy analysis be performed only by those trained to do it? Put another way, do citizens, when they contemplate public policy issues, engage in "real" policy analysis or merely in fuzzy thinking, and can experts put aside their own personal opinions? These are not merely abstract, philosophical issues, but strike at the heart of the policy process, the engagement of citizens, and the incorporation of expertise in policy advice. The European Union grappled with these questions in 2002 as part of its desire to improve "the knowledge base for better policies" (Commission of the European Communities, 2002). It identified several core principles in the use of expert knowledge in the policy process:

accountability, plurality, integrity, openness, participation, effectiveness, coherence, proportionality, and subsidiarity.

The second implication, given that policy analysis should be disciplined and systematic, is that there will be both good and bad analysis. More disciplined and systematic analysis will be superior to the less disciplined and systematic. This implies some intersubjective standard of judgment that will act as a benchmark for all participants in the analytical process. Once again this implies some training, especially in the use of more technically oriented forms of analysis and data generation (e.g., opinion surveys, cost-benefit analysis). Nonetheless, it has to be acknowledged that policy analysis contains an irreducible element of interpretation and perspective, that it is a form of "practical reason" that relies on a variety of techniques, a good deal of judgement, experience, and exploration (Sanderson, 2002). There is no exact science, for example, of structuring policy problems. As we noted earlier, policy problems are almost always complex and multifaceted, and so defining or structuring the problem depends very much on which elements the analyst emphasizes and how those elements are imaginatively combined. This does not mean that all analysis is consequently purely subjective. As was mentioned, a substantial part of policy analysis does rely on specific methodological techniques of data-gathering, research, and assessment. Moreover, in a democratic policy process, policy problems should be debated and exposed to discussion and criticism, and this is a means of correcting mistakes as well as generating intersubjective consensus. But policy analysis has as well to be self-aware and self-critical in an effort to remove as much unintentional bias as possible. One major example of this type of effort is the treatment of gender in policy analysis. Critics of traditional public policy analysis argue that it neglects the interests of women because of the "early adoption of rational, self-interested man as the reference point for both policy development and policy studies" (Burt, 1995, p. 357). A partial solution has been the development in the last decade of specific techniques of **gender-based analysis (GBA)**, which seek to assess the differential impact of public policies, programs, and legislation on women and men. GBA is designed not to simply be an add-on in the analytical process, but a perspective that is woven through each step and phase (Status of Women Canada, 1996). A recent development has been the extension of GBA to analyzing government budgets and their differential impacts on men and women (Bakker, 2006). A complementary concept is **gender mainstreaming,** which is an organizational strategy to ensure that a gender perspective is reflected in all types of organizational activities. The United Nations has made a strong commitment to gender mainstreaming, "ensuring that gender perspectives and attention to the goal of gender equality are central to all activities— policy development, research, advocacy/dialogue, legislation, resource

Chapter 1 Policy Analysis: Concepts and Practice

allocation, and planning, implementation and monitoring of programmes and projects" (United Nations, 2004).

Policy analysis is also complicated by possible cultural biases. An extreme example of policy work that had to grapple with different cultural perspectives is the Royal Commission on Aboriginal Peoples in the mid-1990s. Hundreds of researchers from across Canada were invited to participate, but the Commission was well aware of the problem that Aboriginal peoples had been "studied" for generations and felt very much like the objects of policy rather than its agents. Moreover, the research directors were sensitive to the issue that Aboriginal peoples themselves might see their problems through a different cultural lens:

> The Research Directorate, both in its staffing and commissioning, strives to achieve a balance between Aboriginal and non-Aboriginal researchers, and among Indian, Inuit and Métis. Much of our work will take place outside universities in Aboriginal cultural institutes and communities. We hope that this innovative approach will allow our research to speak in two voices—and be heard by both Aboriginal and non-Aboriginal people in Canada. (Hawkes and Castellano, 1993, p. 7)

The Commission's ethical guidelines for research were even more clear about this juggling act. All Commission research would have to display respect for "the cultures, languages, knowledge and values of Aboriginal peoples, and to the standards used by Aboriginal peoples to legitimate knowledge" (Royal Commission on Aboriginal Peoples, n.d., p. 1). Most public policy issues will not be as strongly marked by cultural differences between participants but, as we noted earlier, values are at the heart of all policy debates, no matter how apparently technical. And values can be strongly linked to "ways of life" or community sensibilities. Consider for a moment the response governments face when they might decide, for rational reasons, to reallocate educational resources by closing schools. Or what municipalities might have to deal with when suggesting name changes to streets.

The third implication is that policy analysis, however much it may draw on other scientific disciplines, is itself a specific form of inquiry. Policy analysis, for example, has a unique focus when compared to other disciplines: public policies themselves and the several elements that comprise them, along with the processes that produce them and the impacts they ultimately have. It has its own traditions of debate, its journals, its schools, and its characteristic intellectual paradigms and issues.

It is important not to paint too rigid a picture of policy analysis. Taking the two elements of the definition—(1) the disciplined application of intellect and (2) public problems—it is easy to see that if we break each one down into its possible elements there is a wide variety of

Figure 1.3 Policy Analysis: Types of Reasoning

Types of Reasoning   Object of Analysis

Normative: analyzes policy in reference to
basic values or ethical principles

Legal: analyzes policy in terms of jurisdiction   Process
and consistency with legislation or the Charter

                                                              Content
Logical: analyzes policy in terms of internal,
vertical, and horizontal consistency and whether
it "makes sense"   Outcomes

Empirical: analyzes policy in relation to
impacts and effects, costs, and administration

possibilities and permutations that might come under the broad rubric of policy analysis. As we will see later in this book, some styles of policy analysis favour advocacy, while others involve managing processes, or even engaging in fundamental philosophical reflection on core ideas that underpin policy debates (Hoppe and Margarita Jeliazkova, 2006). While policy analysis has undoubtedly become professionalized (Radin, 2000), and is a recognized occupational category in government, the work done by policy analysts is not narrowly technical. The "disciplined application of intellect" is really about styles of reasoning, as long as these styles are disciplined and systematic in some recognizable sense. These styles of reasoning are applied to "public problems," but these also have various dimensions: process, content, and outcome, to name only a few. As Figure 1.3 shows, one can reason about (or analyze) policy in several equally legitimate ways: normative, legal, logical, and empirical.

Normative analysis measures some aspect of policy against an ethical standard: secular morality, the Bible, the Koran, the Canadian Charter of Rights and Freedoms, the UN Universal Declaration of Human Rights. This type of analysis is remarkably important in today's world but is rarely acknowledged in the literature on policy analysis (though see Dunn, 2008, Chap. 7). As Peters (2006, Chap. 17) points out, both citizens and politicians analyze and assess public policy in terms of key ethical principles such as fairness, truth, and the concept of desert. We do not judge only on utilitarian grounds, we judge in terms of fundamental norms. This form of analysis is included here both for its importance and because it fits the definition of disciplined and systematic; while one may not agree with the conclusions, at least one can see how they were arrived at.

Legal analysis looks at public policy through the prism of law: constitutionality, consistency with statute, the practices of legal convention. This overlaps slightly with the previous category in that a prime measure of contemporary morality is human rights, and hence constitutional provisions on human rights. But this category also contains questions about jurisdiction and legality in the more technical sense.

Logical analysis deals with questions of consistency and coherence such as were raised earlier in this chapter: is the policy internally consistent, is it vertically consistent, and is it horizontally consistent? This kind of analysis can be done without extensive empirical research and so is a favourite of media pundits. The fact that these pundits shape the opinion of millions of people should underscore how important a form of analysis it is.

Empirical analysis takes logical analysis one step further by actually posing the same questions in the light of empirical evidence; not what might be the likely effect of policy X, but what was its actual effect? Impact questions can be about the direct intended impact, unintended consequences on other targets, or surveys of client satisfaction.

Figure 1.3 also highlights some of the dimensions of policy that can be analyzed: process (the various determinants of a policy, the actors and institutions that shaped it), content (problem definition, goals, instruments), and outcomes (legislation, regulations, actual impact or effect).

Defining policy analysis in this way—as the disciplined application of intellect to public problems—deliberately excludes some "other ways of knowing." It does so because it is itself based on a certain epistemology or system of knowledge. That system is **rationalism,** the characteristic form of knowing in the West that is rooted in the Greek and European civilizations. This is hardly the place to discuss the intellectual history of Western civilization, but it is important to understand what this form of reason implies about how we come to decisions, and what counts as knowledge and what does not. The rational decisionmaking paradigm, a feature of virtually every introductory textbook on policy analysis, is outlined in Box 1.1 (page 21). Note that the procedure is a generic one: it should apply as well to deciding public policy as it does to choosing a mate or one's wardrobe.

Few of us are this systematic when we make everyday decisions, but the more important a decision, the more likely that we will think about it carefully and perhaps approximate this model. Will this make for a better decision? Maybe. But making decisions rationally is not the same as

BOX 1.1   THE RATIONAL DECISIONMAKING MODEL

Choose objectives: The first step in making a decision is knowing what one wishes to do or accomplish. This necessarily involves a statement of the problem as well as of goals.

Consider alternatives: Once the problem and goals are identified, the second step is to identify the means by which the objectives may be attained.

Outline impacts: Each alternative will consist of a bundle of costs and benefits, positive and negative impacts on the problem. Measure them.

Determine criteria: A fourth step is to rank all of the alternatives in order of desirability, but this requires some explicit criterion, such as least cost, for a given objective.

Apply models/scenarios: The final step before actual implementation is the construction of a model or a scenario to help predict and map out the potential empirical consequences of the chosen alternative.

Implement preferred option: Put the preferred option into effect.

Evaluate consequences: What happened, and how well do the real impacts fit with predicted outcomes?

making reasonable decisions. A reasonable or good decision is defined less by the process that produced it than by its appropriateness as a solution to the initial problem. While the rational model could in principle be used to choose a mate, most people would argue that it is more reasonable to make this type of decision with the heart or one's emotions. By the same token, non-Western cultures are often more comfortable with decisionmaking processes that rely less on systematic analysis than on wisdom, intuition, or even "signs" (Suzuki and Knudtson, 1992).

It is worth taking a moment to consider the implications of the rational model for policy analysis and decisionmaking, if only because "rational" seems synonymous with "reasonable" and the opposition of "rationality" and "intuition" seems to give preference to the former. For one thing, the rational model has embedded within it a strong concern with efficiency, which Herbert Simon (one of the most important decision theorists) defined as choosing alternatives that provide the greatest results for the least cost (Simon, Smithburg, and Thompson, 1958, p. 60).

Simon was convinced throughout his long and distinguished career (he was born in 1916, won the Nobel Prize for Economics in 1978, and died in 2001) that social betterment would come from the application of rational techniques to complex decisions. He acknowledged that pure rationality in decisionmaking was an impossibility, and that instead human beings made decisions under various constraints, in a model he described as **bounded rationality** in search of **satisficing** solutions. In 1957 he was excited about the use of the "digital computer and the tools of mathematics and the behavioral sciences on the very core of managerial activity—on the exercise of judgment and intuition; on the process of making complex decisions" (Simon and Newell, 1957, p. 382). Mintzberg (1994) has noted how, for Simon, "the fundamental assumption is that continuous knowledge can be broken down into discrete elements, that is, decomposed for the purposes of analysis. . . . [I]ntuition gets reduced to analysis" (pp. 310–11). The pure rational model presumes certain patterns of thought: it is linear, systematic, self-conscious, purposive, and efficient.

Another way of putting this is that policy analysis, and the rationalism in which it is rooted, is part and parcel of the way "the state sees." James C. Scott (1998) points out the difficulties states had in pre-modern times in fulfilling classic state functions such as raising taxes, conscripting armies, or preventing rebellions. Societies were not "legible" or visible because pre-modern states, confronting patterns of social life that were suited to local conditions, knew very little about the identities, location, holdings, wealth, or personal conditions of their subjects. Scott's book traces the way in which the state developed this knowledge through focusing on and analyzing specific bits of information to the exclusion of others. With simplification "an overall, aggregate, synoptic view of a selective reality is achieved, making possible a high degree of schematic knowledge, control, and manipulation" (Scott, 1998, p. 11). Things we take for granted today, such as standard weights and measures, freehold land tenure and cadastral maps (showing plots of individually owned land), grid systems for the layout of cities, official languages, and even permanent patronyms (inherited last names date only from the twentieth century in Europe) all had to be invented, and they were invented largely to benefit state administration. As Scott (1998) argues, "the modern state, through its officials, attempts with varying degrees of success to create a terrain and a population with precisely those standardized characteristics that will be easiest to monitor, count, assess, and manage" (pp. 81–82). The statecraft that can be exercised on a "legible" society can be either sinister or benign, organized for oppression or public welfare. The point is that rationalism, as a key part of the modernist project, has deep roots in an impulse to centralize, categorize, and control. It should come as no surprise that the first burst of interest in policy analysis occurred just at the time that the United States was preparing to launch massive new social intervention programs in the 1960s and 1970s; new forms of information and "ways of seeing" had to be organized. That these were driven by a desire to improve public welfare is undeniable, but it is also important to realize that in practice rationalism and its offspring, policy analysis, may be closed to more complex social realities grounded in local practice and informal and complex social and economic patterns of behaviour.

This should remind us of the limits of policy analysis and rational technique. It may be that better policy will flow from disciplined analysis (methodologically rigorous, systematic, organized, and geared to the breaking down of complex phenomena into their simple components), but it is no guarantee. As we will note in a moment, there is also the possibility that rational technique might blind us to other, equally legitimate, ways of knowing. But at the very least, we should remember that all of the technique and discipline in the world will still run up against uncertainty. We cannot know everything, and hence our policy interventions may go wrong, fall short, or have unintended consequences. Henry Aaron (2000) has underscored the degree to which the policy sciences tend to ignore the challenges of uncertainty:

> The reason is straightforward. The task is laughably beyond our current analytical capacities. We simply cannot simultaneously handle the direct consequences of a policy change (presuming that our data and models are exactly right); *and* the direct consequences under alternative properly-weighted uncertain contingencies; *and* the direct consequences under plausible models different from the one that we have used; *and* the impacts on future legislation of the different legislative and political environment brought about by current actions; *and* whether it would be better to act now or defer action until the future; *and* if we act now, whether it would be better to implement policy changes promptly or at some time in the future. (pp. 201–02)

The standard definition of policy analysis therefore clearly carries with it some cultural and historical baggage. Even if we substantially relax the definition to include a wider variety of ways of knowing and thinking, it is hard to escape the core assumptions that analysis will demand, at minimum, (1) expertise, (2) reliance of Western science, (3) deductive logic, (4) measurement, and (5) clear and replicable steps or stages. For the last fifty years, this model of rationality has been at the heart of what people do when conducting policy analyses. Indeed, it is far from merely a philosophical framework—it actually forms the foundation for most of the policymaking guides proclaimed by government. The federal government, for example, introduced a *Cabinet Directive on Streamlining Regulation*

(Government of Canada, 2007) that came into effect on April 1, 2007. While dealing explicitly with regulatory analysis, the steps in that analysis are clearly informed by the rational model: identify issues, set objectives, plan for implementation, and measure and evaluate. A similar framework underpins other federal government policy guides such as the *Cabinet Directive on the Environmental Assessment of Policy, Plan and Program Proposals: A Framework for the Application of Precaution in Science-based Decision Making about Risk*, and *A Framework for Science and Technology Advice: Principles and Guidelines for the Effective Use of Science and Technology Advice in Government Decision Making*.

Despite its ubiquity, the rational model has been challenged and criticized for what it leaves out. So what's wrong with being rational? It may seem a bit mechanical and plodding but is hardly sinful or dangerous. In summary, the main challenges and criticisms have been:

The real world is "incremental," not rational. In a famous 1959 article, Charles Lindblom argued that the unforgiving strictures of rational decisionmaking were so unrealistic in terms of the cognitive and political situation faced by most decisionmakers that in fact they made choices by "muddling through." In later work, Lindblom (1979) refined the model, both as a normative and a descriptive framework. In other words, incrementalism better described what really went on and, moreover, it had certain advantages over its apparently superior rival. In the real world of politics and administration, of course, there are multiple decisionmakers with conflicting perspectives and priorities, information is in short supply or contradictory, and everything has to be done immediately. In this situation, Lindblom and others argued, decisions get made on the basis of "successive limited comparisons." In this method, goals and values are not neatly separated from each other or from the process of choice. In making decisions, we often clarify what we want and what we believe only through the process of concrete choices in specific situations. As well, we usually make choices against a backdrop of what has been done before—we move in usually small increments from one situation to the next. Incrementalism seems a sorry standard in many respects, slow, halting, without clear vision or conviction, but it probably captures routine, day-to-day public policymaking in most organizations (Weiss and Woodhouse, 1992).

"Facts" lie at the heart of the rational model, but "facts" are constructed through values and theories. The rational model presumes that there are such things as "facts," but critics point out that facts are always constructed through values and perceptions, or more accurately, through deep theories that structure our cognition of reality. These theories are sometimes chosen rationally in the sense of deliberation among a range of alternatives according to multiple criteria, but "however exhaustive the arguments advanced in support of one position, considered judgments

concerning the best theory will remain contentious and tentative . . ." (Hawkesworth, 1988, p. 87). Frank Fischer and John Forester (1993) have termed this emphasis the "argumentative turn" in policy analysis and planning. For them, policymaking is a "struggle over the criteria of social classification, the boundaries of problem categories, the intersubjective interpretation of common experiences, the conceptual framing of problems, and the definitions of ideas that guide the ways people create the shared meanings which motivate them to act" (Fischer and Forester, 1993, p. 2). The argumentative turn entails, among other things, the critical study of the structure of argument and discourse in policy analysis (Fischer, 1980; Fischer, 2003); the role of values (Fischer and Forester, 1987); and the deep impact of positivism through its associated logic of technocratic mastery (Fischer, 1990). This has been complemented by work such as Dryzek's (1990), exploring the epistemological foundations of policy analysis. This is not merely a methodological debate: for deLeon (1997) as for his colleagues in the "post-positivist" school, the issue is developing a "policy sciences of democracy" (esp. Chap. 4). This usually entails greater emphasis on public engagement and consultation, something which seems to hold the risk of contaminating "rational" policymaking with the uninformed prejudices of interest groups and the public. Recent research, however, suggests that "if you can assemble a diverse group of people who possess varying degrees of knowledge and insight, you're better off entrusting it with major decisions rather than leaving them in the hands of one or two people, no matter how smart those people are" (Surowiecki, 2005: 31). We discuss this question of the "wisdom of crowds" in greater detail in Chapter 6.

Policy analysis actually has relatively little influence on policymaking. The high point in the fortunes of policy analysis and scientific decision-making was in the 1960s, when the United States decided to adopt the Planning-Programming-Budgeting System (PPBS), later adopted in Canada as well, and then made program evaluation mandatory, thus setting off a boom in the industry in the 1970s. A natural question was whether all this activity was having any effect on the policy process. Carol Weiss and her colleagues began a series of studies through the 1970s to answer this question. Their conclusion was that the "implications of explanatory studies and the recommendations from policy-oriented studies seemed to have little effect on either the day-to-day operations of program management or the long-term directions of public policy" (Weiss, 1983, p. 217). If it was clear that policy analysis did not influence the policy process directly, then what contributions did it make? One early argument was that policy analysis and the rest of the social sciences have a broad "enlightenment" function, providing broad ideas, concepts, insights, and theoretical perspectives (Janowitz, 1972). Another version of this image is the "limestone" metaphor, to capture how science enters politics: "It relies on indirect or cumulative interest and requires no action other than the research itself and the presentation of the findings in a readable way. If circumstances permit (and the research has no control over many of them) the work may, in combination with other work with a similar theme and message, seep into the public consciousness" (Thomas, 1987, p. 57).

There is much to these criticisms, and they have had powerful impacts on the way in which policy analysis is theorized and practised. However, in recent years there has been a resurgence of interest in policy and in developing strong **policy capacity**, a resurgence that has been evident both in Canada and abroad. There are several broad explanations for this. In many countries, after a long focus on management of existing resources through the 1990s to deal with deficits and financial constraint, the realization dawned that just "minding the store" was not enough. Countries faced major challenges and rapidly shifting environments, and without guides, strategy, or vision—in short, public policy—they would be rudderless. Other countries, such as those in Central and Eastern Europe, lacked a policy tradition—orders had come down from the Communist Party in Moscow—and so they found themselves grappling with similar imperatives, but from a position that forced them to reinvent and reconsider the assumptions both of their state systems and of policy analysis (as understood in the Western state tradition) itself. The fall 2008 financial crisis left the public sector, and hence intelligent public policy, as the only bulwark against disaster.

Policy is popular again. The next section provides some examples of the international policy movement that is emerging and some of its characteristics. The deeper forces that underlie the rise of this movement will be explored in the next chapter.

The Policy Movement

To understand the recent resurgence in policy analysis one has to understand its rise and temporary decline. The social sciences, particularly economics, political science, public administration, and planning, developed in the late nineteenth and early twentieth centuries. Whereas in continental Europe sociology tended to be the umbrella discipline for all of these, in the Anglo-Saxon tradition of England and North America they developed as separate disciplines. Just as important, political science was distinct from law, another difference from the continental tradition. The idea that these disciplines could be integrated into something distinct—the policy sciences—can be conveniently dated from some key publications by American social scientist Harold Lasswell. As early as 1951, he and colleagues were arguing for a distinct approach they termed the "policy sciences of democracy" and a distinct role for policy analysts

(Lasswell, 1951). In Lasswell's view, the policy sciences would integrate the other social sciences in a multidisciplinary enterprise devoted to dealing with public problems and the policy processes of democracy. It was an ambitious vision but clearly gathered momentum through the 1960s. By 1972, for example, leading American social scientists were seriously debating the possibility that policy analysis might become the integrating medium for the social sciences (Charlesworth, 1972).

The terms "public policy" and "policy analysis" began to be used more frequently in the 1960s as the American government began to try to solve "problems" in a host of areas from racial conflict, urban renewal, transportation, and education (Parsons, 1995, pp. 20–21). Hofferbert (1990) notes that between 1960 and 1975 "national research priorities drew many American social scientists out of the ivory tower and into the political arena, not as politicians or bureaucrats but as experts in the evaluation of public programs" (p. 4). The same was true of Canada. Sutherland (1993) reports that by the mid-1970s "after several years of expansionary budgets and in a climate of general high faith in rationalism, many policy departments and some central agencies had built up good-sized cadres of professional researchers and analysts" (p. 95). Both Hofferbert and Sutherland claim that after this heyday came decline. This was due in part to overweening optimism and the ultimate failure to deliver much except bad news. In the Canadian case as well, the newly elected Conservative government cut 15 000 person-years between 1984 and 1992, hitting staff advisory functions quite hard. As well, the federal Tories were less interested in building internal research capacity than buying the necessary services from think-tanks or universities.

By the late 1990s the pendulum was swinging back, and "policy capacity" and "policy analysis" were once more key terms in debates over governance and appropriate public management. Why? The reasons will be developed in greater detail in the next chapter, but generally had to do with several broad but common factors. First, the collapse of the Soviet Union in 1990–91 ended the Cold War and led to the creation of a host of new states in Central and Eastern Europe (including the Russian Federation). These events required a shift in foreign policy in the West, but also gradually created a demand for training in public administration and policy in these countries. Examples will be given below, but the problem for newly independent countries like the Baltic states and Ukraine was that they had had no tradition of distinct public administration or indeed of policy development. As these states struggled to modernize, it became abundantly clear that good public policy was a key ingredient in the success of post-communist societies. Second, many Western states in the 1990s experienced an unusual degree of political polarization. The Canadian variant was the rise of the Reform (then Canadian Alliance, and finally Conservative) party in the early 1990s and the prominence of the Ontario and Alberta Tory parties as they pursued major program reforms. In the United States, President Bill Clinton had to deal suddenly with a Republican-dominated Congress through the mid-1990s. The rhythms varied, but many European countries saw sharper competition between right and left. The upshot was that, by the end of the decade, debates over policy—and often diametrically opposed policy approaches—were suddenly important. Third, there was a growing sense that the solutions and frameworks of the 1980s would no longer suffice for the modern world (Giddens, 1999; Pal, 1999), and this too led to more concentrated discussion and debate about public policy issues. Fourth, and partly in response to the previous factor, the early 1990s were a decade of public sector reform in the light of new management theories, but eventually the question arose "reform for what?" Changing administrative structures and processes could not be completely divorced from substance. And finally, after a decade of criticism of the traditional state, it was clear that an effective public sector was an important ingredient in social harmony and economic progress, if not survival. Health and educational services, transportation, communications, security, and biotechnology are all affected by, if not dependent on, state action.

If anything, the emphasis on policy capacity has continued, though for complicated and not always mutually consistent reasons. As mentioned above, a key factor has been the realization of the importance of the state and state policy for a host of social and economic activities. The sterile debate of the 1980s and 1990s over a "minimalist state" has been eclipsed by several realities. The post-9/11 international and domestic security situation, as well as the global economic crisis, demands both policy and operational responsiveness by government. Modern economies depend increasingly on new technologies, innovation, and research, and governments find themselves having to design new, more supple, forms of regulation, intervention, and support (*Fourteenth Annual Report,* 2007). A factor peculiar to Europe is the recent accession (January 1, 2007) of Romania and Bulgaria to the European Union (EU), completing the fifth enlargement to 27 countries. Turkey and Croatia are candidate countries. In order to be admitted to the EU, applicant countries must make their laws and most policy frameworks consistent with the "*acquis communautaire,*" or the body of laws, treaties, declarations, and resolutions that make up the EU. This requires a tremendous amount of policy-oriented work.

More detail on these factors will be developed in the next chapter, but the following provides some examples from Canada and the rest of the world on the flavour of this policy movement.

CANADA

The first alarm about Canada's policy capacity was sounded by the Clerk of Privy Council, Jocelyne Bourgon, in 1995 in her Third Annual Report to the Prime Minister on the public service, where she noted that "One of the most striking features of western democratic nations in recent years has been that they have all been engaged in rethinking the role of government and the organization of their public sectors. In many nations the essence of governance is being redefined" (Privy Council Office, 1995). She identified the development of policy capacity as a key priority for the public service over the coming years (Bakvis, 2000).

Bourgon's concern about policy capacity helped propel two important initiatives under her tenure. The first was *La Relève*. After years of downsizing (55 000 public servants had left the federal public service), criticism, pay freezes and cuts, it was time to renew the federal public sector. For our purposes, what was most interesting about the initiative was the assumption of the importance of a well-functioning public sector. As Bourgon put it: "In today's global environment, the quality of the public sector will continue to make a significant difference to the performance of nations. A high quality public sector contributes to competitiveness, provides countries with a comparative advantage in their competition for trade and investment, and contributes to the quality of life and the standard of living of citizens" (Privy Council Office, 1997). The second initiative was the creation of the **Policy Research Initiative (PRI)**, which was directed specifically at enhancing policy capacity. A Policy Research Committee had been established in 1996, involving over thirty departments and agencies. As Lindquist notes, the initiative led to "thematic conferences, workshops with researchers at universities and think tanks, a new journal, the Trends Project with the Social Sciences and Humanities Research Council, and a recruitment program for policy researchers similar to the Accelerated Economist Training Program (Lindquist, 2006: 37). The PRI was embedded in the Privy Council Office, but the emphasis on policy capacity began to wane in the Martin government as it became mired in the sponsorship scandal.

With the Conservative government election in 2006 (and re-election in 2008), somewhat surprisingly given that it was expected to be a short-lived and timid minority government, building policy capacity is once more on the agenda. One reason is that the government had firm priorities when it took over, and though somewhat distrustful of the bureaucracy, demanded that they be developed and implemented. Having massive, successive fiscal surpluses also provided opportunities for new ideas and hence an appetite for policy advice. Finally, in connection with these events, but also in an eerie echo of Bourgon's emphasis on public service renewal, the current Clerk (as of 2008) has also made renewal a top priority. "[I]f the Public Service, as a core national institution, does not renew itself for future as well as current service to the government and people of Canada, it risks becoming less relevant, less useful and less respected as the years go by. If we do not commit ourselves to a continuing process of renewal, the Public Service will not remain a creative national institution, central to the governance and development of our country" (Privy Council Office, 2007: 2). Renewal includes strengthening policy capacity to deal with long-term priorities such as "globalization, security, productivity, ageing, competitiveness and climate change" (Privy Council Office, 2008a). The focus on renewal has engaged deputy ministers, Federal Councils, and a Prime Minister's Advisory Committee on the Public Service (Privy Council Office, 2008b). As an example, the PRI in 2006 was moved from the Privy Council Office to Human Resources and Social Development Canada, with the expectation that it would support the work of policy committees of the Coordinating Committee of Deputy Ministers, thus enhancing policy advice to the federal senior officials' policy community.

INTERNATIONAL EXAMPLES

The Organisation for Economic Co-operation and Development (OECD) is an international body of thirty member states "committed to democracy and the market economy" (OECD, 2008a). Its original membership has expanded beyond North America and Western Europe to include Japan, Australia, New Zealand, Finland, Mexico, the Czech Republic, Slovakia, Hungary, Poland, and Korea. The OECD also has interactions with states in the former Soviet bloc and in Latin America. Much of the focus of its work is on key policy issues, such as ageing, agriculture, biotechnology, education, energy, health, security, sustainable development, trade and transport, and corporate governance.

The OECD also has an interest in governance issues and public sector management, principally through its Directorate for Public Governance and Territorial Development (GOV). Its rationale is as follows:

> Good governance is critical to long-term economic, social and environmental development. The Public Governance and Territorial Development Directorate (GOV) identifies changing societal and market needs, and helps countries adapt their governmental systems and territorial policies. This involves improving government efficiency while protecting and promoting society's longer-term governance values. . . . GOV supports improved public sector governance through comparative data and analysis, the setting and promotion of standards, and the facilitation of transparency and peer review. This involves promoting understanding of the dynamics of public management and territorial development policies in different societal and market conditions, with a view to the long-term interests of all citizens. (OECD, 2008b)

GOV has published several key international reports on governance. For example, a 1995 report entitled *Governance in Transition: Public Management Reform in OECD Countries* argued that member states were facing unprecedented pressures in terms of global competitiveness and new citizen demands, and would require "radical changes" in traditional governance structures and service delivery (OECD, 1995).

In 2003 and in 2005 the Directorate published policy briefs on public sector modernization that surveyed twenty years of OECD member country attempts at reform (OECD, 2003, 2005a). As well, in 2005 it published a longer report that was an update and extension of the 1995 document (OECD, 2005b). The animating theme of all three documents is the notion of the world "pressures" that have made reform inevitable and unavoidable. The 2003 brief mentions the world "pressure" eleven times in eight pages; the 2005 brief mentions it four times; and the longer 2005 report cites it 43 times in 205 pages of text. While there usually is reference to technology, the key pressures that are identified in the texts are budgets and citizens. The budgetary pressures are privileged as a historical source of public sector reforms, but clearly cannot be as prominent as they were a decade ago. Nonetheless, there are references to continuing budgetary pressures due to "demands on social transfer systems" exacerbated by the challenge of an ageing population (the document could not have anticipated the unprecedented financial pressures due to the global financial crisis). But clearly the main pressure that is cited in all three documents is a dissatisfied and somewhat truculent citizenry. The dissatisfaction manifests itself in different ways: demands for more services, demands for more efficient services, disgruntlement about high taxation, a vaguely defined set of inflated "expectations." Though the references are brief, the OECD portrays citizens as somewhat petulant *demandeurs,* whom government officials ignore at their peril. This is not to deny the power of public opinion or public outrage and even demonstrations of violence: the point is the rhetoric and the way it sets up the tone of argument. The nature of the pressure, its legitimacy and its implacable strength, makes reform less a choice than a necessity. Not to reform risks "being out of step" or "not adapting"—in other words to rupture the harmony that should exist between public institutions and citizens.

Through reports like these, the OECD facilitates a global conversation among governments about public management and "modernization." While in the 1990s its approach was closer to "one size fits all" in terms of needed public sector reforms (more efficiency, less spending), by 2005 it had recognized that some mistakes had been made in the past in transferring reform templates directly to countries without thinking about necessary adaptations. It was also emphasizing the importance of organizational culture, values, and the often unique characteristics of different countries as they struggle with reform.

In addition to these sweeping overviews and broad recommendations on modernizing government, the OECD works on several more specific fronts. One is its SIGMA program (Support for Improvement in Governance and Management in Central and Eastern European Countries), which is a joint effort by the OECD and the European Union (under its Phare program, which since 1989 has been channeling EU financial and technical support for transition and reform efforts, and more recently, to prepare countries in Central and Eastern Europe to successfully join the EU). In 2007 it targeted two new EU Member States (Bulgaria and Romania), three EU candidate countries (Croatia, Macedonia, and Turkey) former Yugoslav Republic of Macedonia, and Turkey), Western Balkan countries (Albania, Bosnia and Herzegovina, Montenegro, and Serbia including Kosovo) and Ukraine (SIGMA, 2008). Priority reform areas include anti-corruption and integrity, policymaking and regulatory capacities, and public expenditure management. The importance of policy capacity is clear:

> Sigma activities to support policy-making and co-ordination focus on four sub-areas: policy and strategic capacities; co-ordination structures; regulatory reform, including impact assessment; and management of EU integration.
>
> Sigma assists partner countries in strengthening policy-making capacities and in setting up co-ordination mechanisms at the centre of government, usually in the Office of the Government and/or the Prime Minister's Office, to ensure coherence among sectoral policies of ministries and consistency of government policy-making and implementation. Support is also given to developing methodologies for assessing the impact of legislation on the budget and the economy as a whole—including such aspects as labour market, social and political impact—and on the management, organisational structures and process of adopting the *acquis communautaire.* (SIGMA, 2008)

Another recent OECD project is *Government at a Glance.* It was launched in 2005 as *Management in Government* with the aim of "providing governments with high quality comparative information on the public sector" (OECD, 2007: iii). The report notes that as "public sector reforms continue across the OECD, there is a growing need for improved data to provide a reality check on actions taken and a direction for the future" (OECD 2007: 1). This ambitious project proposes to produce a unified, comparable dataset of government indicators on revenues, inputs, and public sector processes. This is part of an explosion in the last decade of various types of governance indicators (Arndt and Oman, 2006; Levy, 2007), driven by a conviction among international donors that good governance is crucial to development, and having objective data on governance processes in recipient countries is important for investments in aid.

The World Bank is another influential international organization that has turned its attention to governance and policy capacity in recent years. Founded in 1944, the bank currently channels some US$18 billion to more than 100 countries for development assistance loans. In its 1997 annual report, entitled *The State in a Changing World,* the bank highlighted the importance of good governance to sustainable economic development:

> For human welfare to be advanced, the state's capability— *defined as the ability to undertake and promote collective actions efficiently*—must be increased. This basic message translates into a two-part strategy to make every state a more credible, effective partner in its country's development:
>
> *Matching the state's role to its capability* is the first element in this strategy. Where state capability is weak, how the state intervenes— and where—should be carefully assessed. Many states try to do too much with few resources and little capability, and often do more harm than good. A sharper focus on the fundamentals would improve effectiveness. But here it is a matter not just of choosing what to do and what not to do—but of how to do it as well.
>
> But capability is not destiny. Therefore the second element of the strategy is to *raise state capability by reinvigorating public institutions*. This means designing effective rules and restraints, to check arbitrary state actions and combat entrenched corruption. (World Bank, 1997) [emphasis in original]

This was followed in 2000 by a World Bank strategic document entitled *Reforming Public Institutions and Strengthening Governance* (World Bank, 2000). In its most recent reports, the Bank has emphasized empowerment and participation of the poor in the development process, and this has led it to highlight well-functioning public institutions as a key crucible of that participation. By one estimate, World Bank lending for economic reforms fell by 14 percent annually in 2000–2004, but lending on improved governance rose to the point that in 2004, 25 percent of World Bank lending was targeted on law and public administration (Arndt and Oman, 2006: 17).

Not only governments participate in this worldwide movement to develop policy capacity and good governance. There are numerous foundations supporting a host of initiatives to develop democracy and policy capacity. An interesting example of private, nongovernment action is the Open Society Institute (OSI), with headquarters in New York. It serves as the hub for a network of autonomous foundations and networks active in over fifty countries, principally in Central and Eastern Europe, Central Eurasia, the Caribbean and South America, and Africa. The organization is funded by billionaire philanthropist George Soros. According to OSI, "open societies are characterized by a reliance on the rule of law, the existence of a democratically elected government, a diverse and vigorous civil society, and respect for minorities and minority opinions" (OSI, 2008). A representative program of the OSI efforts is the International Policy Fellowships (IPF), administered in cooperation with the Centre for Policy Studies at the Central European University in Budapest, Hungary. Launched in 1998, the program seeks to identify the open society leaders and equip them with policy analysis and advocacy skills so that they may put forward innovative policy solutions in their respective countries, as well as connect with policy analysis networks.

Another good example of a governance/policy oriented global civil society organization is Transparency International (TI). It was established in 1993, and now has a global network of more than 90 locally formed national chapters (Transparency International, 2008). TI's five global priorities in fighting corruption are: corruption in politics; corruption in public contracting; corruption in the private sector; international anti-corruption conventions; and poverty and development. Its thematic areas include access to information, education, judiciary, health, and the Forest Integrity Network. TI is known internationally for its Corruption Perceptions Index and Global Corruption Barometer, both of which provide country rankings. TI also works with international governmental bodies such as the OECD's Anti-Corruption Network for Eastern Europe and Central Asia.

These Canadian and international examples demonstrate the enormous energy that has gone into public sector reform in the last decade, and the prime importance of developing policy capacity as part of the reform agenda. The pace has varied in different countries, as have the circumstances (particularly in Central and Eastern Europe), and even the concepts—sometimes policy is used, sometimes strategy, sometimes horizontal co-ordination. Hood (1998) properly cautions us to be skeptical about the degree of international convergence around "modern" public administration:

> Convergence is a powerful rhetorical theme, because by providing apparently convincing backing for the claim that the same thing is happening everywhere, it suggests (typically by suppressed premiss again) that running with the herd must be the best—or at least the only—thing to do. It is thus hardly surprising that both domestic reformers and international agencies like OECD and the World Bank tend to lay heavy stress on 'convergence' . . . [I]nternational organizations are almost by their

raison d'être committed to a view of international convergence on some single 'best-practice' model which it is their role to 'benchmark' and foster, helping the 'laggards' to catch up with the best-practice techniques of the vanguard. (p. 202)

At the heart of all this international activity, however, is the simple insight that a society's quality of life depends in large measure on the quality of its government, and that the quality of governmental responses to problems depends in large measure on its capacity to think through those problems and develop appropriate and effective solutions. Public policymaking is no more, and no less, than that.

Conclusion

This chapter defined public policy and policy analysis, along with some key associated concepts, and showed how the discipline and practice of policy analysis in its modern guise goes back to the immediate post–World War II era. At the same time, in the second section of the chapter, we showed how after a period of decline, policy and the development of policy capacity through good governance have been enjoying a resurgence, not only in Canada but also throughout the world. We provided some reasons for this shift earlier, but it is important to recall that the interest in policy has been part of a larger effort at **public sector reform.** If reform has been the name of the game, can we expect that the type of policy analysis and the type of policy capacity that is being demanded will be the same as that of the 1960s and 1970s? Will old tools be adequate when the edifice is being drastically renovated?

This book's answer is no. Many of the tools remain useful, as do the concepts, but they are being revised and changed to come to terms with a situation where the role and nature of government is very different from what it was a generation ago. Policymaking and policy analysis have to adapt to at least three fundamental shifts that have occurred in the last decade. First, the nature of some old policy problems has changed, and they have been joined by some entirely new issues. Poverty, for example, which a generation ago was most acute among families with a male breadwinner, is now in many countries a phenomenon concentrated among single mothers. The new problems countries face are often an artifact of new technologies, for example, how to create regulatory frameworks for e-commerce or for the bio-engineering of genetically modified organisms?

Second, many key policy processes have changed. It is almost universally acknowledged that citizens today want a more direct say in both policy development and program implementation. The Internet gives people, nongovernmental organizations, and the private sector unprecedented and instant access to materials and information that previously would have been primarily in government hands. Government departments themselves are different from what they were before—they are generally smaller, more knowledge-based, and focused more on evaluation of results and outcomes. Government responsibilities have been shuffled as well: in most provinces, notably Ontario and Quebec, major provincial responsibilities have been shifted to municipalities and vice versa. Today, policy analysis for a major urban centre in Canada is likely to include issues that previously would have been provincial or even federal responsibilities.

Third, there has been a subtle but important change in the way governments view their relationship with the private sector and civil society. Whereas a generation ago it might have seemed normal for the state to dominate both these sectors, today there is a sense that government actions should in most instances complement markets and collaboratively work with civil society. Until the financial crisis of fall 2008, there was an emerging consensus that in most policy areas, a light touch was better than heavy handed intervention. The collapse of private sector companies around the world (even possibly one or more of the Big Three automakers in North America) forced governments to spend billions on bail-outs and rescue packages, and opened a new debate about the appropriate role of government in shoring up capitalism. Government, and policy, activism may once more be on the public agenda.

At its best, policy analysis provides guidance to governments as they try to address public problems. In practice, of course, governments are political creatures interested in re-election and in power, and so they may eschew "guidance" in favour of more politically motivated behaviour. But from a citizen's perspective, governments are democratically elected to address public problems and provide core public services in the public interest, not in their own interest. The definition of the public interest will be contested of course, but it is this formula that provides the foundation for policy analysis and civic dialogue around policy issues. Policy analysis can then pose its core questions: what is the nature of the problem, what are we trying to achieve, how shall we go about addressing it, and how will we know if we have been successful or not? These are the key questions, but this book argues that the context in which they are asked—both in Canada and around the world—has changed dramatically in recent years. It is to these changes that we now turn.

KEY TERMS

bounded rationality—a term invented by Herbert Simon to capture the idea that most human decisionmaking takes place under various constraints rather than ideal conditions of complete information and unlimited processing capacities

emergent strategies—consistent patterns of behaviour that emerge or form rather than being planned

empirical analysis—takes logical analysis one step further: not what might be the likely effect of policy X, but what was its actual effect?

gender-based analysis (GBA)—a process that assesses the differential impact of public policies, programs, and legislation (proposed or existing) on women and men in terms of their social and economic circumstances, as well as their relationships in key social institutions such as the family

gender mainstreaming—an organizational strategy to ensure that a gender perspective is reflected in all types of organizational activities; championed by the United Nations as a means for achieving gender equality internationally

general goals—policy goals that enjoy a majority consensus or that express the broadest objectives of the policy initiative as a whole

governance—the process of governing or steering complex systems in cooperation with a variety of other actors

horizontal consistency—consistency across policy fields, not just within them

internal consistency—consistency among the three elements of problem definition, goals, and instruments

La Relève—the initiative started by the Clerk of Privy Council, Jocelyne Bourgon, during the mid-1990s to address the "quiet crisis" in the federal public service and rebuild motivation and pride

legal analysis—looks at public policy through the prism of law: constitutionality, consistency with statute, the practices of legal convention

logical analysis—deals with questions of consistency and coherence: is the policy internally consistent, is it vertically consistent, is it horizontally consistent?

normative analysis—measures some aspect of policy against an ethical standard: secular morality, the Bible, the Koran, the Canadian Charter of Rights and Freedoms, or the UN Universal Declaration of Human Rights

policy analysis—the disciplined application of intellect to public problems

policy capacity—the institutional ability to conduct policy analysis and implement its results effectively and efficiently

policy consistency—agreement between the different elements of public policy, embracing horizontal, vertical, and internal consistency

policy development—the process of shaping policy initiatives, from problem recognition to implementation and evaluation

policy framework—a guide to a range of related actions and decisions in a given field

policy goals—the objectives to be achieved by a given public policy

policy instruments—means chosen on how to address the problem and achieve the policy goals

Policy Research Initiative—an initiative directed at developing a sustained demand for policy among a community of collaborating federal departments and the wider research community focused on long-term, research-based, and reflective issues

policy space—the wider field within which a given, single policy operates in relation to others that tackle different elements of the problem

policy-specific goals—goals related to the broader ones but more directly connected to the programs that give the policy effect

policy statement—defines the problem, sets the goals that are to be achieved, and indicates the instruments or means whereby the problem is to be addressed and the goals achieved

policy studies—the broad range of research literature that is relevant to the study of and reflection upon public policy

problem definition—indicates what the problem or issue is and some of the causal factors behind it

public policy—a course of action or inaction chosen by public authorities to address a given problem or interrelated set of problems

public sector reform—attempts to change management practices and institutional design in the public sector to enhance efficiency and effectiveness

rational model—a systematic approach to problem-solving that lays out the problem, reviews options, and makes recommendations based on the intersection between goals and factual circumstances

rationalism—the characteristic form of knowing in the West that emphasizes empirical knowledge, science, objectivity, and systematic analysis

satisficing—the objective in most human decisionmaking to find a workable rather than perfect solution to problems

vertical consistency—consistency between the broad policy framework and the specific programs that implement that framework

FURTHER READINGS

Anderson, J. E. (2006). *Public policymaking: An introduction.* Boston: Houghton Mifflin.

Bardach, E. (2000). *A practical guide for policy analysis: The eightfold path to more effective problem solving.* New York: Chatham House Publishers.

Clemons, R. S., and McBeth, M. K. (2001). *Public policy praxis: Theory and pragmatism: A case approach.* Upper Saddle River, NJ: Prentice-Hall.

Dobuzinskis L., Howlett, M., Laycock, D. (Eds.). (2007) *Policy analysis in Canada: The state of the art.* Toronto: University of Toronto Press.

Dunn, W. N. (2008). *Public policy analysis: An introduction,* 4th ed. Upper Saddle River, NJ: Prentice-Hall.

Howlett, M., and Ramesh, M. (2003). *Studying public policy: Policy Cycles and Policy Subsystems,* 2nd ed. Don Mills, ON: Oxford University Press.

Moran, M., Rein M., and Goodin, R. E. (Eds.) (2006). *The Oxford handbook of public policy.* Oxford: Oxford University Press.

Orsini, M., and Smith, M. (Eds.) (2007). *Critical policy studies.* Vancouver: UBC Press.

Parsons, W. (1995). *Public policy: An introduction to the theory and practice of policy analysis.* Aldershot, UK: Edward Elgar.

Radin, B. (2000). *Beyond Machiavelli: Policy analysis comes of age.* Washington, DC: Georgetown University Press.

Weimer, D. L., and Vining, A. (2005). *Policy analysis: Concepts and practice,* 4th Ed. Upper Saddle River, N.J.: Prentice Hall.

REFERENCES

Aaron, H. J. (2000). Presidential address: Seeing through the fog: Policymaking with uncertain forecasts. *Journal of Policy Analysis and Management,* 19(2), 193–206.

Anderson, J. E. (2006). *Public policymaking: An introduction.* Boston: Houghton Mifflin.

Arndt, C., and Oman, C. (2006). *Uses and abuses of governance indicators.* Paris: OECD, Development Centre Studies.

A Strong Foundation (2000). (Tait Report) *Report of the Task Force on Public Service Values and Ethics.* Ottawa: Canadian Centre for Management Development.

Bakker, I. (2006). *Gender budget initiatives: Why they matter in Canada.* Alternative Federal Budget 2006, Technical Paper 1. Ottawa; Canadian Centre for Policy Alternatives.

Bakvis, H. (2000, January). Country report: Rebuilding policy capacity in the era of the fiscal dividend: A report from Canada. *Governance,* 13, 71–103.

Bird, M., and Stoney, C. (2006). Government approaches to the regulation of sin. In G. Bruce Doern (Ed.), *How Ottawa spends, 2006–2007* (pp. 247–265). Montreal: McGill-Queen's University Press.

Burt, S. (1995). The several worlds of policy analysis: Traditional approaches and feminist critiques. In S. Burt and L. Code (Eds.), *Changing methods: Feminists transforming practice* (pp. 357–78). Peterborough, ON: Broadview Press.

Charlesworth, J. C. (Ed.). (1972). *Integration of the social sciences through policy analysis*. Philadelphia: The American Academy of Political and Social Science.

Colebatch, H. K. (1998). *Policy*. Minneapolis: University of Minnesota Press.

Commission of the European Communities. (2002). *Communication from the Commission on the collection and use of expertise by the Commission: Principles and Guidelines*. COM(2002) 713 Final. Brussels.

deLeon, P. (1988). *Advice and consent: The development of the policy sciences*. New York: Russell Sage.

deLeon, P. (1997). *Democracy and the policy sciences*. Albany: State University of New York.

Desveaux, J. A., Lindquist, E. A., and Toner, G. (1994). Organizing for policy innovation in public bureaucracy: AIDS, energy and environmental policy in Canada. *Canadian Journal of Political Science, 27,* 493–528.

Dobuzinskis L., Howlett, M., Laycock, D. (Eds.). (2007). *Policy analysis in Canada: The state of the art*. Toronto: University of Toronto Press.

Dryzek, J. S. (1990). *Discursive democracy: Politics, policy and political science*. Cambridge, MA: Cambridge University Press.

Dunn, W. N. (2008). *Public policy analysis: An introduction*, 4th ed. Upper Saddle River, NJ: Prentice-Hall.

Dye, T. R. (1984). *Understanding public policy*, 5th ed. Englewood Cliffs, NJ: Prentice-Hall.

Fischer, F. (1980). *Politics, values, and public policy: The problem of methodology*. Boulder, CO: Westview Press.

Fischer, F. (1990). *Technocracy and the politics of expertise*. Newbury Park, CA: Sage.

Fischer, F. (1993). Citizen participation and the democratization of policy expertise: From theoretical inquiry to practical cases. *Policy Sciences, 26,* 165–87.

Fischer, F. (2003). *Reframing public policy: Discursive politics and deliberative practices*. New York: Oxford University Press.

Fischer, F., and Forester, J. (Eds.). (1987). *Confronting values in policy analysis: The politics of criteria*. Newbury Park: Sage.

Fischer, F., and Forester, J. (Eds.). (1993). *The argumentative turn in policy analysis and planning*. Durham, NC: Duke University Press.

Giddens, A. (1999). *The third way: The renewal of social democracy.* Malden, MA: Polity Press.

Government of Canada. (2007). *Cabinet directive on streamlining regulation.* Ottawa.

Graham, G. (1988). "The policy orientation" and the theoretical development of political science. In E. Portis and M. Levy (Eds.), *Handbook of political theory and policy science* (pp. 150–61). New York: Greenwood Press.

Hawkes, D. C., and Castellano, M. B. (1993, January). Research: A challenging agenda. *The Circle* (Royal Commission on Aboriginal Peoples) 2, 1, 7.

Hawkesworth, M. E. (1988). *Theoretical issues in policy analysis.* New York: State University of New York.

Hofferbert, R. I. (1990). *The reach and grasp of policy analysis: Comparative views of the craft.* Tuscaloosa: The University of Alabama Press.

Hood, C. (1998). *The art of the state: Culture, rhetoric, and public management.* Oxford: Clarendon Press.

Hoppe, R., and Jeliazkova, M. (2006). How policy workers define their job: A Netherlands case study. In H. Colebatch (Ed.), *The work of policy: An international survey* (pp. 35–60). Boulder, CO: Lexington Books.

Howlett, M., and Ramesh, M. (2003). *Studying public policy: Policy cycles and policy subsystems,* 2nd ed. Don Mills, ON: Oxford University Press.

Janowitz, M. (1972, July). Professionalization of sociology. *American Journal of Sociology,* 78, 105–35.

Kingdon, J. W. (1995). *Agendas, alternatives, and public policies,* 2nd ed. New York: HarperCollins.

Kraft, M. E., and Furlong, S. R. (2007). *Public policy: Politics, analysis, and alternatives.* Washington: CQ Press.

Lasswell, H. (1951). The policy orientation. In D. Lerner and H. Lasswell (Eds.), *The policy sciences* (pp. 3–15). Stanford, CA: Stanford University Press.

Lasswell, H. (1970). The emerging conception of the policy sciences. *Policy Sciences,* 1, 3–13.

Levy, B. (2007). *Governance reform: Bridging monitoring and action.* Washington, D.C.: The World Bank.

Lindblom, C. (1979, November–December). Still muddling, not yet through. *Public Administration Review,* 39, 517–26.

Lindblom, C. E. (1959). The science of muddling through. *Public Administration Review,* 19, 79–88.

Linder, S., and Peters, B. G. (1989). Instruments of government: Perceptions and contexts. *Journal of Public Policy*, 9, 35–58.

Lindquist, E. (2006). *A critical moment: Capturing and conveying the evolution of the Canadian public service*. Ottawa: Canada School of Public Service.

MacNair, M. D. (2006). In the name of the public good: "Public interest" as a legal standard. *Canadian Criminal Law Review* 10 (2), 175–204.

McCool, D. C. (Ed.). (1995). *Public policy theories, models, and concepts: An anthology*. Englewood Cliffs, NJ: Prentice-Hall.

Mintzberg, H. (1994). *The rise and fall of strategic planning: Reconceiving roles for planning, plans, planners*. New York: The Free Press.

Mintzberg, H., and Jørgensen, J. (1987, Summer). Emergent strategy for public policy. Canadian *Public Administration*, 30, 214–29.

OECD. (1995). *Governance in transition: Public management reform in OECD countries*. Paris: OECD.

OECD. (2003). *Public sector modernisation*. Paris: OECD.

OECD. (2005a). *Public sector modernisation*. Policy Brief. Paris: OECD.

OECD. (2005b). *Modernising government: The way forward*. Paris: OECD.

OECD. (2007). *Towards better measurement of government*. OECD Working Papers on Public Governance, 2007/1. Paris: OECD.

OECD. (2008a). *About the OECD*. Paris: OECD. Retrieved February 26, 2008, from http://www.oecd.org/pages/0,3417,en_36734052_36734103_1_1_1_1_1,00.html

OECD. (2008b). *Directorate for public governance and territorial development*. Retrieved February 26, 2008, from http://www.oecd.org/about/0,3347,en_2649_33735_1_1_1_1_1,00.html

OSI (Open Society Institute). (2008). *What is an open society?* Retrieved February 26, 2008, from http://www.soros.org/about/faq#c_programs_at_osi

Pal, L. A. (Ed.). (1999). *How Ottawa spends: 1999–2000: Shape shifting: Canadian governance toward the 21st century*. Toronto: Oxford University Press.

Pal, L. A., and Maxwell, J. (2004). *Assessing the public interest in the 21st century: A framework*. Ottawa: Canada Policy Research Networks.

Parsons, W. (1995). *Public policy: An introduction to the theory and practice of policy analysis*. Aldershot, UK: Edward Elgar.

Peters, B. G. (2006). *American public policy*, 7th ed. Washington: CQ Press.

Privy Council Office (Canada). (1995). *Third annual report to the Prime Minister on the public service of Canada*. Retrieved February 26,

2008, from http://www.pco-bcp.gc.ca/index.asp?lang=eng&page=clerk-greffier&sub=AnnualReports

Privy Council Office (Canada). (1997). *Fourth annual report to the Prime Minister on the public service of Canada.* Retrieved February 26, 2008, from http://www.pco-bcp.gc.ca/index.asp?lang=eng&page=clerk-greffier&sub=AnnualReports

Privy Council Office (Canada). (2007). *Fourteenth annual report to the Prime Minister on the public service of Canada.* Retrieved February 26, 2008, from http://www.pco-bcp.gc.ca/index.asp?lang=eng&page=clerk-greffier&sub=AnnualReports

Privy Council Office (Canada). (2008a). *The public service of Canada: Too many misperceptions.* Remarks by Kevin Lynch, Clerk of the Privy Council, February 18, 2008. Retrieved February 26, 2008, from http://www.pco-bcp.gc.ca/index.asp?lang=eng&page=clerk-greffier&sub=clerksspeeches&doc=20080218_e.htm

Privy Council Office (Canada). (2008b). *Fifteenth annual report to the Prime Minister on the public service of Canada.* Retrieved February 26, 2008, from http://www.pco-bcp.gc.ca/index.asp?lang=eng&page=clerk-greffier&sub=AnnualReports

Radin, B. (2000). *Beyond Machiavelli: Policy analysis comes of age.* Washington, DC: Georgetown University Press.

Rochefort, D. A., and Cobb, R. W. (1994). Problem definition: An emerging perspective. In D. A. Rochefort and R. W. Cobb (Eds.), *The politics of problem definition: Shaping the policy agenda* (pp. 1–31). Lawrence: University of Kansas Press.

Royal Commission on Aboriginal Peoples. (1991). *The Mandate: Royal Commission on Aboriginal peoples: Background documents* (Ottawa: Royal Commission on Aboriginal Peoples).

Royal Commission on Aboriginal Peoples, (Canada) (n.d.). *Ethical guidelines for research* (Ottawa: Royal Commission on Aboriginal Peoples).

Sanderson, I. (2002). Making sense of 'what works': Evidence based policy making as instrumental rationality? *Public Policy and Administration, 17,* 61–75.

Scott, J. C. (1998). *Seeing like a state: How certain schemes to improve the human condition have failed.* New Haven: Yale University Press.

SIGMA. (2008). *The SIGMA programme.* Retrieved February 26, 2008, from http://www.oecd.org/pages/0,3417,en_33638100_33638151_1_1_1_1,00.html

Simon, H., and Newell, A. (1957). Heuristic problem solving: The next advance in operations research. Reprinted in H. A. Simon. (1982).

Models of bounded rationality: Volume 1: Economic analysis and public policy. Cambridge, MA: MIT Press, 380–89.

Simon, H., Smithburg, D. W., and Thompson, V. A. (1958). *Public administration*. New York: Alfred A. Knopf.

Status of Women Canada. (1996). *Gender-based analysis: A guide for policy-making*. Ottawa: Status of Women Canada.

Stone, D. (2001). *Policy paradox: The art of political decision making*. Rev. ed. New York: W. W. Norton and Co.

Surowiecki, J. (2005). *The wisdom of crowds*. New York: Anchor Books.

Sutherland, S. L. (1993). The public service and policy development. In M. M. Atkinson (Ed.), *Governing Canada: Institutions and public policy* (pp. 81–113). Toronto: Harcourt Brace Jovanovich.

Suzuki, D. T., and Knudtson, P. (1992). *Wisdom of the elders: Sacred native stories of nature*. New York: Bantam.

Thomas, P. (1987). The use of social research: Myths and models. In M. Bulmer (Ed.), *Social science research and government: Comparative essays on Britain and the United States,* (pp. 51–60). Cambridge, UK: Cambridge University Press.

Transparency International. (2008). *Home page*. Retrieved February 26, 2008, from www.transparency.org

United Nations, Office of the Special Advisor on Gender Issues and Advancement of Women. (2004). *Gender mainstreaming*. Retrieved August 5, 2004, from http://www.un.org/womenwatch/osagi/gender-mainstreaming.htm

Vannijnatten, D. L., and MacDonald, D. (2003). Reconciling energy and climate change policies: How Ottawa blends. In G. B. Doern (Ed.), *How Ottawa spends 2003–2004: Regime change and policy shift,* (pp. 72–88). Don Mills, ON: Oxford University Press.

Weiss, A., and Woodhouse, E. (1992). Reframing incrementalism: A constructive response to critics. *Policy Sciences, 25,* 255–73.

Weiss, C. H. (1983). Ideology, interest, and information: The basis of policy positions. In D. Callahan and B. Jennings (Eds.), *Ethics, the social sciences, and policy analysis* (pp. 213–45). New York: Plenum Press.

Wildavsky, A. (1979). *Speaking truth to power: The art and craft of policy analysis*. Boston: Little, Brown & Co.

World Bank. (1997). *World development report 1997: The state in a changing world (summary)*. Washington, D.C.: The International Bank for Reconstruction and Development/The World Bank.

World Bank. (2000). *Reforming public institutions and strengthening governance*. Washington, DC: The International Bank for Reconstruction and Development/The World Bank.

2

Modern Governance:
The Challenges for
Policy Analysis

Policy analysis, in the service of the public interest, makes its contributions by asking certain questions and using certain tools. It cannot make those contributions in a vacuum, however, and the nature of policy work depends on context. As the last chapter suggested, that context has been changing in the last decade. This chapter reviews the key forces underpinning this change: globalization, political culture, and governance. They are closely entangled, and sometimes conflicting, but with broad consequences that make a substantial difference to the nature of policymaking and analysis. Globalization involves deeper and more intense economic and political interdependencies and challenges fundamental assumptions about sovereignty and the role of the nation-state. In Canada as well as other industrialized countries, political culture is less deferential and more individualist and participatory. Changing notions of governance reflect these forces but also have their own dynamic that stresses new forms of **governance** and public management. Subsequent chapters take up the detailed implications of these forces for problem definition, policy design, implementation, agenda-setting, evaluation, and policymaking in turbulent times.

In Chapter 1, public policy was defined as a course of action or inaction undertaken by public authorities to address a problem or interrelated set of problems. Policy analysis was defined as the disciplined application of intellect to public problems. If the nature of public problems changes, if the broad context within which problems arise and are addressed is altered, then both public policy and policy analysis should change as well. This is precisely what has been happening in the past decade in industrialized countries—Canada included—and a revitalized policy analysis has to come to terms with what is different about modern governance. It is a cliché, of course, that our times (like all times!) are marked by change. But it is in the nature of clichés to expose obvious truths, and no truth is more obvious than that we are surrounded and affected by changes of unparalleled magnitude and scope. On a global level, recent years have seen the collapse of the Soviet empire and of apartheid in South Africa, the rise of new security threats and global terrorism, the emergence of the United States as the world's "hyperpower" and the rapid rise of China and India as global military and economic players, continued European Union enlargement, Internet viruses that spread around the world in minutes, the rising threat of pandemics such as SARS, devastating crises in our food supply such as Mad Cow disease and avian flu, that war in Iraq and in Afghanistan, and a global economic crisis. Canada experienced the impact of each of these forces, and had its own developments to contend with: the end of the decade-long Chrétien era in late 2003, the creation of the Canadian Conservative party out of the ashes of the Canadian Alliance and Progressive Conservative parties, and the election of two consecutive minority governments with strong ideas about public policy and public management.

These changes are more than merely numerous—they have altered key social and political systems in both the industrialized and developing world. "Indeed, in Canada, as elsewhere, the impact of the new economic order, the information revolution and the growing populist demand for greater public participation as a means of solving problems is being felt in virtually every sector and in every area of government activity" (Courchene and Savoie, 2003, p. 4). As Lister (2007: 4–5) notes, the impact on the public service "has been a proliferation of complex issues— such as climate change, social exclusion, and public health issues. These problems tend to be long-term, have many causes, and enjoy no clear agreement about what a solution would look like or how it could be achieved. They do not map neatly onto the silos into which we have organized government departments. Many require behavioural change. This comes at a time when the policy levers available to bureaucrats have become more diffuse."

These changes are massive and unrelenting, but the trick is to try to make some sense of the broad pattern and to tease out the implications for policy analysis and governance. This chapter argues that there are three powerful undercurrents beneath the waves of political turmoil and **policy reversal** evident in Canada and throughout the industrialized world. They are globalization, shifts in **political culture,** and new ideas about governance and **public management.** Each of these is multi-faceted, of course, and connected intimately to the others. Nonetheless, it is possible to outline at least a few of their most important features. They have been building for over twenty-five years, and in some respects are so natural a part of our political, economic, and social environment that we take them for granted. A policy analysis that fails to come to grips with these forces and their implications for policy and governance is doomed to irrelevance.

Globalization

Economic Globalization

The modern phenomenon of globalization has to be carefully distinguished from the mere fact of international connectedness. The British Empire was global in scope, and other imperial systems like the Romans' covered enormous tracts of territory. The Moors extended their empire as far as Spain, and the Portuguese in turn established outposts as far away as Goa, India. Marco Polo travelled from the Mediterranean to China in the late 1200s. The city states of medieval Europe had extensive trade connections of their own to the Orient, and vast, complex, and virtually global systems of trade developed by the 1700s around raw materials, sugar, spices, and slaves (Brook, 2007). In short, human history in the last 1000 years has been clearly marked by internationalism that sometimes came close to embracing the entire planet. What is different about the present situation?

American journalist Thomas L. Friedman (1999) captures the differences as well as anyone else. His point of comparison is not the ancient world but the Cold War and what he calls the "**globalization system**" that has replaced it. For Friedman, globalization "is not a phenomenon. It is not just some passing trend. Today it is the overarching international system shaping domestic politics and foreign relations of virtually every country" (p. 7). Globalization has several important features. It is not a static system but a dynamic process that "involves inexorable integration of markets, nation-states and technologies" to an unprecedented degree (ibid.). Its driving idea is **free market capitalism**—the more countries integrate with the world economy and allow global economic forces to penetrate domestic economies, the more they will prosper. It has its own dominant culture—largely American or Western—and so tends to be homogenizing at a certain level (and thus generates reactions against that homogenization). It has its own defining technologies organized around computerization, digitization, satellites, the Internet, mobile communications, and global transportation systems. It has its own international balance of power—between nation-states (the traditional geo-political balance, but wherein the United States is still the only global superpower, though increasingly challenged by China and Russia); between nation-states and markets (global investment markets driven by the "Electronic

Herd"); and between individuals and nation-states (the ability of individuals to act directly on the world stage). While an enthusiast of globalization, Friedman is savvy enough to know that in the real world people live in communities, traditions, customs, and languages that are deeply rooted—what he calls the "olive tree"—and that will bend only so far in the face of global economic, technological, and cultural forces. The policy trick for most states is to come to terms with globalization but also balance it against identity and community.

In understanding globalization, it is important also to understand what it is not. Scholte (2003) identifies what he calls four cul-de-sacs in conceptualizing globalization: globalization-as-internationalization ("the growth of transactions and interdependence between countries"); globalization-as-liberalization ("a process of removing officially imposed restrictions on movements of resources between countries in order to form an 'open' and 'borderless' world economy"); globalization-as-universalization ("a process of dispersing various objects and experiences to people at all inhabited parts of the earth"); and globalization-as-westernization ("social structures of modernity [capitalism, industrialism, rationalism, urbanism, etc.] are spread the world over, destroying pre-existent cultures and local self-determination in the process"). Scholte sensibly argues that understanding globalization in these terms is redundant—the phenomena of internationalization, liberalization, universalization, and westernization have existed much longer than contemporary globalization, and simply redefining these phenomena as globalization does not add anything to our understanding. "Arguments that only build on these conceptions fail to open insights that are not available through preexistent vocabulary. Deployed on any of these four lines, 'globalization' provides no distinct analytical value-added" (Scholte, 2005, 54). Contemporary globalization is characterized by "**globality**," or the sense that the entire planet is a single social space, that people carry on conversations in that space irrespective of territoriality, that they pay collective attention to "global events"—that there is a quality of simultaneity. While globality depends on modern means of transportation (i.e., the spread of SARS as a global event would simply not be possible without modern air travel), it is clear that information and communications technologies and the Internet are a crucial foundation— indeed the very concept of "cyberspace" expresses the notion of a supraterritorial space within which there can be social interactions distinct from those that occur in real space and time (Rheingold, 2003). In this sense, contemporary globalization is defined by globality, which in turn is defined (in large part) by information and communications technologies and the Internet. We take for granted that top-rated movies and songs have a "world-wide release" or that a computer virus can make its way around the world in mere hours.

At the same time, globality in the sense of a single space and time continuum that we all occupy collectively is complemented and complicated by disjunctures in the flows and networks that surround us. Appadurai (1996), for example, proposes that we explore contemporary globalization in terms of five "scapes": ethnoscapes (the movements of people as tourists, migrants, refugees, exiles), technoscapes (Internet and transportation technologies), fincancescapes (unpredictable financial flows), mediascapes (global media in all its forms, TV, videos, movies, audio), and ideoscapes (global flows of ideas and ideologies that are generated locally but then spread globally). For Appadurai, the key to understanding contemporary globalization is the increasing disjuncture among these scapes, the hybridity and plurality of personal experience. The disjuncture among these scapes is created through the absence of any coordinating entity or body—the logic of each scape is only loosely coupled to the others. Take the example of an Inuit teenager living in Iqaluit. She listens to Jamaican reggae on her made-in-China iPod while reading Jane Austen, and eats Florida oranges for breakfast as the snows swirl outside her home. Globality is the sense that these scapes—despite their heterogeneity—merge seamlessly and simultaneously, in an almost ordinary way.

We return to globality later in this section. For many, contemporary globalization is not about scapes and culture, but primarily about major economic transformations in the last fifty years. First, of course, has been the development of a complex international trading system. After World War II, a host of international institutions and conventions were established to create the beginnings of a true international economic system: the General Agreement on Tariffs and Trade (GATT—now superseded by the World Trade Organization or the WTO), the International Monetary Fund (IMF), the World Bank, and the Bretton Woods agreement on currency transactions. The logic behind these initiatives was twofold: first, to create a set of supranational decisionmaking bodies that would create stable and harmonized international regimes dealing with a host of issues from trade to communications; second, to knock down those major barriers between countries that impeded or prevented interactions or communication. The postwar efforts were largely successful on both counts. Figure 2.1 (page 50) shows the increased volume in global trade from 1950 to 2006. The key point is that, despite dips, the long-term trend for world trade has been steadily upward. In 2001, due in large part to the terrorist attacks on the World Trade Center, international trade declined and only began to improve after 2002. However, the trend line seems clear: as borders become more porous, goods, services, and information can travel more freely across political lines. As well, in an often-ignored development, people move as well, and immigration is a major component of contemporary globalization (Sassen, 1998). It is clear that the

Figure 2.1 World Merchandise Trade Volume by Major Product Group, 1950–2006 (Volume Indices, 1950 = 100)

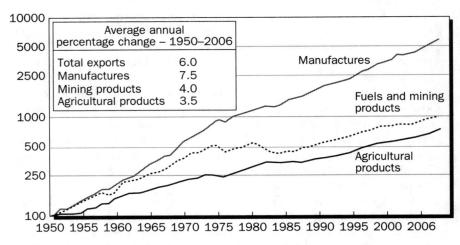

SOURCE: World Trade Organization (2007). *International Trade Statistics 2007.* Chart I.3, p. 2. Retrieved Feb. 2, 2007, from http://www.wto.org/english/res_e/statis_e/its2007_e/its2007_e.pdf.

world economy is subject to turbulence as well, and there may be reversals as well as advances in international economic integration. In 2008 the US economy was on the brink of recession due, among other things, to the housing credit collapse, and that recession was threatening the global economy. However, in a sense this actually illustrates the advance in economic globalization—integration is so deep now in trade and financial markets, that turbulence in one part affects all the others.

In a pre-globalized world, lines on maps mark territories where, through public policy as well as forces of history, society, economy, and governance, "national systems" coincide. At the most elementary economic level, for example, national boundaries marked coherent economic systems. International trade in goods and services could be blocked through public policies that protected domestic markets. The whole idea of a national economy presumes that there is more internal than external trade. In a globalized world, as barriers between and within local markets fall, markets get integrated globally. Companies sell locally, regionally, and internationally, wherever anyone is willing to buy the product. Obviously, domestic policies are not the only impediment to world trade: geography and social factors play a role as well. But these too have been affected by technological changes in the past twenty-five years, making it much easier for firms to manage production and sales processes across widely flung international networks. Known as **"global supply chains,"** or "global value chains," the "key change is that companies are increasingly fragmenting the full range of activities needed to bring a good or service from conception to market—rather than producing entire products within one country. With production broken into smaller parts, companies can then produce or buy each input for a particular good or service from wherever it can be made or provided most efficiently" (Lister, 2007: 5).

Canada, always a trading nation, crossed an important threshold in the 1990s. Interprovincial trade through the 1980s was as important to the country as international trade, both growing yearly at about the same rate. In 1990, however, interprovincial trade flattened and increased only slightly each year, while international exports continued to make gains. By 1996, only P.E.I., Nova Scotia, and the Northwest Territories were exporting more to other provinces than to the rest of the world. As Figure 2.2 shows, total exports flattened between 2000 and 2003, but since that period the country has been relying more and more on international trade. Only Nunavut and the Yukon export more to other provinces than they do internationally, and while interprovincial trade has grown only modestly since 1998, international trade has almost doubled.

Figure 2.2 Interprovincial and International Exports, Canada, 1997–2006 (billions of Canadian dollars)

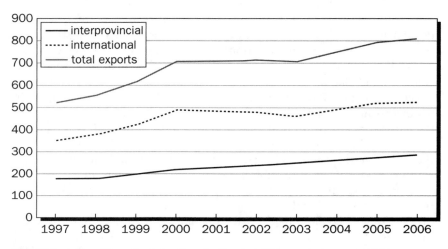

SOURCE: Adapted from Statistics Canada, *Provincial Economic Accounts, 2006 Preliminary Estimates,* Catalogue no. 13-213-PPB, April 2007, pages 324 to 326.

A second economic dimension of globalization is the well-known phenomenon of **transnational corporations** (TNCs). This too has evolved over the postwar period. Multinational companies are not in themselves new—think of the Hudson's Bay Company (chartered in 1670) or the British East India Company (founded in 1600 to trade with Mogul kings in what is now India). But these companies were instruments of an imperial system of mercantilism, tools of imperial governments. What is different about modern multinational commercial firms is that their commercial interests are primary, they operate across the globe, and their national home base is relatively unimportant. As was the case with international trade, the 1990s were a boom period for TNCs and foreign direct investment (FDI). In 1998, FDI rose by almost 40 percent to over $640 billion, most of which was in developed countries. In 2006, global FDI soared by 38 percent to US$1.3 trillion, marking the third consecutive year of growth. But TNCs continue to be important players in the international economy. There are some 78 000 TNCs controlling at least 78 000 foreign affiliates, employing 73 million people abroad. Thus, a good part of what we think of as economic globalization in terms of economic interdependencies among countries is really due to a network of huge corporations and the investments they make and the goods and services they sell.

Country of origin mattered at one time but in the contemporary phase of economic globalization is less and less important. This is because of a shift in the way in which these firms operate. The first phase of multinational development entailed exports to foreign markets of goods produced domestically (e.g., cars made in the United States or Japan exported elsewhere). The second phase was the establishment of production facilities in these foreign markets, facilities that were still quite dependent on the parent corporation for services, inputs, and strategies. A third phase has seen multinational firms begin to operate as transnational firms, that is, to organize their production process into global chains. What this means is that an "American" car will have parts produced in a variety of countries for final assembly somewhere completely distinct from the production of those parts. This is a significant change in the nature of globalization, since it implies a much more tightly integrated international market. As Thurow (1996) noted over a decade ago, "For the first time in human history, anything can be made anywhere and sold everywhere" (p. 113). Global sourcing means that companies will shift production to the most attractive sites, either in terms of expertise or labour costs. Global sourcing presumes an international or global production market, and by the same token an emerging global consumption market. In other words, if production is organized globally, and consumption is increasingly similar in terms of the goods and services that people buy, then it makes less and less sense to talk about "domestic" and "foreign" markets; what seems to be emerging, at least for some goods and services, is a global market or a single economic space. It is important to remember that local markets continue to exist, and local or national markets have institutional advantages (e.g., similar languages or social customs) over international ones.

A final aspect of economic globalization is the increase in capital flows and mobility, dramatically illustrated by the American subprime meltdown and its reverberations throughout global financial markets which had bought toxic mortgages as financial investments. Large financial institutions such as banks, insurance companies, and investment brokers have gradually developed systems to allow virtually instantaneous transfers of capital anywhere in the world. This is based in part on new technology and in part on the emergence of large international institutions and the multinational corporations mentioned above. On top of this are millions of individuals now investing in stocks, bonds, and currencies. In Friedman's colourful phrase, these institutions and individuals together comprise an "Electronic Herd" that stampedes around global markets, often with devastating results. Enormous quantities of liquid capital are shifted from country to country, stock exchange to stock exchange, in response to business opportunities as well as perceived risk. Companies such as Standard and Poor's provide rating services on countries and state enterprises that provide crucial information for international investors. Shifts in capital based on this information have consequences for domestic interest rates, stock prices, and exchange rates. From a policy perspective, for a time the most daunting implication was for governments running large deficits. Deficits are covered by borrowing, and with a long enough string of deficits, governments have to go beyond domestic sources of capital to international ones. Reliance on international investors means keeping them happy, and in recent years these investors were not happy with deficits, what they consider high spending, or indeed anything that undermines their "confidence." A dramatic example of what can happen occurred in 1998 with the capital crisis in Southeast Asia, which soon spread around the world and created what the IMF called "some of the most severe financial market turbulence in the postwar period" (International Monetary Fund 1999, p. 9). The crisis began with weak commodity prices that lowered output in Malaysia, Thailand, and Indonesia, picked up momentum with doubts about the Japanese economy, and then spread to Russia once its government decided to unilaterally restructure its domestic debt and depreciate the ruble. External debt for these countries climbed alarmingly, just as international lending dried up. This reduction of lending capital put pressure on indebted Latin American economies, particularly Brazil. More recently, the US subprime mortgage crisis (which resulted from lending to people who could not really afford rising interest rates, but whose debts were "pooled" and sold to banks and funds around the world) in 2007 "caused a widespread reassessment of risk among lenders and investors, leading to a massive erosion of capital in the financial services industry and a sharp contraction of credit" (Economist Intelligence Unit, 2008: 14).

What does all this mean? Details will be explored in subsequent chapters, but economic globalization has had several consequences that together change the terrain of modern policymaking and analysis. Primarily, the development of international trading regimes means that governments have fewer policy instruments at their disposal to protect domestic markets, what Porter (1990) calls the "home base." In part this is because governments have deliberately entered into agreements to increase trade and investment that constrain their own powers to discriminate in favour of their domestic industries or workforce. The North American Free Trade Agreement and the GATT (administered by the WTO), along with a host of new international trade agreements on intellectual property and trade in services, are prime examples. Dealing with trade disputes around the clash between domestic law and international agreements is now a small governmental cottage industry. As of 2007, for example, Canada was involved in WTO trade disputes against US agricultural subsidies, intellectual property rights in China, Belgian and Dutch government bans on seal products, and Chinese subsidy programs (Foreign Affairs and International Trade Canada, 2008). In some cases, Canadian legislation is a target of other countries under WTO rules (for example, in a dispute with Brazil over subsidies to Bombardier airplanes); in other cases, Canada uses international agreements as the basis for its own complaints (e.g., the infamous softwood lumber case). International agreements of this sort are swords that cut both ways—that is why governments sign them—but they undeniably shift key decisionmaking powers over policy to international organizations. But the reduced capacity of governments is also due to facts on the ground—or on the globe. With current communications and transportation technologies, both companies and people can more easily evade the traditional instruments at the disposal of governments, such as taxation, regulation, and simple surveillance. Moreover, the discipline of the global marketplace, exercised through massive and almost instantaneous capital flows, gives governments less and less room to manoeuvre, and less and less capacity to go it alone. It may drive them to a **"race to the bottom"** as they try to attract international capital through lower and lower standards. Yet another reason that governments have a harder time of going it alone is that globalization induces mutual interdependence and integration so that everyone is interested in everyone else's business. The SARS and Mad Cow crises in 2003 and 2004 were stark reminders of that reality. In the case of SARS, "globality" meant that everyone on the planet was aware of its outbreak in Hong Kong and in Toronto. Indeed, SARS spread through the other emblem of globalization—international air travel. Even though the number of cases was tiny, the economic effects in terms of tourism were huge. Isolated cases of Mad Cow in Alberta saw international global and especially US beef markets clang shut instantaneously.

Does this interdependence and economic integration mean that the state will wither away? Earlier discussions of the impact of globalization assumed that interdependence would reduce government capacity, shift responsibilities upwards to global institutions, and make states less important actors both globally and within their domestic spheres. To the degree that states assume authority over territory, and as we have noted, as territory becomes less and less important as an organizing principle for economic and social life, it would seem that states would indeed wither. The story is more complicated than that, however. For one thing, states remain key institutions in responding to issues that matter to people—social security, economic prosperity and more recently the possibility of a huge global recession, the environment, disasters, and emergencies. They continue to have massive financial and personnel resources at their disposal, much more than any single corporation. For another thing, globalization itself creates an imperative for states to act internationally to pursue the interests of their citizens—climate change, telecommunications regulation, food and safety standards, the list is endless—all require states as the key players in international institutions. Finally, the post 9/11 security state has seen massive growth, not withering, of state capacities in defence, policing, and surveillance. To the extent that terrorist threats are also part of globalization, they have stimulated a strengthening of state powers.

In this more complicated story, states, rather than withering away, are joined by a wider array of actors through international networks of governmental and non-governmental organizations. Sometimes referred to as "multi-centric" (Scholte, 2005: Chap. 6) or "multi-scalar" (Mahon, Andrew, and Johnson, 2007), this captures a world system where these networks provide global governance without a global government as such.

> In a world of government networks, by contrast, the same officials who are judging, regulating, and legislating domestically are also reaching out to their foreign counterparts to help address the governance problems that arise when national actors and issues spill beyond their borders. Global governance, from this perspective, is not a matter of regulating states the way states regulate their citizens, but rather of addressing the issues and resolving the problems that result from citizens going global—from crime to commerce to civic engagement. (Slaughter, 2004: 16)

Indeed, it is important to recall that many aspects of the global economy have in fact been deliberately created by states, even if at the end of the day they cannot completely control them (Pauly, 1997). Moreover, globalization theorists often assume a hypermobility or hyperfluidity of capital and trade that belies the degree of concentration of material facilities and work processes in territorial sites—globalization is in fact "managed" through a small number of "global cities" or sites such as London, Tokyo, Frankfurt, and New York (Sassen 1998, Chap. 10), and these are themselves located in states that still have the capacity to regulate them in various ways. It is an open question as to whether these cities, and their growing interconnectivity around functions like financial investment flows, are the real backbone of economic globalization as opposed to states (Sassen, 2002a). Importantly, global cities such as Shanghai are now emerging in the developing world, and linking up to previous leading cities, creating a truly global network (Sassen, 2002b).

It is also important to remember the adaptability of states, their differential capacity, and their increased importance in a globalized world. Weiss (1998), for example, highlights the importance of states—particularly strong states—in acting as "facilitators not victims" of globalization, and the emergence of catalytic states—such as Singapore—that consolidate networks of national and regional trade and investment. As we noted, states and their networks are important for managing the international trade system, from "rules of origin", to resolving disputes, and to possibly (through a new G-20 mechanism) of actually coordinating global responses to economic crises. Just as importantly, there is the argument that in a globalized world, where factors of production are spread out through global supply chains, competitive advantage increasingly involves massive investments in innovation, science, and technology. Again, the role of government—in collaboration with the private sector and non-governmental institutions—is crucial in creating the regulatory and infrastructural context for success. Laws on intellectual property, funding for universities, regulation of financial investors—all this comes from government. So in the end, economic globalization does not mean the decline of government, but a reconfiguration of its activities, using new instruments and facing new challenges, competitors, and partners.

Another important issue is whether economic globalization is inevitable and uni-directional. The trade and investment figures provided earlier might create an impression of steady growth and steady integration. There are several reasons why this needs to be treated cautiously. First, there is always the possibility of a major downturn. At time of writing, the G-20 was teetering on the brink of recession, despite attempts at a coordinated response to inflate their economies and rescue failing industries. Second, while it might be that **trade liberalization** is in everyone's interest, countries nonetheless try to protect their economies as much as they can, and this can impede institutional progress. The collapse of the Doha round of GATT negotiations and the emergence of regional trade deals is a case in point.

Third, while economic globalization has been accompanied by growing prosperity, it also exposes countries and economies to the cold winds of competition and consequently can engender resistance. As the Pew Global Attitudes survey found in late 2007: "the publics of the world broadly embrace key tenets of economic globalization but fear the disruptions and downsides of participating in the global economy. In rich countries as well as poor ones, most people endorse free trade, multinational corporations and free markets. However, the latest Pew Global Attitudes survey of more than 45 000 people finds they are concerned about inequality, threats to their culture, threats to the environment and threats posed by immigration. Together, these results reveal an evolving world view on globalization that is nuanced, ambivalent, and sometimes inherently contradictory" (Pew Global Attitudes Project, 2007). Indeed, Americans had the lowest level of support for international trade, something that was reflected in promises by both Hillary Clinton and Barack Obama as they competed in February 2008 for the Democratic presidential nomination to tear up the North American Free Trade Agreement. These attitudes and promises reflect the fear that globalization will take away jobs.

The legendary protests in November 1999 against the WTO meetings in Seattle, and similar ones afterward at both WTO and G-8 meetings (notably the 2001 G-8 summit in Genoa) have become the most powerful symbol of resistance against the blind forces of economic globalization. The 2007 G-8 summit in Heiligendamm, Germany, is a good case in point. The summit's agenda, to begin with, illustrated how peak global organizations of this type, while ostensibly dedicated to economic development, actually take on a broad range of governance issues.

> Key issues of the agenda of the G8 Summit 2007 in Heiligendamm included the following: (i) the framework conditions for the global economy, involving the largest emerging economies in the system of global responsibility (strategies for balanced worldwide growth and reduced global imbalances; measures for improved stability and transparency of financial and capital markets; global investment conditions; social dimension of globalisation or "globalisation with a human face"; innovation and protection of IPRs); (ii) climate protection issues (sustainable use of resources; energy efficiency; post-Kyoto efforts); and (iii) African development (good governance; strengthening international and regional partnerships on reform and growth in Africa; fighting HIV/AIDS, tuberculosis and malaria; establishing effective health systems; achieving peace and security). (Federal Government Germany, 2007)

Some 25 000 (police estimate) to 80 000 (organizers' estimate) demonstrators tried to disrupt the proceedings in street clashes with police on

June 2, 2007. About 146 police were injured, some of them seriously. It is important to note that the protests are not merely about the economic dimension of globalization and the role of governments and international organizations like the G-8—as Box 2.1 illustrates, a clash of world views is at stake (O'Brien et al., 2000). The Heiligendamm protest organizers

---

BOX 2.1   **G8 ALTERNATIVE SUMMIT**

G8 2007—THERE ARE ALTERNATIVES!

CALL BY THE INITIATORS FOR SUPPORTING THE INTERNATIONAL
G8-ALTERNATIVE-SUMMIT

Rostock, June 5–7, 2007

In 2007 the summit of the eight richest and most powerful states in the world will take place in Heiligendamm near the City of Rostock on the Baltic coast of Germany. The politics of the G8 have triggered criticism and worldwide protest for a long time. During the 2007 summit in Germany this will be visible in its various forms. One important event will be the Alternative Summit to be held in Rostock from June 5–7. Anyone who is searching for alternatives to globalisation in its current form is invited.

Even though the heads of state and governments of the G8 represent only 13% of the world's population, they will nevertheless deal with questions concerning the world economy, development, environment, war and peace, as well as other issues which concern all of humankind. As usual however, priority will be given to satisfying national interests which are often narrow-minded and short-term.

This will not change in 2007. Revealingly, the German government has declared "investment security" to be the leitmotiv of the summit. The current form of globalisation has produced and continues to produce many losers and very few winners.

One of those losers is social justice. Poverty and social polarisation are increasing worldwide. While the number of people fighting starvation has risen from 840 million to 854 million over the last ten years, the tiny minority of millionaires and the super-rich were able to double their wealth from 16 trillion to 33 trillion dollars. Another group that benefits from this type of globalisation are the so-called 'global players' such as institutional investors and multinational corporations. Simultaneously, poverty and social insecurity are on the rise even in most developed countries.

Another loser is the environment. The current economic model and the corresponding way of life is leading to a catastrophic climate change, destroying bio-diversity, and plundering the planet's natural resources. The very basis for human life on this planet is being destroyed. And the politics of the G8, focussed on unlimited growth and unregulated market dynamics, severely intensify global environmental problems.

Peace and international security are on the losing side as well. More and more causes for conflict are accumulating incessantly. Nationalism, racism, fundamentalism, violence, terror, and war are once again being promoted. Instead of long-term conflict prevention strategies we are witnessing an increasing militarisation of international politics. G8 states are either at war, or in some indirect way involved in armed conflicts. Among the losers of globalisation, women are especially affected. Millions of people are forced into migration or sheer flight by miserable living-conditions. Alongside, the first world is increasing its fortification against migrants.

We cannot allow all this to continue! Globalisation in the interest of the majority of the people works differently. We want a democratic globalisation from below, globalisation of justice and social security. We want fair relations and fair trade between developed and developing countries. We want an economy based on solidarity. The economy must serve the people, not the other way round! We demand a responsible and sustainable treatment of our environment. We stand for peaceful and political solutions of conflicts.

There are alternatives to the politics of the G8. We want to present and discuss them in public. Also, we want to exchange ideas, and collectively work on answers to the many remaining questions.

The Alternative Summit will be held from June 5 (5pm) through June 7 (1pm). Additionally, there will be various connected events that will focus on specific topics. There will be over 120 different workshops in Rostock at the Alternative Summit. The workshops are organized under different topics: Global Justice; Environment, Climate & Energy; Strategies and Alternatives; War and Militarisation; Migration and Racism; Labour and Social Issues; Education; Gender; etc.

SOURCE: Fair World Fair, G8 2007—THERE ARE ALTERNATIVES! www.g8-alternative-summit.org/en/media/Call_1.pdf.

brought various groups together under the banner "another world is possible." Leaflets proclaimed that "The world shaped by the dominance of the G-8 is a world of war, hunger, social divisions, environmental destruction and barriers against migrants and refugees" (Associated Press, 2007). Notably, this world view (unlike the one in Seattle a decade ago) is not against globalization per se. It seeks a just globalization, fair trade, and equitable global solutions to issues like the environment and global warming. Equally significant is the new grammar of social action that these global social movements articulate. They do not organize primarily on the basis of representation of interests or of identity, they engage in performance, theatre, demonstrations, and vivid events that are meant to call attention to dominant codes of power. G-8 protesters performed street theatre and painted themselves green. Falun Gong mobilized 10 000 people in 1999 to participate in a day-long silent demonstration adjacent to Tiananmen Square (McDonald, 2006).

In response to the argument that globalization inevitably leads to a race to the bottom, analysts like Vogel (1995) point to the "California effect": trade can lead to higher environmental standards as political jurisdictions with higher standards "force foreign producers in nations with weaker domestic standards either to design products that meet those standards or sacrifice export markets" (p. 261). Foreign producers then have incentives to force their own countries' governments to increase standards. The California effect—counterintuitive as it might appear — has been observed in other jurisdictions and other policy areas (Vogel and Kagan, 2004), and the reasons are diverse: Western based social movements agitating in developing countries; the disinclination of many low-income countries to simply passively accept damaging corporate policies; the penetration and acceptance of international standards.

Another example of counterintuitive forces at play in modern globalization is what Florida discerns as the rise of the "creative class" (2002, 2005, 2008). His argument highlights two important aspects of contemporary globalization. The first is that it is linked to, if not driven by, fundamental changes in economic production. Obviously, primary resources, manufacturing capacity, availability of capital, and scientific skill matter a lot in the modern economy. But for an increasing number of key goods and services, the primary element is not old-fashioned labour or resource investment, but creativity, often scientific, and just as often cultural or aesthetic. Creativity is the essential element behind the development of new ideas, new products and services, new forms of packaging old products, and is a blend of research, taste, and sensibility. It is what distinguishes products like Apple's iPhone or Peter Jackson's Lord of the Rings trilogy as creativity. Florida argues that this creative class needs to congregate and cluster, and makes special lifestyle demands on cities—demands for pleasing urban surroundings, amenities, and services. To the degree that city planners respond to the creative class, they create urban spaces far from the Dickensian horrors of the industrial revolution. Again, in a counterintuitive development, globalization in this dimension actually drives standards up, not down.

In short, globalization is not an implacable and impersonal juggernaut. Despite its reality, it is both less extensive and intensive than the globalizers would have us believe. It takes place in real space, often in quite limited spaces, and those spaces are subject to some form of policy intervention. Moreover, globalization itself is not merely an economic phenomenon but in large part is politically driven as countries decide that it is in their interests to integrate more closely. Once more, this is an arena of policy and of choice. Finally, citizens will not soon cease to demand the core services and programs of the contemporary welfare state, nor will they hesitate to demand protection from the worst excesses of globalization. The trajectories of all these forces are difficult to predict, but it seems clear now that states, despite a diffusion of their power, remain important. Globalization has not banished geo-politics, though it has created new channels through which geo-politics might flow. As well, the idea that globalization necessarily means relentless and implacable convergence toward the "bottom" (low wages, deregulation, job loss), or a world without policy choices, is without solid foundation. In fact, what is striking is how patterns of convergence and divergence appear simultaneously—even as trade increases and G-8 or G-20 summits are held, major differences over policy arise between the United States, the European Union, Russia, China, and Southeast Asia. The challenge is now not about whether globalization will happen or not, but how this great transformation is managed to make globalization work, especially with the turbulence created by the financial crisis in fall 2008.

CULTURAL GLOBALIZATION

Globalization is about more than economics, however (see Box 2.2). It relies, for instance, on technologies of communication that also have had a dramatic effect on culture. Once again the central issue is the degree to which borders matter less as an element of cohesion in defining national cultures and societies. We have already noted how markets have become uncoupled from territorial boundaries, and the same is increasingly true of culture and communications. One line of argument about this phenomenon is that all around the world people are rapidly becoming the same. The globalization of culture means sameness. To some extent this is true. The massive penetration of American culture through icons such as Coke, McDonald's, Hollywood, and Nike means that there is a pervasive sameness to capital cities no matter where one goes on the planet. Consumers "around the world are beginning to develop similar cultural expectations

BOX 2.2   THE GLOBALIZATION INDEX

The Globalization Index, which is developed by the Centre for the
Study of Globalisation and Regionalisation at Warwick University,
measures the economic, social and political dimensions of globalization for countries on an annual basis over the period 1982 to
2004, and combines these into an overall globalization index, or

Table 1
THE TWENTY MOST SOCIALLY GLOBALIZED COUNTRIES IN 2004

Unit: Score (max. 1)

Country	Score	Rank
Bermuda	1.000	1
Singapore	0.985	2
Hong Kong, China	0.781	3
Switzerland	0.776	4
New Zealand	0.712	5
Austria	0.684	6
Canada	0.683	7
Netherlands Antilles	0.658	8
Sweden	0.643	9
Denmark	0.641	10
United Kingdom	0.630	11
Malta	0.626	12
Iceland	0.622	13
Belgium	0.605	14
Australia	0.595	15
Finland	0.576	16
Netherlands	0.552	17
United States	0.551	18
Barbados	0.504	19
Ireland	0.473	20

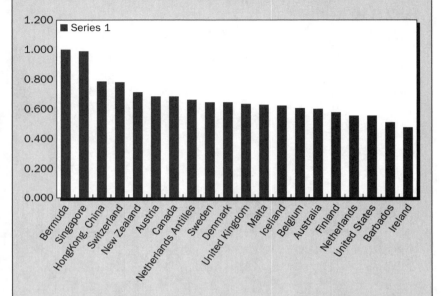

Figure 1 The 20 Most Socially Globalized Countries in 2004

score. The overall globalization index and the economic, social, and political globalization indices are constructed to be consistent over time and across countries. The same variables are used to calculate the index for each year and country, and the variables are normalized to be comparable. The social globalization index is constructed from nine variables, of which four are included in the people globalization sub-index, and five are included in the ideas globalization sub-index. It is worth noting that on the website of the CSGR, there are data available only for the overall globalization index and the economic, social, and political globalization indices (no data available for specific sub-indices and variables).

1. *People globalization sub-index*: (i) foreign stock [stock of foreign population as proportion of total population]; (ii) foreign flow [inflows of foreign population as proportion of total population]; (iii) worker remittances [worker remittances (receipts) as a proportion of GDP].

BOX 2.2 (continued)

Table 2
THE TWENTY LEAST SOCIALLY GLOBALIZED COUNTRIES IN 2004

Unit: Score (max. 1)

Country	Score	Rank
Myanmar	0.002	134
Ethiopia	0.005	133
Nigeria	0.005	132
Madagascar	0.005	131
Mali	0.006	130
Bangladesh	0.008	129
Central African Republic	0.010	128
Mozambique	0.012	127
Cameroon	0.012	126
Malawi	0.013	125
Yemen, Rep.	0.016	124
Chad	0.019	123
Bhutan	0.019	122
Pakistan	0.020	121
Algeria	0.020	120
Nepal	0.022	119
Zambia	0.022	118
Sri Lanka	0.023	117
Papua New Guinea	0.023	116
Djibouti	0.025	115

2. *Ideas globalization sub-index*: (i) phone calls [international outgoing telephone traffic (minutes) per capita]; (ii) Internet users [Internet users as a percentage of population]; (iii) films [number of films imported and exported]; (iv) books and newspapers [sum of value of books and newspapers imported and exported per capita (US$)]; (v) mail [number of international letters delivered and sent per capita].

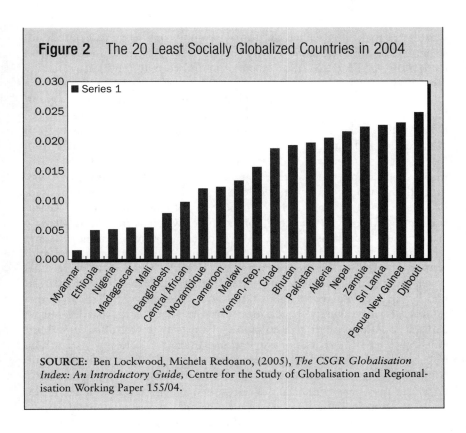

Figure 2 The 20 Least Socially Globalized Countries in 2004

SOURCE: Ben Lockwood, Michela Redoano, (2005), *The CSGR Globalisation Index: An Introductory Guide,* Centre for the Study of Globalisation and Regionalisation Working Paper 155/04.

about what they ought to be able to buy as well as about what it is they want to buy" (Ohmae, 1995, p. 28).

However, this does not mean the consumers want identical products. It actually means that with the erosion of barriers, products can be blends of cultural traditions and expectations and be available anywhere through the "invisible global economy" (Ohmae, 2004). Local cultures do have a resilience and carve out niches for themselves even in the shadows of what Barber (1995) calls "McWorld." Indeed, the counter-argument to this view that globalization means sameness is that it in fact portends a growing awareness of differences and an emphasis on particularities (Cameron and Stein, 2002, p. 12). In this scenario, which seems supported by the tenacity of ethnic differences and conflicts around the world, people retain their local cultural idioms, but globalization no longer makes it possible for them to conceive of their own culture as somehow "natural" and the only single possible world. Communications exposes the differences among peoples everywhere in the world and makes us realize that ours is simply one lifestyle or mode of society. Of course the more sinister reaction is a defensive one—to protect culture against "Western" incursion, and to take the battle into the West itself.

The telecommunications and information revolution has taken a giant leap forward with the Internet. The Internet cuts through traditional debates about the effects of telecommunications and broadcasting on community and culture because it has the potential to globalize and localize at the same time. Accurate numbers are hard to come by, but estimates for December 2007 were that as many as 1.3 billion Internet users around the world (Internet World Stats, 2008). North America, and Europe accounted for about 44 percent of the total, with Africa accounting for only 3.4 percent, for example. Whereas traditional broadcasting media such as TV and film did in fact have a homogenizing dynamic since so much of it was produced for American sensibilities and sent around the world; the Internet has at least the potential to permit the development of differences and indeed of new communities of interest and of affinity. Balanced against this of course are the facts that the Internet is increasingly becoming commercialized and that commercialism is coupled with technological changes that will effectively blur video, TV, and Internet communications. In that situation, it is entirely possible that the American cultural dominance in TV, film, and music will come to colour the Web as well—a sort of "McWeb." Some years ago, with peer-to-peer music sharing services such as Napster and Kazaa, it did appear that the net could circumvent traditional corporate control of cultural products. However, after several court cases, these free services were curtailed (Kazaa was effectively shut down), and iTunes now dominates the per-pay music and video download markets. So while in these cases the middleman has been eliminated to some extent, corporate control of content has not diminished as much as once was hoped. On the other hand, the diversity of content has increased, as distribution costs fall to close to zero, so that even obscure content producers such as garage bands can find an audience and release their work without intermediaries. The Internet has also created "we journalism"—a massive global printing press where anyone can share thoughts and ideas through blogs or personal websites, and of course video images through YouTube and social networking on Facebook and MySpace (we discuss social networking at greater length in Chapter 6).

The convergence of computers and telecommunications and the plummeting costs of the technology suggest that the predicted "death of distance" has indeed arrived (Cairncross, 1997). This is precisely the policy challenge contemporary states face in the cultural field. Cultural affinity has traditionally tended to coincide with territory, so that people define their relevant communities in terms of the territory defined by the state.

Under healthy circumstances (insularity can also be dangerous), this produces a desired degree of **social cohesion** and a foundation for stable community identity and cultural production. Globalization threatens this in a variety of ways. It can annihilate local cultural traditions in favour of some homogenous global standard—McWorld. It can destabilize cultural norms and understandings by "relativizing" them to a host of others and thereby reducing their apparent weight. It can encourage people to define their relevant communities in nonterritorial ways, and thereby weaken national bonds and support for national projects and policies. Governments therefore find themselves with distinctive policy conundrums: while many people welcome increased access to global culture, many resist fiercely and sometimes even violently. This is what Castells means when he refers to the network society and its "systematic disjunction between the local and the global for most individuals and social groups." The effects of globalization are so corrosive that the "search for meaning takes place then in the reconstruction of defensive identities around communal principles" (Castells, 1997, p. 11). Religious fundamentalism, militias, eco-terrorists, deep ecologists—these disparate social movements are symptoms of resistance to the globalized, networked society. Even in its less-threatening form, as the fragmentation of identity and community continues in the face of a "500 channel universe," governments have increasingly turned their attention to issues of social cohesion and national identity. At a more mundane level, governments have to also rethink what they understand as cultural policy—it is probably less possible to protect local culture than it is to support and promote it, perhaps through marketing it internationally.

If culture depends on communication, the communications and information revolution mean that communication is now global, suggesting the emergence of certain global understandings or standards. This is the third aspect of globalization, the development of **international standards** of conduct.

INTERNATIONAL STANDARDS

The best example of these emerging standards is the **human rights** conventions that have evolved since 1945. The United Nations came into being on October 10, 1945, and its Economic and Social Council was instructed to establish a commission to draft an international bill of rights. The UN Charter itself referred to the "principle of equal rights" and the importance of universal respect for "human rights and fundamental freedoms for all." The Council established a Commission on Human Rights that produced the Universal Declaration of Human Rights, which was passed in December 1948. The Universal Declaration was nothing more than that—a declaration without force of international law and without any enforcement mechanism. It recognized the "inherent dignity of and the equal and inalienable rights of all members of the human family" and proceeded to list virtually every conceivable human right from traditional civil and political ones to newer ones such as social security, work, rest, leisure, the right to an adequate standard of living, education, and free participation in the cultural life of the community. At the time these were lofty ideals indeed, and brought together in one document two sets or generations of rights that coincided with the emerging global divisions around the Cold War: civil and political rights central to liberal democracies and social and economic rights championed by socialist and communist states.

The history of human rights since 1948 has seen the progressive elaboration of both standards and institutions to monitor and enforce those standards (Montgomery, 1999; United Nations, 2003). The Universal Declaration, for example, was followed by two International Covenants that did have the force of treaties rather than mere declarations: the International Covenant on Civil and Political Rights and the International Covenant on Economic, Social and Cultural Rights. These were both passed by the UN in 1966 and came into effect in 1976. In addition to these covenants, the UN has passed Conventions for the Suppression of the Traffic in Persons and of the Exploitation of the Prostitution of Others (1951), the Status of Refugees (1954), the Elimination of All Forms of Racial Discrimination (1969), the Elimination of All Forms of Discrimination against Women (1981), against Torture and Other Cruel, Inhuman or Degrading Treatment or Punishment (1987), and on the Rights of the Child (1990). These UN initiatives have been complemented by similar regional conventions; for example in the European Union with the gradual development of citizens' rights through the 1950 Treaty of Rome, the 1961 European Social Charter, and the 1989 Community Charter. The 1997 Amsterdam Treaty gave the European Court of Justice the power to enforce fundamental rights. On July 1, 2002, a permanent International Criminal Court was established at The Hague (though the Rome Statute, which is the foundation for the court, was actually signed in 1998).

Critics often dismiss this dense system of overlapping covenants and declarations as largely meaningless posturing by governments, many of which are energetic violators of the very agreements they have signed. But events such as the 1993 Vienna World Conference on Human Rights and the 1995 Beijing World Conference on Women demonstrate that a global moral community has emerged from these efforts. Human rights violations will continue but no longer invisibly and without impunity. As noted earlier, modern communications technologies make it more and more difficult for authorities to hide their actions; the worldwide exposure of the torture of Iraqi prisoners in May 2004 was a clear indication that digital evidence of inhumane behaviour has the potential to sweep the planet in a nanosecond. Even Canada is not immune to this process: UN human rights committees have sanctioned Canada, for example, in 1993 for Quebec's Bill 178 restrictions on non-French commercial signs, and again in 1995 for federal cuts to social programs. In short, the most important development is less the absence of enforcement mechanisms than the emergence of standards that millions of people, regardless of place or culture, now accept as worthy of enforcement. In large measure, of course, these standards are Western in origin, and so the call for universalism is in part a call for the universal application of a certain view of individual rights and obligations.

As with the other elements of globalization, the implications of the emergence of international standards, many of them contained in conventions and treaties that Canada has willingly signed, are that the policy process and the principles by which it is made are no longer delimited by purely domestic considerations. In most policy fields—from the environment to Aboriginal affairs—governments have to take note of international standards, international agreements that may bind them to those standards, and international reactions to their behaviour. This does not mean that governments are necessarily at the mercy of these standards and agreements; they can still find ways around them if they need to. The simple point is that these standards have a reality that can no longer be ignored, and when mobilized by international actors or institutions, can have a potentially very powerful effect.

Any policies Canada develops will be measured against what other governments have done. In addition to standards and international institutions to monitor them, of course, is the emergence of what some have called a "**global civil society**" of activist NGOs that can be mobilized quickly around domestic policy issues (Keck and Sikkink, 1998). Canada's environmental policies, for instance, are closely watched by various groups around the world such as the Sierra Club and Greenpeace. The Yearbook of International Organizations conservatively estimates that in 2006 there were some 54 000 international NGOs, up from 44 000 in 2004 (Union of International Associations, 2007).

In short, the traditional connection between public policymaking and the territorial boundaries of the nation-state has been severely challenged in the last decade. Both the source of policy problems and their potential solutions now lie as much outside the boundaries of the state as they do within. This is not to say that states are irrelevant or that they cannot tackle major policy issues. The nation-state will remain as a fundamental organizing unit for contemporary industrialized societies, but the sort of control and dominance that they once enjoyed both over the policy process and the intellectual resources required to analyze it is waning.

The ways in which policy problems are defined will change, as will the range of instruments and strategies to deal with them.

The Politics of Difference

Globalization helps us conceptualize changes that have occurred at the international level, along with their effects on domestic politics and policymaking. It would be surprising, however, if these international changes were not accompanied with equally significant changes in the ways in which domestic political communities see themselves and their relations to government. For example, how could international human rights regimes strengthen over the past fifty years without human rights simultaneously becoming more important as standards of civil conduct on the domestic level?

Political culture across the industrialized democracies has indeed changed significantly, no less in Canada than elsewhere. Evidence of this abounds: the collapse of communism in Eastern Europe signalled the triumph of liberal individualist values that seem secure even in the face of the resurgence of authoritarian governments in some countries like Belarus and the Russian Federation; people everywhere seem more prepared to articulate their political concerns in terms of individual and democratic rights; even while Western societies have become more materialistic and consumer oriented, social movements have arisen around the globe to press for "postmaterialist" concerns such as the environment, peace, gender relations, and sexual orientation; and along with an emphasis on the universal rights of individuals there has come a greater sensitivity to the issues of identity and diversity. This section will briefly sketch three developments that set the backdrop to important shifts in political culture: the rise of **postmaterialism,** the increased salience of rights, and the new emphasis on "difference." Together, these comprise what some have called the "**postmodern condition**" of contemporary governance: "some state responses to globalization are fashioning a weaker kind of citizenship, because states sometimes act to diminish their own capacities. Indeed, in several ways the key actor in any citizenship regime—that is the state that confers recognition, establishes rights and responsibilities, provides access to political participation and helps fashion feelings of belonging—has withdrawn from centre-stage" (Jenson, 2003, pp. 313–14).

Postmaterialism in the West consists of a shift away from deference, away from concern with material gain, away from economic issues per se. These are displaced by lifestyle concerns, social, and even spiritual issues, all conducted in a much more participatory mode than was characteristic of the 1960s. "In this process, an emphasis on economic security gradually fades, and universal but often latent needs for belonging, esteem, and the realization of individual intellectual potential become increasingly prominent. Although individuals still value economic and physical security, they increasingly emphasize the need for freedom, self-expression, and improving the quality of their lives" (Abramson and Inglehart, 1995, p. 9). This is a gradual and long-term process that, according to Inglehart, will become evident through generational replacement. The trend is not inevitable, but there is considerable evidence that it has affected most industrial countries in the world. The consequences of a shift to postmaterialist values are potentially profound: greater support for democratic institutions through a new emphasis on self-expression values and human autonomy, and in particular, greater support for participatory democracy and a politics of identity and recognition. Traditional cultures are, of course, resilient, and depending on socio-economic circumstances (a risk to survival) the trajectory of human development can be towards authoritarianism and xenophobia (Inglehart and Welzel, 2005).

Clearly, the growth of postmaterialism has links to the development of what Mary Ann Glendon has called the dominance of "**rights talk**" as a mode of political discourse. In the previous section we discussed the development of international human rights regimes. This development has been mirrored at the domestic level in the elaboration of human rights documents, institutions, and political discourse. She argues that while rights talk is impervious to other more complex languages whereby we regulate our social and political lives, it "seeps into them, carrying the rights mentality into spheres of American society where a sense of personal responsibility and of civic obligation traditionally have been nourished" (Glendon, 1991, p. x). American commentators on the rise of rights talk have been preoccupied with problems of civic dialogue, compromise, and community within their own society, with the shift to what Sandel calls a "procedural republic": "In recent decades, the civic or formative aspect of our politics has largely given way to the liberalism that conceives persons as free and independent selves, unencumbered by moral or civic ties that they have not chosen" (Sandel, 1996, p. 6). Others argue that in fact the rights revolution of the past fifty years, while it had some negative consequences for social solidarity, has produced a more inclusive and tolerant community (Walker, 1998). Canadian analysis has been driven by the patriation of the Constitution in 1982 and its incorporation of a far-reaching Charter of Rights and Freedoms. Along with the traditional liberal-democratic rights of association, expression, and so on, the Charter contains modern clauses on equality and group rights. Canadian courts were granted a constitutionally entrenched power to review all federal and provincial statutes to ensure that they do not violate the Charter. Unsurprisingly, constitutional rights-based litigation mushroomed, foreshadowing a rights revolution (Ignatieff, 2000).

Alan Cairns has been the pre-eminent thinker on the Canadian equivalent of rights talk (1991, 1992, 1993; for a critique of the Cairns thesis, with rejoinder, see Brodie and Nevitte, 1993). His argument consists of several key points. First, the Charter should not be seen in isolation; it reflects, as Glendon notes, an international movement toward specifying and entrenching individual rights against governments. Second, while the Charter in broad terms was a symptom of this development, it nevertheless has several specific effects on Canadian political discourse and practice. Traditionally, Canadian politics has been organized through and around federalism, and its constitution has been a "government's" constitution in the sense that it was primarily about division of powers with little reference to citizens and their rights. The 1982 Charter for the first time brought citizens' rights into the Constitution, but more importantly articulated many of those rights in terms of minority-group identities (racial, ethnic, gender, Aboriginal, disabled, aged, etc.). Third, it is the combination of these constitutional rights and the demographic realities of ethnic, linguistic, and racial diversity in Canada that give the Charter its explosive power. Fourth, this power is being channelled in ways that undermine the "old constitution" of governments and underscore the importance of rights-based citizens' movements. Cairns and others have noted the process whereby the Meech Lake Accord (1987) and the Charlottetown Accord (1992) both collapsed in part before an onslaught of citizens' groups and rights claims (for similar versions of this argument focusing on the failure of these constitutional adventures, see Pal and Seidle, 1993; Lusztig, 1994).

The third element of the changed political culture in industrialized democracies, especially Canada's, is a tension between individual and group rights. The former consist of the traditional collection of civil and political rights that aim to treat individuals roughly the same, regardless of their social and economic differences. The original objective was to build a political community that, for the purposes of public policy, ignored group differences and concentrated instead on equal rights of **citizenship.** This is a noble political ideal and one that still commands substantial support. However, this type of **liberal individualism** was vulnerable to the argument that differences did matter, particularly economic differences, and they impeded the practical achievement of real political equality.

The contemporary version of the argument about difference shifts ground, however. The old argument with liberalism was that differences mattered but essentially that they should somehow be overcome. The objective for **liberal universalism** was still the same. The modern argument of difference challenges the core assumptions of liberal individualism by insisting that differences matter in a positive way, that equal treatment of individuals as abstract citizens ignores fundamental social and cultural characteristics that define identities (though there is a line of thought that special treatment for minorities *as protection* against majorities, is consistent with liberalism; see Kymlicka, 2007). In the words of Iris Young (1990), "To promote social justice, I argue, social policy should sometimes accord special treatment to groups" (p. 158). Kymlicka (1992) describes this position as **cultural pluralism,** and it has fundamental implications for the way we conceive citizenship. It encourages a policy of **multiculturalism,** which Canada pioneered, and which aims both to protect and celebrate cultural diversity.

Liberal individualism insists that equality will best be achieved by treating people as individuals under a system of universally applicable and consistent rules. Cultural pluralism insists that equality can be achieved only by treating people on the basis of their group affiliation and in some cases treating them according to different rules. Of course, not every group characteristic is important; blue eyes or left-handedness is something shared by millions of people but it hardly matters as a basis of group affiliation. Kymlicka (1995), for example, distinguishes between national minorities and ethnic groups and grants more rights to the former. Young (1990) argues that only social groups—defined in terms of salient social, cultural, or racial differences—that have experienced oppression qualify for different treatment. Her list, for example, includes racial minorities (in the American context, Blacks and Hispanics), women, gays and lesbians, people with disabilities, and Aboriginals. These differences are basic and powerful enough to define shared interests, world views, and even cultural norms among members of the group. Moreover, these groups exist in a society marked by inequality and oppression. If groups were different, but these differences were already accommodated and addressed through social and political institutions, there would be little to discuss in terms of public policy. But the "**politics of difference**" argues that in fact these differences are routinely and systematically oppressed. Indeed, it is the fact of oppression that gives these groups special claims within the political system. Note that a "difference perspective" emphasizes **collective identities** as a basis for claims, and urges the importance of those identities in making public policy. It explicitly privileges **cultural identity** as a normative base for making specific, countermajoritarian rights claims on behalf of individuals who are members of specific groups (see Eisenberg, 1994; Fierlbeck, 1996; and Green, 2000).

This cluster of ideas leads to the conclusion that the application of universal rules will serve only to further disadvantage these groups and suppress their legitimate differences. The opposite approach—of different treatment—is evident in policies of employment equity with their differential treatment of women, people with disabilities, visible minorities, and Aboriginals. Multiculturalism policy, though it has had fewer teeth than the equity agenda, has from its beginnings been a program that recognizes and celebrates differences. The whole sorry history of Canadian constitutionalism is rife with what Charles Taylor (1994) calls the **politics of recognition.** The demand—acceded to in 2006 by the federal government—that Quebec be designated a "nation" is based on the firm view that people in that province are distinguished from other Canadians in terms of language, culture, and historical experiences, and that those differences matter enough that they should be the basis of real powers and special treatment. Similar if not even more powerful arguments are made on behalf of "nation-to-nation" relations between Canada's First Nations and the federal government.

From a policy perspective, the impact of postmaterialism, rights talk, and cultural pluralism is complex and often contradictory. For one thing, it has contributed to the widely noted **decline of deference** among the Canadian population and democratic citizenry in other countries. Citizens trust their governments and politicians less than they used to. If they trust less, they inevitably demand a different type of policy process. They want to be consulted, they want to participate, and they want their voices to be heard. "The more fundamental complaint about contemporary democracies is that the institutions and elected representatives have become so remote from the public that no real popular choice of policy can be made. Citizens say in surveys that they do not believe that elected politicians do what their constituents want, but rather pursue their own career interests" (Peters, 2003, p. 83).

Another consequence has been a new emphasis on identity and the politics of recognition. Demographics play an important role in this, and Canadian society is increasingly ethnically and racially diverse, indeed, one of the most ethnically diverse countries in the world. But new sensibilities abound as well, some of them encouraged through government policies like multiculturalism, bilingualism, and equity employment, and recent court decisions (on same-sex marriage, for example). Deeper cultural shifts due to the nature of modernity itself may also be contributing an undertow to an increasing diversity of identities and the notion that people are not bound by destiny to any overriding identity but have choices in defining themselves. People increasingly identify themselves strongly with nonterritorially based groups—religious, ethnic, gender, linguistic, sexual, generational, or some exotic combination. They identify themselves as members of diverse communities and rely on the integrity and health of those communities for their personal well-being. From a policy perspective, this raises two challenges. One is the potential for **social fragmentation** and the importance of supporting some sort of social cohesion. Pluralism and diversity are certainly to be valued in any society, but by the same token, any society worthy of the name shares things in common. Without that, a pleasing diversity can quickly become a scattered collection of mutually exclusive groups. The idea of social cohesion, "a sense of belonging to a community that shares values and a sense of purpose and commitment" (O'Hara, 1998, p. 7) captures the tension of balancing plurality with solidarity. This is not simply an abstract philosophical principle, since social solidarity underpins the willingness of citizens to share burdens and benefits with each other, most notably through the redistribution of the welfare state (Barry, 2001). The second challenge is dealing with thorny issues of "ways of life" and collective rights. Both citizens and policymakers are often willing to compromise on material interests, but ways of life are intrinsically more precious and less negotiable. The result is new difficulties in dealing with some policy questions that are increasingly posed in terms of preserving, protecting, and promoting a way of life, and a certain prickliness on the part of significant segments of the public who feel that public policy should not merely confer benefits but also afford dignity, recognition, and support.

These issues may sound somewhat abstract, but can be illustrated with three concrete issues: Quebec's appointment of a commission to investigate the scope of "reasonable accommodation" to minority groups in the province; the debate over funding of faith-based schools during the 2007 Ontario election; and the controversy over *The Western Standard*'s decision to reprint the notorious Danish cartoons that caused Muslims to riot across Europe in 2006.

The reasonable accommodation issue was precipitated by public complaints in Quebec about insufficient integration of immigrants, particularly Muslim immigrants. In Quebec the issue of immigration is more challenging than in other provinces because of the sense, among both separatists and federalists, that Quebec is a nation (indeed, that sentiment was ratified by a successful motion before the federal parliament in November 2006), usually defined in terms of its society, history, territory, and the French language. Integration of immigrants into the French language did not pose problems, but if those immigrants had significantly different social and religious practices, and at the same time demanded that those practices be accommodated by the majority, there could be difficulties. Isolated cases where Muslims did demand such accommodations (e.g., that windows on a gym be papered so that offensively clad women would not be displayed publicly) ignited Quebec public opinion. Premier Jean Charest struck the Consultation Commission on Accommodation Practices Related to Cultural Differences (CCAPRCD) in February 2007. The Commission decided to interpret its mandate broadly: it "would be to perceive the debate on reasonable accommodation as the symptom of a more basic problem concerning the socio-cultural integration model established in Québec since the 1970s. This perspective calls for a review of inter-culturalism, immigration, secularism and the theme of Québec identity." This is a direct echo of the theme of cultural pluralism discussed earlier. Headed by two distinguished academics, and supported by a fifteen-member advisory committee, the Commission undertook consultations across the province beginning in 2007 and ending in February 2008 (CCAPRCD, 2008a). It received 901 briefs, and released its report on May 22, 2008.

The Commission's basic conclusion was that "the foundations of collective life in Québec are not in a critical situation" (CCAPRCD, 2008b, p. 13). The real problem was one of perceptions, where due to a series of events and isolated cases, there was a broad but erroneous perception that Quebec was facing a crisis of numerous accommodations and major institutional revision. The number of accommodation cases that had found their way to the courts was small, and there was little evidence of any threats to social order or even to basic values. Nonetheless, the Commission pointed out that "interculturalism" as a principle of public policy in Quebec had a special role in balancing integration of immigrants into a French-speaking society with reasonable accommodation for ethnic and religious differences. The balancing act would not be simple: "To summarize, we could say that Québec interculturalism a) institutes French as the common language of intercultural relations; b) cultivates a pluralistic orientation that is highly sensitive to the protection of rights; c) preserves the creative tension between diversity and the continuity of the French-speaking core and the social link; d) places special emphasis on integration; and e) advocates interaction" (ibid., p. 42). The Commission's recommendations emphasized the development of economic opportunities and support for immigrants as much as it did interculturalism in terms of accommodations and institutional changes. A sign of the challenge in translating these philosophical principles into policy practice was the Commission's recommendation that the cross that is prominently displayed in the Quebec national assembly be removed as an affront to the State's neutrality on matters of religion. The government immediately introduced a motion to keep the cross, and it was passed unanimously by all three political parties.

The funding of faith-based schools was not initially a campaign issue in the 2007 Ontario election (CBC News, 2007), until the Conservative leader promised to extend public funding to faith-based schools other than Catholic ones. Ontario is the only province that fully funds both public and Catholic schools (until 1985 that funding was only for elementary schools, but was then extended). Other faiths resented that funding, though it was an accommodation made at Confederation and enshrined in the constitution. Those faith groups even took the case to the United Nations Human Rights Committee, which ruled in 1999 that not funding those groups was discriminatory. When the issue was brought up in the campaign, the Conservatives promised to extend funding as a matter of fairness (as long as those schools followed the Ontario curriculum, hired accredited teachers, and followed provincial educational regulations). They argued that this would bring those schools and faith communities into the wider society. The Liberals vociferously opposed the plan, arguing that it would be divisive and undermine social cohesion. Again, what appear to be abstract philosophical issues of identity and cohesion had solid traction in public debate. The Liberals won the election.

In 2006, the now defunct magazine *The Western Standard,* under publisher Ezra Levant, decided to reprint the Danish cartoons depicting Mohammed, which had generated riots across Europe and in other parts of the world on account of the blasphemy of representing the Prophet in an image. The publication of those cartoons in Denmark offended no Danish law, nor did they offend any Canadian law prima facie. However, Syed Soharwardy lodged a complaint with the Alberta Human Rights Commission, alleging that the cartoons were designed to incite hatred against Islam, and so constituted hate speech, which is a violation of the human rights code. Levant was eventually questioned by the Human Rights Commission (he filmed what he termed his "interrogation" and posted it on YouTube), but the complaint was eventually withdrawn. The human rights code provisions in this instance are designed to protect groups against speech that would incite hatred, and ordinarily that would fall into the category of direct statements intended to accomplish that end. In this instance, the offending material was offensive to the complainant as a religious matter, and so the Commission was actually wading into the waters we discussed above—accommodation of specific minority group practices and characteristics as against the wider society's norms (the cartoons are only offensive to Muslims).

These cases illustrate the challenges of managing diverse democratic societies that try to balance individual rights, group rights, social and community obligations, and a broad rule of law that treats everyone equally. Canada is far from alone in dealing with these issues, and may have some advantages through a long history of immigration and an early adoption (1971) of a formal policy of multiculturalism. France, Germany, and the Netherlands have been grappling with the same issues, as has the UK's Labour government as it launched an effort in 2007 to review its citizenship policy to develop ideals and principles on what binds the nation together.

A final and somewhat contradictory consequence of the shifts in public values described in this section is a growing skepticism of traditional representative institutions. Voter turnout hit a new low of 61 percent in the 2000 election, rose to 64.7% in the 2006 election, and then hit another historic low in the 2008 federal election of 59.1 percent. The decline of deference certainly induces people to be skeptical of politicians, but added to the new emphasis on identity and rights, it makes them suspicious of institutions that represent majoritarian interests. Parliament, political parties, and the electoral system are skewed toward the majority, but the new political culture sees rights as against majority interests, and minority rights as against majority rule. Institutions like the courts, which formally have no representative function, and that appear to be dispassionately concerned only with truth and justice, come off much better in this view (Fletcher and Howe, 2000). It is no coincidence that courts have become much more important in contemporary Canadian public policy just as our political culture has become more rights oriented. This may, however, be a chicken-and-egg issue, since the cultural shifts have themselves coincided with major institutional changes in Canada, such as the adoption and extension of the Charter of Rights and Freedoms, that have given the courts much greater scope for effectively making public policy.

The role of courts in Canadian public policy has not been uncontroversial. Simply because the Charter might have given the courts more scope does not mean that they necessarily had to become major players in policy development. All Canadian legislation must be consistent with the Charter (and the rest of the Constitution), and the courts have the responsibility for adjudicating claims. There are thus three elements at play here: the extent of Charter rights themselves, the willingness and capacity of litigants to take Charter cases to the courts, and the readiness of the courts to make bold decisions. In the conditions of an anemic Charter, supine interest groups, and a somnolent court, constitutional cases would rarely be controversial. In Canada's case, the Charter is robust, interest groups and individual litigants have been active (Brodie, 1997; Mandel, 1994; Hein, 2000), and courts at times have been willing to make bold decisions that increasingly involve "reading in" underlying meaning to constitutional text that does not exist on the surface (Martin, 2003), a practice widely supported by a broad constituency of lawyers and policy advocates (Morton and Knopff, 2000). A more activist court changes the policy process significantly, since policy decisions can arise from a different institutional source with different—largely legal—rationales. In June 2004, for example, the Supreme Court of Canada heard a case that claimed that long waiting lists for surgical procedures violated the Charter of Rights and Freedoms. A year later, in its *Chaoulli* decision, the court narrowly agreed that with long waiting lists in Quebec, citizens should not be prohibited from purchasing private medical insurance. Bit by bit, the courts are re-orienting the fundamentals of the Canadian health system, in part because politicians fear to tinker with what Canadians consider a sacred trust. The impact of courts on public policy has the collateral effect of elevating the importance of legal analysis in governmental policy work and situates agencies such as the federal Department of Justice at the centre of key policy decisions and processes (Kelly, 2000).

The politics of difference, as we have termed it, is a complicated cluster of ideas (rights talk, decline of deference, emphasis on identity), demographics linked to immigration, and institutions (courts). It is important not to exaggerate its impact on contemporary Canada or other industrialized states, but it is also important to take its full measure. For example, Banting et al. (2006: 83) argue that there is no evidence of countries that have adopted strong multicultural programs seeing an erosion of their welfare states, primarily in terms of social welfare redistribution. The mere fact of demographic diversity and difference does not necessarily lead to a decline in political trust or social cohesion, or a willingness to share burdens and benefits through the redistributive welfare state, nor does it automatically mean minorities do not have a sense of belonging. In the Canadian case, the main differences in social cohesion are not primarily due to ethnic differences but to how recent the immigrants' arrival has been. "The longer new immigrants are in Canada, the more their sense of pride and, to a lesser extent, of belonging comes to equal or exceed that of the largest ethnic group" (Soroka, Johnston, and Banting, 2007, p. 23). In comparative terms, the Canadian experience with plurality and multiculturalism has generally been quite successful (Adams, 2007). But the paradox remains that broadscale measures of public opinion can mask the complications at the operative level of public policy (Myles and St-Arnaud, 2006). In that arena, groups may mobilize and articulate discourses of rights and difference that pose substantial challenges to democratic polities. It is clear that things have changed in important ways. The way that Canadians discuss rights, and how they frame policy issues in terms of rights, is vastly different today from a generation ago. There has been an undeniable decline in trust, deference, and engagement with conventional political institutions. Courts have become key policymaking—or at least interpreting—institutions on major policy issues such as health care. The shifting patterns of identity and allegiance have become important considerations in policymaking. All of this is new.

Governance and Public Management

The third major change in the context of policymaking and analysis has been in our concepts of the proper scope of governance by the state and the nature of public management. These are of course entangled with the changes described above in the domestic economy, globalization, and culture shifts, and probably represent the results of outcomes of these changes more than they do independent forces in their own right. Nonetheless, it is a crucial category for policy analysis since it cuts closest to what governments see themselves as properly doing, and the new politics of governance and public management rapidly developed their own dynamics, however much they might be a consequence of deeper factors.

Ideas about governance operate at several distinct levels. The most general is the view of the proper scope and nature of government activity. The 1990s was a decade where policymakers across the ideological spectrum lost confidence in the capacity of government to do things. Conservatives retained less faith than liberals or those on the left, but generally the centre of gravity on these issues shifted perceptibly to the right. In the last two or three years this may have changed, with even Conservative governments at both federal and provincial levels having been markedly expansionist and profligate in their spending and their interventions. The differences are more a matter of tone, but tone sometimes matters. The federal Tories cut the GST when most economists and certainly the opposition parties objected. They decided on a universal child care benefit rather than federally funded daycare centres. But nonetheless, many of the key questions in the debates over governance in the 1990s have not disappeared. Should governments provide services themselves, or should they develop mechanisms for the delivery of these services through either for-profit or nonprofit agencies? Can and should government "correct market failures," or is the medicine worse than the malady (this was a live issue in the November 2008 G-20 summit, with the Bush administration arguing for light government intervention)? To what extent should government encourage the pursuit of what are basically private interests, such as child care or a university education, through the public sphere in the form of either services or legal structures that support such pursuits?

Another, more specific level, concerns the tools that governments realistically have at their disposal for policy development and implementation. Can governments control unemployment and inflation through monetary policy? Can they "create jobs"? Can they solve poverty and eradicate racism? Can they provide adequate housing? Obviously, if one believes that the market can and should do this, the question of policy instruments will not arise at all. However, even in cases where one thinks that the role of government should be minimal, there can be disputes about appropriate tools for governance. The final aspect of governance concerns management practices. Given a certain vision of the role of government and the feasible tools at its disposal for dealing with public problems, how best to organize the administrative machinery of government to achieve those ends?

It is clear that ideas about governance and public management have been changing radically in the last two decades. The movement has coincided with the political ascendancy of the right in most liberal democracies, starting with Ronald Reagan in the United States (elected president in 1980) and Margaret Thatcher in Britain (who became prime minister in 1979). In Canada, the Progressive Conservatives were elected for terms in 1984 and again in 1988, before being almost wiped out in 1993. Interestingly, the Liberals accepted many key elements of the Tory agenda: **deficit reduction** and **government restructuring** being most prominent.

This mimics a pattern in other countries such as New Zealand, where the change in public administration and management was led by left-wing parties. But the gospel of smaller government, balanced budgets, reduced public debt, and new management practices gained converts from both left and right in the 1990s, under the banner of **new public management** (NPM). It became hardwired into most developed democracies, including Canada, but has since been overlaid with other management priorities.

What were its main features? Primarily, there was a belief that what Barzelay (1992, p. 5) calls the "bureaucratic paradigm" of carefully defined roles, reliance on rules and procedures, line and staff distinctions, tight financial control, and central agency oversight, should be replaced with a more client-focused, service-oriented system. Bevir, Rhodes, and Weller (2003) highlighted the following features of the NPM:

> The term refers to a focus on management, not policy, and on performance appraisal and efficiency; disaggregating public bureaucracies into agencies which deal with each other on a user pay basis; the use of quasi-markets and of contracting out to foster competition; cost-cutting; and a style of management that emphasizes, among other things, output targets, limited term contracts, monetary incentives and freedom to manage. . . . It is said to be a global phenomenon. (pp. 1–2)

One of the most widely read examples of the NPM thinking was in a 1992 book entitled *Reinventing Government,* by David Osborne and Ted Gaebler. The most important aspect of the book's argument was its rejection of the hierarchical architecture of most government bureaucracies. Close accountability requires close scrutiny and a minimum of bureaucratic discretion. This traditional system of public administration has many benefits, but it is also in large part responsible for the stereotypical inflexibility and unresponsiveness of government bureaucracy. The result very often is costly, lumbering organizations that are driven by rules rather than results. Creativity is stifled, problem-solving is discouraged in favour of following routine, and significant resources are devoted simply to managing people within the system, rather than achieving policy goals. Osborne and Gaebler distilled ten principles of reinventing government from the cases they reviewed. These principles were grounded in the assumption that government is necessary, but it does not necessarily have to act like government.

> Most entrepreneurial governments promote *competition* between service providers. They *empower* citizens by pushing control out of the bureaucracy, into the community. They measure the performance of their agencies, focusing not on inputs but on *outcomes.* They are driven by their goals—their *missions*—not by

their rules and regulations. They redefine their clients as *customers* and offer them choices—between schools, between training programs, between housing options. They *prevent* problems before they emerge, rather than simply offering services afterward. They put their energies into *earning* money, not simply spending it. They *decentralize* authority, embracing participatory management. They prefer *market* mechanisms to bureaucratic mechanisms. And they focus not simply on providing public services, but on *catalyzing* all sectors—public, private, and voluntary—into action to solve their community's problems. (Osborne and Gaebler, 1993, pp. 19–20)

Kenneth Kernaghan (2000a) provides a useful list that contrasts what he calls "bureaucratic" with "post-bureaucratic" organizations. It is presented in Figure 2.3 (page 83). Note that the characteristics on the post bureaucratic side lend themselves to a variety of different configurations—decentralized organizations, for example, could be completely privatized ones or public agencies with greater responsibility for their own actions.

In the United States, the Clinton administration launched a **National Performance Review** on government, headed by Vice-President Al Gore, in March 1993. Its first report contained 384 recommendations for improving federal governmental performance, touching on virtually every agency and program in the American federal government. Despite criticisms that the process was stalled within months of the release of the report, Kettl and DiIulio (1995) conclude that it led to real change, for example, in governmental culture, procurement practices, and cuts to some government agencies. By the second Clinton–Gore term, the effort had shifted to trying to imbed reinvention as a permanent feature of federal government agencies, and so the NPR was rechristened as the National Partnership for Reinvention in Government. The priorities enunciated at the time included better service delivery, partnerships, and efficiency. These were joined by an emphasis on customer satisfaction and more online services. The election of George W. Bush in 2000 signalled a new direction in public management priorities for the United States government. Bush supported the mantras of efficiency and smaller government, but was much more ideologically enthused by reliance on market mechanisms to achieve public policy goals. Moreover, his one overarching public management initiative in the early part of his first term was more community-based delivery of public services and programs, but, in particular, with an emphasis on faith-based organizations (principally charities, but churches as well). Bush created the White House Office of Faith-Based and Community Initiatives almost immediately on taking office, and it became the centrepiece of his "compassionate conservativism." This was NPM in the sense of community partnerships,

Figure 2.3 Bureaucratic versus Post-bureaucratic Organization/Management

Bureaucratic Organization	Post-bureaucratic Organization
Policy and Management Culture	

Organization-centred
  Emphasis on needs of the
  organization itself
	Citizen-centred
	  Quality service to citizens (and
	  clients/stakeholders)

Position power
  Control, command and
  compliance
	Participative leadership
	  Shared values and participative
	  decision making

Rule-centred
  Rules, procedures and
  constraints
	People-centred
	  An empowering and caring milieu
	  for employees

Independent action
  Little consultation, cooperation
  or coordination
	Collective action
	  Consultation, cooperation and
	  coordination

Status quo-oriented
  Avoiding risks and mistakes
	Change-oriented
	  Innovation, risk taking
	  and continuous improvement

Process oriented
  Accountability for process
	Results oriented
	  Accountability for results

Structure	

Centralized
  Hierarchy and central controls
	Decentralized
	  Decentralization of authority and
	  control

Departmental form
  Most programmes delivered by
  operating departments
	Non-departmental form
	  Programmes delivered by wide
	  variety of mechanisms

Market Orientation	

Budget driven
  Programmes financed largely
  from appropriations
	Revenue driven
	  Programmes financed as far as
	  possible on cost recovery basis

Monopolistic
  Government has monopoly
  on programme delivery
	Competitive
	  Competition with private sector
	  for programme delivery

SOURCE: K. Kernaghan, *The Post-Bureaucratic Organization and Public Service Values*, March 2000. International Institute of Administrative Studies, 2000, published by Sage Publications Ltd. Reprinted by permission of Copyright Clearance Center.

and in the sense of a skepticism of traditional government bureaucracy, but with a new focus on charitable organizations. The 9/11 terrorist attacks eclipsed this initiative and indeed put the Bush administration on a completely different track with respect to public sector management. From a champion of small government, Bush was transformed into a champion of strong, robust, and at least in connection with things pertaining to security, muscular and interventionist government. In the largest centralizing move in American peacetime, Bush released the National Strategy for Homeland Security, passed the Homeland Security Act, and created the Department of Homeland Security with 180 000 employees. Funding for homeland security tripled in the first two years to US$30 billion. The new department brought together the security services, Coast Guard, border control, emergency preparedness agencies, and immigration, along with several others. From that point on, the demands of fighting terrorism induced large and intrusive government at the national level, as well as massive spending to create the largest deficit in United States history.

The Bush administration also had a management agenda, one that was announced before the 9/11 terrorist attacks (Office of Management and Budget, 2002). The agenda laid out five management priorities—human capital development, competitive sourcing, improved financial management, e-government, and integration of budget and performance information. A clear emphasis has remained on performance reporting, and executive agencies are expected to report quarterly on their performance against the five management priorities as well as a series of program initiatives. Box 2.3 shows the December 31, 2007 scorecard. The graphic displays executive agencies, and gives a dark (success), medium (mixed results), and light (unsatisfactory) rating along each dimension.

The British example is perhaps more relevant to the Canadian context because Britain too is a parliamentary democracy, and because it has not mixed NPM principles with religious fervour or a new massive security apparatus. In Britain today, three-quarters of "government employees" do not work for traditional departments but instead for executive agencies that have been contracted to provide certain services. The wide range of reforms has been under way since Margaret Thatcher's prime ministership, but two initiatives, the **Next Steps** program and the **Citizen's Charter,** illustrate the early goals of the organizational revolution that took place in the United Kingdom (Jenkins and Gray, 1993; Doern, 1993). Tony Blair's "New Labour" victory in 1997 carried the government reform agenda forward with even greater vigour.

Next Steps had its origins in the Financial Management Initiative of 1982, which tried to underscore the importance of management in government by introducing better practices and giving managers greater autonomy over budgets and operations as long as they met certain

BOX 2.3

Executive Branch Management Scorecard

	Current Status as of December 31, 2007					Progress in Implementing the President's Management Agenda				
	Human Capital	Competitive Sourcing	Financial Perf.	E-Gov	Budget/Perf. Integration	Human Capital	Competitive Sourcing	Financial Perf.	E-Gov	Budget/Perf. Integration
AGRICULTURE	●	○	●	○	●	○	●	○↓	●↑↑	●
COMMERCE	●	○	●	○	●	●	●	●	●↑↑	●
DEFENSE	○	○	●	○	○	●	○	○↓	○↑	●
EDUCATION	○	●	●	○	●	●	●	●	●↑	●
ENERGY	●	●	●↑↑	●↑	●	●↑↑	●	●	●↑	●↑
EPA	●↑	●	●	●	●	●	●	●	●	●
HHS	●	●	●	○	○↑	●	●	●	●↓	●↑
DHS	○	○	●	○	○	○	○↑	○	●↑	○↓
HUD	○	●	○	○	●	●	●	●	●↑	●
INTERIOR	●	●	○	○	○	●	●	●	●	●
JUSTICE	●	●	○↑	○	●	●↑	●	●	●	●
LABOR	●	●	●	●	●	●	●	●	●	●
STATE	●	○	●↓↓	○↓	●	●	○↓	○↓	●↑	●
DOT	●	○	○↑	●	●	●	●↑	●	●↑	●
TREASURY	●	○	●	●	●	●	●	○↓	●↑	●
VA	●	●	●	●	○	●	○↑	○	●	●
USAID	○	○↑	●	●	●	●↑	●	●	●↓	●
CORPS	●	○	●	●	●	●	●↑	●	●	●
GSA	●	○	●	●	●	●	●	●	●↑↑	●
NASA	●	●	●	○↑	●	●	○↓	●	●↑↑	●
NSF	○	●	●	●	●	●↓↓	●	●	●	●
OMB	●	●	●	●	●	●	●	●	●	●
OPM	●	●	●	●	●	●	●	●	●↑	●↑
SBA	○	○	●↑	○	●	○	○	●	●↑	●
SMITHSONIAN	○	●	●	●	●↑↑	●↑	●	●	●	●
SSA	●	●	●	●↑↑	○	●	●	●	●↑↑	●

↑↓ Arrows indicate change in status since evaluation on Dec 31, 2007.

↓↑ Arrows indicate change in progress since previous quarter.

SOURCE: White House (United States) (2007). *The President's Management Agenda: The Scorecard of December 31, 2007.* Retrieved February 15, 2008, from http://www.whitehouse.gov/results/agenda/FY08Q1-SCORECARD.pdf.

performance and output targets. By the late 1980s the reform had bogged down, and so efforts were redoubled to take the "Next Steps" of the original Financial Management Initiative in decentralizing government services. The plan called for as many agencies as possible to be converted to "departmental executive agencies" that would essentially act as businesses delivering public services. The chief executive officer of each Next

Step agency was to negotiate a contract with the department specifying performance goals and targets but would then have substantial freedom to operate the "business" as he or she saw fit.

In a little over a year, eight agencies were created. By April 1993, there were 89 such agencies employing almost two-thirds of the civil service. By 1998, 377 500 civil servants worked in 138 Next Steps agencies and four departments with Next Steps business lines. These are not privatized agencies; they remain part of government and their employees are still civil servants. But they are stand-alone organizations with only loose connections to core ministries. The key change is the introduction of substantial managerial autonomy. Each agency has a framework document or agreement that is negotiated between the parent department and the Treasury and is subject to some renegotiation later by the chief executive officer. The framework document differs for each agency, though all outline the agency's objectives and targets, resource management guidelines, and the pattern of agency–department relations. The result is the provision of government services in markedly new ways. The Next Steps agencies, for example, no longer need to follow general government guidelines on expenditures as long as they work within their framework agreement. Agencies can set salary levels and classify jobs as they see fit. Managers can take risks, be more entrepreneurial, and the agency as a whole can respond more effectively to its "customers." In 1998 the government decreed that for the most part the creation phase of Next Steps agencies was over and that the focus would now shift to performance improvement.

This emphasis on decentralization was matched with a new emphasis on service and performance. The U.K. Citizen's Charter was introduced by John Major in 1991 after he had assumed the prime ministership from Margaret Thatcher. Whereas Next Steps introduced fundamental organizational changes, the Charter was designed to alter bureaucratic practices in order to raise the quality of public services. The Citizen's Charter applied across the British government, and was joined to a program called Service First. There was also an improved **Charter Mark** program. The Charter Mark program was a scheme to judge public sector organizations on their performance with customers and clients. Any agency that provides services directly to the public, and voluntary agencies that receive at least 10 percent of their funds from public sources, could apply to receive a Charter Mark. Applications are made to assessors, based on six service standards (strong performance standards; serving customers; fairness, accessibility, and choice; continuous improvement; effective resource management; and contribution to the quality of life in the community) and empirical evidence that customers agree that those standards have been met. The Charter Mark program continues but, as a result of a 2006 review and report to the UK government, will be gradually phased out (Herdan, 2006). But the phase out is actually in favour of more robust performance measures and higher standards of self-assessment by organizations serving the public. The report and the government's response was part of a larger initiative to transform public services: "We agree that the new standard should be more focussed on robust testing of outcomes for customers. In particular, effective measurement of satisfaction and the use of other citizen perspective measures are important for public service organisations across all service channels" (Cabinet Office, 2006:4).

The emphasis on service and more importantly the tailoring of services to citizens/customers, started in 2002 with the Blair government's new framework on social services delivery. The overarching goal of the strategy was customer satisfaction with the quality and variety of services, but also personalization of those services, on the understanding that the universalistic welfare state of the postwar period did not adequately respond to the different needs of individuals. The plan was premised on four key principles (national standards, devolution to the front line, flexibility to deliver diverse services, expanded choice for customers), which were to be buttressed with a new, more robust performance measurement and standards regime (Office of Public Services Reform, 2002). The most recent thinking in the UK government is dedicated to continuing to extend this service-oriented and personalized approach to the public sector:

> The vision at the heart of this paper is to create self-improving institutions of public service, independent of centralised state control, drawing on the best of public, private and third sector provision. These institutions must be free to develop in the way they need to, responsive to the needs and preferences of citizens, and with a flexible workforce that is able to innovate and change. Out of this vision will come a new concept of modern public services: one built around the user of the service. (Cabinet Office, 2007: 7)

In 2008, the British Prime Minister, Gordon Brown, reconfirmed this new direction in services and the nature of public management: "we have got to tailor our public services to the needs of people and their aspirations, and that means instead of the old uniform provision of standardised provision, we are going to have to think carefully about how public services can meet the individual needs of people" (Brown, 2008).

Canada did not go as far as the United Kingdom or other leaders in NPM such as New Zealand and Australia, and its administrative practices diverged sharply from the Bush administration. At the provincial level, the governments of Alberta under Ralph Klein and Ontario under Mike Harris attracted the most attention in the 1990s. The Alberta government passed a Deficit Elimination Act that committed it to that goal for 1996/97 but actually achieved a balanced budget a year earlier through deep spending cuts. It restructured its welfare services, closed hospitals, consolidated school boards, and privatized its liquor stores (Bruce, Kneebone, and McKenzie, 1997). A Conservative government was elected in Ontario in 1995 on the platform of its Common Sense Revolution, which promised virtually the same policy configuration as Alberta's (Ibbitson, 1997). In the words of Mike Harris, "I am not talking about tinkering, about incremental changes, or about short term solutions. After all, the changes we have all experienced in our personal lives have been much more fundamental than that. It's time for us to take a fresh look at government. To re-invent the way it works, to make it work for people" (Progressive Conservative Party of Ontario, 1995, p. 1). The high rhetoric, however, actually reflected massive changes under way in all the provinces. Lindquist and Murray (1994) concluded that all provincial governments had been engaged in downsizing, delayering, and focusing on service quality. While Alberta and Ontario led the way, governments in British Columbia under Gordon Campbell and in Quebec under Jean Charest each implemented NPM principles.

At the federal level, the early vehicle of public sector reform was the **Program Review** exercise, launched in 1994. The scope and impact of the review hit home with Canadians only in the February 1995 federal budget statement. The language of that budget was as uncompromising as that in the Common Sense Revolution: "The Program Review will lead to long-standing structural change in what government does" (Department of Finance, 1995, p. 32). Program Review was guided by six tests or questions: "serving the public interest; necessity of government involvement; appropriate federal role; scope for public sector/ private sector partnerships; scope for increased efficiency; affordability" (Department of Finance, 1995, p. 34). These tests were explicitly linked to a deficit-reduction strategy that the federal government finally decided to embark upon seriously in 1995 (Greenspon and Wilson-Smith, 1996). Compared to some other countries, Canada's federal public sector reform effort was at first primarily fiscally driven. This set up two dynamics. The first was directly harnessed to the fiscal program and sought to implement wide-ranging public sector reforms to achieve more effective and efficient governance. The lead agency on this front was the Treasury Board, and it carried forward a program of management reform through the late 1990s under the rubric of "**Getting Government Right**." The other dynamic was a reactive one, as the public sector sought to implement reforms to deal with the consequences of fiscal cuts; this was spearheaded primarily by the Clerk of the Privy Council, whose efforts under *La Relève* were briefly described in Chapter 1.

The *Getting Government Right* (1997) initiative was organized around several key themes. Together they summarize Ottawa's reform efforts, which, while they were not structurally radical, did have a wide scope in covering both services and programs as well as their presentation to Parliament and to the public: modernizing program delivery (service clustering, transparency of regulatory procedures, cost-recovery where appropriate); alternative service delivery; partnering with other levels of government and the private sector; greater strategic oversight for central agencies like the Treasury Board; better accountability to Parliament and to the public.

The next phase of management reform from the Treasury Board was the president's 2000 report entitled *Results for Canadians*. The president pointed out that the management framework articulated in the document did not mark a departure from Getting Government Right, but a consolidation. The framework was to be guided by a four step agenda: recognize that the federal government must build a "citizen focus" into all its activities and services; highlight the importance of public service values; focus on achieving results for Canadians; and promote "discipline, due diligence and value for money in the use of public funds." (*Results for Canadians*, 2000). *Results for Canadians* did not depart markedly from the 1997 approach, except that it emphasized structural changes in the federal government much less. In a sense, Ottawa had undergone whatever organizational changes it was prepared to stomach (indeed, federal employment began to grow again so that by 2003 it was at pre-Program Review levels). What was new was an emphasis on values and democratic accountability. As well, the focus on results was much greater—larger efforts were to go into developing indicators of program performance and reporting on them. In 2001 and 2002, the government produced government-wide performance reports for the country as a whole, taking the process beyond simply reporting at a departmental or agency level.

In its report on its *Plans and Priorities 2003–2004*, the Treasury Board cited the importance of both *Getting Government Right* and *Results for Canadians* as the core of the federal government's management framework (Treasury Board of Canada, 2003). It highlighted again the importance of service quality improvements, particularly in reference to the Government On-Line initiative, an $880 million program over six years to make the most commonly used federal government services available and accessible to all Canadians online (Government On-Line, 2003). It also referred to the introduction of a comprehensive package of reforms to the federal public service—the Public Service Modernization Act. The core of this initiative was to encourage all federal managers (deputy heads) to use more flexible definitions of merit in their hiring decisions, and give them wider authorities over hiring and staffing in their organizations. This was intended to streamline the often cumbersome human resource practices in the federal government.

By 2003, then, the public sector reform process at the federal level had emphasized performance, results, service, and a leaner, more partnered and decentralized institutional framework—and these were all consistent with NPM. Accountability was a key item, but submerged within the overall emphasis on performance. This began to change in 2003, first with the alleged scandal of $1 billion lost in grants and contributions from Human Resources and Development Canada (Good, 2003), and then with the sponsorship scandal and the Gomery Inquiry that investigated it (Commission of Inquiry into the Sponsorship Program, 2006; Perreault, 2006). Gomery in particular had fed the public imagination for almost two years with televised testimony of alleged kick-back schemes, weeping and contrite corporate executives, and even former Prime Minister Chrétien pulling golf balls out of his briefcase. The Conservatives capitalized on this and made a new **Federal Accountability Act** (FAA) the centrepiece of their election campaign. Once they won, they moved quickly to ensure that the FAA was the first piece of major legislation put forward by the new government.

The FAA is a sweeping piece of legislation that aims to change both political and public management practices in the Canadian federal government (Federal Accountability Action Plan, 2006). Among its highlights are new restrictions on party financing (a complete ban on contributions by unions, corporations, and other organizations; an annual limit of $1000 in donations by individuals); tougher conflict of interest guidelines (now enshrined in legislation with a new Conflict of Interest and Ethics Commissioner who can initiate formal investigations); a new independent Commissioner on Lobbyists, coupled with tougher standards on disclosure of contacts between lobbyists and decisionmakers; a new Parliamentary Budget Office to give objective analysis to Parliament on the nation's finances and economic trends, with the power to demand data from departments; a new Public Appointments Commission to oversee the selection process for government boards, commissions, agencies, and Crown corporations; tighter government procurement provisions; enhanced powers for the Auditor General to "follow the money"; and new whistleblowers provisions through the Public Servants Disclosure Protection Action, with access to a more independent Public Service Integrity Commissioner as an officer of Parliament. One of the more interesting if obscure provisions of the FAA was the designation of deputy heads of departments as "**accounting officers.**" This is a convention that has been used in Britain for over one hundred years, and is also accepted in Ireland, South Africa, and India. The basic idea is that deputy heads are personally responsible for the administration and management of their departments, and are accountable to Parliament and the public. This goes against the Canadian tradition of full ministerial responsibility for both policy and management of departments, a tradition that Gomery argued allowed ministers as well as officials to effectively avoid their responsibilities. The legislation fudged the issue by defining deputy heads as accounting officers consistent with the principle of ministerial responsibility, but Parliament (House of Commons, 2007) and the government (Privy Council, 2008) took a different view of what this meant in terms of the answerability of officials.

The state of public sector reform at the federal level in mid-2008 is therefore quite complicated. On the one hand, the NPM reforms in the mid-1990s and early 2000s have been hard-wired into the system, institutionalized, and embedded in review and performance appraisal mechanisms. For example, the **Management Accountability Framework (MAF)**, developed in 2002, "sets out the Treasury Board's expectations of senior public service managers for good public service management. The MAF is structured around ten key elements that collectively define "management" and establish the expectations for good management of a department or agency" (Treasury Board of Canada, 2007). Those ten elements are summarized in Figure 2.4. Note that they include both "hard" and "soft" elements of NPM: risk management, accountability, results and performance, balanced against people, stewardship, accountability and public service values.

Figure 2.4   Management Accountability Framework

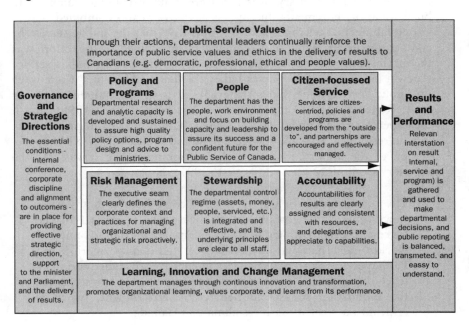

SOURCE: *Management Accountability Framework*, URL: http:www.tbs.sct.gc.ca/maf-crg/documents/booklet-livret-eng.asp, Treasury Board of Canada Secretariat, 2005. Reproduced with the permission of the Minister of Public Works and Government Services Canada, 2009.

Overlaying these NPM legacies are two new developments. One is a new public management regime with an unusually forceful emphasis on ethics and accountability. This is not because Canada is especially corrupt (for amusing examples of US federal government ethical lapses, see the Department of Defense's *Encyclopedia of Ethical Failure,* 2006); indeed, the Gomery Commission showed that overall the system worked quite well and that the scandal was due to a handful of rogue politicians and public servants. But the mood in Ottawa has changed (possibly across the country as well), and there is an extraordinary emphasis on probity. Ironically, an emphasis on probity and conduct translates into an emphasis on procedure and a web of formal and complex rules, and so this new overlay to some extent runs against the grain of the NPM optimism that government could become less bureaucratic, more nimble, agile, and responsive (Lépine, 2007).

The second development is a fresh emphasis on public sector renewal, particularly with respect to human resources. In November 2006 the Prime Minister appointed an Advisory Committee on the Public Service, co-chaired by Don Mazankowski (a former minister in the Mulroney government), and Paul Tellier (a former Clerk of the Privy Council). The committee's mandate was to focus on several key challenges for the federal public sector, primary of which were a major demographic shift (a huge wave of retirements due in the next five years) combined with a strong labour market that makes it imperative that the public service be competitive in attracting and retaining talent. Joined to this effort was the establishment of an Associate Secretary to cabinet for public service renewal (as of mid-2008, James Lahey), a Deputy Ministers' Committee on Public Service Renewal, an external Advisory Committee on Senior Level Retention and Compensation (it has existed since 1998), and a revamped Canada Public Service Agency with a new strategic focus on human resources. This all signaled a new, and somewhat un-NPM appreciation of the importance of a well-functioning public service. As the Advisory Committee put it in its first (2007) report:

> The first premise for our work as a committee is that a well-functioning and values-based public service is critical to the success of every country in today's complex and interconnected world. As a national institution, a high-quality, merit-based Public Service is part of Canada's comparative advantage and a key to competitiveness in the global economy. It also helps provide the foundation for sound democratic government, which is critical to a positive business climate in Canada.
>
> The traditional mission of the Public Service is to provide professional, non-partisan advice and support to government, and

high-quality programs and services that are responsive to the changing needs of Canadians. This means developing policies and programs that serve not just one sector or region but all Canadians, and not just for today but also for the longer term. The benefits—often unseen—that Canadians enjoy from the work of public servants include everything from effective regulation in various areas to border services, cultural institutions, and the federal contribution to Canada's broader criminal justice system. Federal programs touch Canadians in almost every facet of their daily lives. (Advisory Committee on the Public Service, 2008)

In its second (2008) report the Committee continued to push the importance of excellence in the public service, more stream-lined recruitment and performance measures, and a re-organized human resource management structure within the federal government (Advisory Committee on the Public Service, 2008).

NPM in the 1990s and early 2000s was a global phenomenon, celebrated by the OECD, and argued to have similar characteristics no matter what the national context (Kettl, 2005; Lynn Jr., 2001). As Pollitt (1995) put it: "One senses an 'official line' advanced, with local inflections, by most national government leaders" (p. 204). This official line coalesced around a strong political emphasis on certain techniques: decentralization of budgeting, performance indicators, performance-related pay, an emphasis on quality and standards, the contractualization of relationships, and evaluation coupled with a concern about value for money. We should remember, however, that academic versions of the NPM, as well as some practical real-world examples, suggest a variety of sometimes inconsistent models (Peters, 1995). The emphasis on empowerment and the distrust of bureaucracy, for example, is just as likely to lead to a greater emphasis on broad political participation in policymaking as it is market-based prescriptions (Denhardt and Denhardt, 2000, 2003). And the enthusiasm with which new visions of governance have been seized by politicians has not been mirrored by analysts. For many students of public administration, wide-sweeping changes were often implemented without public consultation or popular mandates (e.g., New Zealand), and for others the NPM was yet another postwar fad that recognized the market as the only credible model for human organization (Savoie, 1995). As well, as more research has been conducted on the actual fortunes of NPM around the world, it is clear that the Canadian experience of variation, differential acceptance, and uneven implementation is true around the world (Bevir, Rhodes, and Weller, 2003; Christensen and Laegried, 2002). Different countries implemented differently, selecting some elements and not others, and the success of implementation depended on a host of institutional and political variables.

The mix of public sector reform trends in Canada by 2008 consisted of some holdovers from the NPM movement—a continued emphasis on efficiency, somewhat smaller government if possible and where possible, and more work on service, performance, and results measurement. However, the sobering realities of a post 9/11 world, coupled with increasingly complex problems defined either by nature (pandemics, climate change) or by technology, or by a possible world-wide recession, made it clear that government is not going to wither away. Increasingly, the quality of government has come to be recognized as a key instrument in domestic stability and prosperity, as well as for international competitiveness. In the Canadian case, the sponsorship scandal changed political discourse and injected a high premium on accountability and ethics into discussions of public sector reform. The important point to keep in mind, however, is that these changes, however difficult they may be to align, do make for a very different public sector context for policymaking in the first decade of this century. There are greater pressures on performance, accountability, service, and probity than ever before. This complicates the policy environment considerably, but for perhaps the first time in twenty years, the balance is tipping towards a more positive assessment of the public service and the role that the public sector plays in social and political life. This poses challenges, but opportunities as well.

Conclusion

Are the forces described in this chapter stable, and will they last? Yes and no. Globalization, increasing cultural diversity, the decline of deference, and the information revolution are impossible to reverse, and impossible to avoid. Governance, or our systems of public policy development and administration, are reactions to these forces, and can be expected to change and vary over time. Governing is about making choices, and choices are still very much available despite the inevitability of these forces. For example, the budget cutting, downsizing, and restructuring that characterized the mid-1990s was indeed compelled in part by globalization, but governments handled it in different ways. Ten years later, governments still have substantial room to manoeuvre. In 2006 the Conservatives made key choices on implementing the FAA, on reducing the GST, and on changing course from an institutional daycare option favoured by the previous government to a Universal Child Care Benefit (giving parents $100 per month for each child under the age of six). The government of British Columbia introduced a carbon tax—the first in North America—in its 2008 budget. And both federal and provincial governments will have major choices to make in dealing with recession.

The changed context for policymaking does not mean the end of choices, simply different constraints, and different choices within those constraints. While some governments in Canada will continue to have fiscal room, there will now be new pressures on where to target funds as deficits loom. But those choices will not be made by governments of the type familiar in the 1990s; we have moved and continue to move from a bureaucratic model to something different. Forms and processes of governance have changed, as have the problems they tackle and the means at their disposal. This book is about the new constraints, the new choices, and the new tools available to policymakers. The themes developed in this chapter will weave through the rest as we explore what it means to go beyond policy analysis. The next chapter looks more closely at the first key phase of policymaking, problem definition, and its link to the agenda-setting process.

KEY TERMS

accounting officer—designation of a deputy head of a federal department as personally responsible and accountable to Parliament for the administration and management of his/her department

Charter Mark (UK)—a scheme to engage independent assessors to judge and certify public sector organizations on their performance with customers and clients

Citizen's Charter (UK)—introduced by John Major in 1991 and designed to alter bureaucratic practices by publicly stating government service obligations to citizens

citizenship—traditional collection of civil and political rights that aim to treat individuals roughly the same, regardless of their social and economic differences

collective identities—widely shared characteristics such as race or language that are politically salient as a way of orienting oneself in politics

cultural identity—a normative base for making specific rights claims on behalf of individuals who are members of specific cultural groups

cultural pluralism—the condition wherein a political community is marked by a wide variety of cultural groups, and for whom those cultural differences are salient as a basis of claim or grievance

decline of deference—the decline in citizens' trust and confidence in their governments and increasing desire to be consulted, to participate, and to be heard in policy development

deficit reduction—a fiscal policy to reduce and eventually eradicate the budget deficit

Federal Accountability Act—major piece of public sector reform legislation introduced by the Conservative government in 2006 to deal with political party financing, lobbyists, and whistleblowers, and to strengthen a host of institutions such as the Auditor General

free market capitalism—a type of capitalism that emphasizes smaller government, the minimum of controls and regulations, and wide scope for markets in the delivery of goods and services

Getting Government Right—a program of federal management reform led by the Treasury Board Secretariat through the late 1990s, which sought to implement wide-ranging public sector reforms to achieve more effective and efficient governance

global civil society—an emerging series of networks of activist NGOs and connected nongovernmental institutions that can be mobilized quickly around policy issues

global supply chain—also known as global value chain, represents the distribution of corporate functions (management, finances, communication, production) across the globe

globality—the sense that the entire planet is a single social space, that people carry on conversations in that space irrespective of territoriality, that they pay collective and simultaneous attention to "global events"

globalization system—the idea that globalization is not simply a matter of greater interdependence but is also a system with its own dynamics and logic

government restructuring—substantial and wide-reaching structural change in public administration and management, usually intended to reflect new public management objectives of efficiency and effectiveness

human rights—the recognition of the inherent dignity and of the equal and inalienable rights of all members of the human family

international standards—either formal or informal standards developed by the international community that are intended to supplement and sometimes override domestic standards

liberal individualism—insists that equality will best be achieved by treating people as individuals under a system of universally applicable and consistent rules

liberal universalism—the preference to treat individuals according to a universally applicable set of rules, not those tailored to specific group differences

Management Accountability Framework (MAF)—a set of ten principles or measures against which the performance of senior federal public service managers' performance will be assessed

multiculturalism—a policy of protecting and celebrating the cultural diversity of different groups within a society, and ensuring that there is no discrimination on those grounds

National Performance Review (US)—a program of public sector reform of the Clinton administration, headed by Vice-President Al Gore, in March 1993, touching on virtually every agency and program in the American federal government

new public management—focus on performance appraisal and efficiency; disaggregating and decentralizing public bureaucracies; the use of market mechanisms and of contracting out to foster competition; financial management; partnerships

Next Steps (UK)—the plan in the late 1980s to convert many traditional departments into "departmental executive agencies" that would essentially act as businesses delivering public services

policy reversal—the changes in key policies during the early 1990s that have altered key social and political systems built up in the postwar period in both the developed and developing world

political culture—people's orientations of support and trust toward the political system

politics of difference—an emphasis on rights, discourse, culture, and group-specific differences as the foundation of politics and policy

politics of recognition—the recognition and celebration of "difference" and the view that differences must be recognized and validated

postmaterialism—the broad cultural shift around the world but particularly in the West away from material concerns to questions of identity and lifestyle

postmodern condition—term used to describe the amalgam of conditions consisting of the rise of postmaterialism, the increased salience of rights, and the new emphasis on "difference"

Program Review—the federal Liberal government's policy in the mid-1990s of management reform and program-by-program assessment according to six criteria as a means for reducing the deficit and enhancing efficiency

public management—the process of directing the public sector as a whole as well as the specific agencies within it

race to the bottom—competition among countries for investment by lowering of standards

rights talk—a mode of political discourse that emphasizes the salience of individual and group rights

social cohesion—a sense of belonging to a community that shares values and a sense of purpose and commitment

social fragmentation—the process of losing social cohesion

trade liberalization—the process of lowering trade barriers of every sort such as duties and nontariff barriers, to encourage trade and investment flows

transnational corporations—commercial firms that operate in numerous countries, not simply for the sale of their products, but to organize production itself

FURTHER READINGS

Banting, K., Courchene, T. J., and Seidle, F. L. (Eds.). (2007). *Belonging?: Diversity, recognition and shared citizenship in Canada* (39–86). Montreal: Institute for Research on Public Policy.

Barzelay, M. (2001). *The new public management: Improving research and policy dialogue.* Berkeley: University of California Press.

Holton, R. J. (2005). *Making globalization.* Basingstoke, UK: Palgrave.

Inglehart, R. (Ed.). (2003). *Human values and social change: Findings from the values surveys.* Leiden, Netherlands: Brill.

Kettl, D. F. (2005). *The global public management revolution.* 2nd Ed. Washington, DC: Brookings Institution.

Ritzer, G. (Ed.). (2007). *The Blackwell companion to globalization.* Malden, MA.: Blackwell Publishing.

Scholte, J. A. (2005). *Globalization: A critical introduction.* 2nd. Ed. Basingstoke, UK: Palgrave.

Stiglitz, J. E. (2003). *Globalization and its discontents.* New York: W. W. Norton.

Stiglitz, J. E. (2006). *Making globalization work.* New York: W. W. Norton.

REFERENCES

Abramson, P. R., and Inglehart, R. (1995). *Value change in global perspective.* Ann Arbor: University of Michigan Press.

Adams, M. (2007). *Unlikely utopia: The surprising triumph of Canadian pluralism.* Toronto: Viking Canada.

Advisory Committee on the Public Service (Canada). (2007). *Report to the Prime Minister, 2007.* Retrieved March 3, 2008, from http://www.psagency-agencefp.gc.ca/PSR-RFP/PMAC-CCPM/pmacps_ ccfppm_ e.asp

Appadurai, A. (1996). *Modernity at large: Cultural dimensions of globalization.* Minneapolis, MN.: University of Minnesota Press.

Associated Press (2007). 146 German police officers injured in violent G8 protests. Retrieved February 11, 2008, from http://www.cnn.com/2007/WORLD/europe/06/02/g-8.protest.ap/index.html

Banting, K., et al. (2006). Do multiculturalism policies erode the welfare state? An empirical analysis. In K. Banting and W. Kymlicka (Eds.). *Multiculturalism and the Welfare State: Recognition and Redistribution in Contemporary Democracies* (pp. 49–91). Oxford: Oxford University Press.

Barber, B. R. (1995). *Jihad vs. McWorld*. New York: Times Books.

Barry, B. (2001). *Culture and equality: An egalitarian critique of multiculturalism*. Cambridge: Policy Press.

Barzelay, M. (1992). *Breaking through bureaucracy: A new vision for managing government*. Berkeley: University of California Press.

Bevir, M., Rhodes, R.A.W., and Weller, P. (2003). Traditions of governance: Interpreting the changing role of the public sector. *Public Administration* 81 (1), 1–17.

Brodie, I. (1997). *Interest groups and the Supreme Court of Canada*. Ph. D. dissertation. University of Calgary.

Brodie, I., and Nevitte, N. (1993, June). Evaluating the citizens' constitution theory. Canadian *Journal of Political Science, 26*, 235–59.

Brook, T. (2007). *Vermeer's hat: The seventeenth century and the dawn of the global world*. New York: Viking.

Brown, G. (2008). "Q and A session on globalisation." Retrieved February 15, 2008, from http://www.pm.gov.uk/output/Page14523.asp

Bruce, C., Kneebone, R. D., and McKenzie, K. J. (Eds.) (1997). *A government reinvented: A study of Alberta's deficit elimination program*. Toronto: Oxford University Press.

Cabinet Office (UK) (2006). *The customer voice in transforming public services: The government response*. Retrieved March 2, 2008, from http://www.cabinetoffice.gov.uk/upload/assets/www.cabinetoffice.gov.uk/chartermark/gov_response_bernard.pdf

Cabinet Office (UK), (2007). *Building on progress: Public services*. Retrieved March 2, 2008, from http://www.cabinetoffice.gov.uk/upload/assets/www.cabinetoffice.gov.uk/strategy/building.pdf

Cairncross, F. (1997). *The death of distance: How the communications revolution will change our lives*. Boston: Harvard Business School Press.

Cairns, A. C. (1991). *Disruptions: Constitutional struggle, from the Charter to Meech Lake*. (D. E. Williams, Ed.). Toronto: McClelland and Stewart.

Cairns, A. C. (1992). *Charter versus federalism*. Montreal: McGill-Queen's University Press.

Cairns, A. C. (1993). The fragmentation of Canadian citizenship. In W. Kaplan (Ed.), *Belonging: The meaning and future of Canadian citizenship* (pp. 181–220). Montreal: McGill-Queen's University Press.

Cameron, D. R., and Stein, J. G. (2002). Street protests and fantasy parks. In D. R. Cameron and J. G. Stein (Eds.), *Street protests and fantasy parks: Globalization, culture, and the state* (pp. 1–19). Vancouver: UBC Press.

Castells, M. (1997). *The information age: Economy, society and culture. Vol. II: The power of identity.* Oxford: Blackwell.

CBC News (September 17, 2007). How provincial governments finance religious schools. Retrieved February 13, 2008, from http://www.cbc.ca/ontariovotes2007/features/features-faith.html

CCAPRCD. (2008a). *Home page.* Retrieved February 13, 2008, from http://www.accommodements.qc.ca/index-en.html

CCAPRCD. (2008b). *Building the future: A time for reconciliation.* Abridged report. Retrieved June 10, 2008, from http://www.accommodements.qc.ca/documentation/rapports/rapport-final-abrege-en.pdf

Christensen, T., and Laegried, P. (Eds.) (2002). *New public management: The transformation of ideas and practice.* Hampshire: Ashgate.

Commission of Inquiry into the Sponsorship Program and Advertising Activities (Gomery Inquiry). (2006). *Restoring accountability: Recommendations.* Ottawa. Public Works and Government Services of Canada.

Courchene, T. J., and Savoie, D. J. (2003). Introduction. In T. J. Courchene and D. J. Savoie (Eds.), *The art of the state: Governance in a world without frontiers* (pp. 1–27). Montreal: Institute for Research on Public Policy.

Denhardt, R. B. and Denhardt, J. V. (2000). The new public service: Serving rather than steering. *Public Administration Review* 60 (6): 549–559.

Denhardt, R. B. and Denhardt, J. V. (2003). *The new public service: Serving, not steering.* Armonk, N.Y.: M.E. Sharpe.

Department of Defense (US) (2006). *Encyclopedia of ethical failure.* Washington, D. C. Retrieved on June 10, 2008, from www.dod.mil/dodgc/defense_ethics/dod_oge/Encyclopedia_of_Ethical_Failures_2006_Full_Version.doc

Department of Finance (Canada). (1995). *The federal budget.* Ottawa: Ministry of Finance.

Doern, G. B. (1993). The UK citizen's charter: Origins and implementation in three agencies. *Policy and Politics, 21,* 17–29.

Economist Intelligence Unit (2008). *Country Report: United States of America*. London, UK: EIU. Retrieved February 9, 2008, from http://store.eiu.com/product/50000205US.html?ref=featuredProductHome

Eisenberg, A. (1994, March). The politics of individual and group difference in Canadian jurisprudence. *Canadian Journal of Political Science, 27*, 3–21.

Federal Accountability Action Plan. (2006). *Turning a new leaf*. Ottawa. Retrieved March 3, from http://www.faa-lfi.gc.ca/docs/ap-pa/ap-pa_e.pdf

Federal Government (Germany) (2007). *G8 Summit 2007, Heiligendamm*. Retrieved February 11, 2008, from http://www.g-8.de/Webs/G8/EN/Homepage/home.html

Fierlbeck, K. (1996, March). The ambivalent potential of cultural identity. *Canadian Journal of Political Science, 29*, 3–22.

Fletcher, J. F., and Howe, P. (2000, May). Public opinion and the courts. *Choices, 6*.

Florida, R. (2002). *The rise of the creative class: And how it's transforming work, leisure, community and everyday life*. New York: Basic Books.

Florida, R. (2005). *The flight of the creative class: The new global competition for talent*. New York: HarperBusiness.

Florida, R. (2008). *Who's your city? How the creative economy is making where you live the most important decision of your life*. Toronto: Random House.

Foreign Affairs and International Trade Canada (2008). *Dispute settlement*. Retrieved February 11, 2008, from http://www.international.gc.ca/trade-agreements-accords-commerciaux/disp-diff/ index.aspx?lang=en

Friedman, T. L. (1999). *The Lexus and the olive tree: Understanding globalization*. New York: Farrar, Straus, Giroux.

Getting Government Right. (1997). Ottawa: Minister of Public Works and Government Services Canada.

Glendon, M. A. (1991). *Rights talk: The impoverishment of political discourse*. New York: The Free Press.

Good, D. (2003). *The politics of public management: The HRDC audit of grants and contributions*. Toronto: University of Toronto Press.

Government On Line (2003). *2nd Annual Report*. Retrieved August 6, 2004, from http://www.tbs-sct.gc.ca/report/gol-ged/2003/gol-ged02_e.asp

Green, J. (2000, March). The difference debate: Reducing rights to cultural flavours. *Canadian Journal of Political Science, 33*, 133–44.

Greenspon, E., and Wilson-Smith, A. (1996). *Double vision: The inside story of the Liberals in power*. Toronto: Doubleday.

Hein, G. (2000, March). Interest group litigation and Canadian democracy. *Choices, 6.*

Herdan, B. (2006). *The customer voice in transforming public services.* The Independent Report from the review of the Charter Mark Scheme and Measurement of Customer Satisfaction with Public Services. London: Cabinet Office.

House of Commons (Canada). (2007). *Protocol for the appearance of accounting officers as witnesses before the Standing Committee on Public Accounts.* Retrieved March 3, 2008, from http://cmte.parl. gc.ca/ Content/HOC/committee/391/pacp/reports/rp2798921/391_PACP_ Rpt13/391_PACP_Rpt13-e.pdf

Ibbitson, J. (1997). *Promised land: Inside the Mike Harris revolution.* Scarborough, ON: Prentice-Hall.

Ignatieff, M. (2000). *The rights revolution.* Toronto: House of Anansi.

Inglehart, R. and Welzel, C. (2005). *Modernization, cultural change, and democracy: The human development sequence.* New York: Cambridge University Press.

International Monetary Fund. (1999). *International capital markets: Developments, prospects, and key policy issues.* Retrieved August 6, 2004, from http://www.imf.org/external/pubs/ft/icm/1999/index.htm

Internet World Stats (2008). *Internet usage statistics.* Retrieved February, 14 from http://www.internetworldstats.com/stats.htm

Jenkins, B., and Gray, A. (1993). Reshaping the management of government: The Next Steps initiative in the United Kingdom. In F. L. Seidle (Ed.), *Rethinking government: Reform of reinvention?* (pp. 73–109). Montreal: Institute for Research on Public Policy.

Jenson, J. The frontiers of citizenship: Reflections. In T. J. Courchene and D. J. Savoie (Eds.), *The art of the state: Governance in a world without frontiers* (pp. 311–21). Montreal: Institute for Research on Public Policy.

Keck, M. E., and Sikkink, K. (1998). *Activists beyond borders: Advocacy networks in international politics.* Ithaca: Cornell University Press.

Kelly, J. B. (2000, Winter). Bureaucratic activism and the Charter of Rights and Freedoms: The Department of Justice and its entry into the centre of government. *Canadian Public Administration, 42,* 476–511.

Kernaghan, K. (2000a, March). The post-bureaucratic organization and public service values. *International Review of Administrative Sciences, 66,* 91–104.

Kettl, D. F., and DiIulio, Jr., J. J. (Eds.). (1995). *Inside the reinvention machine: Appraising governmental reform.* Washington, DC: The Brookings Institution.

Kettl, D. F. (2005). *The global public management revolution*. 2nd Ed. Washington, DC: Brookings Institution.

Kymlicka, W. (1992). *Recent work in citizenship theory*. Ottawa: Multiculturalism and Citizenship Canada.

Kymlicka, W. (1995). *Multicultural citizenship: A liberal theory of minority rights*. Oxford: Clarendon Press.

Kymlicka, W. (2007). Ethnocultural diversity in a liberal state: Making sense of the Canadian model(s). In K. Banting, T. J. Courchene, and F. L. Seidle (Eds.), *Belonging?: Diversity, recognition and shared citizenship in Canada* (39–86). Montreal: Institute for Research on Public Policy.

Lépine, G. (2007). *The web of rules: A study of the relationship between regulation of public servants and past public sector reform initiatives*. Toronto: Public Policy Forum.

Lindquist, E. A., and Murray, K. B. (1994, Fall). Appendix: A reconnaissance of Canadian public administrative reform during the early 1990s. *Canadian Public Administration, 37*, 468–89.

Lister, M. (2007). *Government and globalization: What kind of public service does Canada need in order to thrive in the Knowledge Economy?* Toronto: Public Policy Forum.

Lusztig, M. (1994, December). Constitutional paralysis: Why Canadian constitutional initiatives are doomed to fail. *Canadian Journal of Political Science, 27*, 747–71.

Lynn Jr., L. E. (2001). Globalization and administrative reform: What is happening in theory? *Public Management Review, 3*, pp. 191–208.

McDonald, K. (2006). *Global movements: Action and culture*. Oxford: Blackwell.

Mahon, R., Andrew, C. and Johns, R. (2007). Policy analysis in an era of "globalization": Capturing spatial dimensions and scalar strategies. In M. Orsini and M. Smith (Eds.), *Critical policy studies* (41–64). Vancouver; UBC Press.

Mandel, M. (1994). *The Charter of Rights and the legalization of politics in Canada*. Rev. ed. Toronto: Thompson Education Publishing.

Martin, R. I. (2003). *The most dangerous branch: How the Supreme Court of Canada has undermined our law and our democracy*. Montreal and Kingston: McGill-Queen's University Press.

Myles, J. and St-Arnaud, S. (2006). Population diversity, multiculturalism, and the welfare state: Should welfare state theory be revised? In K. Banting and W. Kymlicka (Eds.). *Multiculturalism and the Welfare State: Recognition and Redistribution in Contemporary Democracies* (pp. 339–354). Oxford: Oxford University Press.

Montgomery, J. D. (1999). Fifty years of human rights: An emergent global regime. *Policy Sciences, 32*(1), 79–94.

Morton, F. L., and Knopff, R. (2000). *The Charter revolution and the Court Party*. Toronto: Broadview Press.

O'Brien, R., Goetz, A. M., Scholte, J. A., and Williams, M. (Eds.). (2000). *Contesting global governance: Multilateral institutions and global social movements*. Cambridge, MA: Cambridge University Press.

Office of Management and Budget (USA). (2002). *The President's management agenda*. Retrieved March 2, 2008, from http://www .whitehouse.gov/omb/budget/fy2002/mgmt.pdf

Office of Public Services Reform. (2002). *Reforming our public services: Principles into practice*. Retrieved March 2, 2008, from http://www .pm.gov.uk/files/pdf/Principles.pdf

O'Hara, K. (1998). *Securing the social union*. CPRN Study No. 02. Ottawa: Canadian Policy Research Networks.

Ohmae, K. (1995). *The end of the nation state: The rise of regional economies*. New York: The Free Press.

Ohmae, K. (2004). *The next global stage: Challenges and opportunities in our borderless world*. Upper Saddle River, N.J.: Wharton School Publishing.

Osborne, D., and Gaebler, T. (1993). *Reinventing government: How the entrepreneurial spirit is transforming the public sector*. New York: Penguin.

Pal, L. A., and Seidle, F. L. (1993). Constitutional politics 1990–92: The paradox of participation. In S. Phillips (Ed.), *How Ottawa spends, 1993–94: A more democratic Canada?* (pp. 143–202). Ottawa: Carleton University Press.

Pauly, L. W. (1997). *Who elected the bankers? Surveillance and control in the world economy*. Ithaca: Cornell University Press.

Perreault, F. (2006). *Inside Gomery*. Toronto: Douglas and McIntyre.

Peters, B. G. (1995). The public service, the changing state, and governance. In B. G. Peters and D. J. Savoie (Eds.), *Governance in a changing environment* (pp. 288–320). Montreal: Canadian Centre for Management Development and McGill-Queen's University Press.

Peters, B. G. (2003). Democracy and political power in contemporary western governments: Challenges and reforms. In T. J. Courchene and D. J. Savoie (Eds.), *The art of the state: Governance in a world without frontiers* (pp. 81–108). Montreal: Institute for Research on Public Policy.

Pew Global Attitudes Project. (2007). *World Publics Welcome Global Trade—But Not Immigration*. Retrieved February 27, 2008, from http://pewglobal.org/reports/display.php?ReportID=258

Pollitt, C. (1995). Management techniques for the public sector: Pulpit and practice. In B. G. Peters and D. J. Savoie (Eds.), *Governance in a changing environment* (pp. 203–38). Montreal: Canadian Centre for Management Development and McGill-Queen's University Press.

Porter, M. E. (1990). *The competitive advantage of nations*. New York: Free Press.

Privy Council Office (Canada). (2008). *Accounting officers: Guidance on roles, responsibilities and appearances before Parliamentary committees 2007*. Retrieved March 3, 2008, from http://www.pco-bcp.gc.ca/ index.asp?lang=eng&page=information&sub=publications&doc= guidemin/ao-adc/2007/account-guideonrole2007_e.htm

Progressive Conservative Party of Ontario. (1995). *The common sense revolution*. Toronto: Progressive Conservative Party of Ontario.

Results for Canadians. (2000). Ottawa. Retrieved March 3, 2008, from http://www.tbs-sct.gc.ca/res_can/rc_1_e.asp#pre

Rheingold, H. (2003) Smart mobs: *The next social revolution*. Cambridge, MA: Perseus Publishing.

Sandel, M. J. (1996). *Democracy's discontent: America in search of a public philosophy*. Cambridge, MA: Harvard University Press.

Sassen, S. (1998). *Globalization and its discontents*. New York: The New Press.

Sassen, S. (2002a). Locating cities on global circuits. *Environment and Urbanization*, 14 (1): 13–30.

Sassen, S. (2002b). (Ed.) *Global networks, linked cities*. New York: Routledge.

Savoie, D. J. (1995, Spring). What is wrong with the new public management? *Canadian Public Administration*, 38, 112–21.

Scholte, J. A. (2003). *What is globalization: The definitional issue—again*. Institute on Globalization and the Human Condition, McMaster University, Working Paper Series.

Scholte, J. A. (2005). *Globalization: A critical introduction*. 2nd Ed. Basingstoke, UK: Palgrave.

Slaughter, A.-M. (2004). *A new world order*. Princeton: Princeton University Press.

Soroka, S. N., Johnston, R., and Banting, K. (2007). Ties that bind? Social cohesion and diversity in Canada. In K. Banting, T. J. Courchene, and F. L. Seidle (Eds.), *Belonging?: Diversity, recognition and shared citizenship in Canada* (1–40). Montreal: Institute for Research on Public Policy.

Statistics Canada (2007). *Provincial Economic Accounts, Annual Estimates—Tables and Analytical Document*. Catalogue no. 13-213-PPB, pp. 324–326. Retrieved February 5, 2008, from http://www.statcan.ca/bsolc/english/bsolc?catno=13-213-P

Stiglitz, J. E. (2006). *Making globalization work*. New York: W. W. Norton.

Taylor, C. (1994). *Multiculturalism: Examining the politics of recognition*. Princeton: Princeton University Press.

Thurow, L. C. (1996). *The future of capitalism: How today's economic forces shape tomorrow's world*. New York: William Morrow and Co.

Treasury Board of Canada. (2003). *Plans and priorities. 2003–2004*. Ottawa.

Treasury Board of Canada. (2007). *Management accountability framework: Frequently asked questions*. Retrieved March 3, 2008, from http://www.tbs-sct.gc.ca/maf-crg/faq_e.asp

Union of International Associations. (2007). *The yearbook of international organizations*. Retrieved February 27, 2008, from http://www.uia.org/organizations/home.php

United Nations. (2003). *The globalization of human rights*. Geneva: United Nations University Press.

United Nations Conference on Trade and Development (2007). *World Investment Report 2007: Transnational Corporations, Extractive Industries and Development*. New York and Geneva: United Nations. Retrieved February 7, 2007, from http://www.unctad.org/en/docs/wir2007_en.pdf

Vogel, D. (1995). *Trading up: Consumer and environmental regulation in a global economy*. Cambridge, MA: Harvard University Press.

Vogel, D. and Kagan, R. (2004) (Eds.). *Dynamics of regulatory change: How globalization affects national regulatory policies*. Berkeley: University of California Press.

Walker, S. (1998). *The rights revolution: Rights and community in modern America*. New York: Oxford University Press.

Weiss, L. (1998). *The myth of the powerless state*. Ithaca, NY: Cornell University Press.

World Trade Organization (2007). *International Trade Statistics 2007*. Retrieved Feb 2, 2007, from http://www.wto.org/english/res_e/statis_e/its2007_e/its2007_e.pdf

Young, I. M. (1990). *Justice and the politics of difference*. Princeton, NJ: Princeton University Press.

CHAPTER

3

Problem Definition in Policy Analysis

Policymaking is in large measure about trying to solve problems, and so the nature of those problems—how they are defined—is central to the entire process. But defining problems is not merely a technical exercise; it entails political and strategic manoeuvres, insofar as problem definition sets the tone for successive stages in the process. Framing problems draws on a wide variety of ingredients, from scientific expertise to conventional wisdom and rhetoric. In a democracy, it always means shaping arguments in ways that capture public attention and support. This process is connected to interests and institutions, of course, but the study of problem definition and framing clearly underscores the importance of ideas in policymaking. The second part of the chapter explores ways in which both the substance and the process of problem definition are changing in the face of the forces described in Chapter 2.

The core of any public policy is the triad of problem definition, goals, and instruments. Know them, and you know the policy. But if we view policy more dynamically, which of these elements comes first, or what is the prime mover in the policy response? There is universal agreement that the key factor is the problem or at least the definition of a situation considered problematic (Geva-May and Wildavsky, 1997, p. 1). As Dunn puts it: "Problem structuring is a central guidance system or steering mechanism that affects the success of all subsequent phases of policy analysis. Regrettably, policy analysts seem to fail more often because they solve the wrong problem than because they get the wrong solution to the right problem" (Dunn, 2008, p. 72). Policies are responses to problems, and so the character and shape of the problem will deeply affect the nature of the response. At the most extreme, if a problem is not widely recognized at all, there will be little or no policy response. The existence of widespread and systematic poverty in the United States in the late 1950s was largely ignored, for example, until the publication of Michael Harrington's *The Other America: Poverty in the United States* (1962). The same could be said of modern environmentalism; until Rachel Carson's *Silent Spring* (1962), the notion that what we were doing to the environment was a problem simply did not occur to many people. A striking Canadian example comes from research conducted by the Canadian Advisory Council on the Status of Women in 1987 on domestic abuse: the study entitled *Battered but Not Beaten* by Linda MacLeod took something from the shadows of private family life and exposed it as a major social problem. In recent years there was a sudden burst of reports across North America about the looming "crisis" of obesity. While fat and dieting have been features of contemporary culture for years, obesity suddenly emerged as a policy problem whereas before it had been visible only as a personal issue. In March 2004, for example, the American Centers for Disease Control and Prevention announced that obesity would soon overtake smoking as the leading cause of preventable death, and media were festooned with stories about the connections between obesity and diabetes, the impact on the elderly, and the rising "epidemic" of obesity among the young (linked to sedentary lifestyles, fatty foods, and video games). All of these cases illustrate the fact that policy problems do not simply "exist out there"—they have to be recognized, defined, structured, and made visible.

It would seem that there should be another end of the continuum to complement problem invisibility, a point where problems are so well defined and understood that the policy response seems obvious and uncontroversial. In fact, there are very few of these, at least with respect to proposed solutions. On some issues, such as child pornography, consensus appears overwhelming about both the character of the problem (universally despised) and the solution (a strong prohibition). However, in concrete cases there is still much room for debate. For example, in January 2000 the Supreme Court of Canada heard a case involving the possession of what qualifies under the law as child pornography. John Robin Sharpe had been charged with possession of fictional stories and sketches involving minors and sex, had argued his own case in the British Columbia lower courts, and had been acquitted. The Supreme Court listened to arguments in his defence that these materials did no harm to real children and that Canada's child pornography laws were too broad, and in February 2001 basically upheld the law, though with some reservations. So it is clear that problems are not simply either recognized or not: they have to be discerned, shaped, articulated, and defended. There are so many different elements that can conceivably go into a problem definition—including both facts and values—that people may see the same situation quite differently, even if they agree on its general aspects, and so will offer very different solutions.

The idea that people disagree in their perceptions of problems and solutions is hardly news, so it may come as a surprise to learn that until the last decade, policy analysis held out the hope of trying to "get it right," in other words, to achieve the correct definition of the problem.

As Stone (2002) puts it:

In conventional policy analysis textbooks, as well as in the larger rationality project, a problem definition is a statement of a goal and the discrepancy between it and the status quo. In this conception, problem definition is a matter of observation and arithmetic—measuring the difference between two states of affairs (p. 133).

Almost twenty years ago, a leading text could refer to the possibility of making "mistakes" in the problem definition or initiation phase of policy design (Brewer and deLeon 1983, p. 35). The idea of "making mistakes" would strike Stone (2002) as very odd since, to her, problem definition "is a matter of representation because every description of a situation is a portrayal from only one of many points of view...[and it] is strategic because groups, individuals, and government agencies deliberately and consciously fashion portrayals so as to promote their favored course of action" (p. 133). When everything is open to interpretation, there is no clearly superior way of discerning a situation, and so all interpretations are equally valid. This explains the problem-saturated policy environment within which we live. The media, interest groups, experts, analysts, think-tanks, and political parties subject us to a constant barrage of crises and problems. Not only is the number of problems apparently large, but also the range of solutions seems bewilderingly wide.

Governments do not have infinite resources or time, however, and every government faces the ultimate test of having to choose among definitions and solutions and doing what it was elected to do—govern. It is this combination of epistemological variety and political reality that shapes the agenda of questions that occupy the literature on problem definition: (1) by what political and intellectual processes are problems defined, (2) what are the generic elements of a problem definition, (3) how are some problems chosen to be on the political/policy agenda while others languish in obscurity, and (4) what impact does problem definition have on subsequent stages of the policy process? The good news is that most of the answers to these questions are interesting and insightful. The bad news is that they are not systematic nor could they really be expected to be. Problem definition has a strong socio-psychological dimension; it is one component in the imaginative construction of reality, with heavy doses of professional skill, creativity, intuition, and serendipity. Moreover, problem definition is embedded in fluid political and policy processes, where accident and luck play a strong role. It is not surprising, therefore, that the literature is dominated by case studies that, while interesting themselves, often conclude that "it all depends."

However, the questions, and some of the general answers to them, are worth exploring, if only because they do provide an organized way of thinking about problem definition and formulation. Contemporary policy analysis needs to go beyond this to recognize that some key elements of both the substance and process of problem definition have changed dramatically in the last decade in response to the forces described in Chapter 2. In terms of the substance of public policy problems, **globalization**, diversity, and the role of government in actually causing problems rather than solving them are new parameters within which any policy analysis will have to take place. Recently, some new frames of reference, or what we will term below **"ideas in good currency"** seem to have made inroads in policy debates. The tools needed to deal with policy problems in this new environment are different from those in the past, and this chapter closes with a consideration of the demands this places on analysts.

Problem Definition: Key Issues

What constitutes a problem? The most common definition in the field is that a problem is a "substantial discrepancy between what is and what should be" (Dery, 1984, p. 17), or to put it another way, policy problems "are unrealized needs, values, or opportunities for improvement" (Dunn, 2008, p. 72). There are three components to these definitions: reality (what is, the unrealized needs or values), a desired state of affairs (what should be, the improvement), and the gap between them (the discrepancy). But why should the simple fact of a discrepancy or gap between reality and the ideal constitute a problem? Clearly it does not, and note that the definitions address what should be, and not what could be. There have to be realistic opportunities for improvement. So this is a first clue on the nature of problem definition—it is incomprehensible without some understanding of the goals being pursued or the standards being used to judge "what should be."

If standards are always involved in defining the desired state of affairs, the other key ingredient is discerning the gap or discrepancy. Indeed, this is the first phase in the process of problem definition. Before problems can be defined they have to be recognized or sensed. This is a primordial stage in problem definition in that it usually involves just a first tremor that something is wrong, a sense of unease, that there is a difference between reality and our preferred standard. Strict constructionists (in the sense that all problems are socially constructed) like Deborah Stone (2002) see this as a highly unpredictable and strategic process and, moreover, one that is contingent on core assumptions, world view, and social location. It is widely agreed, however, that values, perceptions, and interests play a huge role in this phase, since recognition depends on attention, and attention depends on relevance and an ability to notice and care about signals coming in from the environment around us. How likely is someone with a secure job who lives a middle-class lifestyle to notice or care about urban homelessness or Aboriginal suicide?

While the role of selective perception has a measure of truth to it, too strong an emphasis on mutually exclusive values tends to underestimate the degree to which some standards whereby we recognize nascent problems and public issues are in fact widely shared and hard-wired into the political process itself. **Problem recognition**, according to Kingdon (1995), is often stimulated by widely agreed-upon **indicators** and routine monitoring that turns up dis epancies or patterns that hint that something is amiss:

> Fairly c en, problems come to the attention of government deci-
> sion m ers not through some sort of political pressure or per-
> ceptual eight of hand but because some more or less systematic
> indicat simply shows that there is a problem out there. Such
> indicat s abound in the political world because both govern-
> menta nd nongovernmental agencies routinely monitor various
> activit and events: highway deaths, disease rates, immuniza-
> tion r s, consumer prices, commuter and intercity ridership,
> costs entitlement programs, infant mortality rates, and many
> other: p. 90)

Kingd goes on to say that while pressure campaigns and dramatic events ar ertainly important in attracting notice to a problem, in fact people pa attention "rather straightforwardly because there actually is a demonstr le problem that needs their attention" (p. 93). This occurs in those ins ices where there is a reasonable degree of consensus about the indicato and what they mean. Canadian debates about poverty, for example re normally based on the low income cutoffs (LICO) developed by atistics Canada. These cutoffs, however, were never intended to be a easure of poverty but rather an indicator of when the consumptio of an "average" package of goods would become difficult (Sarlo, 96, Chap. 2). Moreover, the LICO is a relative measure—it measure low income as a proportion of income spent on certain goods (food, shelter, and clothing) above what other Canadian families of the same size spend. Another approach is an absolute measure of low income or poverty, which tries to determine what it would take at a minimum to survive. But even here, the definitions of these "market basket measures" can vary from bare necessities to something more elaborate. The National Council of Welfare has made the point that poverty is a very complicated condition, and no single indicator will capture all its dimensions:

> Poverty indicators are not developed in isolation. They are tools we use to achieve our vision and goals. Our vision and overarching goals must be set before we can look at which indicators can help us plan, monitor and assess our progress so we know whether we have been successful. Certainly, for an anti-poverty strategy, one key type of indicator will be direct measures of poverty, which are usually based on income. We may need to start, however, by discussing what we mean by poverty in Canada. Then we can figure out how best to measure it. Given the many dimensions of poverty, we may not be able to find one measure that gives us a perfect picture. We need to remain open to the idea that it may turn out to be more useful to develop or adopt multiple measures of poverty. (National Council of Welfare, 2007)

Nonetheless, despite debates and a variety of measures, when the numbers of Canadians who fall below the LICO increases, there are immediate concerns about possibly rising poverty in the country. Changes in other indicators such as the gross national product (GNP), the exchange rate, crime statistics, productivity rates, literacy, aging, teenage pregnancies, and smoking (to choose just a few), also convey messages. When the indicator shows a positive development, there is a general sense that "things are going well" (e.g., increases in GNP, productivity, and literacy). When the indicator shows a negative development, this signals that perhaps there is a problem that needs attention (e.g., increases in crime, pregnancies, and smoking).

Indicators come in various forms. Sometimes they are simply routinely produced by programs and government departments—annual reports, unemployment statistics, Statistics Canada data, and government-sponsored research reports and studies. Interest groups, think-tanks, and foundations of course have an interest in either highlighting indicators that support their cause or their orientation or in developing research that casts light on suspicions they have about a given issue or problem. These types of indicators are different from what Kingdon calls "**focusing events**," which can be sudden catastrophes or crises that grab attention. One of the most chilling of these was the SARS (Severe Acute Respiratory Syndrome) epidemic. The first known outbreak occurred in Foshan City, Guangdong Province, China, on November 16, 2002. At that time it was not recognized as SARS, but simply as an unusual respiratory ailment. Almost two months later, the World Health Organization (WHO) received an e-mail describing an unusual contagious disease that had left more than 100 people dead in Guangdong Province. In the next few days, Chinese authorities revealed that some 300 people were ill, and five had died, but that this was simply a case of atypical pneumonia, and that the outbreak was under control. Then followed a series of deaths and illnesses in Hong Kong that were ascribed to avian flu. By the end of the month, there were reports and rumours of as many as fifty hospitals in Guangzhou (in Guangdong Province) with ill patients. The mystery disease began to spread beyond China, as a Canadian woman and an American man both made their way homeward. The American man stopped over and became ill in Hanoi, and by March 5 the Canadian woman was dead in Toronto and five relatives were hospitalized. Still no one knew precisely what the disease was or where and how it was spreading. By mid-March the WHO had given SARS its name and issued a travel advisory on the suspicion that the disease was spreading through international flights. It was not until mid-April that the causative agent in SARS was identified—a completely new coronavirus, unlike any other human or animal member of the coronavirus family (World Health Organization, 2003). The 2003 epidemic affected 8098 people worldwide, of whom 774 died.

SARS was unusual in that it attracted worldwide attention very quickly. By themselves, most focusing events are not so mysterious and dramatic, and usually have to be supplemented by other factors such as a receptive public mood, energetic politicians, interest groups willing to push the issue, or some sense that trends are developing beyond acceptable thresholds. It is in the character of focusing events that they galvanize debate and discussion, but the most that happens at this stage is the development of a sense that there may be a problem that needs attention and further research. For example, the horrific footage of Robert Dziekanski, a Polish immigrant, being tasered and eventually dying on October 14, 2007 in the Vancouver airport sparked a national debate on police use of tasers. The topic had barely ever been mentioned before, but as more incidents of taser use arose in the following months, a host of questions arose: how do tasers actually work; what voltage is safe; are police overusing tasers? New Brunswick, Newfoundland and Nova Scotia all launched reviews of tasers. Amnesty International produced research purporting to show that 310 people had died in North America as a result of taser use (*Globe and Mail*, 2008: A17). The RCMP's Commission on Public Complaints also reviewed taser use in the force, and recommended limits to its use (*Globe and Mail*, 2007a: A24) Even the UN got into the act, with its Committee Against Torture proclaiming that use of tasers constituted a form of torture. In the United States, the National Institute of Justice (the research agency for the Department of Justice), launched a panel to investigate the effects of tasers on internal organs, metabolic pathways, and the cardiac and respiratory systems. The Institute believed that "major questions remain to be answered about taser safety" (*Globe and Mail*, 2007b: A28).

So, as Kingdon and others have pointed out, indicators or events—whether in the form of routine reports or focusing events—have to be interpreted. In themselves they mean relatively little. Another good example was the evolving debate over government deficits in the 1990s and what they meant. The numbers were indisputable and widely accepted—the issue was what those numbers meant, what the underlying causes of deficits were, and what might be done about them. To simplify only slightly, the argument gradually emerged in the 1980s and 1990s that deficits were caused by overspending, were a drag on the economy, and were reaching unsustainable levels. The counterargument—that deficits were an occasionally necessary instrument to stimulate the economy and would self-correct once economic activity took off again—gradually lost force. There now appears to be a broad consensus on both left and right—as demonstrated by Canadian party positions in the 2006 and 2008 elections, and positions taken on recent federal and provincial budgets—that deficits are unacceptable and economically counterproductive. But this consensus, fragile as it is, took almost two decades to develop in Canada (and Canada's string of federal surpluses is unique among G-7 countries). Governments spend of course, and because of a reasonably buoyant economy in the last decade, have been able to pull off the magic trick of reducing taxes and debt, spending more, and avoiding deficits. Even the Ontario government, which in 2005–06 ran deficits, proudly noted that in 2007 it was in balance, and on track for five consecutive balanced budgets (Ontario Ministry of Finance, 2007). This boast was rendered obsolete by the global financial crisis, and by November 2008 the Ontario government was projecting at least a $500 million deficit, and Ottawa was considering the possibility as well, though with marked reluctance.

Problem definition or structuring is the arduous process of taking some indicator that a problem exists—such as lagging productivity or average income—and answering three fundamental questions. The first question is about the indicator itself and its relation to the phenomenon it is representing. This means being both clear about that phenomenon, and about the "fit" between it and the indicator. We noted above that poverty can be defined in several ways, for example as a lack of material resources (basic food and shelter) or it might be defined as well as social exclusion, the inability to fully participate in one's community. A different concept of poverty demands a different measure or indicator, or perhaps some combination of several indicators to get a handle on the full complexity of the issues. The second question is also about the indicator but now shifts to causality. Why did this happen and how? What matrix of cause and effect is at work? In both of our examples, the central question is why? What is the cause of SARS or low productivity or poverty? In the SARS case it might be atypical pneumonia or a completely new strain of a pathogen. In the productivity case, it might be low rates of capital investment, high taxes, cyclical variations, or low levels of innovation and scientific research. For poverty, it could be a lack of education or skills that bars people from good jobs. Each one of these hypotheses would have to be considered and tested in some fashion. The third question is about what action to take in the event that there is a "real" problem at stake. Is this a problem that can be solved, and who should solve it? Most importantly, is this a problem that government should solve? Is it in the public sphere, or is it a matter either for private initiative or nongovernmental collective action? The answers seem obvious in the case of SARS and poverty reduction, but perhaps less so in the case of productivity.

It is rare for these questions—particularly the first two on the nature of the phenomenon/indicator and the causal matrix that might underlie it—to be answered in detail except by specialists. The range of specialists that will be engaged in a policy issue will vary with the substance of that issue; economic problems will engage economists, environmental problems will engage experts in biology and environmental sciences, and so on. But policy problems are different from more general research problems in that the objective is to address and if possible solve the problem in some practical way. Accordingly, a key aspect of determining these questions and developing answers to them is what Dunn (2008) calls "**problem structuring**" (p. 72). He points out that some problems are well structured (few decisionmakers and a small set of alternatives), while some are moderately or ill-structured. Ill-structured problems are marked by high levels of uncertainty and competing objectives and alternatives (p. 79). In this case, policy analysis must rely on creativity, insight, and judgment in helping to shape a workable understanding of the problem. Nonetheless, there are generic techniques that can be used to help scope out the nature of a policy problem. Box 3.1 (page 116) outlines some of the major ones described by Dunn. These techniques and steps are far from infallible, but they do provide some conceptual tools to help move beyond the recognition stage to problem definition and problem structuring, particularly when there are a large number of stakeholders and a variety of different views, assumptions, and arguments about the nature of the problem.

Few of us, however, have the time to be that well acquainted with a problem definition or to apply these techniques independently. Most of us, even in cases where we are quite interested in a given policy issue, will tend to summarize it in what Baumgartner and Jones (1993) call "**policy images**." Policy images are a "mixture of empirical information and emotive appeals" that explain the issue and justify the public policy response (p. 26). Moreover, since these images are shorthand, they convey more than information; they give a sense of the tone of the issue in positive or negative terms. Baumgartner and Jones cite the changing tone in the policy image surrounding civilian nuclear power from a largely positive association with economic progress to a negative connotation linked to

BOX 3.1   METHODS OF PROBLEM STRUCTURING

METHOD	DESCRIPTION
Boundary analysis	This is a technique to canvass the whole range of existing definitions and conceptualizations of a given problem. Involves: (1) saturation sampling: multi-stage process of contacting or canvassing all stakeholders involved in an issue, until no new stakeholders can be added or named, (2) problem representations: develop a full list of all problem representations held by stakeholders, (3) boundary estimation: plot the frequency of new elements added to the problem definition until the frequency of additions approaches zero.
Classification analysis	This involves breaking down the problem phenomenon into logically distinct categories or classes. There is no clear rule about this; but, for example, in addressing the problem of poverty, one would want to go beyond just two classifications (those who fall below the poverty line, and those who do not) to include gender, race, disability, age, and so on. The problem might appear quite differently for different groups (and hence invite different solutions), but we also get a better sense of the causal factors at work with a more complex classification scheme.
Hierarchical analysis	This is a technique for identifying possible causes of a problem. Three classes are used: possible causes, plausible causes, and actionable causes. Possible causes are factors, that, however remote, may have some bearing on the problem. Plausible causes are ones that are more conventionally highlighted in the research or debates on the issue. Actionable causes are ones that can be addressed by governments.
Synectics	This technique relies on the use of analogies to see if new policy problems have sufficiently similar characteristics to older ones that the previous problem definitions and solutions can provide some guidance. For example, in

	thinking about the legalization of marijuana, one might consider the analogy of Prohibition policies against alcohol in the 1930s.
Brainstorming	A family of techniques, more or less formal, to generate ideas, goals and strategies. Can involve informal and unstructured exchange to scenario writing.
Multiple perspective analysis	Deliberately review the problem situation from three perspectives: (1) the technical perspective: cost-benefit analysis, econometrics systems analysis, (2) organizational perspective: focus on institutional rules and processes, and the following of standard operating procedures, (3) personal perspective: view problems and solutions in terms of individual perceptions and values.
Assumptional analysis	Aims at developing a synthesis of the different assumptions that stakeholders have about the issue or problem. Involves canvassing the full range of solutions proposed for the issue or problem, and using that as a vehicle for analyzing and challenging the assumptions that underlie the problem definition.
Argument mapping	A technique to map and classify the different components of policy arguments made by stakeholders—components such as arguments based on statistics, on authority, on values, on intuition or judgement.

SOURCE: Dunn, W.N. (2004). *Public Policy Analysis: An Introduction*, 3rd ed. (Englewood Cliffs, NJ: Prentice Hall), Chap. 3.

environmental damage. A policy issue may be framed in various images, depending on the interests and actors in the field. Stable policy fields tend to coalesce around one dominant policy image, and policy challenge and change is largely about mobilization through the "redefinition of the prevailing policy image" (p. 239). We mentioned attitudes toward deficits earlier: it seems likely that a stable policy image has coalesced around the question of deficits in that they are now almost universally considered undesirable.

Problem structuring or definition therefore involves various techniques aimed at probing an issue that has been signalled in some way as a possible policy problem. The process of problem definition is one of shaping a persuasive argument about the nature of the problem and, of course, the solution. Of what does that argument and persuasion consist? Rochefort and Cobb (1994) offer a scheme that captures some of the key elements, summarized in Box 3.2.

BOX 3.2　　　　　　**ASPECTS OF POLICY ARGUMENTS AND PROBLEM DEFINITION**

Causality (what kinds of causal factors lie behind the problem?)	• Individual causation versus systemic (the former stresses choices and culpability; the latter stresses impersonal and unavoidable forces). • Intentional versus accidental causes. • Causes due to the nature of values systems. • Complex causal systems versus simple causal agents
Severity (How bad is the problem, and how bad is it likely to get?)	• This distinguishes between the acknowledged existence of a problem (e.g., recession) and how serious it is likely to become. • Severity is usually measured against some backdrop or context, such as trend lines ("this will soon go away" or "this is getting worse"), specific populations ("this is a big problem only for group X"), or what is considered normal or deviant.
Incidence (What is the scope and impact of the problem?)	• Who is affected generally? • What subgroups are affected and how? • What patterns of incidence are most important?
Novelty (Is this new?)	• Is the issue or problem new? • Is it unexpected?

Proximity (How "close" is the problem?)	• This refers to how close a problem "hits home." • Depends on how "home" is defined (i.e., children are valued for any social group's survival, so by definition anything that affects children negatively is bad).
Crisis (How pressing is the problem?)	• Largely a rhetorical device to signal severity and proximity.
Problem populations (Who will be targeted in the policy response?)	• Problem definitions can also define the people who are potential targets of policy interventions. • Deserving vs. undeserving of assistance. • Sympathetic vs. deviant definitions of groups. • Definitions that emphasize capacities vs. those that emphasize dependency.
Instrumental vs. expressive orientations (How important is the process of solving the problem in comparison to the solution itself?)	• Difference between focusing on ends (the instrumental intent to solve the problem) and the means (the degree to which what you do expresses an important symbol or value—e.g., refusing to negotiate with terrorists even if it harms hostages).
Solutions (What can be done?)	• Solutions sometimes actually precede the problem and help shape it (e.g., a commitment to vouchers as a policy instrument to deal with a host of problems). • Are solutions available—can something actually be done to solve a problem, or is action taken merely for its own sake or for symbolism?

SOURCE: Adapted and amended from Rochefort and Cobb. (1994). "Problem definition: An emerging perspective." In D. A. Rochefort and R. W. Cobb (Eds.), *The politics of problem definition: Shaping the policy agenda* (pp. 1–31). Lawrence: University Press of Kansas.

Not every problem definition or **policy argument** will contain all these characteristics, but most will be present. The definer has to deal with the question of causation. Without an idea of why the problem exists there is no way to figure out what to do about it. The "**causal images**" we use can differ in their emphasis on individual responsibility or systemic sources. Is poverty a result of individual decisions and choices or of large economic forces? Definitions can also differ in the degree of complexity of their causal portraits. Inevitably, however, policy action can be taken only across a narrow range of factors so that the causal assumptions in most policy-relevant problem definitions are usually limited. The severity of the problem is another important characteristic. A problem may be acknowledged, but it might be innocuous enough not to matter in policy terms (e.g., lack of physical fitness of the general population). This often gets connected to the incidence of the problem in the sense of how different groups in the population are affected. Concerns about violence against women or date rape focus on the incidence and severity of these phenomena on women.

Novelty, proximity, and crisis are all elements that help heighten the urgency of a problem. The way in which a problem definition portrays potential target populations of policy interventions has received more attention in recent years (Schneider and Ingram, 1997; 2005) on the sound assumption that policies are more than just instruments for solving problems: "Public policies that serve democracy need to garner support, stimulate civic engagement, and encourage cooperation in the solution of problems" (Ingram and Schneider, 2006: 180). Policies also convey signals about how policymakers picture recipients of government programs. Welfare programs are typically paternalistic, conveying the image that welfare recipients cannot plan their own lives and must be watched carefully for fraud. Premier Mike Harris once famously defended his welfare reforms on the grounds that they would ensure that welfare moms would not spend their cheques on beer. Having a negative image as a target population (e.g., prostitutes, drug users) can interfere with clear-eyed policy responses to the problems faced by that population. This is another aspect of the symbolic or expressive dimension of policy. Often what matters most about a problem is not whether it *can* be solved or managed but *how* it will be solved or managed. This is because of the simple fact that what we do (in this case, collectively as a political community) says much about who we are.

We can apply some of these categories to our earlier examples of SARS. Obviously, causality behind the crisis was a key element, but it was not simply a matter of a medical emergency, but an organizational one as well. This may seem odd in the SARS case, since the virus was eventually identified. But this is an epidemiological cause; the problem of the *epidemic* was due to how it was contained and dealt with, and this was more a matter of hospital, health, and immigration organization. China, for example, was widely blamed for not reporting the first cases for months. In Toronto, there were complaints about the emergency response system and the practice of rotating nurses among hospitals (thus potentially spreading the disease). The severity of SARS was acutely high, since people died and the economic impact was devastating. The incidence of SARS in North America was limited to Toronto in the end, but the fear at the time was that it might spread, and spread rapidly. Thus while it remained a local problem, it had national and even international dimensions. In terms of novelty, the SARS tragedy was unexpected and frightening. This added to the sense of crisis. While it did not have a problem population per se, the elderly were more at risk with SARS. The SARS issue forced consideration of procedural questions—testing and the appropriate protocols for health authorities and the WHO. Finally, SARS was susceptible to a "solution" for two reasons. First, the pressure was intense because of the nature of the epidemic. The fact that it was an international crisis mobilized international resources through the WHO to track its source. Second, quarantine and immigration controls could plausibly contain the epidemic, even if they could not cure the disease.

There is no science of problem definition, and providing the sort of checklist found in Box 3.2 is at best an approximation of the elements that go into the process of persuading others that a problem exists and that it should be addressed. What is clear, however, is that much of the time the process of problem recognition and definition is one of making arguments and persuading others (Majone, 1989; Fischer, 2003). **Constructivists** emphasize that there can be no absolutely conclusive proof of anything outside a shared paradigm of understandings. Within those worlds, of course, according to their own canons, it is possible to make a case that will be widely judged as "more true" than the next. Across those worlds, different values and standards of evidence and persuasion will make it difficult to come to firm and widely accepted conclusions. However, there is neither an infinite variety of conceptual paradigms nor of standards of what constitutes good argument. While rhetoric and presentation are always important, there are both inherent constraints within issues themselves, as well as broadly shared understandings at any given point in time that form a common backdrop for the debate about public policy issues. Dunn's (2008) illustrations of **boundary analysis** show that, for example, in asking a group of twenty people what criteria they use to judge the severity of a problem (e.g., cost, social impact), the number of criteria is not infinite. The first person asked might list a dozen criteria. The second person, in adding new ones, might offer eight. And so on, until no one can think of any more to add. The "boundary" or complete set of criteria is reached fairly quickly. People will still disagree over weights and interpretation, but they do so on a foundation of commonly agreed criteria, which is an important first step.

In another example, Milward and Laird (1996) examined five cases of agenda-setting (supply-side economics, the greenhouse effect, child abuse, drunk driving, and comparable worth) and argued that the way in which an issue is framed is "critically important to the success of the issue on the public agenda" (p. 63). Some of these issues, such as child abuse and drunk driving, were clearly framed, and this clarity contributed to their success on the public policy agenda. "A clearly framed issue is one that succinctly states what the problem is in plausible terms and embodies an easily understood solution" (p. 64). Moreover, issues are not infinitely malleable but have characteristics that make them more or less amenable to clear framing. Changing the tax treatment of certain types of investments, for example, is difficult to personalize, but child abuse and drunk driving both leave victims that can put a human face directly onto a policy problem. Issues that are driven by powerful underlying demographics, such as pensions today because of the greying of the boomers, develop an urgency that can move them up the agenda quite rapidly. The same is true of issues that have no credible opposition. As Milward and Laird argue, there are no "spokespersons for 'killer drunks' or child abusers" (p. 70).

Issue framing or problem definition consequently has two dimensions. The first is analytical and emphasizes the logical elements that make up an argument or claim. William Dunn (1993; 2008, Chap. 1, 8), for example, offers a schema to decipher the different statements that comprise any policy argument. *Policy-relevant information* (I) is the data or evidence at the policy analyst's disposal. A *policy claim* (C) is the conclusion of the policy argument, usually in the form of a recommendation on how to tackle the problem. A *warrant* (W) is an assumption that permits the analyst to move from the information to the claim. Warrants come in different forms—appeals to authority, to intuition, to values, and so on. *Backings* (B) are statements that provide support for warrants or neutralize possible criticisms or objections. Finally, *qualifiers* (Q) are statements that express the degree of confidence or certainty in the policy claim (e.g., "very likely" or "probably").

Take the question of legalization of marijuana, possession of which is currently a criminal offence in Canada and the United States. The policy-relevant information (I) in this instance would consist of medical evidence on the impact of marijuana use, the costs of enforcement, the rate of arrests for different groups, the effect of criminal records, number of illegal grow houses, and so on. Those in favour of decriminalization would make that policy claim (C), based on several possible warrants (W): everyone uses it, whether it is legal or not; recreational use does not lead to addiction or impaired health, at least not any more than reasonable alcohol consumption; government has no role in regulating a substance like this. Backing (B) would come from statements producing evidence or arguments to support the warrant in question, and qualifiers (Q) would indicate the likelihood of a surge in addictions or drug use. Those opposing decriminalization would begin with much the same information (I), but of course make a completely opposite policy claim (C). The warrants (W) might be empirical (e.g., relaxation of controls will lead to a surge in use; the negative health effects are not negligible; the difficulty of enforcing regulations), or moral (e.g., society is already too hedonistic). Backing (B) and qualifiers (Q) would be adduced to make the case stronger. As Dunn points out, understanding the structure of policy arguments helps us understand that often the same policy-relevant information (I) can lead to very different claims (C), based on different assumptions, values, and perspectives on the evidence (W). For example, there are provisions in Canada for the medical use of marijuana, a case where additional considerations about a specific population (those suffering ailments that marijuana can alleviate) are brought to bear.

Policy arguments can also be viewed from the perspective of rhetoric. In this view, the analytical statements are less important than structural elements of language that stimulate almost unconscious reactions to the argument. For example, there is growing interest in the way in which policy arguments are actually framed as narratives or as stories. We are all familiar with certain archetypal "story lines," and a policy argument that can tap into one of these draws on the power of the narrative structure itself. Arguments about social policy and the deficit, for example, can be seen as "redemption stories." In the past, goodwill and good intentions built a welfare state to meet important needs, but then temptation led us astray and we indulged in excesses and financial debauchery. Our problems got worse, but we ignored them and continued our profligate ways. Now the only option is a complete renunciation of our past sins, and with much pain and suffering we will be redeemed. No wonder finance ministers have sounded like preachers in recent years. Their "narrative line" has been about nothing less than weakness, temptation, and eventual, if painful, redemption. In the last five years, as the economy has continued to perform well and many governments across the country see ballooning revenues, the story line is shifting from punishment to reward. After years of sacrifice and high taxes, now that the deficit has been eliminated, ordinary citizens deserve rewards for their suffering. Part of this reward story—as told by critics of government—is that those governments would rather hold back the reward and spend the money themselves for political gain. Demands for tax cuts coming from the right depend on policy-relevant information and good argumentation, but this rhetorical narrative gives their policy claims a considerable boost (cuts to the GST and income taxes were explicitly defended on the grounds that this was "not the government's money"). Ironically, years of tax cuts and high spending may leave governments little choice but to run deficits as they face the need to keep the economy afloat.

Consider the way in which certain words are used to tilt meaning and stimulate reactions. **Labels** are summary words that convey subtle but powerful meanings: "axis of evil" versus "enemies," "gay" versus "homosexual," "homeless" versus "vagrant," "user fee" versus "tax," "sex-worker" versus "prostitute," "pro-life" versus "anti-abortion," "smart regulation" versus "deregulation." Intense policy battles are often fought over labels, because labels are often the first way in which the public is acquainted with a policy issue. **Metaphors** are another weapon in the linguistic arsenal. Consider some of the most famous: Cold War, Iron Curtain, Third World, pork barrel, social safety net, spaceship Earth, global village, and of course, war metaphors such as the War on Poverty, line in the sand, and so on—and these do not even include the ubiquitous sports metaphors! What Dunn calls synectics (see Box 3.1)—the use of analogies to think through the nature of policy problems—also has its rhetorical dimension in the use of metaphors. If people accept that spanking "is *like* child abuse," a good deal of the policy argument has been won. To return to marijuana, whether it is "*like* alcohol" or "*like* cocaine" will tilt the policy argument in very different directions. Medical analogies also can sway thinking: for example, the terms epidemic, quarantine, virus, infection, healthy.

As Kingdon (1995) points out, getting people to see new problems or see old ones in new ways, "is a major conceptual and political accomplishment" (p. 115). At any given time, there is a host of problems competing for public attention. Some are old and familiar, some are new twists on old issues, and a very few are completely new. The first hurdle is the one mentioned earlier, of providing persuasive indicators that something of importance is actually going on. The next step is a fuller description or definition that will likely take into account some or all of the elements outlined in Boxes 3.1 and 3.2. A critical aspect of this process is one that was briefly alluded to earlier: defining the problem as one that falls in the public sphere, and indeed as a problem to which the government can offer a credible and feasible response. Even if successful in all this, however, the problem still has to be positioned high enough on the public agenda to receive attention. This normally entails neutralizing opposition to change, since any given status quo will have its supporters who will often fight vigorously to defend their benefits or reject what they see as wrong-headed policy (Cobb and Ross, 1997). This is the process of **agenda-setting.** Why do some problems or issues get onto the agenda when others do not, and what explains the relative positions of issues on that agenda?

We already have referred to the importance of issue-framing, and to the vague but important principle of some broad public consensus that determines which ideas (and issues) are plausible and important. At any given time, the number of such "ideas in good currency" as Donald Schon (1971) termed them, is quite limited. They change slowly, and lag behind present circumstances, but provide a point of reference for policy debates. According to Schon, beneath every policy debate "there is a barely visible process through which issues come to awareness and ideas about them become powerful" (p. 123). Some examples of ideas in good currency from the 1950s included competition with the Russians, the space race, and basic research. Certainly the 1990s list would have included competition, sustainable development, and fiscal prudence. The new millennium seems to have generated a few of its own ideas in good currency: tax cuts, investment in health care, innovation through investments in science and technology, the need to tackle climate change, the importance of security and defence against terrorists. Kingdon (1995) captures much the same idea with the notion of the "**national mood**":

> People in and around government sense a national mood. They are comfortable discussing its content, and believe that they know when the mood shifts. The idea goes by different names—the national mood, the climate of the country, changes in public opinion, or broad social movements. But common to all of these labels is the notion that a rather large number of people out in the country are thinking along certain common lines, that this national mood changes from one time to another in discernible ways, and that these changes in mood or climate have important impacts on policy agendas and policy outcomes. (p. 146)

Baumgartner and Jones (1993; also see Jones, 1994; and True, Jones, and Baumgartner, 1999), while emphasizing the turbulence and change in American politics, note also that periods of policy stability are marked by substantial consensus over policy images: "One of the clearest findings from our research is the extent to which a prevailing conception of a policy issue dominates both press coverage and official behavior during periods when policy subsystems are especially strong" (p. 238). Part of this stability is due to the need by decisionmakers to winnow the tremendous amount of information produced in the political system and in policy subsystems. Jones and Baumgartner (2005) argue that policy systems are typically "information rich" and so the problem that decisionmakers have is selecting relevant information, responding appropriately to signals conveyed by that information, and prioritizing decisions through prioritizing problems. Moreover, information is often ambiguous, incomplete, or contested, making the job even more difficult. Consequently, attention can only be fixed on a limited set of problems and information flows at any given time. Indeed, a coping strategy in this type of cacophonous environment is to deliberately ignore signals, to avoid paying attention.

Combined with institutional structures in the political system that process information selectively (for example, the Canadian parliamentary system has fewer access points for interest groups than the American congressional system), the entire policy process—and agenda-setting—has a strong coefficient of drag, of stability: "If we put together the limits of human information processing and the characteristics of democracies that encourage error correction, we get a model of politics that is very static but reluctantly changes when signals are strong enough" (Jones and Baumgartner, 2005, p. 19).

Ideas in good currency and the policy images that dominate a given policy field at any given time help clarify the boundaries and constraints in agenda-setting, and facilitate information processing and the reduction of informational "noise." The political system as a whole can handle only a limited number of issues at one time (Soroka, 2007). It is rare for new ideas and new issues to come out of nowhere. Fresh policy proposals typically are framed in ways that resonate with existing ideas in good currency, but, if they fail, they drop off the agenda into a sort of twilight zone for policy innovations that might be mobilized again later, when the opportunity affords itself. This process of ideas struggling for attention and then fading away has supported the image of an agenda-setting cycle where issues arise, enjoy some intensive debate and perhaps success, and then gradually fall off. An early and influential example of this image was Anthony Downs's "**issue attention cycle**" (1972), but a cyclical image underpins most discussions of agenda-setting. Baumgartner and Jones (1993) borrowed the idea of "**punctuated equilibrium**" (which they have since subsumed under a broader theory they term "disproportionate information-processing"; see Jones and Baumgartner, 2005) to convey a process that simultaneously combines long stable periods of policy consensus followed by bursts of change around new issues and new policy images. Research on Canadian data shows little evidence for either an issue attention cycle or for punctuated equilibria, possibly because the parliamentary system gives "extensive agenda-setting powers to governments by, among other things, curtailing public and media access to information" (Howlett, 1997, p. 27; also see Soroka, 2002). Nonetheless, the work described in the previous paragraphs is as much about decision-making as a psychological state as it is about agenda-setting through institutions. Many of the informational processing dynamics could still hold at the individual level, even while parliamentary institutions provide a more stable platform for the development and maintenance of policy priorities. And there are enough examples of surprises, reversals, and disequilibria in the Canadian system to warrant some skepticism about its overall stability.

A great deal of the agenda-setting process is contingent on unpredictable factors and personalities, or as Kingdon puts it, the "opening of

policy windows." Windows sometimes open regularly (e.g., cabinet shuffles and budget speeches), but who jumps through successfully or not is still a matter of chance and skill. It is clear that some issues are driven onto the agenda by fundamental characteristics of a political community and economy itself: in Canada, for example, the perennial questions of Quebec and of our relationship to the United States. Modern welfare states have a wide range of important redistributive social programs that are of vital importance to recipient groups (e.g., pensions and the elderly), and so issues of this type are usually high on the public agenda. Massive changes in economic circumstances, or powerful shifts in technology, also have a way of rippling through the political system and generating issues for public discussion. But these structural explanations can illuminate only the broad shape of the public agenda. Much depends on political jockeying, **policy entrepreneurs,** and combinations of complex and unpredictable forces. The best that one can hope for in this field is a grasp of the institutions and the routines they generate (Howlett, 1998), the actors, and the opportunities, as well as the importance of shaping a coherent problem definition. As we will argue shortly, however, the dynamics and circumstances of problem definition have changed significantly in the last decade, and some of the old assumptions no longer apply.

What is the relation of problem definition to policy solutions? The conventional argument in the literature is that the way in which a problem is defined has a dramatic impact on the proposed solutions. At one level this makes sense: if you have to hit a nail, use a hammer, or something that hammers, which could just as easily be a shoe or a brick. Problem definition shapes solutions primarily because of the causal explanations that are its heart. Unemployment, for example, is a problem, but to deal with unemployment we need to know what causes it. If it is due to an international recession, there is not much the government can do to insulate the economy. If it is due primarily to a skills shortage, then the answer may be training programs. According to Statistics Canada (2005) 12 million Canadians fall below the basic standard of literacy, but how to deal with this? Better early education? Better diagnosis of persons with reading disabilities? Adult literacy programs? The solution would depend on the fundamental causes at work.

There are, nonetheless, important variances between problem definition and solutions. First, problems are not always so easily defined. Many social problems are "squishy" in that they don't lend themselves to mathematical formulation and are politically controversial (Strauch, 1976, p. 134), or "messy" in that they are deeply entangled with other problems (Ackoff, 1976, p. 21). The less clear the causal underpinnings of a problem, or the more irreducibly complex a problem appears, the less likely unique solutions can be derived from the definition. Second, even if the causal connections are clear, it is not always feasible to deal with "root" causes. Sometimes, Band-Aid solutions are all that we have. Third, most problem definitions deal with clusters of issues and raise questions about what governments should do across a range of options. This poses the question of what combination of solutions to apply and what emphasis government should place on any single solution. Just as there is no science of problem definition, there is no clear science of solutions.

Problem Definition: Beyond Old Categories

The preceding section sketched out the conventional theories of problem definition and agenda-setting. But, as Chapter 2 argued, the context within which policy analysis is practised today has changed substantially, and some of the key assumptions about the reality to which these theories apply—the substance as well as process of problem definition and agenda-setting—need to be re-examined. This section comes at problem definition and agenda-setting from this angle: what are the implications of globalization, culture shift, and governance for the ways in which we define public policy problems? Problem definition cannot be easily disentangled from the other phases of the policy process, but this chapter will concentrate on the emerging societal policy agenda and ideas in good currency. More detailed aspects of policy design, implementation, and evaluation will be taken up in subsequent chapters.

THE EMERGING POLICY AGENDA

With a new context for policymaking, we should expect both a new agenda and a new sense of the sources of policy problems. One of the most important changes in the sources of policy problems is that many of them are now generated beyond our borders due to the phenomenon of globalization. As was argued in Chapter 2, the dynamics of globalization and internationalization mean that borders are much more permeable. But that permeability is coupled with a new level of integration in the international political economy. It is important not to exaggerate this phenomenon. There have been many areas of public policy in the past— finance, communications, foreign policy, agriculture, trade, to name a few—that have traditionally been highly exposed to international forces and tightly integrated into international systems. By the same token, there remain many policy areas today that will continue to be insulated from the direct influence of these international forces or systems, for example, health care, social security, or overland transportation. Rather, what has happened is that the intensity of international exposure has increased in many policy fields traditionally marked by global influences, and a host of other areas have been indirectly affected by these wider forces. Observers noted in November 2008, as governments struggled to deal with the international reverberations of the US sub-prime mortgage crisis, that foreclosures in Nebraska were being felt by small investors in Norway. Policy-making systems have essentially shifted away from a preponderant concern about problems generated domestically within national borders to problems generated internationally. The policy challenge is how to respond to these new types of problems. While globalization takes pride of place in the new pantheon of sources of policy challenges, it is not alone. Technology is another obvious candidate, both in its own terms and because of its close connection to economic competitiveness through innovation. And most recently, the issues of international terrorism and emergencies are much on the public mind.

One window on the range of policy challenges posed by these and other phenomena is the Policy Research Initiative (PRI) discussed in Chapter 1. The PRI supports the government's medium-term agenda and takes its guidance from a Deputy Ministers' Steering Committee, and so its research agenda provides a sense of what is considered important within the government of Canada. The current research agenda consists of seven broad areas of investigation (Policy Research Initiative, 2008). The first is improving measuring and reporting of the impacts of federal science and technology. The federal government spends about $6 billion of the $28 billion annually expended in Canada on R&D, and this project is intended to develop better measures of its impact on the Canadian economy and society. This is consistent with the 2007 *Mobilizing Science and Technology* policy released by the government with an additional $1.9 billion in expenditures. Innovation is the key to competition in a modern, globalized economy, and so governments at all levels are doing all they can to enhance innovation through support of science and technology.

A second major area of research also resonates with the public sector reform theme that we explored briefly in Chapter 1. This effort is directed at international regulatory co-operation, as part of a broader international initiative to improve the quality of regulation: "However, most developed nations have begun to recognize that the quality of their regulations can be a key strategic asset. Consequently, the Organisation for Economic Co-operation and Development's (OECD) regulatory reform program now focuses on means to improve "regulatory quality" across member countries" (Policy Research Initiative, 2008). There are three sub-projects within the larger one: regulations, prosperity and competitiveness; Canada–US regulatory co-operation; and regulatory reform and capacity building.

The remaining areas of research address the environment (climate change and freshwater management) and broad demographics of the Canadian population (population 2017, youth, and cultural diversity). The cultural diversity theme is particularly interesting, since it was highlighted in Chapter 2 as a key challenge to contemporary policy-making (we address some aspects of climate change in the next chapter):

Issue

It is believed that Canada's diversity, if properly nurtured, becomes its strength. Canada's approach to ethno-cultural diversity, especially its multiculturalism policy, has won accolades internationally. In practice, however, managing ethno-cultural diversity remains a work in progress subject to the constant evolution of social realities. Based on empirical evidence in Canada and abroad, this project identifies the opportunities and pressures in fostering inclusive citizenship in a multicultural Canada that is increasingly diverse with successive waves of immigration.

Background

Broadly defined, Canada's multicultural diversity is a product of three cultural drivers: Aboriginal Peoples, the English and French-speaking Charter groups, and immigrants. In particular, successive waves of immigration since the 1970s have made Canada ever more diverse in ethnicity, culture, and language. This third driver, the focus of this project, is instrumental in bringing forth Canada's multiculturalism policies. By 2017, one in five Canadians will come from a visible minority group. The number of allophones is also rising. While fewer people have professed religious affiliations, Islam remains the fastest growing religion. Moreover, as the world is more connected economically and, to some extent, politically, world events and foreign policies often have domestic impacts.

Multiculturalism resonates with Canadian values such as equality, tolerance, and mutual respect. Since its inception in 1971, multiculturalism policy has evolved from that of celebrating differences to institutional accommodation, and more recently to inclusion and full participation. In theory and intent, Canada's policies and legislation regarding ethno-cultural diversity are tools for building inclusive citizenship, reducing barriers to social and economic participation of marginalized groups, and sharpening Canada's economic edge in face of globalization. (Policy Research Initiative, 2008)

Another useful place to look for emerging policy agendas—new drivers that to some extent cut across the political—is the government's Speech from the Throne (SFT) that launches a new session of Parliament. SFTs are or course partisan documents as well, and every government will try to position itself advantageously with respect to the opposition. But by the same token, a SFT does set a governmental agenda for at least two years if not longer, must command reasonably broad support, and reviews major policy challenges and opportunities as the government sees them.

The October 16, 2007 SFT was entitled *Strong Leadership. A Better Canada* (Canada, 2007). It had five broad priorities. The first was "Strengthening Canada's Sovereignty and Place in the World," principally by asserting sovereignty in the Arctic and committing more resources to the military for the Afghanistan mission. The speech referred to the importance of being "back as a credible player on the international stage" and cited the mission in Afghanistan and the desire to extend it beyond 2009 to 2011 (which was approved by Parliament in 2008). A second thrust was "Strengthening the Federation and our Democratic Institutions," which from a Conservative point of view entailed limiting the federal spending power and having a more clearly delineated division of jurisdictions between federal and provincial governments. The section on economic policy also highlighted international factors: "This is a time of economic uncertainty and volatility in the wider world. . . . Canada is not immune from this turbulence." It would invest in trade hubs such as the Windsor–Detroit corridor and the Atlantic and Pacific gateways. In addition, however, it would have to support traditional industries such as forestry and fisheries, helping "workers as these industries adjust to global conditions . . ." The same logic of international drivers was evident in the section on climate change, where the government acknowledged that as a global problem, climate change needed a global solution and consequently engagement with the international community. While the SFT did address issues that are almost entirely domestic—safe streets and the quality of life of Aboriginal Canadians—the bulk of it dealt with policy issues that had a strong international component.

That international emphasis was considerably amplified in the November 19, 2008 SFT, entitled *Protecting Canada's Future* (Canada, 2008). Somewhat leaden given the circumstances, it marked a cautious continuation of a tested agenda for a new government. Its first commitment was the reform of global finance: "The first order of business must be to put the international financial system on a sounder footing." Its second was a possible reversal of its anti-deficit position of the past decade: "Ongoing, unsustainable deficits are quite rightly unacceptable to Canadians. These structural deficits must never return. At the same time, in a historic global downturn, it would be misguided to commit to a balance budget in the short term at any cost, because that cost would ultimately be borne by Canadian families." This statement was accompanied by signals about responsible spending, putting grants and contributions under a "microscope," a review of public sector compensation, and possible restraints on equalization payments. As for spending priorities, several sectors and departments could be heartened: student financial assistance, Aboriginal education, investments in new machinery, the automotive and aerospace industries, fisheries, mining, and forestry, and infrastructure. There were promises on supporting science and technology, culture, and international investment opportunities. The other big ticket items were energy (expanding the pipeline network to the North, as well as nuclear energy), climate change (a North American cap and trade system), and an increase in the Universal Child Care Benefit. Most of these were simple extensions of commitments made in 2007, or incremental changes at best. As Conservatives, the government also had to include closing sections on "safety" (crime, guns, food, and national security), on Afghanistan (ending the military mission in 2011), Senate reform, and continued public sector renewal (with a hint of substantial rationalization of the federal government's human resource management apparatus, as outlined by the Prime Minister's Advisory Committee on the Public Service).

Ideas in Good Currency

We noted in the first section of this chapter that problem definition is a crucial phase in the policy process but that it is not unconstrained. Better or worse arguments can be made, and not all issues can be addressed simultaneously. Moreover, there is a rhythm to the agenda-setting process wherein issues rise and fall (and maybe rise again!) and jostle for position. A good deal of the success of policy entrepreneurs and policy communities in getting their issues on the agenda depends on good luck and political skill, but luck and skill have to be placed against the backdrop of what Schon calls "ideas in good currency" or others term the "public mood." The two are not quite the same, since ideas in good currency may not necessarily reflect (at least in the first instance) a groundswell of public opinion. Indeed, the public mood might be influenced by a sense of changes in important structuring ideas, ideas that many people might at first find unfamiliar or even disagreeable, but that over time they will come to accept as a standard of importance and plausibility. The evolution of the sense of what constitutes "national security" in the face of terrorism since 9/11 is a case in point.

Any list of such core ideas will have a strong dose of subjectivity to it, but at the same time, if the concept of ideas in good currency has any validity at all, a well-constructed list should "sound right" to most people who hear it. First, consider what might plausibly have been a list from the 1970s and early 1980s, before the influence of the Reagan revolution in the United States and its echo in the Mulroney regime, and just around the time of the passage of the Canadian Charter of Rights and Freedoms. Its central tone or themes were equity, cooperation, a strong national government, "made in Canada" solutions, social justice, and social needs. While being careful not to exaggerate—after all, despite their sabre-rattling, the Mulroney Conservatives passed employment equity legislation and more than doubled the federal debt—it is clear that the mid-1980s was a transition period to something with a different emphasis in the 1990s, an emphasis which we to some extent have described in Chapter 2. Certainly, from the vantage point of 2009, the flavour and tone of what counts as "common sense" in public policy today has changed. Note, however, that it is a matter of tone and emphasis and not of a complete sea change in public discourse. As most analysts cited in the first section of this chapter argue, new ideas do not completely displace old ones in public discourse, and indeed some of the older ones float in a purgatory of lost causes, to ascend again to political heaven when the time is propitious.

While these major changes have affected almost everything that governments do (and we will be looking at these effects in later chapters), at the level of ideas in good currency, the single most important change has been in the perceptions surrounding the fiscal capacities of government. In policymaking, of course, as in most things, money always matters. But what has changed dramatically is the sense of how much money governments have and what they should do with it. It has been a change, however, not simply in rhetoric, but in reality as well. Canadian governments since the mid-1960s, when they launched major, expensive social programs such as Medicare and the Canada Pension Plan, and certainly since the oil crisis and inflation of the mid-1970s, have constantly wrung their hands and worried publicly about rising deficits and overspending. While they took periodic and often quixotic action on the budgetary front—with perhaps first prize for budgetary bluster going to the Mulroney Conservatives in their almost decade-long, and ultimately futile fight against the deficit—deficits continued to rise. Before the mid-1990s, the last time the total government sector in Canada (on a national accounts basis) was in surplus was in 1974 (Doern, Maslove, and Prince, 1988, p. 17). By 1992, Canada had the second-highest level of total government debt as a percent of gross domestic product (GDP) after Italy (Purchase and Hirshhorn, 1994, p. 29). Through the 1980s, Canadian governments continued to borrow to cover their deficits, piling up the public debt (even as they raised taxes) as interest rates began to climb and economic performance slowed. In this sense, the deficit was "structural" rather than "cyclical" in that the debt itself was so large that not even an economic upturn would do much to reduce interest payments. The key policy consequence of a willingness to run deficits was the absence of a need to make hard choices among programs, or cut ones that did not seem to work.

That, at least, is the narrative that now suffuses public opinion on government spending and certainly was the leitmotif in budget-cutting exercises at the provincial and federal levels since the early 1990s. While in the 1980s there used to be debate about whether the deficit was a "real problem" or whether it was merely an artifact of high interest rates, a sluggish economy, and tax privileges for the wealthy, by the late 1990s all political tendencies, both left and right, agreed that deficits were bad. The debate then shifted to ways of dealing with it, either on the expenditure side with program cuts (which most governments have done), the revenue side (some arguing for higher taxes on corporations and the middle class, while most governments have opted for revenue generation through various fees and charges), or lower interest rates. The shift in what Kingdon calls the "national mood," along with government determination to reflect that mood (or lead it), has been remarkable. By mid-1996, seven of ten provinces had balanced budgets. Saskatchewan and Alberta led the way, and the 1996 Ontario budget echoed the importance of deficit elimination (the Harris government cut the provincial deficit by $3 billion or 27 percent in its first year in office). By 2005–06 and 2006–07, all Canadian governments were posting surpluses (Department of Finance, 2008: 218). The idea of "fiscal prudence" was in such good currency that all four major national political parties pledged during the 2004 and 2006 federal election campaigns that they would not run deficits, as did Stephen Harper again in the 2008 election.

The effects of this new emphasis on the fisc, or the national treasury, in problem definition have been profound (we will revisit the effects on other stages in the policy process in later chapters). If the deficit is the problem, then it implies the government itself is a problem, since the deficit is a reflection of government activity and management. No ministerial musings on the deficit, from Canada to the United Kingdom to New Zealand, have been complete without an explicit attack on the style of government that produced it. The ferocity with which government itself is attacked as a source of problems varies from conservatives to liberals, but the general view is that at a minimum, government should "get itself right," and in doing so will provide the best "solution" to its own negative impact on the economy and society. Given the financial crisis of late 2008, these convictions may be reversed. The US government is at historic levels of debt, and faces a mountain more as it tries to throw financial life preservers to leading American companies. The government of Ontario faces a deficit, as might Ottawa. But since the source of the financial crisis seems to have been unsecured borrowing and undisciplined lending, it will be difficult for governments to go too far into the red.

With the virtual elimination of deficits across the country (though they will return with an economic slow-down as the US goes into recession in 2008), the nature of policy debate changed as well. In an era of surpluses, the issue became whether these surpluses should be "invested" in new programs or returned to taxpayers through tax cuts. Predictably, the right urged tax cuts, while the left urged new spending, and the national Liberals did a little of both. In addition to tax cuts, however, the Conservatives were able to ratchet up spending in their budgets 2007–08, as well as pay down the debt. The cuts to the GST in particular were most strongly opposed by Liberals and NDP, both on policy grounds (it would be better to cut income taxes rather than consumption taxes) and political grounds (the cuts withdrew billions of dollars of federal revenues that would be difficult to recapture for another party in government if it tried to raise taxes). Soaring revenues allowed the federal Conservatives to avoid deficits, but simultaneously pay down debt, increase expenditures, and cut taxes. In 2006–07 the federal debt stood at $467.3 billion, down from its peak of $562.9 billion in 1996–97. The federal debt-to-GDP ratio was 32.3 percent, down from its peak of 68.4 percent in 1996–97. Total spending however was up 6.3 percent over 2005–07, and the Tories promised $60 billion in tax relief for individuals, families, and businesses from 2007–12 (Department of Finance, 2007).

It is in the nature of democratic governance that there will typically be differences in opinion about public policy and hence relatively few ideas or policy images that command wide consensus. However, we might mention five others that approach the solidity of support enjoyed by the idea of fiscal prudence among the public. The first is perhaps the most obvious—globalization. The consensus here is not on the desirability of convergence or integration—there is sensible disagreement about how far Canada should go in accepting globalization—but rather with respect to the inevitability of global pressures and the sense of a multipolar and multithreat world. Canadians know that globalization is a powerful reality and has to be dealt with across a variety of policy fronts, from defence to peacekeeping to working with the United States. The second is the importance of health care. Every poll in recent years has shown that health care is a top concern for most Canadians. Again, there is room for legitimate disagreement over how to deliver health care services, but health care itself is a major priority. The third is the importance of reform to our democratic institutions. At both the national and provincial levels, there has been a wave of small and large reforms, as well as rhetoric about more to come. British Columbia has experimented with open Cabinet meetings and held a referendum (defeated) on proportional representation, as did Ontario in 2007 (also defeated). In June 2004 Ontario announced that it was moving to fixed election periods (the first Thursday in October every four years), and the federal government passed legislation in 2007 to have fixed elections every four years on the third Monday in October, unless Parliament is dissolved earlier (as it was in September, 2008). All major federal parties have pledged institutional reforms as well, most notably the Conservative government with Senate reform (as of 2008, fixing the term of Senators to eight years). The fourth is the importance of the environment and climate change. Public support for environmentalism waxes and wanes, but it is clear that there has been a secular increase in sensibility toward ecological damage and the responsibility that citizens and governments have toward protecting the environment and dealing with the threat of climate change. The federal Conservative government initially downplayed this issue, being openly critical of the feasibility of the Kyoto commitment, but soon realized that public opinion was on the other side of the issue. The final one is a new consensus around the need to deal with security issues and international terrorism. Again, there is room for disagreement, for example, on the war in Afghanistan, but most Canadians acknowledge that government has to focus on internal security threats, deal with the border in new ways, and maintain a vigilance that even a few years ago would have seemed extreme.

Conclusion

No one should read this chapter as claiming that everything about our processes of problem definition and framing has suddenly shifted to the United Nations or consists of nothing more than carping about money. There are still plenty of policy problems bubbling at all levels that are primarily domestic in origins and solutions: drugs, crime, literacy, water quality, housing, waste disposal, education—in short, things that matter to people on a daily basis. The simple point of this chapter is that the context and processes of problem definition are never set in stone and that they have changed in important ways in the last decade, and indeed in the last year. Some of the sources of policy problems have a completely different character today: globalization, technology, and the environment, for example. Others are quite new: the aging of society and dropping productivity. Still others have affected the nature of traditional domestic problems, for example, international terrorism and epidemics. And as we argued in Chapter 2, there has also been a change in approaches to governance, in what we consider possible and acceptable for governments to do in addressing these problems.

And yet there are several paradoxes at the heart of these changes. One is that the nature of these issues (e.g., globalization and technology) is such that they are closely entangled. This has led to laudable demands that policy thinking today be more "horizontal" and cross-cutting, since the issues are more diffuse and interconnected. The aging of the population, for example, is linked to economic issues (productivity and training), to social programs (pensions), and to immigration. The danger, however, is that problem definition will become an exercise in thinking about everything at once. In addition to horizontality, there is also pressure on how to maintain both coherence and focus in problem definition.

This is reflected in an almost limitless range of problems and issues that governments could conceivably address. While on the one hand governments are challenged to connect the dots between issues like human capital, early childhood education, and immigration, or between terrorism, security, privacy, and border controls, on the other hand there remains general skepticism about how effective government in general and in particular can actually be.

In practical terms, what does this all mean for doing policy work and developing coherent and workable policy problem definitions? It is important to re-emphasize the distinctions between problem recognition and problem definition. In countries like Canada, even though there is likely a greater degree of agenda control by government, there is a constant stream of data, information, and arguments about the range of existing and emerging problems that require a policy response. A crucial part of good policy work remains the analysis and development of those data into something more detailed—a problem definition that brings together data, research, analysis of causal links, and logical arguments. Moreover, there are techniques and guides (as described in the first part of the chapter), to help this process along. However, the contemporary policy analyst must at the same time be aware of the changed context within which that work takes place. She requires an appreciation of existing research, international trends, and the broad domestic policy agenda. She must have a grasp of "ideas in good currency" and contemporary sensibilities about the nature of the "public" and the "private" and the appropriate role for government. She needs an understanding of the complex matrix of cause and effect that infuses almost any policy issue and in particular the nature of global forces and their effects on local problems. Finally, she has to be able to take her work beyond problem definition to policy design. That is the subject of the next chapter.

KEY TERMS

agenda-setting—the social and political process of determining what issues to address and in what priority

argument mapping—a technique to map and classify the different components of policy arguments made by stakeholders, such as arguments based on statistics, authority, values, intuition, or judgment

assumptional analysis—aims at developing a synthesis of the different assumptions that stakeholders have about the issue or problem. Involves canvassing the full range of solutions proposed for the issue or problem and using that as a vehicle for analyzing and challenging the assumptions that underlie the problem definition

boundary analysis—a technique to canvass the whole range of existing definitions and conceptualizations of a given problem

brainstorming—a family of techniques, more or less formal, to generate ideas, goals, and strategies; can involve informal and unstructured exchange to scenario writing

causal images—a shorthand conceptualization of complex cause-and-effect relationships

classification analysis—breaking down the policy problem phenomenon into logically distinct categories or classes

constructivism—philosophical position that there can be no absolutely conclusive proof of anything outside a shared paradigm of understandings

focusing events—sudden catastrophes or crises that grab attention

globalization—the progressive exposure of domestic economies and polities to a wide range of international forces, and the increased interdependence that comes with it

hierarchical analysis—a technique for identifying possible causes of a problem by classifying causes as possible causes, plausible causes, or actionable causes

ideas in good currency—broad ideas about public policy that are widely shared without much commentary or debate and that change slowly over time but form the backdrop for policy discussion

indicators—atypical or routine monitoring that turns up discrepancies or patterns that hint that something is amiss and lead to further development and analysis of the problem definition

issue attention cycle—a portrayal of public policy going through cycles of attention, reaction and action, and quietude

issue framing—a way of depicting a policy issue or problem in broad, understandable if somewhat simplified terms

labels—summary words that convey subtle but powerful meanings: "homosexual" versus "gay," "vagrant" versus "homeless," "tax" versus "user fee"

metaphors—in a policy context, words or phrases that convey powerful meanings through an implicit comparison, such as the "Cold War," "Iron Curtain," or "social safety net"

multiple perspective analysis—a technique to review the problem situation from three perspectives: (1) the technical perspective: cost-benefit analysis, econometrics, and systems analysis; (2) the organizational perspective: focus on institutional rules and processes, and following standard operating procedures; and (3) the personal perspective: viewing problems and solutions in terms of individual perceptions and values

national mood—an inchoate, broad, but nonetheless real consensus among the population around some national issue

policy argument—an organized set of claims about a policy problem and recommended solutions that include such characteristics as causality, severity, novelty, crisis, instruments, and solutions

policy entrepreneurs—actors who shape the public agenda and can quickly and effectively mobilize around a policy issue when they see or sense an opportunity

policy images—a mixture of empirical information and emotive appeals that explain the issue and justify the public policy response

policy windows—unpredictable openings in the policy process that create the possibility for influence over the direction and outcome of that process

problem recognition—the stage at which there is an emerging sense that there may be a problem that needs attention and further analysis, usually based on indicators or some event that signals an issue

problem structuring—the intellectual process of shaping the problem definition

punctuated equilibrium—a process that simultaneously combines long stable periods of policy consensus followed by bursts of change around new issues and new policy images

synectics—a technique that relies on the use of analogies to see if new policy problems have sufficiently similar characteristics to older ones that previous problem definitions and solutions can provide some guidance

FURTHER READINGS

Baumgartner, F. R., and Jones, B. D. (1993). *Agendas and instability in American politics*. Chicago: University of Chicago Press.

Dery, D. (1984). *Problem definition in policy analysis*. Lawrence: University Press of Kansas.

Dunn, W. N. (2008). *Public policy analysis: An introduction*. 4th ed. Upper Saddle River, NJ: Prentice Hall.

Jones, B., and Baumgartner, F. R. (2005). *The politics of attention: How government prioritizes problems*. Chicago: University of Chicago Press.

Kingdon, J. W. (1995). *Agendas, alternatives, and public policies*, 2nd ed. New York: HarperCollins.

Moran, M., Rein, M., and Goodin, R. E. (Eds.) (2006). *The Oxford handbook of public policy*. Oxford: Oxford University Press.

Soroka, S. (2002). *Agenda-setting dynamics in Canada*. Vancouver: UBC Press.

REFERENCES

Ackoff, R. L. (1976). *Redesigning the future: A systems approach to societal problems*. New York: John Wiley and Sons.

Baumgartner, F. R., and Jones, B. D. (1993). *Agendas and instability in American politics*. Chicago: University of Chicago Press.

Brewer, G. D., and deLeon, P. (1983). *The foundations of policy analysis*. Homewood, IL: The Dorsey Press.

Carson, R. (1962). *Silent spring*. Boston: Houghton Mifflin.

Canada. (2007). *Strong leadership. A better Canada*. Speech from the Throne, October 16, 2007.

Canada. (2008). *Protecting Canada's Future*. Speech from the Throne, November 19, 2008.

Cobb, R. W., and Ross, M. H. (Eds.) (1997). *Cultural strategies of agenda denial: Avoidance, Attack, and Redefinition*. Lawrence, Kansas: University Press of Kansas.

Conservative Party of Canada. (2004). *Platform 2004*.

Department of Finance (Canada). (2007). *Annual financial report of the government of Canada—Fiscal year 2006–2007*. Retrieved February 27, 2008, from http://www.fin.gc.ca/afr/2007/afr2007e.pdf

Department of Finance (Canada). (2008). *The Budget plan 2008: Responsible leadership*. Retrieved February 27, 2008, from http://www.fin.gc.ca/ec2007/pdf/EconomicStatement2007_E.pdf

Dery, D. (1984). *Problem definition in policy analysis*. Lawrence: University Press of Kansas.

Doern, G. B., Maslove, A. M., and Prince, M. J. (1988). *Public budgeting in Canada: Politics, economics, and management*. Ottawa: Carleton University Press.

Downs, A. (1972). Up and down with ecology: The issue attention cycle. *Public Interest, 28*, 38–50.

Dunn, W. N. (1993). Policy reforms as arguments. In F. Fischer and J. Forester (Eds.), *The argumentative turn in policy analysis and planning* (pp. 254–90). Durham, NC: Duke University Press.

Dunn, W. N. (2007). *Public policy analysis: An introduction*. 4th ed. Englewood Cliffs, NJ: Prentice Hall.

Fischer, F. (2003). *Reframing public policy: Discursive politics and deliberative practices*. New York: Oxford University Press.

Geva-May, I., and Wildavsky, A. (1997). *An operational approach to policy analysis: The craft*. Boston: Kluwer Academic Publishers.

Globe and Mail. (December 14, 2007a). Restrict the use of tasers. A24.

Globe and Mail. (November 24, 2007b). Again, a taser and a death. A24.

Globe and Mail. (February 11, 2008). Push-button policing: Why talk when you can shock? A17.

Harrington, M. (1962). *The other America: Poverty in the United States*. New York: Macmillan.

Howlett, M. (1997). Issue-attention and punctuated equilibria models reconsidered: An empirical evaluation of the dynamics of agenda-setting in Canada. *Canadian Journal of Political Science, 30*(1), 3–30.

Howlett, M. (1998). Predictable and unpredictable policy windows: Institutional and exogenous correlates of Canadian federal agenda-setting. *Canadian Journal of Political Science, 31*(3), 495–524.

Ingram, H., and Schneider, A. L. (2006). Policy analysis for democracy. In M. Moran, M. Rein, and R. E. Goodin (Eds.), *The Oxford handbook of public policy* (169–89). Oxford: Oxford University Press.

Jones, B. D. (1994). *Reconceiving decision-making in democratic politics: Attention, choice, and public policy*. Chicago: University of Chicago Press.

Jones, B. D., and Baumgartner, F. R. (2005). *The politics of attention: How government prioritizes problems*. Chicago: University of Chicago Press.

Kingdon, J. W. (1995). *Agendas, alternatives, and public policies*, 2nd ed. New York: HarperCollins.

MacLeod, L. (1987). *Battered but not beaten: Preventing wife battering in Canada*. Ottawa: Canadian Advisory Council on the Status of Women.

Majone, G. (1989). *Evidence, argument, and persuasion in the policy process*. New Haven: Yale University Press.

Milward, H. B., and Laird, W. (1996). Where does policy come from? In B. G. Peters and B. A. Rockman (Eds.), *Agenda for excellence 2: Administering the state* (pp. 38–75). Chatham, NJ: Chatham House Publishers.

National Council of Welfare. (2007). *Solving poverty: Cornerstones # 4*. Information Kit, June 2007. Retrieved February 25, 2008, from http://www.ncwcnbes.net/documents/researchpublications/Research-Projects/NationalAntiPovertyStrategy/2007InformationKit/FS5-Cornerstone4ENG.pdf

Ontario Ministry of Finance. (2007). *Ontario budget 2007*. Retrieved on March 4, 2008, from http://www.ontariobudget.ca/

Policy Research Initiative. (2008). Retrieved on March 4, 2008, from www.policyresearch.gc.ca

Purchase, B., and Hirshhorn, R. (1994). *Searching for good governance*. Kingston, ON: Queen's School of Policy Studies.

Rochefort, D. A., and Cobb, R. W. (1994). Problem definition: An emerging perspective. In D. A. Rochefort and R. W. Cobb, (Eds.), *The politics of problem definition: Shaping the policy agenda* (pp. 1–31). Lawrence: University Press of Kansas.

Sarlo, C. A. (1996). *Poverty in Canada*. 2nd ed. Vancouver: The Fraser Institute.

Schneider, A. L., and Ingram, H. M. (1997). *Policy design for democracy*. Lawrence: University Press of Kansas.

Schneider, A. L., and Ingram, H. M. (2005). (Eds.). *Deserving and entitled: Social constructions and public policy*. Albany: State University of New York.

Schon, D. A. (1971). *Beyond the stable state*. New York: W. W. Norton and Company.

Soroka, S. (2002). *Agenda-setting dynamics in Canada*. Vancouver: UBC Press.

Soroka, S. (2007). Agenda-setting and issue definition. In M. Orsini and M. Smith (Eds.), *Critical policy studies* (pp. 185–210). Vancouver: UBC Press.

Statistics Canada (2005). *Building on our Competencies: Canadian results of the International Adult Literacy and Skills Survey 2003*. Catalogue no. 89-617-XIE. Retrieved February 26, 2008, from http://dsp-psd .pwgsc.gc.ca/Collection/Statcan/89-617-X/89-617-XIE2005001.pdf

Stone, D. (2001). *Policy paradox: The art of political decision making*. Rev. ed. New York: W. W. Norton and Company.

Strauch, R. E. (1976, Winter). A critical look at quantitative methodology. *Policy Analysis, 2*, 121–44.

True, J. L., Jones, B. D., and Baumgartner, F. R. (1999). Punctuated-equilibrium theory: Explaining stability and change in American policymaking. In P. A. Sabatier (Ed.), *Theories of the policy process* (pp. 97–116). Boulder, CO: Westview Press.

World Health Organization. (2003). *SARS: Chronology of a serial killer*. Retrieved March 9, 2008, from http://www.who.int/csr/don/2003_07_04/en/

CHAPTER

4

Policy Instruments and Design

Policy design is a mix of inspiration and technique. The inspiration comes in framing the policy issue (discussed in Chapter 3) in ways that make sense of the problem and provide a broad sketch of how to tackle it. The technique (though not without its creative side either) comes in the detailing of what tools to use, and in what combination, to achieve a given end. The tools will vary with the task at hand, sometimes involving expenditures, sometimes regulation, partnerships, or the exchange of information. Policy design usually will draw on all of these and more, and then be bundled into programs. The conventional discussion of policy instruments usually proceeds by laying out the basic categories and outlining some of the objective characteristics of each of the instruments; when and why, for example, regulation makes more sense than direct program provision by government. This chapter will honour that format in briefly describing the main categories, but it will also show how the menu of choices has changed in recent years. While the reality of instrument choice has always been more constrained than theory might suggest, the old, full menu of the past has been replaced with something closer to a table d'hôte with a more limited, but in some respects more novel, range of items. At the same time, there are new pressures on governments to do traditional things with traditional tools, intervene less, and also intervene more with unprecedented instruments and interventions. Choosing what to do, why to do it, and how, has never been more interesting, or more challenging.

Policies are best thought of as creative solutions to challenging puzzles rather than just dry legislation and programs. The creative dimension breaks through conventional definitions of the issue and comes up with something people had not thought of before. This does not mean, of course, that those creative solutions are the correct ones, only that they offer an unanticipated or surprising approach. For example, many American states have added a new tool to deal with delinquent taxpayers. The normal approach around the world is fines and punishments, but these can be both time-consuming and expensive. A new approach is to publicize the names of taxpayers who have outstanding tax bills on the Internet. Going by names like CyberShame and DelinqNet, delinquent taxpayer lists now appear on state revenue department websites. In Wisconsin, for example: "A provision of the state budget that passed in October dramatically lowered—from $25 000 to $5000—the threshold of unpaid taxes, penalties, interest and costs to have a taxpayer's name on the Revenue Department's on-line list of delinquent taxpayers. As a result, the 5 500 names now on the list are expected to grow to more than 19 000. The change might make Wisconsin the state with the most tax scofflaws listed on the Internet. Other states—Connecticut and South Carolina's "Debtor's Corner," for example—list only those who owe the most. Missouri lists only businesses, and California lists "only the top 250 taxpayers who owe more than $100,000 in income taxes" (Milwaukee Journal Sentinel, 2007).

Policy design is about choosing the most appropriate instrument to deal with the policy problem as it has been defined in order to achieve a given policy goal. This implies that a key criterion in instrument choice and policy design is effectiveness—getting the job done. Efficiency—getting the job done with the least resources—is typically considered another key criterion. The reality of politics means that popularity and re-election cannot be left out of the mix of motives; indeed, they may be overpowering at times. But if one adds the inevitably creative aspect of policy design to the range of criteria by which that design might be judged, it is clear that coming up with a list of tools is no easy task. In fact, while lists abound, and while there is some agreement on at least the major policy instruments and their characteristics, there is little agreement (or knowledge) of how and when particular mixes of instruments should be used in policy design. Like a list of the letters in the alphabet, the keys on a piano, or all the possible ingredients in five-star French cooking, the best that an inventory could provide is a sense of the possibilities of language, music, or cuisine. Choice and design are marked as much by art and circumstance as they are by technique.

Nonetheless, thinking through at least the major categories of ingredients is a useful exercise. The first section of this chapter will do this with brutal economy, splitting only enough hairs to make sense of major alternatives and some of the broad dynamics of choice. Policy instruments will be distinguished here from implementation, which we take up in Chapter 5. There is an overlap between the two, of course, but policy instruments usually refer to the technical means of achieving a goal, such as a **tax** or a **regulation**, while implementation refers to the organizational structure and processes to execute that instrument. Policy instruments and implementation overlap most obviously in cases where a particular organizational format is the technical means of achieving the policy goal, such as a **partnership** between a nongovernmental agency and a government department. We take this up in Chapter 6.

Thinking about instruments and policy design also helps clarify the relationship among policy, programs, and instruments. As we argued in Chapter 1, policy is a framework, a map, or a guide. It connects a problem definition (or clusters of problems) with goals and objectives, and a selection of instruments (means or tools) whereby the problem will be overcome and the objectives met. To be actualized or made real, policies have to be expressed or implemented through programs, and any given policy (if it is broad enough) will likely have several programs, which in combination will tackle different aspects of the broader problem (this also raises the issue of horizontal consistency). These programs, in turn, consist of bundles of instruments or policy tools (expenditures, taxes, regulations). Figure 4.1 shows this set of relationships both conceptually and with respect to the example of Canadian Aboriginal policy. The broad policy framework is set by the 1997 document *Gathering Strength*, which was announced shortly after the report of the Royal Commission on Aboriginal Peoples. That framework or guide then informs a variety of programs. The figure shows only one program, Aboriginal Business Canada (ABC), but illustrates how ABC relies on a mix of policy instruments such as loans, information, and different client targets.

Figure 4.1   Policy, Programs, and Instruments

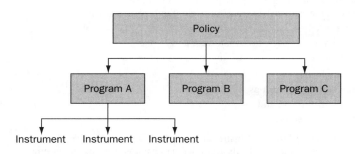

Canada's Aboriginal Policy, Programs, and Instruments

Policy
Gathering Strength: Canada's Aboriginal Action Plan
Gathering Strength looks both to the past and the future. It begins with a Statement of Reconciliation that acknowledges the mistakes and injustices of the past; moves to a Statement of Renewal that expresses a vision of a shared future for

(continued)

Figure 4.1 (continued)

Aboriginal and non-Aboriginal people; and outlines four key objectives for action to begin now:

- Renewing the Partnerships speaks to bringing about meaningful and lasting change in our relationships with Aboriginal people;
- Strengthening Aboriginal Governance is about supporting Aboriginal people in their efforts to create effective and accountable governments, affirming treaty relationships, and negotiating fair solutions to Aboriginal land claims;
- Developing a New Fiscal Relationship means arriving at financial arrangements with Aboriginal governments and organizations which are stable, predictable, and accountable and will help foster self-reliance; and
- Supporting Strong Communities, People and Economies focusses on improving health and public safety, investing in people, and strengthening Aboriginal economic development.

Programs (a sample)

- Aboriginal Business Canada
- Claims
- Climate Change
- Corporate Initiatives
- Departmental Audit and Evaluation Branch Reports
- Economic Development
- Education
- Inuit Relations Secretariat
- International Relations Directorate (IRD)
- Infrastructure and Housing
- Lands and Trust Services
- Northern Affairs Program
- On-Reserve Matrimonial Real Property
- Self-Government
- Social Policy and Programs
- Sustainable Development
- Water Quality

Program: Aboriginal Business Canada
ABC provides support to Aboriginal entrepreneurs for a range of activities including business planning, start-up, expansion, and marketing.

We provide eligible majority-owned Aboriginal enterprises with:

- financial assistance;
- business information and resource materials; and
- referrals to other possible sources of financing or business support.

We work with clients:

- of all Aboriginal heritage groups;
- on-reserve and off-reserve; and
- in urban, rural, and remote areas.

Working with Aboriginal Financial Institutions
ABC works with a network of 54 Aboriginal Financial Institutions, including Aboriginal Capital Corporations, Aboriginal Community Futures Development Corporations, and other Aboriginally-owned or controlled lending institutions.

These organizations act as developmental lenders (providing loans to enterprises that are not yet ready to secure business loans successfully from banks) and offer business advisory services.

Some of these organizations have diversified their operations and act as third-party delivery agents for the Aboriginal Business Canada program, primarily in rural and remote communities.

The theme of this book is that the world of policymaking is changing, and so the bulk of the chapter will take up these new dynamics and also link the question of **instrument design** to a question that increasingly troubles policymakers: how to fashion democratic and cooperative social institutions as vehicles for the other things that a people might wish to accomplish collectively.

Inventory and the Dynamics of Instrument Choice

The technical means whereby we pursue goals are a reflection of the ways in which we perceive problems and the goals that we are pursuing. For example, income security programs made their appearance as full-blown policy instruments only when Western governments (grudgingly) came around to the view, during the Great Depression in the 1930s, that income inequality was a problem and that it was a legitimate goal of government to try to redistribute income. Any inventory of policy instruments will therefore be a snapshot of what is considered legitimate and efficacious at any given time. There is a sense of appropriateness or legitimacy to the use of policy instruments that varies in much the same way as Chapter 3 argued that "ideas in good currency" will change from time to time. This sense of what is legitimate rests on several ethical foundations, and in a country like Canada, principally on a cluster of ideas such as equality, equity, liberty, and rights. There is no point in trying to define these ideas, since they are constantly contested, but it is fair to say that at this point in Canadian history, most of us look to the Charter of Rights and Freedoms and the courts for inspiration as to the proper scope and limits of government action in our lives. Policy analysts have to know which way the wind is blowing in these areas, or instruments that they may recommend for good policy reasons may turn out to have little or no legitimacy among the wider public. The government of Singapore, for example, has had a ban on chewing gum as part of its Regulation of Imports and Exports, though since 2004 it has allowed the import of chewing gum with therapeutic value. Visitors to Singapore will see this on the government's website: "The prohibition on the import of chewing gum except for those of therapeutic value is absolute" (Visit Singapore, 2008). This would be considered outrageous in Canada. Context matters. The City of London, after the July 7, 2007 subway terrorist bombings, massively increased its on-street video surveillance network, to the point that almost everyone is being recorded every second. Again, twenty years ago, this level of government intrusion would have been strenuously resisted.

The history of attempts to classify governing policy instruments begins with Kirschen (1964). His system presented sixty-two different types of economic policy instruments, and the various contributors to the field since have tried various ways of combining aggregate categories with the more finely grained instruments within them. Doern and Phidd (1992, p. 97), for example, argue that there are really only five broad categories: (1) **self-regulation**, (2) **exhortation**, (3) **expenditure**, (4) regulation (including taxation), and (5) public ownership. Based on earlier work by Doern and Wilson (1974), this typology assumed that as one moves from the first category to the last, one moves roughly along a continuum of **legitimate coercion**. The argument was that all government in a liberal democracy involves some degree of imposition or coercion and that politicians generally prefer to use the least coercive instrument possible. Within these broad categories, Doern and Phidd (1992) identify as many as twenty-six finer "graduations of choice" such as grants and subsidies, **guidelines**, and speeches (p. 112).

Another well-known typology by Hood (1994; Hood and Margetts, 2007) developed what he called the "NATO scheme," standing for the different resources that governments have at their disposal to effect policy change. N stands for **nodality** or information resources, A for authority, T for treasure or money, and O for organization or personnel. These struck Linder and Peters (1989) as too broad, and in their article on the question, they developed their own schema that tries to draw on several existing schemes, including Hood's. Four basic classes appeared over and over again in the literature they reviewed, but not always the same four, and so they combined them into a group of seven major categories of policy instruments: "(1) direct provision, (2) **subsidy**, (3) tax, (4) contract, (5) authority, (6) regulation, (the only consensus class), and (7) exhortation" (p. 44). They too provide a finer gradation of choice, based on their view that what really matters is the way in which policymakers themselves subjectively perceive the choices that they have before them. The problem is that this gradation does not mesh very well with other attempts at classification (e.g., McDonnell and Elmore, 1987; Schneider and Ingram, 1990; Howlett and Ramesh, 2003), all of which adopt a different classificatory principle (e.g., government resource versus impact or ends).

Yet another classification system for policy tools or instruments comes from Lester Salamon (2002). He defines a policy tool or instrument as "an identifiable method through which collective action is structured to address a public problem" (p. 19). Salamon is particularly interested in the degree to which modern governments are in fact "third-party" governments. "What is distinctive about many of the newer tools of public action is that they involved the sharing with third-party actors of a far more basic governmental function: the exercise of discretion over the use of public authority and the spending of public funds" (p. 2). Box 4.1 provides a list of the policy instruments highlighted by Salamon.

BOX 4.1   TOOLS OF GOVERNMENT

GOVERNMENT CORPORATIONS AND GOVERNMENT-SPONSORED ENTERPRISES

A government corporation is a government agency, owned and controlled by government, which is set up as a separate corporate entity legally distinct from the rest of the government of which it is a part. This form is often used for activities that are expected to be revenue producing and potentially self-sustaining; however, this need not be the case.

ECONOMIC REGULATION

Economic regulation controls the entry and exit of firms (entry controls), prices (price controls), and/or output (production controls). . . . economic regulation is aimed at ensuring competitive markets for goods and services and at avoiding consumer and other harms when such markets are not feasible. Economic regulation addresses the behaviour of firms.

SOCIAL REGULATION

Social regulation is aimed at restricting behaviours that directly threaten public health, safety, welfare, or well-being. These include environmental pollution, unsafe working environments, unhealthy living conditions, and social exclusion.

GOVERNMENT INSURANCE

Government insurance is a tool through which governments agree to compensate individuals or firms for losses from certain specified events. Eligible recipients are typically charged a fee, or premium, for participation in the insurance program, and participation is often mandatory. Government insurance programs can be operated directly by government agencies or indirectly with the aid of private insurers. In either case, government typically bears the financial responsibility for covering any claims that exceed the pool of resources assembled in the program. Government insurance programs differ from private sector ones in two ways: government insurance tends to be offered for risks that the private sector would be unwilling to cover, and government insurance is

BOX 4.1 (continued)

not usually designed to make a profit (it has social or economic objectives).

PUBLIC INFORMATION

Information is a tool for eliciting desired policy outcomes. Policy-makers inform an audience of target actors about a policy issue or pattern of behaviour to influence what people think, know, or believe when they engage in target behaviour. People change what they do because public policy has changed what they think or has changed what they think about, without necessarily changing anything else about the situation.

CORRECTIVE TAXES, CHARGES AND TRADABLE PERMITS

Corrective charges and tradable permits are a class of policy tools that involve using prices and other market mechanisms to create financial incentives for individuals to change their behaviour in ways that reduce social harms or secure benefits for society at large. In contrast to social regulation, which uses a command and control approach, taxes and charges rely on financial penalties or rewards—it alters the costs and benefits of targeted behaviours, and lets individuals or firms make their own choices.

PROCUREMENT CONTRACTING

Procurement contracting, as a tool of government, is a business arrangement between a government agency and a private entity in which the private entity promises, in exchange for money, to deliver certain products or services to the government agency. The private entity may be a for-profit or a non-profit agency.

PURCHASE-OF-SERVICE CONTRACTING

Purchase-of-service contracting essentially involves an agreement under which a government agency enlists a private organization to deliver a service to an eligible group of "clients" in exchange for money. This type of contracting differs from procurement contracting since the good or service is being purchased for third parties, not for the government itself.

GRANTS

Grants are payments from a donor government to a recipient organization (typically public or nonprofit) or an individual. More specifically, they are a gift that has the aim of either "stimulating" or "supporting" some sort of service or activity by the recipient, whether it be a new activity or an ongoing one. Through this device, a governmental agency (the "grantor") participates in the provision of a service, while leaving to another entity (the "grantee") the task of actual performance.

LOANS AND LOAN GUARANTEES

In a direct loan, the government itself lends money directly to borrowers. It then services that loan (i.e., collects scheduled repayments from the borrowers) and forecloses or otherwise attempts to collect on the loan if a borrower cannot make scheduled payments. When the government guarantees a loan, a private lender, such as a commercial bank or mortgage lender, makes the loan to the borrower. The government enters into a contractual agreement to make full or partial payment to the lender in case the borrower defaults on the guaranteed loan. The private lender originates the loan, secures the government guarantee, and services the loan according to government regulations or minimum standards.

TAX EXPENDITURES

A tax expenditure is a provision in tax law that usually encourages certain behaviour by individuals or corporations by deferring, reducing, or eliminating their tax obligations.

VOUCHERS

A voucher is a subsidy that grants limited purchasing power to an individual to choose among a restricted set of goods and services (e.g., food vouchers, educational vouchers).

TORT LIABILITY

Tort liability, as a tool of government, is the establishing of a right of persons or other entities to seek compensation or injunctive relief through the judicial system for harm that they have experienced

BOX 4.1 (continued)

caused by the negligence or other wrongful conduct of other persons or entities. This right is ordinarily established in court-recognized common law, but may also be created by statutory law or by administrative regulation. Tort law is thus an alternative to administrative regulation and other tools as a mechanism for preventing harm. Tort law relies on court actions brought by injured parties to seek remedies for harms that they have suffered.

SOURCE: Salamon, Lester M. (Ed.). (2002). *The tools of government: A guide to the new governance.* Oxford: Oxford University Press. By permission of Oxford University Press, Inc.

Given this rich variety of classifications and lists, how to proceed? Vedung (1998) defines policy instruments as the "set of techniques by which governmental authorities wield their power in attempting to ensure support and effect or prevent social change" (p. 21). The important thing about this definition is that it reminds us that policy, programs, and ultimately the policy instruments that give them effect are about *deliberately achieving some desired outcome*, and that moreover, "social change" is ultimately a result of human behaviour. The question of instruments therefore is really about the resources and techniques that governments have at their disposal to achieve certain outcomes through affecting human behaviour. In a phrase, it often involves making people do things or stopping them from doing some other things. It is for this reason that most classifications of policy instruments stress the degree of coercion that is involved. Salamon (2002) defines coercion as the most salient dimension in understanding policy tools, and suggests that it "measures the extent to which a tool restricts individual or group behaviour as opposed to merely encouraging or discouraging it" (p. 25). The state, even the downsized and globalized one discussed in Chapter 2, has the monopoly of legitimate force in most societies, as well as the capacity to issue **binding rules** and **prohibitions**. It is useful therefore to consider the degree of state involvement and the degree of state coercion embedded in any policy instrument, as long as we understand that the choice of instrument assumes some grasp of what level of coercion will be accepted as legitimate in society. For example, as a general trend, it seems that public opinion in most Western countries is skeptical of "high-end" coercive policy instruments such as state monopolies or smothering regulations. On the other hand, in Canada at least, there appears to have been a trend favouring more coercive instruments being used against sex offenders or those who violate speech and equity codes, as well as potential security threats.

Since there is no universally accepted typology, and since most typologies of instruments emphasize different criteria, the one offered in this chapter (see Figure 4.2) is deliberately eclectic. We begin by presuming that the policymaker's purpose is to achieve an outcome in terms of (1) the behaviour of individuals; (2) political, social, or economic conditions; or (3) services provided to the public. It would be possible to state the latter two in terms of behavioural changes as well; for example, the desired outcome of reducing poverty could be achieved through changed behaviours such as employers paying higher wages due to increased minimum wage levels or the poor themselves being able to purchase more necessary goods and services because of tax breaks or subsidies. However, since much policy discussion takes place around conditions (e.g., poverty, unemployment, productivity, crime) and services (e.g., health, education, water quality monitoring), there seems little benefit in jettisoning the terms. Now, given the fact of some desired outcome or policy objective (based on an assessment of the problem), what tools are at the policymaker's disposal for achieving it? Figure 4.2 provides three broad categories. The first is to do nothing. In a sense, the option of doing nothing is not really a choice of instrument—it is simply inaction. As we noted in Chapter 1, we refer here to deliberate inaction, a conscious choice. We discuss this in more detail below, but the logic of highlighting this as a choice is to underscore the point that doing nothing often makes sense when it turns out that a perceived policy problem was not really a problem at all, or that the cost of intervention exceeds the benefits, or that other forces will achieve the desired outcome in the absence of government action.

The next two categories contain the two broad families of interventions or policy instruments that governments can choose to achieve their objectives. The first entails acting indirectly in the sense that the objectives are being pursued through the actions and behaviour of citizens, organizations, or firms. This can be done through affecting the information or values that underpin behaviour (information or exhortation instruments); the calculus of monetary costs, benefits, and resources (expenditure instruments); or stipulating rules and sanctions attached to certain behaviours (regulatory instruments). Within this family of instruments, information-based tools are generally considered to be less coercive than expenditure-based tools, and both of these are considered less coercive than regulation-based tools. The continuum is not perfect—as we note below, taxes are probably more coercive than self-regulation through **voluntary codes**. As well, in some respects, acting indirectly in our sense actually involves quite coercive state powers (e.g., the criminal justice system). However, it captures a rough scale effect as we move from

Figure 4.2   Policy Instruments: A Classification

GOVERNMENTS CAN...

Do nothing [Static response]
Rationales:
  Problem-related
  Resource-related
  Precedent-related
  Self-corrective system

Act indirectly....
  Affirmative/Promoting   *Negative/Restraining*
  Information   encourage   dissuade
                                        argument
                                        persuasion
                                        facts/data
  Expenditures   cash transfer   taxes
                     grants   user charges
                     subsidy/contribution   service fees
                     loans   fines
                     tax expenditure
                     voucher

  Regulation   permissions   criminal law
                   licences   non-criminal prohibitions
                   recognitions

Behaviour

Condition

Service

Act directly....
State Agency
    department
    social agency
State Corporation

Third party partnership/contract
    nongovernmental organization
    nonprofit corporation
    company

one category to the other. The other axis, borrowing from Vedung (1998), is between affirmative/promoting and negative/restraining (p. 26). Tools drawing on information, expenditures, and regulation can either promote certain behaviours or outcomes, or prohibit or restrain them.

In the second family of instruments, the state acts directly and is ultimately accountable for achieving its objectives. The most obvious and conventional way to do this is through the use of the state's own resources to change conditions or provide services. For example, Revenue Canada, as a department, used to collect taxes for the federal government. Now taxes are collected through the Canada Revenue Agency, which, however, is still an agency (though at arm's length) of government. Many provincial and municipal governments, in dealing with the housing problems of poor people, directly provide social housing through special agencies. Canada used to have a large number of public enterprises or state corporations, most notably Air Canada and Petro Canada before they were privatized but also the still-surviving Canadian Broadcasting Corporation. Whatever the form—a department, agency, or corporation—in all three instances the government is achieving its policy objective through the marshalling of its own resources and organizational capacity and not working through citizens, nongovernmental organizations (NGOs), or the private sector. It is doing it itself. However, another form of direct action is through partnerships or **contracts** with third parties such as NGOs, nonprofit agencies, or companies. This subcategory admittedly stretches the definition of direct action slightly, but it is included here because the state is still formulating its objectives, determining acceptable outcomes, signing the contract for service delivery, providing the funds, and monitoring performance. It is also ultimately responsible for those outcomes.

It is important to understand that in the run of normal or routine politics, the range of instrument choice is generally limited by the existing array that is already embedded in the policy field. Policymakers think through their options on the basis of what is currently in the field or underpinning policy efforts. If evaluation shows that some instruments are not working, they can be amended, but as long as normal politics is incremental politics, the temptation is to build upon already existing and fairly finely graduated policy instruments. In periods of greater policy turbulence, policymakers will actually begin to think in broader instrument categories, because in turbulent times policies are often fundamentally restructured, forcing a consideration of instrument types. We discuss the new dynamics of instrument choice in the second half of this chapter; the changes in governance in the past decade have indeed been turbulent, and with them have come new debates and new approaches to instrument choice. In the sections below, we briefly outline the key characteristics of each instrument. We begin, however, by briefly outlining the logic of "doing nothing."

DOING NOTHING

"Doing nothing" may appear as a "nondecision," which indeed it is if it has no rationale beyond either ennui or a simple desire to remain unengaged. As we argued in Chapter 1, however, a deliberate choice not to intervene, made after an analysis of the problem, should be considered a policy decision—what we will call here **"static response."** There can be several good rationales for declining to intervene. Together they comprise a coherent set of considerations that should be part of any systematic process of instrument choice, even though "doing nothing" does not seem intuitively to fit the notion of an "instrument" or tool. The four rationales that follow presume that a potential problem or opportunity has presented itself to policymakers in some fashion, and that a careful analysis was undertaken about the nature of the problem and the appropriate response.

Problem-related rationales: The analysis indicates that in fact there is either no problem after all or a problem that is not within the government's current priorities or its jurisdiction. In May 1999, for example, the CRTC announced that it would not extend its regulation to the Internet because it "concluded that the new media on the Internet are achieving the goals of the Broadcasting Act and are vibrant, highly competitive and successful without regulation" (CRTC, 1999). This decision was reversed less than ten years later, in May 2008, when the CRTC concluded that the Internet was no longer a distinct technology and delivery channel, and that the lines between it and broadcasting were increasingly blurred (e.g., YouTube or Joost). Another example of static response was Canada's refusal to join the war against Iraq. Prime Minister Chrétien and his cabinet did not believe that Iraq had weapons of mass destruction, nor did they believe that the invasion would defeat terrorism. This was a deliberate decision not to act (Chrétien, 2007: 317–18).

Resource-related rationales: The analysis indicates that there is indeed a problem, and that it falls within the government's general priorities and its jurisdiction. Nonetheless, given resource constraints and other more pressing demands, the government cannot allocate resources for this problem. A prime example of this through the late 1990s was the federal government's acknowledgment that the health care system was in trouble but that it could not afford to put more money into it. This changed dramatically by 2004, when all governments were vying to put more money into health care. At that point, defence was a good candidate for resource-related rationales: while everyone recognized that more money needed to go into the Canadian military, the sheer magnitude required made some decisionmakers balk. Again, this was reversed with the election of the Conservatives in 2006, who decided to channel more money into the military.

Precedent-related rationales: A problem exists, but the analysis raises the concern that a policy intervention might set a precedent that could place unmanageable demands on government. In the tainted blood scandal, for example, Ottawa refused to compensate hepatitis-C victims who had contracted the disease from blood products before 1986 in the fear that this would open a floodgate of compensation claims that would go beyond the $1.1 billion the federal and provincial governments were already paying out (Orsini, 2002). The same worry has been behind Ottawa's careful approach to "redress" policies for ethnic groups that endured historical injustices (e.g., the Japanese, Chinese, Ukrainians, Aboriginals) (James, 2007).

Self-corrective system rationales: In this case, while it is accepted that there may be a problem, it is also assumed that there is also a coherent system (e.g., social, cultural, religious, economic) at work that over time may correct it spontaneously, without the need for government intervention. Market-based rationales are the most familiar example of this these days; in cases of high prices, monopoly power by single firms, etc., the argument is that market competition over time will correct the problem. For example, in contrast to when oil prices soared in the 1980s, and the federal government tried to shield Canadians through the National Energy Program, the increase in energy prices that started in 2006 was ignored. Prime Minister Harper remarked that Canadians would simply have to get used to higher prices (CTV, 2006).

Static response appears like an empty category, a nullity or absence of action, but is increasingly important at least as part of the instrument selection/policy analysis process. The term is slightly misleading—"doing nothing" does require analysis and a decision not to respond directly. However, in an era that remains skeptical of excessive government intervention and more attuned to the efficacy of markets and civil society, it is no longer assumed that as soon as a problem presents itself that government on its own should be reaching for active policy instruments. People will expect responses to problems, but not always government policy responses. It should also be noted though that static response is a difficult thing for governments to do. To appear to ignore a problem—as the Conservatives did in 2006 with increases in energy prices—is politically risky.

INFORMATION-BASED INSTRUMENTS

Information-based policy instruments include government-directed "attempts at influencing people through transfer of knowledge, communication of reasoned argument, and **moral suasion** in order to achieve a policy result" (Vedung and van der Doelen, 1998, p. 103). Of course, all serious policies and programs depend on information in the minimal sense of making people aware of their existence, but Vedung (1998) makes the useful distinction between information as an independent policy instrument and information on a metapolicy instrument that supports others (p. 49). Information-based policy instruments can include flyers, pamphlets, booklets, training, advertisements, reports, websites, and portals. Information-based instruments are considered the least coercive of all policy instruments since there is no obligation to act on the information and no supplementary inducement or penalty. Some forms of information can be designed to dissuade behaviours—a good example is the graphic health warnings on cigarette packages—while others are designed to encourage or promote certain behaviours—for example, *Canada's Food Guide* helps us know how many legumes to consume per week. Other forms of information are just that—information that citizens require in order to make decisions and take actions. Government now places enormous quantities of information on the web that is useful to citizens—information about programs, about services, and forms and applications. Most interestingly, since many government services are essentially exchanges of information (applying for licences, paying taxes, making inquiries), information instruments can also be interactive, with information flowing both ways. We discuss information in relation to services in Chapter 5; here we will focus on information as an instrument to tackle policy problems.

A key principle behind information-based instruments is that behaviour is based on knowledge, beliefs, and values. Assume that the government's policy objective is to reduce smoking. If knowledge, in the sense of facts at the smoker's disposal, is incorrect or incomplete (e.g., the addictive qualities of nicotine), or beliefs are wrong (e.g., that smoking has no ill-health effects), or values are counterproductive (e.g., it's "cool" to smoke), then smoking behaviour will continue unabated. Presumably, an information campaign that would enlighten smokers would change their behaviour, since it would appear to be manifestly in their interest to reduce or quit smoking. But of course we know that this is not always the case, and it alerts us to the fact that information-based policy tools work best when knowledge, beliefs, and values are consistent with direct and immediate self-interest. Even when "enlightened" by government information campaigns, smokers may continue to smoke because they like it, because they discount the negative health effects far into the future, because they struggle with temptation even though they know and try better (Schelling, 1984), or because they want to defy what they perceive as a hectoring, paternalistic government program (the boomerang effect).

There is a paradox about information-based instruments—as benign as they might appear, the most powerful way to change behaviour is to change the knowledge, beliefs, and values upon which it is based. The former communist regimes in Europe and every existing authoritarian government in the world understand that very well. So did Plato in *The Republic*. The use of information/exhortation in democratic states can seem much less objectionable; it is remarkable, for example, how public attitudes toward the environment have changed in only one generation and have become the foundation for acquiescence to blue-box programs, anti-littering campaigns, and picking up after your dog in the park. This is all to the good. But there can be concerns. In Canada, the federal government has for decades been the country's single largest advertiser. There is a fine line between promoting public policies and programs, and self-promotion for the government of the day. Other levels of government in Canada have not been left behind. And as the opening example from this chapter indicated, information can be used in a somewhat discomfiting way as a "**shaming**" instrument—in a sense, this is the use of information *about* rather than information *for*. Our behaviour might be changed not because our beliefs have been affected by an information campaign but because of information about us that has been provided to others. The use of shaming as a policy instrument is more widespread than we might assume. Product labelling, for example, can be used to induce companies to remove ingredients that are deemed harmful to the consuming public. Regulatory agencies can issue lists of "worst offenders" (for example, polluters), deliberately using the publicity as a way of inducing change. Graham describes this as "democracy by disclosure": "Stated simply, such strategies employ government authority to require the standardized disclosure of factual information from identified businesses or other organizations about products or practices to reduce risks to the public" (Graham, 2002, p. 138). The interesting thing about the new disclosure instruments is that unlike warning labels that tell people what to do or articulate a harm or risk, mandatory disclosure simply puts factual information in the public domain (e.g., nutritional labelling), and lets people make up their own minds about risk. It can also be used as an instrument to increase transparency, as is the case in the federal government's proactive disclosure policy, where travel and hospitality expenses of senior officials and contracts over $10 000 are posted on department websites. The combination of public disclosure laws (and the United States is considerably ahead of Canada in this respect), assiduous researchers and critics, and modern media, give information a potency that is sometimes underestimated. We address some new aspects of information/exhortation in the second part of the chapter.

EXPENDITURE-BASED INSTRUMENTS

From the policymaker's point of view, virtually every policy instrument involves expenditure—even giving a speech will entail the cost of speechwriters and distribution of materials. So money is a ubiquitous and universal resource that governments use to affect policy, and rarely, if ever, can expenditure as an instrument be avoided. The point about expenditure-based policy instruments, however, is that it is money itself that is the direct instrument. In this instance, governments are not trying to achieve their objectives or outcomes by changing the information that undergirds behaviour, but rather the calculus of costs, benefits, and financial resources that individuals or organizations undertake before they do something. Producing Canadian films, for example, is risky because of the high probability of not making a profit. Government subsidies and tax breaks can change that equation and induce more Canadian filmmaking. Canadians who live in poverty and who might not be able to afford a proper diet or housing can be aided through **cash transfers** in the form of income security or assistance payments.

In 1998 the Auditor General of Canada undertook a special audit of the **grants** and **contributions** practices of several departments, primarily Industry Canada and Heritage Canada. As the report pointed out, the "provision of grants and contributions to individuals, businesses and not-for-profit organizations is one of the most important ways that the Government of Canada pursues its program objectives" (Auditor General of Canada, 1998). The report provided a useful definition of grants and contributions:

> Grants are unconditional transfer payments for which eligibility and entitlement may be verified. If an individual or organization is eligible for a grant, the appropriate payment can be made without requiring the recipient to meet any future conditions. In contrast, the payment of a contribution is subject to performance conditions that are specified in a contribution agreement. The recipient must continue to show that these conditions are being met in order to be reimbursed for specific costs over the life of the agreement. The recipients' use of contributions can also be audited by the government, whereas this is usually not a requirement for a grant. (Auditor General, 1998)

In Figure 4.2 we have distinguished between cash transfers, grants, and subsidy/contributions. In Canadian usage, transfers usually apply to payments by government to individuals or other governments that do not involve any form of exchange and have only minimal conditions attached to them. Equalization payments and the Canada Health and Social Transfer (CHST) are prime examples of cash transfers from the federal government to the provinces. Provincial governments also transfer cash to their municipalities to support a wide range of programs. Old Age Security and the Canada Child Tax Benefit are examples of transfers to individuals. The key point is that a cash transfer tends to be provided for broad support rather than in connection with a specific project or endeavour. Grants, even while they have few if any performance conditions attached, are usually provided in connection with a more specific endeavour (e.g., student educational grants). However, in a technical sense grants tend not to be too closely calibrated to the actual costs of engaging in that endeavour. Contributions and subsidies, on the other hand, have more numerous and detailed conditions, usually demand some measure of performance, and are more carefully calculated to defray some specific proportion of the cost of the endeavour. They differ from loans in that the latter must be repaid. Tax expenditures accomplish much the same thing as contributions or subsidies, but through the mechanism of reducing taxes for specific activities and thereby increasing the benefits. Perhaps the most publicly visible tax expenditure in Canada is the Registered Retirement Savings Program (RRSP) where interest in special accounts is tax free and contributions are tax deductible, though the device is used routinely to support everything from small businesses to **investments** in high technology and research. The 2008 federal budget introduced the Tax-Free Savings Account (TFSA) which is similar to the RRSP, but where contributions are not tax deductible, interest can grow tax free, and withdrawals are not taxed either. **Vouchers** are typically "coupons" for stipulated amounts of money that may be redeemed under certain conditions—the best known example is Food Stamps in the United States, although vouchers are increasingly being used to provide educational services, housing, child care, transportation, and health care (Steuerle and Twombly, 2002). In the United States, vouchers have become the dominant form of federal housing assistance (Center on Budget and Policy Priorities, 2007). While the United States probably leads the world in reliance on vouchers, they are routinely used around the world: Accor Corporate Services, for example, operates in 40 countries and distributes vouchers for everything from milk to clothing to millions of recipients on behalf of public service providers. (Accor Services, 2008). The OECD points out that vouchers can be in the form of coupons—an "explicit" voucher—or in the form of reimbursements or direct payments for goods or services from approved suppliers. "The extent of use of these three forms of vouchers is significant in some sectors in OECD member countries, with their use being mainly focused on housing, education (primary and secondary), childcare (nursery education), and care for the elderly" (OECD, 2005, 146).

Expenditure instruments pose substantial management challenges in terms of ensuring that conditions are met and monies are spent appropriately, with some result. The Auditor General has been evaluating grants and contributions by the federal government for over twenty years, and in 1984 identified eight critical management processes for grant and contribution programs: "stating objectives clearly; establishing unambiguous terms and conditions; informing potential applicants of program guidelines; reviewing and approving applications diligently; making payments properly; monitoring individual grants and contributions appropriately; providing good information to management; and assessing program effectiveness" (Auditor General, 1998). Despite this, the government's record on grants and contributions was marked by consistent problems:

> In summary, our audits of the management of grant and contribution programs over the past 21 years have produced a long series of consistent observations. Our 1977 audit found problems in compliance with program authorities, weaknesses in program design, instances of poor controls, and insufficient performance measurement and reporting. Subsequent audits have made similar observations. While we have found signs of specific improvements in some areas when we followed up on these audits, overall we have continued to find the same problems each time we have audited grant and contribution programs. (Auditor General, 1998)

The sponsorship scandal in early 2004 involving the Ministry of Public Works and contracts with the Quebec communications firm Groupaction simply illustrated that the government still was challenged in handling the spending instrument. The Auditor General's review of the matter found "an appalling disregard for the Financial Administration Act, the Government Contracts Regulations, Treasury Board policy, and rules designed to ensure prudence and probity in government procurement" (Auditor General, 2002, p. 1). The Gomery Commission agreed: "Many factors contributed to what has been described as the "sponsorship scandal": inappropriate political interference in administrative matters, acceptance by public servants of such interference, excessive concentration of power in the Prime Minister's Office, carelessness and incompetence and blatant disregard of Treasury Board policies, greed and venality" (Commission of Inquiry, 2005, p. 438). To be fair, public sector financial management is complex, and because of its political/bureaucratic environment, is susceptible to all sorts of game-playing (Graham, 2007; especially Chaps. 6 and 8, and Appendix 1). As well, many of the challenges to managing large spending programs are systemic—ironically, in 2000, in the Human Resources and Development Canada "scandal" over a billion dollars lost in employment training funds (eventually it was determined that it was only $85 000) might have been in part caused by new public management practices that led to decentralized decision-making and little oversight and information (Good, 2003). Since then, the machinery designed to manage public money has become even more complex. Whereas once the expenditure process could be summarized as a struggle between "spenders" (most departments) and "guardians" (the Department of Finance and Treasury Board), it now is characterized by "spenders, guardians, priority setters (the Prime Minister's Office and the Privy Council Office) and financial watchdogs (the Office of the Auditor General) . . ." (Good, 2007, p. 4). To some extent this has further complicated budgeting and expenditure management, without necessarily improving it. Serious and on-going review of continuing expenditures (the "A" base) remains weak, as does monitoring the link between expenditures and performance (ibid., p. 308).

The negative/restraining side of expenditures is to increase the costs of some activities. Governments tax, of course, to get revenue. They can have policies about taxation, in terms of the fairness and incidence of the tax regime. They can also use taxes as deliberate policy instruments. For example, "sin taxes" on alcohol and cigarettes are a means of discouraging their use (Bird and Stoney, 2006). The distinction between taxes and other types of government levies such as user charges or fees is increasingly blurred, but in principle taxes have a compulsory aspect and generally are not connected to any specific service. Income and property taxes do have a discretionary component in that if someone decided not to work or live in a dwelling, he or she would not be liable for those taxes—but in practice, of course, they are almost unavoidable. Non-smokers do not pay cigarette taxes, but smokers who do pay those taxes do not receive any specific government service in return. Both **user charges** and **service fees** have a service component in them and so are not usually viewed as taxes. In the case of user charges, the service component is quite general and the charge therefore is levied on a category of person or user. Examples include access to and use of facilities such as airports (many now levy an "improvement charge") or municipal dumps. A service fee usually is connected to some specific service rather than general use; for example, receiving a passport. In practice, the terms are often interchangeable, and for cosmetic reasons policymakers often prefer to use the term "fee" rather than "tax." Whatever term is used, the precise amounts of any levy and its attendant conditions (e.g., when, how, and on which payers) are complex questions of public finance.

REGULATION

Regulation draws on the most fundamental resource a government has, its capacity to command and prohibit. "Regulatory instruments are used to define norms, acceptable behavior, or to limit activities in a given society. The law, backed up with the threat of sanction, represents the 'stick' used to prescribe or prevent certain types of human behavior" (Lemaire, 1998, p. 59). That capacity depends on a blend of legitimacy and effective sanctions for disobedience, with the greatest weight on legitimacy. If governments merely have power without authority, they will have little capacity to command and have citizens obey. It is the legitimacy of their commands as perceived by the majority of citizens that permits them to efficiently use sanctions against the minority that disobey. A great deal of public policy is about achieving outcomes through ensuring certain actions or behaviours. Regulatory instruments rely on rules to prohibit or promote selected actions or behaviours. This has an admirable directness to it—"thou shalt" or "thou shalt not"—but we have classified them here under "indirect" instruments since in most cases, regulation is understood to involve government rules aimed at certain activities undertaken by individuals, organizations, or firms to achieve certain outcomes.

It is important to understand that what we conventionally define as regulation is actually "**secondary legislation**," a form of law. To understand regulation, we need first to understand the nature of law. Most of what government does stems from law in one way or another. The issue here is the use of law or rules themselves to achieve policy objectives. Stipulating rules to achieve those objectives seems both reasonable and effective. The use of criminal law prohibitions against murder or child abuse, or even noncriminal prohibitions such as driving on the left side of the road, is simple and clear. There are several considerations however, that, while fundamental, are often overlooked in the policy literature. The first is that there are different types of legal instruments (Keyes, 1996). It is possible to distinguish among

- *Legislation or statute* (including delegated legislation—or regulation—based on **statute**);
- *Decisions* (legal ones about what a statute means);
- *Contracts* (applicable to the parties and legally binding);
- *Quasi-legislation* (issued by administrative authorities in the form of internal or nonbinding rules, policies, and guidelines); and
- *Incorporation by reference* (bringing another instrument such as a code of conduct into a statute and giving it the force of law).

Distinctions can be made among these in terms of (1) their legal effect and (2) the procedures used to formulate them. Legal effect has two dimensions: generality (the number of people it is directed to) and degree of binding (imposition of some threat or sanction). Statutes normally affect large numbers of people and are binding on all. This is also true of delegated **legislation** or regulatory authority, but there is a constraint in that courts will demand a clear legal authority for using this power. **Decisions** are instruments that apply law, not make it. They are specific rather than general. Contracts are even narrower, binding only on the parties to the contract. Quasi-legislation has no binding legal effect generally—but, for example, Canada Revenue Agency bulletins interpreting the meaning of legislation can have practical effect and can be authoritative to the degree that the courts accept them. Ganz (1987) defines **quasi-legislation** as "a wide spectrum of rules whose only common factor is that they are not directly enforceable through criminal or civil proceedings" (p. 1). She points out that the lines between these two categories are increasingly blurred and that it does not depend on form—a circular may be legally binding but a "law" in practice may not (for example, police routinely ignore personal use of small amounts of marijuana). There has been huge growth in statutory and extrastatutory rules in a plethora of forms: codes of practice, guides, notes, circulars, white papers, policy notes, development briefs, tax concessions, notices, codes of conduct, codes of ethics, and conventions. The main reasons for the use of quasi-legislation are always the same: flexibility and lack of technicality (Baldwin, 1995, p. 4). Flexibility means that rules can be changed easily and quickly. Of course, what appears as flexibility and simplicity from one perspective can seem like "back-door legislation" and confusion from another.

Finally, **incorporation by reference** is quite a powerful and flexible form of rule-making because it can combine instruments that would otherwise stand separate and give them the force of law. A statute that incorporates a regulatory code of conduct developed by an industry association, for example, takes the privately developed code and gives it the force of law. Moreover, depending on drafting, the incorporation can be dynamic in the sense that any amendments made to the code subsequent to the passage of the legislation also automatically get reflected in the legal instrument (there is, for obvious reasons, some debate over this). The law without the code is one instrument, and the code without the law is another. Combined, they form a hybrid that is more than the sum of its parts.

The type of instrument can be linked to the procedure for making it. The reason is that the characteristics of the body making a legal instrument determines how well suited it is to making it. For example, strong compliance with a rule usually depends on people knowing and accepting it, and this knowledge and acceptance improves when people have a chance to participate in the making of the rule. Some types of decision-making bodies are better at involving certain groups of people than others. The logic is that the wider the legal effect and more binding the nature of the rule, the closer one gets to authoritative and generally representative institutions such as Parliament. Delegated legislation and quasi-legislation usually do not bring people into the decisionmaking process as effectively as Parliament potentially can. The narrower the legal effect, and the more valued consensus is among a small group of participants, the more one will rely on forms of rules approaching the quasi-legislative, or discretionary end of the continuum.

Regulation is therefore a distinct type of rule-making available to governments. It is termed "secondary legislation" because, unlike quasi-legislation, it requires a statutory basis. As the 2003 *Cabinet Directive on Law-Making* makes clear,

> Canada's system of responsible parliamentary government is based on the rule of law. This means that laws must be made in conformity with the Constitution. The Crown retains very few regulatory powers that are not subject to the legislative or law-making process. For example, regulations governing the issuance of passports or medals and honors are still made under the royal prerogative. Parliament may delegate regulatory authority to Cabinet (the Governor in Council), a person (such as a Minister of the Crown) or a body (such as the Atomic Energy Control Board). However, this authority remains subject to the will of Parliament and regulations made under this delegated authority are referred to as subordinate legislation. (Privy Council Office, 2003)

Affirmative/promoting uses of regulation include permissions, licences, recognitions, and self-regulation. **Permissions** are simply permits or enablements with few if any conditions attached—for example, a hunting permit or a city declaration that bars can stay open later for a special event. **Licences** are more complicated in that they involve a mix of prohibition, permission, and condition. This is the classic formula of the regulator: first, generally prohibit some action (e.g., broadcasting TV signals, driving a vehicle, fishing for salmon, doing brain surgery); second, specifically permit that action for individuals or organizations who will respect some pre-defined criteria or conditions. The licence conditions can be as detailed or as scant as the regulator likes. Of course, a key ingredient is defining sanctions for the unlawful (i.e., unlicensed) practice of the regulated act. Use of "regs," as seasoned policy analysts like to call them, is a marvelously flexible instrument in that it can define prohibited acts quite precisely and can attach equally precise conditions to the licensee. Keeping track of regulations can be difficult, and a new tool has been developed entitled "RegWatch" to identify Canadian, foreign, and international standards referenced in Canadian federal law.

Regulation can also entail "**recognition**" or defining the *bona fide* actors in a policy field. The most benign is simply to recognize certain individuals or organizations for some policy-relevant quality that they have or have achieved. Under the Indian Act, for example, the federal Department of Indian Affairs and Northern Development keeps a registry of all Indians so defined for purposes of the legislation (essentially those individuals descended from Indian bands with whom the federal government struck treaties in the nineteenth and twentieth centuries). Appropriately enough, they are known as status Indians, and other Indians are described as non-status or non-treaty Indians. For the purposes of the Indian Act and what it permits, prohibits, and provides, it matters a great deal if one is status or non-status. Another example is the Green logo designed by Environment Canada or the U.K. Charter Mark discussed in Chapter 2. Products or services that meet certain standards can display the logo and thereby send a signal to consumers. Government is simply lending its authority to designate some actors as complying with the larger policy purpose. That designation carries a certain advantage to its recipients.

A species of regulation is government-sanctioned self-regulation, where the state delegates its regulatory power not to a state agency but to a nongovernmental organization or association. The professions (medicine, law, engineering) are the main examples and involve the delegation of government powers to set mandatory standards and discipline infractions. The assumption policymakers have made is that these professions can be trusted not to take the short-term view or operate primarily for economic gain. In other cases, government accredits organizations to conduct official activities, and may incorporate the results into legislation, thereby giving those activities the force of law. A good example is the National Standards System, which is managed by the Standards Council of Canada, a Crown corporation. The Council accredits organizations to develop, test, and apply standards. Most standards (and there are thousands, covering almost every conceivable product and many services) are voluntary, though some are incorporated by reference into international law. In another strategy, government can help organizations develop their own voluntary codes of conduct. Voluntary codes also go by other names: codes of conduct, codes of practice, voluntary initiatives, guidelines, and nonregulatory agreements. Successful codes are said to have the following characteristics: (1) buy-in from leaders of the relevant organizations; (2) rank and file support; (3) a clear statement of objectives, obligations, and rules; (4) transparent development and implementation; (5) regular flow of information; (6) an effective dispute-resolution system; (7) meaningful incentives to participate; and (8) negative repercussions for failure to join or comply (Industry Canada, 1998, pp. 7–8). The government's role in voluntary codes is that of a catalyst, facilitator, and sometimes endorser. In those cases where volunteer codes affect business or industrial sectors, government is also interested in the degree to which the codes may impede competition.

Regulations can broadly be classed as economic, social, or environmental, though each of these will have subsets based on the object (e.g., prices, safety) or targets (e.g., specific industries). Economic regulation typically addresses such factors as pricing, advertising, and labelling, competition, some aspects of production, profits, and disclosure of financial information. The classic rationale for economic regulation is that markets are not working efficiently. This may be due to monopolies (the historical case for public utility regulation), oligopolies (hence competition regulation), or the simple occurrence of various forms of behaviour designed to maximize profits at the expense of workers and consumers (e.g., collusion, false advertising, union busting). Social regulation is designed to protect us less as consumers than as persons or citizens. This somewhat vague formulation is fairly clear when it comes to health and safety standards such as fire regulations. Though these frequently apply to products and services, they also affect our use of spaces and buildings as citizens. It is a lot less clear what criteria regulators have in mind as they move into the cultural realm with broadcasting regulations (e.g., Canadian content, nonstereotyping), and social justice regulations such as employment equity or speech codes. Environmental regulation struggles with the standards issue as well, since the science is often not precise enough to determine what the allowable limits of many toxic substances might be. Nor can we easily know the effects of the interaction of hundreds of thousands of substances in the air, land, and water.

ACTING DIRECTLY

The preceding categories of instruments are indirect in that they involve working through citizens or organizations to achieve public goals. Governments can sometimes decide to achieve the conditions or service goals they have in mind by marshalling their own resources toward those ends. A good example is education. Parents need to have their children educated, but governments can elect to provide that education directly themselves, or they may provide parents with the funds (usually through some form of voucher) that they could then redeem for services as they see fit, from either government providers, the private sector, or some mix. Any service directly provided by government, from garbage collection to education, will involve the expenditure of often very substantial amounts of money. In 2007, for example, provincial and territorial governments spent a total of $308 billion on health ($101.4 billion), social services ($53.8 billion), and education ($74.3 billion). This represented 74 percent of total expenditures in that year (Statistics Canada, 2007). So "direct provision" is less an alternative to spending money than it is a means of spending money that reflects a different policy logic. It is a logic reflected in the questions listed in Box 4.2 (see on the next page). Take municipal garbage collection as an example. The need in this case is the removal of refuse, and municipal governments have traditionally provided this service directly by raising general tax revenues to cover the cost. Traditionally no fees have been attached. Municipal governments have had both the authority and the fiscal capacity to deliver the service. The nub of the issue is in questions 4 and 5. Are there alternative service providers? Absolutely.

BOX 4.2 — QUESTIONS TO ASK ABOUT DIRECT PROVISION OF SERVICE INSTRUMENTS

1. What is the need or the problem, and what service or bundle of services will meet that need?
2. Do we have the legal capacity to provide the service?
3. Do we have the resources to provide the service?
4. Are there alternative service providers?
5. Is there a compelling policy reason to provide the service directly (e.g., safety, uniformity of standards, recipients cannot choose appropriate service levels, retaining agency capacity in the program field)?
6. If the service is provided publicly, should there be fees attached?
7. If the service is provided privately, will recipients be able to pay for it, or should there be some subsidy?
8. If there is a subsidy, should it be paid to providers or recipients?
9. If the service is provided privately, by what sort of entity (e.g., for-profit or nonprofit).
10. If the service is provided privately, what oversight/regulation should government provide?

The garbage business in North America is huge. What is the compelling policy reason to directly collect garbage with city workers rather than through a contract for service with a private company? Typically, the argument from public sector unions has been that the level of service (and the wages and working conditions of sanitary workers) will decline if private companies get into the act. Apart from that, most people care only that the can at the curbside is emptied weekly. This is essentially a question of efficiency. If public sector workers can collect the garbage as efficiently as a private sector company can, there usually is little reason to change. Question 6, however, has risen with a vengeance in recent years. As the costs of garbage collection and recycling have increased dramatically across North America, and as pressure to hold the line on taxes has mounted, more and more municipal governments have decided to charge some sort of fee for collection. This can get quite creative, from charges per can or bag to limits on the number of bags one can put out. The logic in both cases is the same: what was once a "free" service now has a direct cost attached to it. The other questions deal with the ways in which government can either support or regulate the private provision of services. As we shall see in Chapter 5, "**alternative service delivery**" or some variant of the term has become an important issue in the implementation of public policy. More and more jurisdictions are answering question 4 in the affirmative, but question 5 in the negative, and then the game turns into one of deciding how to structure a private sector/public sector partnership. Another implementation issue is, if the service is to be provided through a public agency, how should that agency be designed? Should it be a direct-line department, or an arm's-length entity like a public or Crown corporation?

As the list of questions on service delivery suggests, governments can either provide the service directly or regulate the provision of the service by third parties, or they can do a mix of both. Policy instruments are not mutually exclusive but are usually combined in packages to deal with the different dimensions of the problem.

The preceding has covered most of the major categories of instruments. What can we conclude from the discussion? First, no list is ever complete, and there are some instruments that some authors would include as separate categories (e.g., Crown corporations) and others would place under a broad category such as direct provision. Second, the sliding scale of authority idea is only moderately helpful in distinguishing these instruments. A high government charge on a service I need to use regularly will seem a lot more coercive to me than even the most detailed regulations covering a service I rarely access. Equally, a persistent series of hectoring ads about what the government believes to be naughty behaviour may seem more paternalistic than the income tax I am forced to pay once a year. This point takes on even greater force when we consider a third conclusion: no instrument is an island. Since they tackle clusters of problems, government policies use clusters of programs. These program clusters in turn bundle together groups of instruments. Education, for example, mixes big spending, direct service delivery, taxation (special education taxes), and lots of regulations.

This crude inventory has shown us what instruments we can choose and some of the rationales behind their choice. But what actually explains instrument choice? Theoretically, some instruments are substitutable, meaning that from the point of view of cost and at least the major outcome desired by policy, it makes little difference which instrument you use. Postsecondary education is currently funded in part by federal government transfers to the provinces. For years, federal ministers have mused about converting that transfer to vouchers that would go directly to students. The money would be exactly the same, and it could flow only into postsecondary institutions. The big difference would be the change from a cash transfer to governments to a voucher for students. The other aspect of this issue is comparing the pattern of instrument choice across governments. Expenditures across the OECD countries on health, education, and income security are much closer than the means used to provide these services.

Linder and Peters (1989) provide a model for understanding the links between the broad policy system variables and decisions that policymakers themselves undertake in given situations. They emphasize the importance of systemic variables, organizational characteristics, problem features, and the profile of individual decisionmakers. Systemic variables include such broad factors as national policy style, political culture, and prevailing social cleavages. Organizational variables include the way that the sponsoring department is structured, its history, and its connections with its relevant policy communities. The problem context embraces questions such as how crowded the policy domain is, the political constraints of using a specific instrument, and the requirements of political support (Bressers and O'Toole, 2005). Finally, individual level variables comprise perceptions, values, and experience of the policymaker. This schema operates almost like a funnel, channelling these larger forces down from the systemic level to the individual decisionmakers. Of course, national policy style and political culture are not actors on the policy stage; they have influence only through the decisionmaker's implicit or conscious application. The current debate in some provincial jurisdictions over the use of private management companies to run public hospitals is an interesting illustration. This is contracting out to a third party in a policy area that jealously protects its public character. The decision to use this instrument will certainly depend on cost considerations and effectiveness (the problem context), but also on what is feasible or acceptable in that political regime (style and political culture).

New Dynamics

As we have argued throughout this book, the nature of governance is changing because of globalization, technology, culture, and new approaches to public management and statecraft. While the impacts on problem definitions are powerful, as we saw in Chapter 3, they are still somewhat difficult to conceptualize because problem definition and agenda-setting are such complex processes in their own right. In this chapter and in Chapter 5, we see clear evidence for new ways of making policy.

Spending Instruments

The first edition of this book appeared in 1997, when governments across Canada were in the midst of seriously attacking deficits that had built up over almost a quarter century. From 1998 to 2008, the federal government ran a string of large surpluses, and projected surpluses (though smaller) for 2009–11 as well. In 2006–07, all provincial/territorial governments were in surplus as well. Given the angst in the mid-1990s over deficits (which had been a constant feature of federal budgets since the early 1970s, piling up the national debt annually) this was a singular achievement, and one that distinguished Canada from most other OECD countries. Much of this achievement came from a sustained U.S. economic boom in the same period, and in 2006–07 a spike in resource prices. As we argued in the previous chapter, the global financial crisis in 2008 raised the spectre of deficits once again. Governments have been able to spend more—and they have done so with enthusiasm—but at the same time most of them have tried to pay down debt. In addition, new pressures stemming from global and continental competition have induced new configurations and new types of spending instruments. In order to understand this, we need to briefly review the political background to Canadian fiscal policy in the last decade.

Serious fiscal restraint began for the federal government in the mid-1990s with program review that forced policymakers to ask six fundamental questions (see Chapter 2) about each program they administered and to reconsider modes of delivery (i.e., their instruments). Provincial governments went through similar exercises, under different guises, and took somewhat longer to achieve balance. At the federal level, total expenditures in 1992–93 were $161 billion; by 1997 they dropped to $149 billion. Much of that drop was achieved through cuts in transfers to the provinces, particularly in health and social services, with predictable results across the country. Federal spending started to increase again after 1997, stemming from an unbroken string of surpluses.

During the late-1990s period of restraint, the magnitude and unavoidability of the cuts faced by most spending departments in most jurisdictions across Canada demanded a fundamental re-evaluation of lines of business. When funding drops by 20 percent or 30 percent in two years, something has to change, and that change cannot be incremental. Another consequence of this period of restraint was a greater interlinkage in designing policy. In part, this stemmed as well from the growing appreciation of the interconnectedness of policy fields. Sustainable development, for example, can be defined to include health and social stability, in which case almost anything becomes relevant as "environmental policy." And as fiscal concerns permeated policymaking over the past decade, almost everything came under the purview of departments of finance. Added to this were shifts in economic theory that highlighted the importance of human capital for competitiveness in high-technology, information-based industries—encouraging social policy to merge to a large extent with economic policy. Nonetheless, reduced spending capacity helped this new appreciation of linkages and leverage to emerge as well.

In this period of restraint, most government departments had to reassess their priorities, cut some programs, reduce spending on others, and downsize their staff and other resources. They had to focus their programs more tightly, budget carefully, and try to demonstrate results. After almost a decade of continuous surpluses, have these disciplines disappeared under the political pressure to spend, or has something fundamental changed in the way in which governments view the "spending instrument"? Once surpluses appear, of course, the political pressure to spend increases dramatically. The policy advantage governments had during deficit days was that they would quite plausibly argue that they could not afford new programs. Balanced budgets, and particularly surpluses, demolish that riposte and force policymakers once again to make choices about how to respond to new demands. As well, the natural tendency of any elected politician is to respond positively to demands for new programs and expenditures. Despite these pressures, however, it appears that the experience of the past decade has had a profound effect on how the Canadian public and their elected governments view spending.

There now seems to be solid, emerging cross-political orthodoxy against running deficits, if at all possible (Campbell, 1999, p. 141). All federal parties in the 2004, 2006, and 2008 elections promised not to run deficits, and it was only the global financial crisis that opened the door to the newly elected Conservatives in November 2008 to contemplate running a "temporary" deficit. Equally significant, while the newly elected McGuinty government in Ontario brought down a deficit budget in May 2004, it also committed itself to a four-year plan to reach balance—which it achieved, with some pride. Several things appear to have happened over time. First, countering previous economic orthodoxy, deficits did not seem necessary to stimulate the economy. Second, once large surpluses were achieved, they were much more congenial from the point of new spending programs. Third, from a political perspective, actively avoiding deficits became a mark of solid financial management—both Liberals and Conservatives have celebrated the importance of prudent financial management. The pull of this orthodoxy was evident in the federal government's grudging willingness to entertain a deficit in 2009, but not "structural deficits."

Nonetheless, there continues to be an appetite among the Canadian public for focused spending in various areas, particularly in health care, and governments cannot be blind to spending pressures that are associated with changing demographics and a certain minimum maintenance of infrastructure and core services, not to mention economic survival. As we noted earlier, about 70 percent of all provincial government spending is on health, education, and social services, and not surprisingly, these are the top priorities for citizens as well. After the shocks of transfer cuts in the mid-1990s, and facing a constant barrage of criticism from provincial leaders and rising concerns from ordinary Canadians about the quality of health care, the federal government began to respond in various ways. It started to put money back into the system: in 2001 Ottawa established the Commission on the Future of Health Care in Canada (the Romanow Commission), which paved the way for the Health Care Renewal Accord of February 2003 ($34.8 billion over five years). In the June 2004 election, all three national parties pledged to support the Accord and to add even more money. In 2007, federal government spending on health care was up by nearly 5 percent over 2006, in part because of new expenditures for the Patient Wait Time Guarantee Trust (Department of Finance, 2007b: 57).

The issue therefore is not spending per se. Even the allegedly fiscally phobic Conservative Party of Canada has increased spending each year since being elected in 2006, and was resigned to a deficit for 2009. Another interesting indication that spending is viewed more carefully these days is the emphasis on making "investments." Almost all major government spending initiatives are now described as "investments." An investment implies a return of some sort, a benefit or a profit, and so is rhetorically more useful to contemporary policymakers. This emphasis on investments and boutique spending programs marked the government's policies until late 2008, but the spending instrument may come back with a vengeance. Defence and health care were givens for increased spending, but new financial demands to support the ailing automotive industry, and even mining and forestry, put new pressures on government coffers. The 2008 Speech from the Throne clearly indicated a reluctance to engage in long-term or "structural" deficits, but it looked like big spending was back, and indeed some respected economists argued that sustained deficit spending was needed to save the Canadian and global economies from collapse.

There is likely to be continued pressure on the spending instrument, though it will be used cautiously and somewhat reluctantly. There has been another important change in public attitudes and public policy discourse, however, which might upset this equation—the popularity of tax cuts. It should be remembered that a good part of the success in erasing deficits and achieving balanced budgets in the late 1990s was through increased tax rates and increased tax revenues. Alberta led the way in first reducing taxes after it had achieved balanced budgets, and then in 2001 moving to a flat tax rate of 11 percent on taxable income and substantially increased personal exemptions. Tax cuts were a major feature of federal budgets between 2000 and 2003, and again all three national parties offered some degree of tax relief in the June 2004 election (the Liberals with only minor reductions for seniors and those with disabilities; the Tories with major personal and corporate cuts; the NDP with increased taxes on the wealthy combined with reductions for middle- and lower-income groups). It is clear however that tax-cutting as an economic strategy is more comfortable for the right, whereas the left will emphasize "fairness" in taxation with targeted and relatively minor reductions. The federal Conservatives carried on in 2006 and 2007 with successive cuts to the GST, and major cuts to income taxes (the government's 2007 Economic Statement proudly proclaimed $60 billion in cuts over six years to individuals, families, and businesses).

The pressure for tax reductions may not disappear entirely, at least as an instrument for economic stimulus, but given demands for higher spending, the scope for reductions is likely to be smaller. To this might be added a strong sense that government grants and contributions are often badly managed, and that money is wasted in hundreds of small and large ways in Ottawa and provincial capitals. This perception stemmed in large part from the HRDC and sponsorship scandals discussed earlier, but occasional stories like the one in Box 4.3 serve to sharpen public skepticism, and officials and policymakers will have to show how their spending programs and management of public money are beneficial, efficacious, and prudent. This shift in public mood was the foundation for the Federal Accountability Act, as well as the new policy on grants and contributions announced in 2008.

BOX 4.3 THE PRIVACY COMMISSIONER'S TRAVEL EXPENSES

Below are excerpts from the Auditor General's 2003 report on the travel and hospitality expenses of former Privacy Commissioner Radwanski. In part it contributed to the introduction of "proactive disclosure" policies publicly stating on departmental web sites what senior officials have spent recently on hospitality and travel expenses.

126. The former Commissioner and the Senior Director General flew business class wherever possible, even on short domestic flights. Both almost always stayed at expensive hotels and ate at costly restaurants.

127. Hotel costs of the former Commissioner and his Senior Director General usually exceeded the published guideline rates allowed to government employees. Our audit determined that in about 80 percent of their domestic travel, they exceeded the

BOX 4.3 (continued)

Treasury Board guidelines for accommodations by 70 percent on average. In 60 percent of their international travel they also exceeded Treasury Board accommodation guidelines, and by 50 percent on average. On three nights in London, England, for example, the former Commissioner and the Senior Director General each spent more than $500 per night on hotel accommodations. None of their travel claims included documentation to justify exceeding the guideline limits, even though Treasury Board policies require such justification.

128. We also found that two hotel rooms at $330 each per night had been booked in Washington, DC for two nights. Although the hotel rooms had been paid for, they were not used on the first night; on the second day they were used, according to the former Commissioner, only as a place to "freshen up" and make telephone calls after a two-hour flight.

129. The cost of meals claimed during travel usually exceeded Treasury Board guidelines. Our review of domestic and international travel found that spending on meals exceeded the guidelines over 60 percent of the time. Examples of unreasonable meal expenditures include over $300 in London on lunch for two and over $100 in Hawaii and $100 in London on breakfast for two. On three occasions, in Hawaii, Brussels, and London, the former Commissioner and the Senior Director General spent over $550 per day on meals for two.

130. Travel meal expenditures are not to include alcohol. We calculated that during all the international trips of the former Commissioner, over $31,000 was paid for meals and refreshments. Taking into account that Treasury Board meal allowances for international travel vary by city to reflect the cost of living, we estimated that government employees with similar itineraries would have been entitled to claim about $14,000. Using his "discretion," therefore, the former Commissioner incurred about $17,000 more than that for meals and refreshments abroad—more than twice the amount set out in the guidelines. . . . In our opinion, this was an abuse of the discretion accorded to a deputy head.

SOURCE: *Report of the Auditor General of Canada – September 2003*, Office of the Auditor General of Canada. Reproduced with the permission of the Minister of Public Works and Government Services, 2008.

The government established a Blue Ribbon Panel on Grants and Contributions in June 2006. Its report, entitled *From Red Tape to Clear Results*, was released in February 2007 (Blue Ribbon Panel, 2006), and became the catalyst for a three-year government Action Plan to reform the administration of grants and contributions. The Panel noted that the federal government annually spends over $27 billion on more than 800 grant and contribution programs, spread over 50 departments and agencies. Its report was intended to suggest changes that would make those programs more efficient and effective, while at the same time ensuring accountability. To that end, its recommendations were geared to making the programs more responsive to clients, clarifying objectives, providing better service, and simplifying—without compromising—reporting, accountability, and audit functions. The government received the report enthusiastically, and launched an Action Plan in 2008 to implement the Panel's recommendations over a three-year period (Treasury Board of Canada Secretariat, 2008). The first part of the plan was the development of a new Policy on Transfer Payments, to go into effect on October 1, 2008. The next steps included the development of a new service policy for the departmental administration of grants and contributions, and the designation of six "vanguard" departments to develop business plans (Canadian Heritage, Canadian International Development Agency, Economic Development Agency of Canada for the Regions of Quebec, Health Canada, Human Resources and Social Development Canada/Service Canada, Indian Affairs and Northern Development). Their common areas of focus were: "simplification of funding programs and agreements; streamlining, standardization, and harmonizing of the application process; introduction of flexible risk management practices; establishment of service standards; identification and implementation of best practices; improved access to information via technology; and enhancement of stakeholder engagement" (ibid.)

TAXATION

Canadian governments tackled their deficits in the 1990s by cutting some expenditures, but they also benefited from increased tax revenues. As Purchase and Hirshhorn (1994) show, total tax revenues in Canada "increased from 31.3 percent in 1983 to 37 percent in 1992" (p. 36). Moreover, while corporate taxes actually declined in this period, "taxes on individuals have increased sharply" (p. 37). Federal government revenues were $116 billion in 1993–94; in 2000–01 they were $162 billion; and in 2002–03 they were $177 billion. In 2007–08, they were projected to total $245.5 billion, up 4 percent from 2006–07, and up 10.5 percent from 2005–06 (Department of Finance, 2008: 199–202). While most Canadians welcomed the eradication of government deficits in the 1990s, they were not entirely pleased with the high taxes they had to pay to achieve it. Taxes did begin to decline from that period, but even in 2007 the federal government admitted that: "Personal and corporate income taxes as a percentage of GDP are higher in Canada than in all other G7 countries" (Department of Finance, 2007a: 19). As we noted above, all three major national parties favour tax reductions of some sort, with the key difference being their magnitude and incidence, and the Conservative government has moved aggressively to cut both corporate and personal income taxes, not to mention the GST, a signature slash.

A countertrend to reduced income taxes is an increase in user charges and service fees. The deepest reasons for this are also the murkiest, and perhaps the most controversial: as citizens become more resistant to redistributive government, they become more resistant to redistributive (i.e., general) taxation. Fees and charges seem to link services more directly to beneficiaries. Through user charges and service fees, special benefits enjoyed by only a minority of citizens are paid for in whole or in part by that minority. In the 1990s, studies showed that user fees accounted for as much as 17 percent of Ontario's government revenues and that reliance on them, by at least Ontario municipal governments, was increasing (Sproule-Jones, 1994, p. 7). A June 2000 report of the federal Standing Committee on Finance noted that while user charges contributed a negligible amount to Ottawa's revenues (about 2.4 percent), there were some 391 of them spread over 47 departments and agencies (Standing Committee on Finance, 2000). The government had encouraged departments to rely more on user charges and cost recovery in its 1997 Cost Recovery and Charging Policy, which was changed to the External Charging Policy in 2003. In 2003 there were "400 external charging programs in 47 departments and agencies resulting in thousands of different fees" (Treasury Board of Canada, 2003). In 2005–06, federal government revenue from user charges was $1.9 billion, spread out across 51 departments (Treasury Board of Canada, 2007).

The latest taxation twist has been **carbon taxes**, linked to new and more aggressive action to counter climate change caused by greenhouse gas emissions. As we noted earlier, a tax—used as a policy instrument and not simply to raise revenue—is a device to make targeted behaviours more expensive and hence less attractive. In this broad sense, a tax (as a charge that is a disincentive) can be levied on almost anything, assuming that it cannot be easily evaded. Carbon taxes have an additional quality in that they are designed to both expose and levy the costs of externalities on those who produce them. A company that pollutes the air or water does not usually have to take into account the cost of this external effect on others when it prices its products. In February 2008, British Columbia was the first North American jurisdiction to levy a full (i.e., not focused on one type of emission) revenue neutral carbon tax, following Quebec with its 2007 tax on hydrocarbons. The federal Liberals followed in June 2008 with a new environmental plan entitled "Green Shift," the centrepiece of which was an ambitious, national carbon tax in the amount of over $15 billion over four years, to be completely offset by reductions in personal and corporate taxes. The idea is not new: Finland has had a carbon tax since 1990, Sweden since 1991, the UK since 2001, and New Zealand since 2005 (Carbon Tax Center, 2008). It is the carbon in fossil fuels that contributes to climate change, and proportions of carbon in different fuels are known quite precisely (e.g., coal emits more carbon than natural gas). This is the platform for taxing emissions or developing other measures such as **cap and trade**.

The British Columbia carbon tax was a trendsetter in several respects (British Columbia, 2008). The tax hit all fossil fuels, initially at a rate of $10 per tonne of greenhouse gas emissions, tripling by 2012. The tax was to be revenue neutral, meaning that whatever was raised would be returned to taxpayers. This is an important point, since a carbon tax is regressive—it hits low-income consumers of gas, oil, and electricity the hardest. The British Columbia budget introduced a low-income Climate Action Tax Credit of $100 per adult and $30 per child (paid quarterly), and promised to reduce both personal and corporate income taxes. On top of this, it introduced a Climate Action Dividend of $100 in June 2008 for each provincial resident to offset the life-style changes that they were being asked to make. The government projected revenues from the carbon tax of $1.85 billion over three years, all of which it said would be returned to taxpayers through off-setting tax reductions and credits.

The pressure to deal with climate change through some form of taxation or regulation has been building steadily. In January 2008 the National Roundtable on the Environment and the Economy concluded that Canada could substantially reduce its carbon emissions by 2050 through either carbon taxes or a cap and trade scheme (National Round Table on the Environment and the Economy, 2008). The federal Standing Committee on Finance recommended in 2008 that the federal government develop tax incentives to encourage truck owners and operators to reduce their greenhouse gas emissions (Standing Committee on Finance, 2008). The federal government's response in March 2008 to these pressures, and to the British Columbia example, was to regulate rather than tax. Its *Turning the Corner* strategy (first announced in 2007) on greenhouse gas emissions had regulated caps for industry that it claimed would result in a 20 percent overall reduction by 2020. The tar sands were specifically targeted with requirements that all new plants starting after 2012 would have to use carbon capture and storage (beneath the ground) technologies. New regulations would apply to sixteen sectors, "including oil sands, oil and gas, power plants, refineries, chemical and fertilizer plants, pipelines, cement, metals, smelters, and pulp and paper" (Government of Canada,

2008). The government also proposed a one-time carbon credit for firms that had taken past actions to reduce emissions, as well as the establishment of a carbon trading market (see Regulation, below).

REGULATION

Just as the character of expenditures and taxes as policy instruments has changed, so has regulation. The pressures on regulatory instruments have been somewhat contradictory. Initially, as part of downsizing government in the 1990s and related to cuts in spending, there was also a movement to deregulate on the grounds that excessive regulation did as much harm to the economy as deficits did, if not more. The OECD noted, for example, a strong trend among its members to "reforming and reviewing" regulation (OECD, 2007). Regulatory instruments rely on the use of authority, and to the extent that government lost some legitimacy in the late 1990s, so it lost its authority, and with that came an increasing distaste for government "red tape." As well, in the same period, both international agreements and economic and technological forces constrained the use of regulatory instruments in many traditional areas such as telecommunications and broadcasting, utilities, foreign investment, and marketing boards. On the other hand, especially after 9/11, SARS, the collapse of Enron and WorldCom, and debates about the safety of GSM foods, the public appetite for re-regulation began to grow. Public discourse shifted to recognizing the need for regulations in a complex, risk-saturated modern world, and even recognizing that effective regulatory systems (since every country has to have regulations of some sort in the same broad areas of economy, health, and safety) can be a competitive advantage. We will try to make sense of these contradictory pressures by addressing constraints on regulation, demands for regulation, and shifts in regulatory venues.

The constraints on the use of regulatory instruments come principally from four sources: international trade agreements, technology, economics, and cost. A large subset of economic regulatory instruments has been devoted in one fashion or another to the protection of domestic industries from excessive internal or foreign competition. Classic examples include regulations that prevented foreign banks from operating in Canada, regulations that gave domestic Canadian oil companies advantages over foreign-owned competitors, foreign investment guidelines, broadcasting rules that protected Canadian advertisers and cable companies, and agricultural marketing boards for everything from milk to potatoes. The 1989 Free Trade Agreement, and its successor, the North American Free Trade Agreement (NAFTA), with Canada, the United States, and Mexico, expressly forbids some forms of regulation that would advantage domestic industries over competitors from the partner countries. Agricultural marketing boards, for example, are facing intense pressures under the NAFTA provisions on agriculture and food products. While environmental, health, and cultural regulations are in principle shielded from NAFTA, the larger free-trade logic of the agreement increasingly puts these provisions under pressure. The World Trade Organization (WTO), the successor to the GATT, was explicitly designed to establish clearer and more efficient institutional mechanisms to deal with a wider variety of trade issues (e.g., services, farming, and manufactured goods), and has a major focus on technical barriers to trade (regulations).

> The Technical Barriers to Trade Agreement (TBT) tries to ensure that regulations, standards, testing and certification procedures do not create unnecessary obstacles. However, the agreement also recognizes countries' rights to adopt the standards they consider appropriate—for example, for human, animal or plant life or health, for the protection of the environment or to meet other consumer interests. Moreover, members are not prevented from taking measures necessary to ensure their standards are met. But that is counterbalanced with disciplines. A myriad of regulations can be a nightmare for manufacturers and exporters. Life can be simpler if governments apply international standards, and the agreement encourages them to do so. In any case, whatever regulations they use should not discriminate. The agreement also sets out a code of good practice for both governments and non-governmental or industry bodies to prepare, adopt, and apply voluntary standards. Over 200 standards-setting bodies apply the code. The agreement says the procedures used to decide whether a product conforms with relevant standards have to be fair and equitable. It discourages any methods that would give domestically produced goods an unfair advantage. The agreement also encourages countries to recognize each other's procedures for assessing whether a product conforms. Without recognition, products might have to be tested twice, first by the exporting country and then by the importing country (World Trade Organization, 2008).

As we note below, however, internationalization has also provided a fresh context for "**re-regulation**" that brings domestic policy targets into a wider, international regime. This can actually strengthen domestic regulation, not constrain it. A decade ago, Doern and colleagues pointed out that in fact there has been an increase in some business framework and environmental regulation, and that in contrast to the conventional view that the previous two decades have been primarily an era of deregulation, "it is evident that, overall, the density and extent of rule making by, or on behalf of, the state has increased" (Doern et al., 1999a, p. 5). This is in part due to pressures in health and safety regulation, often driven by technology. Food products, clean air standards, water quality, and the impact of biotechnology across a host of areas drive a demand for more, not less, regulation. Another important change to regulation as a governing instrument and as part of policy design has been the internationalization of regulatory regimes. If we think of regulation in its broadest sense—rules and standards about conduct, backed by sanctions of some sort—then many of our domestic regulatory regimes are becoming linked with international ones. This reflects one side of the process of globalization discussed in Chapter 2. As the forces and factors important to policy shift to the international level, governments increasingly have to cooperate at that level in order to continue to have some influence on their domestic practices: "Not only are fundamental trade rules crossing borders and affecting practices in various 'domestic' regulatory realms, but newer 'crosswalks' institutions are being negotiated between heretofore separate international realms, such as competition, the environment, intellectual property, and investment" (Doern et al., 1999a, p. 21).

These organizational constraints on regulatory instruments mirror the constraints that some of these instruments face as a result of technological and economic changes. The key to conventional regulatory instruments is the government's ability to first forbid some activity or outcome and then permit it under certain conditions. This assumes that the activity or outcome in question can indeed be controlled and monitored. When regulatory authorities can be bypassed, then the regime collapses or becomes irrelevant. Substantial changes in technology and competitive markets were the foundation for the massive deregulation movement in trucking, airlines, and energy in the 1980s (Schultz, 1994). Before the advent of satellite dishes, for example, what Canadians watched on TV could be controlled by the regulator. It was less clear what the CRTC could do about what Canadians watched in a 500-channel TV universe where most of those channels are being broadcast by entities beyond the CRTC's control. This explained the CRTC's initially cautious approach to new, Internet-based media (CRTC, 1999). As noted above, in the last decade the lines between the Internet and broadcasting have become increasingly blurred, and so the CRTC in 2007 launched its New Media Project "to examine the cultural, economic, and technological issues associated with new media broadcasting and what actions, if any, the CRTC should take to ensure that the Canadian new media broadcasting environment meets the objectives of the Broadcasting Act" (CRTC, 2008). This was followed in May 2008 with a public notice for comments on the scope of future regulatory activity in this field.

These forces help us understand the constraints and limits on regulatory instruments, forces that lie behind much of what has been labelled "deregulation" in the past decade. However, there are countervailing pressures that make regulatory instruments attractive, and that in fact mean that what has been going on is better described as "re-regulation" in some areas and even an intensification of the state's regulatory role in others. Ironically, the argument that government should be reduced and restructured can work to the advantage of regulatory instruments. The downsizing comes principally in expenditures and direct service provision, leaving a stronger role for governments in the establishment of framework legislation or regulation: "Deregulation in Canada has resulted in a more focused and likely more robust regulatory role by government. Case studies of deregulation in various sectors show that major deregulatory actions have been accompanied by refinements and creations of new regulatory instruments" (Doern et al., 1999b, 394). Governments, so the argument runs, should steer not row, and this draws them toward regulatory instruments that focus more on frameworks and outcomes than minute rules. As well, some areas of regulation remain quite popular with the public, whatever the apparent rising antipathy to government as a whole. Mad Cow and SARS were simply the most visible instances where people expected governments to act forcefully, but there have also been scares of potable water and genetically modified foods. Indeed, even as major areas of economic regulation were being cut back in the 1980s, social regulations were, in some cases, actually increasing. Human rights legislation, regulations against discrimination, and efforts to control violence and pornography have enjoyed continuing support. Moreover, the forms of regulation may adapt. Prince (1999) reminds us of the importance of what he calls civic regulation: rule-making "with respect to numerous social aspects of human behaviour and needs, moral conduct and standards, intergovernmental relations, and human rights and civil liberties" (p. 204). He agrees that this arena of state regulation is probably expanding due to pressures for "intervention and protection from citizens, interest groups, social movements, and governments" (p. 221). Certainly, the shift to postmaterial values and rights discourse discussed in Chapter 2 is part of the reason for this, along with an increasing insistence by more "business-minded" governments on standards of conduct by recipients of social assistance and other forms of public aid.

The trends in regulation are therefore complicated. First, it is undeniable that there has been a combination of pressures in the last two decades to re-examine the effects and the management of economic regulations. This has been driven in part by technological changes (e.g., in communications and in financial services) and partly by deliberate decisions to deregulate taken by conservative governments around the world. The Canadian variant was several reviews of regulation undertaken in the 1970s, which eventually yielded the Regulatory Impact Assessment

Statement regime of the mid-1980s (Mihlar, 1999) and the Government of Canada Regulatory Policy (1999), which has since been replaced by the Cabinet Directive on Streamlining Regulation (Government of Canada, 2007). Second, while some regulatory agencies and their oversight have been weakened, for instance in transportation, resources, and utilities, they have also become in some instances more focused and strategic. Third, new areas of civic and environmental and even economic regulation have arisen that are being managed by all three levels of government, sometimes alone but often in concert. As we noted above, the federal government's response to climate change was deliberately regulatory, and not based on carbon taxes. The regulatory regime for carbon trading will be one of the most complex ever attempted in Canada:

> To be eligible to generate offset credits, projects must be within the scope of the Offset System, and must achieve real, incremental, quantified, verified and unique reductions of greenhouse gases.

> The credit creation process is as follows:

> - A Protocol Developer creates a quantification protocol for the project type and Environment Canada approves the protocol
> - A Project Proponent applies to have their project registered
> - Environment Canada registers the project
> - A Project Proponent reports the greenhouse gas reductions achieved from a registered project and ensures that a verifier has provided a reasonable level of assurance on the reductions claim
> - Environment Canada certifies the reductions and issues offset credits.

> Each offset credit will represent one tonne of carbon dioxide equivalent. Offset credits will be tradable and bankable within the unit tracking system. The proposed industrial air emissions regulations will set out the conditions under which regulated entities will be able to use offset credits for compliance. (Environment Canada, 2008)

Fourth, domestic regulation is increasingly affected by international factors, institutions, and decisions, and in many cases "bridges" between domestic and international regulatory agencies are being constructed in order to facilitate harmonization of standards. This is true of the climate change, for example, where standards are being harmonized around post-Kyoto agreements. Fifth, the rhythms of regulation and deregulation vary considerably by country. The United States—which often seems to set the tone in policy discussions—has accepted deregulation and minimal state intrusion as a matter of rhetorical faith, whereas Canada and many European countries have been considerably more cautious (Peters, 1998; Wilks and Doern, 1998). However, for Canada, pressure has been increasing since 9/11 to "merge, collapse, or rationalize levels of regulation" with the United States (Doern and Johnson, 2006: 5).

A perfect illustration of these developments can be seen in the federal government's attempt to rethink regulation in the early 2000s. It established the External Advisory Committee on Smart Regulation in 2003, and asked it to develop a regulatory strategy for the twenty-first century, based on a sense that the context for regulation was increasingly challenging: "the speed of modern society has resulted in an explosion of new technologies, the rapid flow of commerce and instant access to information. Businesses are continually innovating to meet changing consumer needs, cut production costs and increase their market shares. In a knowledge-based economy, regulatory regimes have to adapt quickly to sustain effective protection and keep pace with innovation and entrepreneurship" (External Advisory Committee on Smart Regulation, 2004).

The concept of "smart regulation" has several components. Possibly the most important driver is a sense of rising competitive pressures, particularly international ones, a more rapid cycle of innovation and technological development, coupled with public concerns about health, safety, and consumer choice. The basic saw-off is between providing companies with light, flexible, and responsive regulatory regimes that allow them to bring products to market quickly and capitalize on a clear, consistent, but not overbearing regulatory system, and making sure that that regulatory system continues to protect consumers while not patronizing them. This balance can be seen clearly in the area of consumer protection where

> there has been a significant supply-side focus to many of the federal reforms, undertaken in the past decade or more, that affect the consumer interest. These reforms were designed to remove constraints that prevented or impeded markets from providing industrial customers and final consumers with a wide range of goods and services at competitive prices. Examples of these supply-side levers include trade liberalization, reforms of competition policy and other marketplace laws, regulatory reforms to establish more competitive markets in previously highly regulated sectors, privatization of some major federal crown corporations, and the innovation, productivity and competitiveness agendas of past Liberal governments. (Ireland and Webb, 2007: 275)

New Emphases: Information, Partnerships, Internationalism, and Institutional Design

The mark of the inventive policy designer is the ability to come up with new ways of doing things, and there have been some fresh techniques or devices both discussed and implemented in some countries in recent years (e.g., tradable pollution permits). This section will focus, however, on four categories of policy instruments and how emphasis has shifted to make them comparatively more important than ever before.

As we noted above, information is typically considered to be a weak and relatively unobtrusive instrument in the government toolkit. We also noted, however, somewhat less benign uses of information through "regulation by shaming" and the robust use of advertising, exhortation, and public awareness campaigns. In fact, information as a technique in delivering policy outcomes may be gaining importance for at least four reasons. The first is that spending, regulatory, and taxation instruments have been constrained in the new governance environment. By comparison, information is often less expensive as an instrument and gives the impression of being less invasive.

The second reason is somewhat more complex, but reflects the new approaches to public management discussed in Chapter 2, and which we will take up again in Chapter 5 in greater detail. Two major emphases in this new thinking are **"citizen engagement"** and better accountability mechanisms from government to the public. While these are clearly related, the first refers to bringing citizens and groups into the decision-making process, while the second refers more to techniques of providing **transparency** in public decisionmaking. The Federal Accountability Act has several provisions for transparency and reporting, such as proactive disclosure, whistleblowing legislation, and greater powers for public watchdogs. As we will note in Chapter 5, the emphasis in recent years on performance measurement and results is also part of a new emphasis on stronger accountability regimes. It is now widely assumed that engagement, transparency, and accountability may in themselves become factors in policy development. In short, if governments promise to do certain things, and their promises and their performance are a matter of public record, sooner or later that information will be used to hold them accountable. The Social Union Framework Agreement (SUFA) for example, was signed by Ottawa and nine provinces and the territories in 1999 (Quebec did not sign) to provide a new framework for the development of social policy in Canada. As Prince notes: "The SUFA is an interesting mixture of policy-tool characteristics. An administrative agreement among first ministers, the accord is an exercise in exhortation and symbolism. . . . It contains a series of . . . public pledges by government leaders that have no legal status . . . " (Prince, 2005: 296).

The third reason that information is becoming a more important resource and instrument for governments is due to the explosion of information and communications technologies (ICTs). ICTs are important drivers changing the way that citizens and consumers get goods and services from government and the private sector. Every level of government across the country is experimenting with ways of using information in new ways to manage program delivery and handle policy problems. It is simply a given now that information technology is a major economic driver, and that knowledge and innovation are the key comparative advantages now for firms as well as national economies. The federal government's vision of "e-government" or "government on-line" is also emblematic of a focus on information as a main conduit of interaction between governments and citizens. The federal government, for example, launched its Government On-line initiative in 1999, with the objective of converting 130 of its most widely used services to an electronic platform, where they could be accessed 24/7 by all Canadians, anywhere in the country or the world (Government of Canada, 2006). The project was declared a success in 2006 and was ended. The project had been such a success that the Canadian government was ranked first internationally for its electronic service delivery five years in a row by Accenture in its global survey (Brown, 2007). Thirty-four departments and agencies were involved in the project. Many of these services were simply informational, but many also were "transactional" in the sense that there would be two-way communication between clients and government, and interactive access to services on-line that would previously only have been available at a government office. The Canadian Revenue Agency, for example, provides "the following on-line services to its business clients: filing a return; registering a business; getting information on corporations, sole proprietors and partnerships, e-commerce, GST/HST Netfile; keeping records; making requests; payroll services; making an electronic payment; downloading or ordering forms and publications." As we will discuss in more detail in Chapter 5, e-government or government on-line is more than just about the delivery of services, it has broader implications for public management and public policy as a whole. "E-government has had a significant impact on public administration, changing the environment in which the public service operates, adding new concepts and methods to its operations and changing the relative weight and relationships among established elements of public administration" (Brown, 2005: 247). This is a case of information as a policy instrument both being used by government, but also fundamentally changing the practice and organization of government.

Information has become more important for a fourth reason as well. As governments have become more active in the realm of civic regulation such as antidiscrimination, they inevitably get into the persuasion game, since the policy problems here are primarily attitudinal (Hood and Margetts, 2007).

Policy concerns about health and lifestyle in this period also contributed to the importance of changing hearts and minds on key issues such as exercise and eating habits. Contemporary concerns about violence, stereotyping, and abuse ensure that policy instruments that both convey information and try to exhort certain behaviours will remain important. In addition, however, governments increasingly find themselves working with partners for the delivery of programs, as will be explained in Chapter 5. This interdependency depends on the exchange of information and the building up of relationships. The more that government finds itself operating in networks, relying on partners, and enhancing and facilitating the capacities of societal actors to do things, the more its primary role is to provide critical information, help circulate it, and encourage policy learning. This can go beyond simple distribution of information to calling attention to new policy problems—providing leadership, in short.

A new emphasis on partnerships is another development in policy targets and hence policy instruments. Partnerships will be discussed in greater detail in Chapters 5 and 6, but the basic logic is that government can either get out of some of the things that it has traditionally done and leave them to the private or nonprofit sectors, or it can continue to do those things in partnerships with those sectors. An example is care for the elderly, which is provided primarily by for-profit and non-profit organizations that receive the bulk of their funding from provincial governments. The first mode suggests an oversight capacity for government once the service has been devolved. The second implies a direct partnership with a community association, industry group, or NGO. If partnerships are conceived of as a policy instrument, then they will not simply appear; they have to be created. This requires some skill, as well as a grasp of the different types of partnering that can be undertaken (e.g., one of consultation versus a roundtable format or working together to implement programs).

The third new emphasis in policy is the international system itself. The traditional organization of the foreign policy dossier called for a single foreign affairs department that would channel issues from domestic departments into the international system. With the internationalization of so many policy fields, and with the substantive policy expertise in fact lodged in "domestic" departments, more and more of these departments are engaged in international negotiations. The Department of Foreign Affairs and International Trade tries to coordinate this at the national level, but the sheer scope of international representations by every government body, from local municipalities to federal departments, makes it a difficult task. Yet, international agreements and international negotiations are becoming a routine instrument in the pursuit of domestic policy. Moreover, it is not simply a matter of single policy fields being projected upward to the international level but linkages across policy fields being developed by international agencies and communities of practice (Slaughter, 2004).

A final, unconventional category that seems to be attracting increasing attention is procedural (Howlett, 2000) or institutional instruments (Kirschen, 1964). Governments "increasingly come to rely on the use of a different set of 'procedural' tools designed to indirectly affect outcomes through the manipulation of policy processes" (Howlett, 2000, p. 413). Many of these instruments are aimed less at delivery of policy and programs than at the restructuring of relationships either within the state or between the state and social partners. Webb offers a vision of what he calls "sustainable governance" that highlights not only the institutional dimension of policy instruments, but the combination of institutions and actors and instruments that are active within a given policy field: ". . . sustainable governance involves a combination of governmental and nongovernmental institutions, processes, instruments, and actors, it entails more than simply a question of instrument choice. . . . Sustainable governance is a concept that attempts to recognize and draw on the largely untapped potential of the private sector, the third (voluntary) sector, and individual citizens to assist in governing in the public interest" (Webb, 2005: 243).

Another way to see this category of instruments is as focusing on organization or network-type targets. Organizational instruments take the state itself—its structure and management—as a target of public policy. As Osborne and Gaebler (1993) famously argued, there is a continuing role for government but not in its bureaucratic guise. It is necessary to restructure government so that incentives to perform efficiently and well are clear and pervasive. **Performance indicators** and pay linked to performance help do that. Other mechanisms are designed to introduce market forces into the provision of public services, from contracting out to full privatization.

Network targets are primarily groups and individuals in civil society, outside the state. The role of government is to facilitate and empower rather than to deliver and direct. Adjustment programs, capacity building, the dissemination of information, participation and partnerships, rights enforcement, funding interest groups, and developing stakeholder networks—all of these make sense only if organizations and individuals are granted high levels of autonomy and legitimacy as policy actors in their own right, not merely as recipients of government programs. As McDonnell and Elmore (1987) argue, policy instruments in this category have the character of "inducements" rather than mandates and hinge on "how much variation policymakers are willing to tolerate in the production of things of value" (p. 15). If individuals, organizations, and communities are to have choice and autonomy, then the tolerance for variation has to increase substantially. Framework policy, decentralization, and information policy instruments clearly presume that policy outcomes will depend on a degree of "co-production" with other actors. Of course, "**co-production**" also means a greater degree of mutual interdependence—governments cannot control all processes and outcomes. Therefore, this approach also requires a greater tolerance for potential failure and the possibility that partners will both make mistakes and have to learn from them. It puts the policy designer less in the position of being an "engineer" than an "animateur," relying primarily on process values and politics (Linder and Peters, 1995). We will return to these types of instruments in the next chapter.

Conclusion

We should address two questions in closing this chapter. First, is there a uniform tilt to the new toolbox of policy instruments? Second, what does the evolution of the toolbox tell us about modern governance?

Readers will have noticed that there does appear to be a tilt to the way in which instruments and policy design have been going. At one time we might have said the tilt was towards smaller and leaner and less intrusive government. Now, the reality is probably something closer to prudential caution, sobriety about the influence of government, coupled with strong and even expansionist actions in certain sectors with retreats in others. Until recently, deficit pressures and citizen disaffection caused governments to be cautious (within the political calculus of re-election). New pressures on spending and pump-priming now seem insurmountable. The rhetoric of cutting back on government reached a high point in the early 2000s, but after 9/11 and other social and political challenges, it became more muted. For reasons that we explored in Chapter 1, the importance of governance for economic performance and social stability has had a renewed appreciation—the subprime and financial sector crisis in fall 2008, for example, led to nationalizations of mortgage lending institutions and banks in the US and UK, along with massive financial bailouts in other countries (including Canada) to keep the financial system solvent. We would argue that legacies remain from the NPM era, but that they have been overlaid by a new willingness to use government policy instruments, as long as they are used prudently and as much as possible in alignment with market forces.

Other factors lie behind this complicated shift in governance. First, as we noted in Chapter 2, postmaterialist values are not uniformly pro-market, for example, when it comes to the environment. Second, there is substantial angst about some major social policy questions such as youth crime, violent pornography, decaying family structures, racism, school behaviour, and educational performance, not to mention a host of health and safety concerns. It is far from clear that governments or citizens in these areas are prepared to accept the old nostrums of minimal government and market mechanisms. Third, the same market forces that drive globalization and competitiveness generate anxieties about jobs, communities, and lifestyle. Some more extreme scenarios draw a grim portrait of highly polarized societies, with a small elite of global citizens jetting off to their next conference or business meeting while the majority drifts in a world of intermittent employment, corroded infrastructure, and the commercialization of virtually every aspect of life. Finally, it is important not to overestimate the ease with which global pressures penetrate national social, economic, and political systems. The institutional configuration of these systems can make it more or less easy for global pressures to be channelled through to governments (Neville, 2002). For example, despite globalization and two free trade agreements with the United States, Canadian and American health and social policy systems remain very different.

The policy literature is coming to recognize this, principally by urging the importance of values in public policy. Though this is a larger issue than instrument choice, the discussion in this chapter has shown that the tilt of the toolbox is to maximize individual choice and more careful, if possibly more extreme, government intervention than anything seen in the recent past. But public policy is not purely instrumental; it sends signals to citizens about who they are and how they should behave. For better or worse, it gives them a picture of appropriate social and political relations. Policy implementation that depends increasingly on market mechanisms and individual choice will encourage citizens to see their relations to government and to each other as primarily ones of exchange—a set of quasi-economic transactions for individual benefit. As Aaron, Mann, and Taylor (1994) point out: "In the jargon of the social scientists, analysts have begun to recognize that values and norms are not 'exogenous,' or independent of public policy. And the idea that values can change, combined with the recognition that responses to policies depend on people's preferences—that is, their values—leads to thinking about how public policy might change values directly or indirectly and thereby change the responses of public policies themselves" (p. 3). Their point is twofold: (1) effective public policies depend on a certain temperament of cooperation and support from citizens, and to neglect the nurturing of that temperament would be a huge mistake, and (2) governments have a legitimate, though carefully balanced, role in supporting and developing some key social values, such as trust, community, and empathy. This can extend to policy designs that might have an element of paternalism to them. For example, most people discount the future in relation to the present, and most people weigh current losses more heavily than future benefits. These are among the reasons why many people, absent any external mechanisms, find it hard to quit smoking or drinking, stick to diets, save for their retirement, and invest in their education. There is a case to be made the government has a (paternalistic) role in combating these tendencies through health information campaigns and regulatory regimes or public pension systems that force people to save (Thaler and Sunstein, 2003; 2008).

These are ultimately questions of policy design for democracy, an issue that the literature on policy instruments often avoids and that practising policymakers usually sidestep. But it is worth asking these questions. What effect will downsized government have on citizenship? How far should we go in encouraging individual self-reliance before eroding common bonds and a public space? Marc Landy (1993), for example, defines citizenship as "a station that lies between self-absorption and absorption with abstractions. . . . It involves an ongoing effort to synthesize questions of 'what is best for the world' with 'what is best for me'" (p. 20). This is a vision that stresses duty, responsibility, and democratic deliberation. March and Olsen (1995) define the civic temperament this way: "democratic civility achieves its primary claims by stimulating empathetic feelings in citizens, attitudes that allow for sympathetic consideration of the plights and possibilities of others, capacities for feeling sorrow and joy in concert with others. Civility in conflict is encouraged by encounters of understanding, generosity, and restraint" (p. 61). Schneider and Ingram (1997) are concerned about "degenerative policy designs" that, in their view, "send different messages to different target populations, but these messages encourage most of the target groups to take only their own interests into account in their expectations of government thereby leading to irresponsible citizenship and the demise of community" (p. 197).

These phrases sound soft when compared to the tough talk usually associated with developing economic competitiveness. That tough talk has served in the past to justify smaller government. Some recent economic thinking about what truly makes economies competitive, however, suggests that these softer policy targets may be vitally important. Work on **social capital**, for example, seeks to explain both efficient government and competitive economies in terms of social bonds of association and trust. The phenomenal success of Robert Putnam's *Making Democracy Work* (1993) and *Bowling Alone* (2000) suggests that concerns about social capital cut across ideological lines. Francis Fukuyama (1995) has argued that economic performance depends on social capital and is a function of trust, which he defines as the "expectation that arises within a community of regular, honest, and cooperative behaviour, based on commonly shared norms, on the part of other members of that community" (p. 26). Both economic and political "performance" can be seen as forms of "collective action" problems, where what is rational from a collective point of view (say, a clean environment) runs up against incentives for individuals to free-ride and maximize their self-interest (say, the profits that can be made when all your competitors install antipollution equipment but you do not). If people cooperate, they are all better off. Community and social cohesion have become watchwords for government policy throughout North America.

The above should help provide the answer to our second question about what the toolkit tells us about modern governance. As has been mentioned many times in this book, modern governments have had their hands tied by fiscal pressures, internationalization, and shifts in ideology that demand less intervention. There seems to be limited tolerance for deficit spending, and there is pressure to at least hold the line on taxes, if not reduce them. Internationalization means that the domestic economy is much more exposed to global competition, and investors sit ready to judge government policy by pulling out of currency and bond markets if they see something they dislike.

This is not the whole story, however. As we noted earlier in this chapter, the same forces of globalization that constrain governments create powerful pressures for them to act on behalf of their domestic constituencies. Governments remain massively involved in health, education, infrastructure, innovation, and social security, and by 2008 most governments in Canada could count on healthy revenues and even surpluses. New issues such as public security, climate change, Aboriginal self-government, information technologies, and building and maintaining social capital also demand attention. Information resources and technologies of power (e.g., surveillance) have also improved considerably. We noted above that governments may be forced to use more informational policy instruments to change hearts and minds around life-style issues. But it is not simply information that we are talking about. If one takes seriously the notion that the modern welfare state should be redefined to become a more positive instrument in supporting personal autonomy and self-esteem, and that life-style circumstances can undermine these qualities, then "policy must be interventionist, rather than just of the safety-net type . . . positive outcomes will presume lifestyle change" (Giddens, 2007, 122). This kind of intervention, which we see around issues like smoking regulations, bans on trans fats, carbon capture, mixes instruments in novel and more muscular ways.

What is different is that policymakers have to be a bit more clever than they once were. Without the easy option of throwing money at a problem (even the financial crisis has its limits), and with these new demands, policy suddenly requires more imaginative use of available instruments. If internationalization threatens an important domestic industry, the trick is to find a way, within the rules, to help. If government cannot do something on its own, it needs to create the conditions to work with others to achieve the objectives. Both of these are tricks about converting policy tools into implementation, the subject of the next chapter.

KEY TERMS

alternative service delivery—the use of nontraditional means to deliver public services, e.g., commercialized firms, partnerships, single-window service centres

binding rules—rules or regulations that have the coercive power of law behind them

cap and trade—a regulatory tool that caps carbon emissions and then allows companies over their limit to purchase allowances on markets that have been made available by companies below their limit

carbon tax—a tax on the carbon content of fossil fuels

cash transfer—money provided by the government for broad support rather than in connection with a specific project or endeavour

citizen engagement—bringing citizens and groups directly into the decisionmaking and policy implementation process

contract—a binding agreement between two or more parties

contributions—cash transfer subject to performance conditions that are specified in a contribution agreement

co-production—production of goods or services jointly by various partners

decision (legal)—rendered by an adjudicative body; the application of law

deregulation—the process of reducing the number, incidence, and cost of regulations

exhortation—the use of information resources to make direct appeals

expenditure—disbursement of monies

grants—cash transfers with few if any performance conditions attached, though other requirements may be built into the grant

guidelines—codes or frameworks to guide action, without coercive support

incorporation by reference—when legislation refers to other legislation or codes, particularly those developed by private parties, and thereby gives them the force of law

instrument design—the generic term for the selection and calibration of different policy instruments through programming to achieve policy objectives

investment—a cash payment that implies a return of some sort, a benefit, or a profit

legislation—laws formally passed by an elected legislature and ratified by the executive

legitimate coercion—the application of force backed by law

licence—permit to engage in activities that may involve a mix of prohibition, permission, and conditions

loan—cash transfer that requires eventual repayment

moral suasion—the ability to persuade others based on one's institutional prominence or authority

nodality—the generic category of information resources at the disposal of governments

partnership—working jointly and cooperatively with others, in some formal arrangement, for the production and delivery of goods and services

performance indicator—some measure of how well a service or activity is doing, either through financial or output measures, or client satisfaction

permission—regulatory device that permits a certain activity under specific conditions

policy design—the process of choosing the most appropriate instrument to deal with the policy problem as it has been defined in order to achieve a given policy goal

procedural policy instrument—instrument that alters institutional rules and arrangements to try to induce behaviour

prohibitions—regulatory device that forbids certain activities under certain conditions

quasi-legislation—regulations and legal decisions that have the force of law but that have not been duly passed by the legislature

recognition—regulatory device that uses the government's capacity to recognize certain qualities or achievements as a "sign of approval"

regulation—the generic category of policy instruments that rely on the government's capacity to command and prohibit

re-regulation—a process of developing new regulatory regimes for arenas that had been previously regulated in more traditional formats

secondary legislation—regulations announced under the regulatory powers of a statute and that therefore have the force of law without necessarily being passed by the legislature

self-regulation—the delegation of the state regulatory power to a nongovernmental organization or private association

service fee—fee attached to the provision of some service, such as issuing a passport

shaming—publication of unwelcome information in order to force targets to change their behaviour in order to protect their reputations

sin tax—traditionally, taxes levied on cigarettes and alcohol

social capital—the degree to which members of a community trust each other and engage in reciprocal relations based on that trust

static response—a deliberate choice not to intervene, made after an analysis of the problem

statute—a duly passed act of the legislature

subsidy—cash transfers that are closely calibrated to the costs of engaging in an activity that the government regards favourably

tax—a compulsory levy that is not generally connected to any specific service and is intended to provide general purpose revenues to the government

tax expenditure—the technique of foregoing certain owed taxes (and hence losing or "spending" tax dollars) in order to subsidize an activity

transparency—clear accountability, reporting, and publication provisions for the provision of services as well as the decisionmaking process

user charge—the charge levied on a category of person or user of a service, not the service itself

voluntary code—standards or codes developed by private sector organizations themselves; sometimes known as codes of conduct, codes of practice, voluntary initiatives, guidelines, and non-regulatory agreements

vouchers—"coupons" for stipulated amounts of public financial support attached to a service that may be redeemed under certain conditions

FURTHER READINGS

Bardach, E. (2000). A practical guide for policy analysis: The eightfold path to more effective problem solving. New York: Chatham House Publishers.

Bemelmans-Videc, M.-L., Rist, R. C., and Vedung, E. (Eds.) (1998). *Carrots, sticks and sermons: Policy instruments and their evaluation* (pp. 59–76). New Brunswick, NJ: Transaction Publishers.

Eliadis, P., Hill, M.M., and Howlett, M. (Eds.) (2005). *Designing government: From instruments to governance.* Toronto: University of Toronto Press.

Hood, C. (1984). *The tools of government.* London: Macmillan.

Hood, C., and Margetts, H. Z. (2007). The Tools of Government in the Digital Age. New York, N.Y.: Palgrave Macmillan.

Salamon, L. M. (Ed.) (2002). *The tools of government: A guide to the new governance.* New York: Oxford University Press.

Schneider, A. L., and Ingram, H. (1997). *Policy design for democracy.* Lawrence: University Press of Kansas.

REFERENCES

Aaron, H. J., Mann, T. E., and Taylor, T. (Eds.). (1994). *Values and public policy*. Washington, DC: The Brookings Institution.

Accor Services. (2008). About us. Retrieved March 9, 2008, from http://www.accorservices.com/EN/OurOffer/Benefits/Pages/PublicBenefits.aspx

Auditor General of Canada. (1998). Annual report 1998. Grants and contributions: Selected programs in Industry Canada and Department of Canadian Heritage. Ottawa.

Auditor General of Canada. (2002). Report to the Minister of Public Works and Government Services on three contracts awarded to Groupaction. Ottawa.

Baldwin, R. (1995). *Rules and government*. Oxford: Clarendon Press.

Bird, M., and Stoney, C. (2006). Government approaches to the regulation of "sin." In G. B. Doern (Ed.), *How Ottawa spends 2006–2007: In from the cold: The Tory rise and the Liberal demise* (pp. 247–65). Montreal: McGill-Queen's University Press.

Blue Ribbon Panel on Grant and Contribution Programs. (2006). *From red tape to clear results*. Retrieved on June 13, 2008, from http://www.brp-gde.ca/pdf/Report_on_Grant_and_Contribution_Programs.pdf

Bressers, Th. A., and O'Toole, L. J. (2005). Instrument selection and implementation in a networked context. In P. Eliadis, M. M. Hill, and M. Howlett (Eds.), *Designing government: From instruments to governance* (pp. 132–53). Toronto: University of Toronto Press.

British Columbia. (2008). *Budget and fiscal plan, 2008/09–2010/11*. Retrieved on March 15, 2008, from http://www.bcbudget.gov.bc.ca/2008/bfp/default.aspx?hash=2

Brown. D. (2005). Electronic government and public administration. *International review of administrative sciences*, 71 (2), 241–54.

Brown, D. (2007). The government of Canada: Government on-line and citizen-centred service. In S. Borins et al., *Digital state at the leading edge* (pp. 37–68). Toronto: IPAC and the University of Toronto Press.

Campbell, R. M. (1999). The fourth fiscal era: Can there be a "post-neo-conservative" fiscal policy? In L. A. Pal (Ed.), *How Ottawa spends 1999–2000: Shape shifting: Canada governance toward the 21st century* (pp. 113–49). Toronto: Oxford University Press.

Carbon Tax Center (2008). "Introduction." Retrieved March 5, 2008, from http://www.carbontax.org/

Center on Budget and Policy Priorities (2007). *Introduction to the Housing Voucher Program*. Retrieved March 2, 2008, from http://www.cbpp.org/5-15-03hous.pdf

Chrétien, J. (2007). *My years as Prime Minister*. Toronto: Alfred A. Knopf.

Commission of Inquiry into the Sponsorship Program & Advertising Activities (Gomery Inquiry) (2005). *Who is responsible? Fact finding report*. Ottawa: Minister of Public Works and Government Services.

CRTC. (1999). Public notice 1999–84. Retrieved March 14, 2008, from http://www.crtc.gc.ca/archive/ENG/Notices/1999/PB99-84.HTM

CRTC. (2008). New Media Project Initiative Overview. Retrieved June 13, 2008, from http://www.crtc.gc.ca/eng/media/media3.htm

CTV. (2007). Higher gas prices here for a while: Harper. Retrieved on March 9, 2008, from http://www.ctv.ca/servlet/ArticleNews/story/CTVNews/20060419/gas_mackay_060419/20060419?hub=TopStories

Department of Finance. (2007a). *Advantage Canada: Building a strong economy for Canadians*. Retrieved on March 14, 2008, from http://www.fin.gc.ca/ec2006/plan/pltoce.html

Department of Finance (Canada). (2007b). *Annual financial report of the government of Canada—Fiscal year 2006–2007*. Retrieved February 27, 2008, from http://www.fin.gc.ca/afr/2007/afr2007e.pdf

Department of Finance (Canada). (2008). *The budget plan 2008: Responsible leadership*. Retrieved February 27, 2008, from http://www.fin.gc.ca/ec2007/pdf/EconomicStatement2007_E.pdf

Doern, G. B., and Phidd, R. W. (1992). *Canadian public policy: Ideas, structure, process* (2nd ed.). Toronto: Nelson.

Doern, G. B., and Wilson, V. S. (Eds.). (1974). *Issues in Canadian public policy*. Toronto: Methuen.

Doern, G. B., et al. (1999a). Canadian regulatory institutions: Converging and colliding regimes. In G. B. Doern et al. (Eds.), *Changing the rules: Canadian regulatory regimes and institutions* (pp. 3–26). Toronto: University of Toronto Press.

Doern, G. B., et al. (1999b). Conclusions. In G. B. Doern et al. (Eds.), *Changing the rules: Canadian regulatory regimes and institutions* (pp. 389–406). Toronto: University of Toronto Press.

Doern, G. B. and Johnson, R. (2006). Multilevel regulatory governance: Concepts, context, and key issues. In G. B. Doern and R. Johnson (Eds.), *Rules, rules, rules, rules: Multilevel regulatory governance* (pp. 3–26). Toronto: University of Toronto Press.

External Advisory Committee on Smart Regulation. (2004). *Smart regulation: A regulatory strategy for Canada*. Retrieved March 14, 2008, from http://epe.lac-bac.gc.ca/100/206/301/pco-bcp/committees/smart_regulation-ef/2006-10-11/www.pco-bcp.gc.ca/smartreg-regint/en/index.html

Fukuyama, F. (1995). Trust: The social virtues and the creation of prosperity. New York: Free Press.

Ganz, G. (1987). Quasi-legislation: Recent developments in secondary legislation. London: Sweet and Maxwell.

Giddens, A. (2007). Over to you, Mr. Brown: How Labour can win again. Cambridge: Polity Press.

Good, D. A. (2003). The politics of public management: The HRDC audit of grants and contributions. Toronto: University of Toronto Press.

Good, D. A. (2007). The politics of public money: Spenders, guardians, priority setters, and financial watchdogs inside the Canadian government. Toronto: University of Toronto Press.

Government of Canada. (1999). *Regulatory policy*. Retrieved March 14, 2008, from http://www.tbs-sct.gc.ca/ri-qr/ra-ar/default.asp@language=e&page=publications&sub=governmentofcanadaregula.htm

Government of Canada (2006). *Government on-line 2006: Annual report*. Retrieved on March 14, 2008, from http://www.gol-ged.gc.ca/rpt2006/rpt/rpt00_e.asp

Government of Canada. (2007). *Cabinet directive on streamlining regulation*. Retrieved March 14, 2008, from http://www.regulation.gc.ca/directive/directive-eng.pdf

Government of Canada. (2008). *Turning the corner: Taking action to fight climate change*. Retrieved on March 15, 2008, from http://www.ec.gc.ca/doc/virage-corner/2008-03/pdf/572_eng.pdf

Graham, A. (2007). *Canadian public-sector financial management*. Kingston: School of Policy Studies, Queen's University, and McGill-Queen's University Press.

Graham, M. (2002). *Democracy by disclosure: The rise of technopopulism*. Washington, DC: Brookings Institution.

Hood, C. (1984). *The tools of government*. London: Macmillan.

Hood, C., and Margetts, H. Z. (2007). The Tools of Government in the Digital Age. New York, N.Y.: Palgrave Macmillan.

Howlett, M. (2000, Winter). Managing the 'hollow state': Procedural policy instruments and modern governance. *Canadian Public Administration*, 43, 412–31.

Howlett, M., and Ramesh, M. (2003). *Studying public policy: Policy cycles and policy subsystems*. 2nd ed. Toronto: Oxford University Press.

Industry Canada. (1998). *Voluntary codes: A guide for their development and use*. Retrieved March 14, 2008, from http://www.ic.gc.ca/epic/site/oca-bc.nsf/vwapj/volcodes.pdf/$FILE/volcodes.pdf

Ireland, D., and Webb, K. (2006). Consumer protection through free markets, small government, and individual responsibility? The federal approach, 1993–2007. In G. B. Doern (Ed.), *How Ottawa spends, 2007–2008: The Harper Conservatives—Climate of change* (pp. 273–91). Montreal: McGill-Queen's University Press.

James, M. (2007). The permanent-emergency compensation state: A "postsocialist" tale of political dystopia. In M. Orsini and M. Smith (Eds.), *Critical policy studies* (pp. 321–46). Vancouver: UBC Press.

Keyes, J. M. (1996). Power tools: The form and function of legal instruments for government action. *Canadian Journal of Administrative Law and Practice*, 10, 133–74.

Kirschen, E. S., et al. (1964). *Economic policy in our time* (3 vols.). Amsterdam: North-Holland.

Landy, M. (1993). Policy shapes and citizenship. In H. Ingram and S. R. Smith (Eds.), *Public policy for democracy* (pp. 19–44). Washington, DC: The Brookings Institution.

Lemaire, D. (1998). The stick: Regulation as a tool of government. In M.-L. Bemelmans-Videc, R. C. Rist, and E. Vedung (Eds.), *Carrots, sticks and sermons: Policy instruments and their evaluation* (pp. 59–76). New Brunswick, NJ: Transaction Publishers.

Linder, S. H., and Peters, B. G. (1989). Instruments of government: Perceptions and contexts. *Journal of Public Policy*, 9, 35–58.

Linder, S. H., and Peters, B. G. (1995). The two traditions of institutional designing: Dialogue versus decision? In D. L. Weimer (Ed.), *Institutional design* (pp. 133–60). Dordrecht, Netherlands: Kluwer.

March, J. G., and Olsen, J. P. (1995). *Democratic governance*. New York: Free Press.

McDonnell, L. M., and Elmore, R. F. (1987). *Alternative policy instruments*. Santa Monica, CA: Center for Policy Research in Education.

Mihlar, F. (1999). The federal government and the "RIAS" process: Origins, need and non-compliance. In G. B. Doern et al. (Eds.), *Changing the rules: Canadian regulatory regimes and institutions* (pp. 275–92). Toronto: University of Toronto Press.

Milwaukee Journal Sentinel. (2007). New year brings reminder from past: More delinquent taxpayers will be on the web list in 2008. Retrieved March 1, 2008, from http://www.revenue.wi.gov/news/071226.html

National Round Table on the Environment and the Economy. (2008). *Getting to 2050: Canada's transition to a low-emission future*. Retrieved on March 15, 2008, from http://www.nrtee-trnee.ca/eng/publications/getting-to-2050/Getting-to-2050-low-res-eng.pdf

Neville, A. (Ed.) (2002). *Policy choices in a globalized world*. New York: Nova Science Publishers.

OECD. (2005). Modernising government: The way forward. Paris: OECD.

OECD. (2007). Cutting red tape: Comparing administrative burdens across countries. Paris: OECD.

Orsini, M. (2002, September). The politics of naming, blaming and claiming: HIV, Hepatitis C and the emergence of blood activism in Canada. *Canadian Journal of Political Science*, 35, 475–98.

Osborne, D., and Gaebler, T. (1993). Reinventing government: How the entrepreneurial spirit is transforming the public sector. New York: Penguin.

Prince, M. J. (1999). Civic regulation: Regulating citizenship, morality, social order, and the welfare state. In G. B. Doern et al. (Eds.), *Changing the rules: Canadian regulatory regimes and institutions* (pp. 201–27). Toronto: University of Toronto Press.

Prince, M. J. (2005). From welfare state to social union: Shifting choices of governing instruments, intervention rationales, and governance rules in Canadian social policy. In P. Eliadis, M. M. Hill, and M. Howlett (Eds.), *Designing government: From instruments to governance* (pp. 281–302). Toronto: University of Toronto Press.

Privy Council Office (Canada). (2003). *Cabinet directive on law-making.* Retrieved March 9, 2008, from http://www.pco-bcp.gc.ca/index.asp?lang=eng&page=information&sub=publications&doc=legislation/lmgcabinetdirective_e.htm

Purchase, B., and Hirshhorn, R. (1994). *Searching for good governance.* Kingston, ON: Queen's School of Policy Studies.

Putnam, R. (1993). *Making democracy work: Civic traditions in modern Italy.* Princeton, NJ: Princeton University Press.

Putnam, R. (2000). Bowling alone: The collapse and revival of American community. New York: Simon and Schuster.

Salamon, L. M. (Ed.) (2002). *The tools of government: A guide to the new governance*. New York: Oxford University Press.

Schelling, T. C. (1984). The intimate contest for self-command. In T. Schelling, *Choice and Consequence*, (57–82). Boston: Harvard University Press.

Schneider, A., and Ingram, H. (1990). Behavioral assumptions of policy tools. *Journal of Politics*, 52, 510–29.

Schneider, A. L., and Ingram, H. (1997). *Policy design for democracy.* Lawrence: University Press of Kansas.

Schultz, R. (1994). Deregulation Canadian-style: State reduction of recasting? In I. Gow and L. Bernier (Eds.), *A downsized state? Canada and Québec compared* (pp. 129–47). Montreal: Presses de l'Université du Québec.

Slaughter, A.-M. (2004). *A new world order*. Princeton: Princeton University Press.

Sproule-Jones, M. (1994). User fees. In A. M. Maslove (Ed.), *Taxes as instruments of public policy* (pp. 3–38). Toronto: University of Toronto Press.

Standing Committee on Finance (Canada). (2000). *Challenge for change: A study of cost-recovery*. Retrieved June 12, 2008, from http://cmte .parl.gc.ca/cmte/CommitteePublication.aspx?COM=158&Lang=1& SourceId=36476

Standing Committee on Finance (Canada). (2008). *Taxing to Prosper: Canada's System of Taxes, Fees and Other Charges*. Retrieved March 5, 2008, from http://cmte.parl.gc.ca/Content/HOC/committee/392/ fina/reports/rp3253372/finarp03/04-toc-e.htm

Statistics Canada (2007a). Public Sector Statistics: Financial Management System 2006/2007. Catalogue no. 68-213-XIE. Retrieved March 7, 2008, from http://www.statcan.ca/english/freepub/68-213-XIE/68-213-XIE2007000.pdf

Steuerle, C. E., and Twombly, E. C. (2002). Vouchers. In L. M. Salamon (Ed.), *The tools of government: A guide to the new governance* (pp. 445–65). New York: Oxford University Press.

Thaler, R. H., and Sunstein, C. R. (2003). Libertarian paternalism. *American Economic Review*, 93, 175–179.

Thaler, R. H., and Sunstein, C. R. (2008). *Nudge: Improving decisions about health, wealth, and happiness*. New Haven: Yale University Press.

Treasury Board of Canada Secretariat. (2003). *Treasury Board President Announces Revised External Charging Policy*. Retrieved March 5, 2008, from http://www.tbs-sct.gc.ca/media/nr-cp/2003/0903_e.asp

Treasury Board of Canada Secretariat. (2007). *Report of the President of the Treasury Board on the Provisions and Operation of the User Fees Act*. Retrieved March 5, 2008, from http://www.tbs-sct.gc.ca/report/ orp/2007/ufa-lfu/ufa-lfu_e.asp

Treasury Board of Canada Secretariat. (2008). *The Government of Canada action plan to reform the administration of grant and contribution programs*. Retrieved on June 13, 2008 from http://www.tbs-sct.gc.ca/ gcr-esc/docs/2008/ragcp-rapsc-eng.asp

Vedung, E. (1998). Policy instruments: Typologies and theories. In M.-L. Bemelmans-Videc, R. C. Rist, and E. Vedung (Eds.), *Carrots, sticks and sermons: Policy instruments and their evaluation* (pp. 21–58). New Brunswick, NJ: Transaction Publishers.

Vedung, E., and van der Doelen, F. C. J. (1998). The sermon: Information programs in the public policy process—Choice, effects, and evaluation. In M.-L. Bemelmans-Videc, R. C. Rist, and E. Vedung (Eds.), *Carrots, sticks and sermons: Policy instruments and their evaluation* (pp. 103–28). New Brunswick, NJ: Transaction Publishers.

Visit Singapore. (2008). About Singapore. Retrieved March 3, 2008, from http://www.visitsingapore.com/publish/stbportal/en/home/about_singapore/faq/customs.html

Webb, K. (2005). Sustainable governance in the twenty-first century: Moving beyond instrument choice? In P. Eliadis, M. M. Hill, and M. Howlett (Eds.), *Designing government: From instruments to governance* (pp. 243–80). Toronto: University of Toronto Press.

Wilks, S., and Doern, G. B. (1998). Conclusions. In G. B. Doern and S. Wilks (Eds.), *Changing regulatory institutions in Britain and North America* (pp. 376–95). Toronto: University of Toronto Press.

World Trade Organization. (2008). *Technical explanation of WTO Agreement on Technical Barriers to Trade*. Retrieved on March 14, 2008, from http://www.wto.org/english/tratop_e/tbt_e/tbt_e.htm

CHAPTER 5

Policy Implementation

S ay "implementation" and you say "organization." Whereas Chapter 4
dealt with policy instruments—the means or techniques of getting
things done—this chapter addresses the challenges of organizing and
delivering outcomes through those instruments. The policy literature often
states that no one paid much attention to implementation until the 1970s,
but this is wrong. Policy analysts themselves did not pay much attention to
it, but the field of public administration has concentrated on implementation for most of its history, since a good deal of administrative science, or
management, as it is now called, deals with harnessing personnel and other
resources in order to get things done. The subject of implementation brings
public administration and public policy analysis about as close as they ever
come. Even then, the policy literature has paid less attention to organizational details than the political and intellectual constraints in implementation. This chapter will pick up the discussion from Chapter 4 and look at
design questions (how we achieve our objectives) from the point of view of
organizing services and programs. Implementation studies have the reputation of being the dismal science of policy studies, since much of the work
here tends to emphasize how tough it is to get anything accomplished.
However, in contrast to theory, the practice of public administration and
policy implementation has been undergoing a revolution in recent years.
With **decentralization,** partnerships, client focus, quality service standards,
performance and results, subsidiarity, special operating agencies, privatization, commercialization, accountability, and ethics, the list of new management practices and emphases is long. As one would expect, there is
considerable debate whether these new forms of policy implementation represent improvements or decline, and whether there are uniform trends.

Implementation and policy design are conceptually distinct, though they
overlap in practice. Think of design as the blueprint for the policy and

DESIGN AND IMPLEMENTATION

DESIGN	IMPLEMENTATION	
	Effective	*Ineffective*
Strong	Success	Implementation Failure
Weak	Design Failure	Total Failure

implementation as its execution. Looked at in this way, the relationship between the two aspects of the policy process raises an interesting question: is it possible for badly designed policies to be well implemented, and good policy designs to be badly implemented? Box 5.1 illustrates a rough set of relationships that can exist between implementation and design. A well-designed policy with good implementation is almost a definition of success: a good idea well executed. There is another degree of success however, which might be thought of as implementation failure—a good idea that suffers from inadequate execution. It must be said that this explanation of failure is the refuge of many a policy designer. The idea was fine, but the follow-through was responsible for less than spectacular results. More on this in a moment. One point to keep in mind is that there is still hope—since the design is sound, failure is a matter of organization, personnel, or resources. It is also possible to have design failure—the policy is badly designed in terms of problem definition or instruments or goals, but is executed reasonably well. Total failure—and total misery— occur when both design and implementation are seriously flawed. To be realistic, most policies will have shortcomings in design and in implementation; what we are considering here is very weak design combined unhappily with very weak implementation.

We can see from these crude categories that implementation makes a distinct contribution to the success or failure of a policy.

> The study of policy implementation is crucial for the study of public administration and public policy. Policy implementation is the stage of policymaking between the establishment of a policy, such as the passage of a legislative act, the issuing of an executive order, the handing down of a judicial decision, or the promulgation of a regulatory rule, and the consequences of the policy for the people whom it affects. If the policy is inappropriate, if it cannot alleviate the problem for which it was designed, it will probably be a failure no matter how well implemented. But even a brilliant policy poorly implemented may fail to achieve the goals of its designers. (Edwards, 1984, ix)

The design phase is about determining the problem, the goals, and the most appropriate instruments for a solution. Even if all of that goes well, and the conceptualization of the policy problem is broadly correct, the follow-through can fail. Knowing this, of course, the smart designer builds considerations about implementation into the policy design from the beginning, though this too can raise problems if we presume that there should be both some degree of flexibility in the way policies are implemented as well as input from below. In this chapter we will assume that the policies are well designed and concentrate on principles and mechanisms of implementation. The first section quickly reviews some of the conventional wisdom of the policy literature, while the second reviews the exploding world of new forms of public management and service delivery.

Implementation Theory

Recall the discussion of instruments and policy design in the last chapter. In elaborating a set of programs that combine various instruments in order to put the policy into effect, what would one want in order to ensure success?

Box 5.2 (page 208) draws on Hogwood and Gunn's (1984) classic list of requirements (Chap. 11). The image of the successful implementer that arises from this list of requirements is someone or some organization that has brains, strong planning capacity, resources, authority to act, and complete understanding of the goals. It is, in short, a world without friction, without scarcity, without confusion, miscommunication, conflict, or misunderstanding. It is also a world of hierarchy and power, where the implementer decides and those decisions cascade down to the final point of delivery without obstruction or misinterpretation. Little wonder, then, that perfect implementation almost never happens, and, as Hogwood and Gunn (1984) conclude, some degree of failure "is almost inevitable" (p. 198).

The Hogwood and Gunn list of requirements is developed from the administrator's or implementer's point of view. Another approach that picks up many of the same variables, but also incorporates some system-level considerations, was offered by Sabatier and Mazmanian (1981). Box 5.3 summarizes the framework. It hinges on three broad categories of variables. First, the tractability of the problem: some issues, like traffic congestion, are easier to deal with than others, like disposal of nuclear waste. A good causal theory, a relatively narrow range of targeted behaviour, a small population target group, and a small desired change in behaviour as a result of policy make implementation more successful, all other things being equal. Second, Sabatier and Mazmanian also incorporate legislative and institutional variables. The statute should be clear, and

BOX 5.2   ELEMENTS FOR SUCCESSFUL IMPLEMENTATION

No insurmountable external constraints	• Usually organizations and individuals that will not cooperate, but can include acts of nature
Adequate time and sufficient resources	• Time, money, and people
Required combinations	• Time, money, and people in the right order and mix
Valid theory	• Good design, especially cause-and-effect relationships
Causal connections are reasonable, clear, and direct	• Focus on causal variables that can realistically be addressed by public policy, rather than, for example, large systemic ones that are resistant to intervention
Dependency relationships are minimal	• Authority is not fragmented or dispersed
Agreed objectives	• Everyone sings from the same song sheet; no dispute about ends
Correct sequence of tasks	• Doing first things first, and so on
Communication	• Clear communication and understanding
Compliance	• No sabotage, recalcitrance, or rebellion

SOURCE: Hogwood, B.W., and Gunn, L.A. (1984). *Policy analysis for the real world*, Oxford: Oxford University Press, Chap. 11.

the implementing agency well resourced. Linkages to cooperating agencies should be designed with a minimum of veto points and strong lines of accountability. The statute should be implemented by agencies or individuals sympathetic to its goals, and outside access to the decisionmaking process should be skewed toward supporters rather than critics.

BOX 5.3   A CONCEPTUAL FRAMEWORK OF THE IMPLEMENTATION PROCESS

TRACTABILITY OF THE PROBLEM

1. Availability of valid technical theory and technology
2. Diversity of target-group behaviour
3. Target group as percentage of the population
4. Extent of behavioral change required

ABILITY OF STATUTE TO STRUCTURE IMPLEMENTATION	**NONSTATUTORY VARIABLES AFFECTING IMPLEMENTATION**
1. Clear and consistent objectives	1. Socioeconomic conditions and technology
2. Incorporation of adequate causal theory	2. Media attention to the problem
3. Financial resources	3. Public support
4. Hierarchical integration with and among implementing institutions	4. Attitudes and resources of constituency groups
5. Decision-rules of implementing agencies	5. Support from sovereigns
6. Recruitment of implementing official	6. Commitment and leadership skills of implementing officials
7. Formal access by outsiders	

SOURCE: Sabatier and Mazmanian. (1981). The implementation of public policy: A framework of analysis. In D. A. Mazmanian and P. A. Sabatier (Eds.), *Effective Policy Implementation* (p. 7). Lexington, MA: Lexington Books.

A third category is broad socioeconomic and political variables that determine the fate of implementation. These overlap in part with forces discussed in Chapter 3, maintaining the sense in the public and the political system that the problem to which the policy is being directed is important and requires attention. In sum, the chances of successful implementation, which Sabatier and Mazmanian define as "the translation of

statutory objectives into the policy decisions of implementing agencies,"
are maximized if

> the statute stipulates unambiguous objectives; assigns implemen-
> tation to sympathetic agencies who will give it high priority;
> minimizes the number of veto points and provides sufficient
> incentives to overcome resistance among recalcitrant officials;
> provides sufficient financial resources to conduct the technical
> analyses and process individual cases; and biases the decision-
> rules and access points in favor of statutory objectives. Confor-
> mity of policy decisions with statutory objectives is also very
> dependent on the ability of supportive constituency groups and
> legislative/executive sovereigns to intervene actively in the
> process to supplement the agency's resources and to counter
> resistance from target groups. (pp. 21–22)

Even this is a daunting list—it highlights clear objectives, sympathetic
agencies, authority, resources, fidelity to statute and rules, leadership, and
public support—showing why the study of implementation appears to be
the dismal science of policy analysis (Hupe and Hill, 2002). The book that
arguably kicked off interest in implementation by policy analysts was by
Jeffrey L. Pressman and Aaron Wildavsky (1984), with the appropriately
pessimistic title: *Implementation: How Great Expectations in Washington
Are Dashed in Oakland: Or, Why It's Amazing that Federal Programs
Work at All, This Being a Saga of the Economic Development Administration as Told by Two Sympathetic Observers Who Seek to Build Morals
on a Foundation of Ruined Hopes*. The book examines an urban employment scheme called the Oakland Project, announced in 1966. At the time,
Oakland had an unemployment rate of 8.4 percent, concentrated among
inner-city blacks. The program was to spend $23 million on a variety of
public works projects and would be administered by the Economic
Development Administration (EDA). Some 3000 jobs were to be created
through an innovative scheme whereby employers seeking EDA loans or
support would have to submit an employment plan showing how they
would recruit target group members. As Pressman and Wildavsky pointed
out, the Oakland Project enjoyed wide political support, and was well
funded, with monies in place. Yet three years later, only $3 million had
been spent, most of that for a freeway overpass and architects' fees. Why
did the Oakland Project fail?

From the beginning, "the success of the EDA program depended on
agreement among a diverse group of participants with differing organizational objectives" (p. 30). The project had, at minimum, fifteen different sets of actors, some within the same agency. They included, among
others, five different sets from within the EDA itself: the Department of
Health, Education, and Welfare; the Department of Labor; the U.S. Navy;

the City of Oakland; and Black leaders. Beyond this there were all the private sector actors who were supposed to create jobs with the help of EDA funds. Levels of commitment, perceptions of urgency, and capacity varied enormously among these actors. Moreover, the implementation process was marked by a sequence of tasks that had to be completed or agreements struck before the process could move on. Pressman and Wildavsky called these "**decision points**" that required "clearance" by multiple sets of actors in order for implementation to go forward. They hypothesized that 30 decision points required a cumulative total of 70 **clearances.** Assuming an 80 percent probability of agreement on each clearance point, the chances of completion were one in a million. Even if one assumed an unrealistically high probability of 99 percent for each clearance, the odds for successful implementation were only about one in two. "However you look at it, the ultimate probability of success is very low" (p. 107).

One might argue that the Oakland Project succumbed to the fragmentation that characterizes the American political system. It is true that parliamentary systems like Canada's have a higher degree of executive dominance and institutional capacity to implement from the top down (Atkinson, 1993; Pal and Weaver, 2003). But Canada's is also a federal system, which reduces the executive dominance to some degree at the centre. The other notable feature of the Oakland Project was the high consensus around it. In cases where principles differ; where problem definitions are widely divergent; or where actors have incentives to impede, delay, or frustrate, it could be expected that policies will face even greater odds against implementation.

Fortunately, things are not so grim. Subsequent work has shown that the probability of successful implementation increases if one adopts assumptions that are plausible, but only slightly different from those held by Pressman and Wildavsky in their study. After all, things do get accomplished, however imperfectly. The Pressman–Wildavsky implementation model consists of a chain of statistically independent nodes or clearance points with an attached probability. Relax the model in five ways and the probability for clearance increases substantially (Alexander, 1989). First, it is unrealistic to assume that actors will make only one attempt at clearance. They may persist in multiple tries. Second, clearance points are not always independent; they might be packaged or bundled in ways so that one clearance ripples through several others. Third, there is a bandwagon effect at times where previous clearances actually increase the probability of future clearances. This usually happens in threshold decisions where a certain number of agreements are necessary before a large payoff can be received. This puts pressure on holdouts. A good example is labour negotiations, where both sides try to "build momentum" on a series of minor issues before they tackle the larger ones. Fourth, program-reduction strategies may be used to shorten the "**decision chain.**" If the proposed program is being held hostage at one clearance point because of some feature that requires agreement from reluctant supporters, it is possible to cut out that component and proceed to the next decision point. Finally, one can assume higher probabilities of clearance than 99 percent in some instances, and this has a marked effect on overall clearance probabilities.

All of these techniques, in one way or another, involve trying to make the implementation process more controlled. But what if, as Eugene Bardach (1977) asked, "the character and degree of many implementation problems are inherently unpredictable" (p. 5)? Bardach took the dynamic conceptualization of implementation first developed by Pressman and Wildavsky—dynamic in the sense that it occurs over time—and arrived at the notion of "games" as a way of understanding the essentially defensive nature of implementation:

> The idea of "games," therefore . . . directs us to look at the players, what they regard as the stakes, their strategies and tactics, their resources for playing, the rules of play (which stipulate the conditions for winning), the rules of "fair" play (which stipulate the boundaries beyond which lie fraud or illegitimacy), the nature of the communications (or lack of them) among players, the degree of uncertainty surrounding the possible outcomes. The game metaphor also directs our attention to who is not willing to play and for what reasons, and to who insists on changes in some of the game's parameters as a condition of playing. (p. 56)

In reflecting on what makes the implementation game successful, what enables implementers to deal with its inevitably unpredictable character, Bardach offered several strategies. First, avoid implementation designs that rely on complex management systems, large organizations, and lots of clearances. Implement through the market, if possible; deliver cash directly to people rather than services that require elaborate bureaucracies, and aim at small and feasible targets. Second, engage in scenario-writing to work out different possible consequences of a string of actions and interactions. Third, and most importantly, fix the game in the sense of "repairing" it when it goes off the rails and in the sense of "adjusting certain elements of the system of games . . . so as to lead to a more preferred outcome" (Bardach, 1977, p. 274). This amounts to paying attention to the policy-formation process (Winter, 1990, pp. 25–26).

If the prospects for implementation were as bleak as some of the earlier literature suggested, then policymaking would seem a hopeless enterprise. It may be that we have unrealistically high notions of what constitutes policy success. Ironically, because perceptions of government became more negative over the 1970s and 1980s, the public sector may be presumed to be doing worse than it actually is: "by adopting new ways of looking at and evaluating public policymaking, we have ourselves constructed a significant number of the fiascoes we subsequently 'observed'" (Bovens and t'Hart, 1996, p. 146). However, the lessons of implementation cannot be ignored. It is difficult to make things happen, and it becomes increasingly difficult the further removed the situation is from the preconditions identified by Hogwood and Gunn. It can also be more difficult than it need be, if we expect perfect implementation through control. If top-down control is our standard, if we see implementation as the formal elaboration of some unitary design, then almost by definition that is unlikely to happen, given what we know about the limits of organizations and the impact of politics on decisionmaking. Majone and Wildavsky (1984) urged an image of implementation as evolution, not as control:

> Implementation is evolution. Since it takes place in a world we never made, we are usually right in the middle of the process, with events having occurred before and (we hope) continuing afterward . . . . When we act to implement a policy, we change it. When we vary the amount or type of resource inputs we also intend to alter outputs, even if only to put them back on the track where they were once supposed to be. In this way, the policy theory is transformed to produce different results. As we learn from experience what is feasible or preferable, we correct errors. To the degree that these corrections make a difference at all, they change our policy ideas as well as the policy outcomes, because the idea is embedded in the action. (p. 177)

Implementation is therefore an execution process, an elaboration, a realization of schemes and conceptions, the building of links in often long chains of decision and agreement. It can also be seen as a process of communications, an "implementation subsystem full of messages, messengers, channels, and targets" (Goggin et al., 1990, p. 33). It takes place in a world of multiple powers and authorities, organizations, and personalities, and therefore is inevitably a struggle. Even this fails to capture the reality, since it still implies an evolution from the design or blueprint, when in fact what may be happening is closer to the loop or cycle mentioned in the preceding quote, where implementation is a function of combined "top-down" and "bottom-up" processes. Indeed, some students of implementation have been so impressed by the degree to which the fortunes of policies are determined at the final point of delivery that they have urged a "**backward mapping**" technique to work out what the policy should actually be, as opposed to more conventional "**forward mapping**."

> Forward mapping . . . begins at the top of the process, with as clear a statement as possible of the policymaker's intent, and proceeds through a sequence of increasingly more specific steps to define

what is expected of implementers at each level. At the bottom of the process, one states, again with as much precision as possible, what a satisfactory outcome would be, measured in terms of the original statement of intent . . . . [Backward mapping] begins, not with a statement of intent, but with a statement of the specific behavior at the lowest level of the implementation process that generates the need for a policy. Only after that behavior is described does the analysis presume to state an objective; the objective is first stated as a set of organizational operations and then as a set of effects, or outcomes, that will result from these operations. Having established a relatively precise target at the lowest level of the system, the analysis backs up through the structure of implementing agencies, asking at each level two questions: What is the ability of this unit to affect the behavior that is the target of the policy? And what resources does this unit require in order to have that effect? In the final stage of analysis the analyst or policymaker describes a policy that directs resources at the organizational units likely to have the greatest effect. (Elmore, 1982, pp. 19, 21)

In sum, the conventional work on implementation has tended to highlight its multidimensionality, difficulty, ambiguity, and a growing realization of its importance. The multidimensionality arises from the understanding that implementation can be viewed as an organizational process, something internal to bureaucracies and focused on the challenge of balancing discretion with accountability. Implementation can also be viewed primarily as a political process of bargaining among actors who, while not necessarily equal in resources, can each affect outcomes. It can also be seen from the perspective of individuals, personalities, and leadership capacities, either in organizations or political structures. The difficulty of implementation lies in the high demands for success. As Hogwood and Gunn (1984), as well as Sabatier and Mazmanian (1981) illustrate, it is a lot easier to outline the requirements for successful implementation than to actually fulfill them. The ambiguity of implementation reflects the complex symbiosis between theory and practice: policy is initially nothing more than ideas or conceptualizations, while implementation is the specific means of execution and elaboration in practice. Theory guides practice, but practice must, of necessity, add details that were never contemplated in the origins of the policy. Finally, the importance of implementation comes through precisely this contribution of practice—it is, in effect, the test of the policy theory (assuming it goes well). By testing, we learn. So a properly designed implementation process should provide a mechanism for **policy feedback**, learning, and improvement.

Implementation, however, is not a matter of merely empirically deciding what works and then developing checklists of factors to consider as one plugs along. As Linder and Peters (1990) note, looking at policy from the top down, the "implementation solution" criterion seems to be clarity, so that compliance can be ensured down the line. From the bottom up, however, the main criterion appears to be flexibility and discretion, and hence policy design should emphasize simplicity (pp. 64–65). Bardach (1977) made the same point: "even when we know what ought to be done, and can get political leaders to agree to mandate it, government is probably ill-suited to do the job. At the very least, it is likely that the bureaucratic and regulatory strategies government has traditionally relied upon are ineffective if not mischievous" (p. 4). The factors that we consider to be important in implementation, in other words, depend on the way in which we perceive governance. To take an extreme example, if the scope of government were to be reduced to its nineteenth-century proportions of maintaining public safety and infrastructure such as roads and sewers, it is unlikely that any student of public policy would dream of implementation as a major issue. Implementation is a concern only when there are lots of complex policies to implement. Moreover, the nature of the issues and challenges we confront in implementation also depend on the modes of implementation that we characteristically use. When governments deliver services like education directly themselves, accountability and compliance are more or less presumed to flow from the line relationships that extend down from the ministry to the local schools. Imagine a situation where all educational services were delivered by third parties, and the ministry's role was to develop curricula and distribute support to parents in the form of vouchers. Key implementation issues would suddenly become related to compliance with curricular guidelines and fraud in the use of the vouchers.

Like everything else in policymaking, the world of implementation has changed significantly in the last two decades. The main trend in the 1980s and 1990s and into the early 2000s was new public management (NPM), briefly described in previous chapters. This involved downsizing the state, decentralization, a focus on performance and results as well as on service orientation, partnerships, and an emphasis on market mechanisms. Again, as previously mentioned, the specific pattern of reforms varied by country, and Canada's version was considerably less enthusiastic than some others. Nonetheless, many key principles were adopted and implemented at all levels of government. There is no clear successor to NPM as a broad management philosophy, but there have been some developments in management theory and practice in the last decade that have overlain NPM, and created yet another distinctive environment for the implementation and management of public policy in Canada. Similar tendencies are evident in other OECD countries.

Public Management Developments: NPM and Beyond

The broad outlines of the philosophical premises of NPM were sketched in Chapter 2. These premises imply a different form of governance and different types of agencies and accountability relationships. Not surprisingly, to the degree that the NPM took root in Canada, it had an influence on mechanisms of implementation. Though NPM has been overtaken by other developments in public management thinking, it has left an imprint on how governments in Canada and elsewhere act.

The sources of the NPM are various. Politically, the first wave of radical governmental reform came with the Thatcher regime in Britain in the late 1970s and early 1980s. According to Savoie (1994), these initiatives became one of the key inspirations for the Mulroney-era changes to the public service (p. 231). The massive changes undertaken by the New Zealand government in the mid-1980s were another harbinger of things to come. Intellectually, the management revolution was led by gurus such as Peters and Waterman (1982) and Osborne and Gaebler (1993). While the political roots of the NPM were initially in the conservative end of the political spectrum, gradually governments of every political stripe accepted at least part of the message and reformed their internal structures and connections with social partners. In New Zealand, change was initiated by a Labour government. In Canada, the Saskatchewan NDP government was the first to balance its budget, ahead of Conservative Alberta. In the United Kingdom, it was Tony Blair's "New Labour" government that spearheaded substantial public sector reforms focusing on performance.

The broad appeal of NPM ideas (despite the variable uptake among different countries) suggests that deeper forces were at work: the bundle of factors described in Chapter 2 that links globalization, technology, and shifts in postwar paradigms to the nature of the nation-state. In May 2000, for example, the Clerk of the Privy Council argued that globalization would force more public involvement, more partnerships, and more focus on service delivery (Privy Council Office, 2000). It is important to note the conflicting pressures behind these forces since they help explain some of the confusing characteristics of the NPM. On the one hand, the NPM was all about reorganization and restructuring and relied heavily on market terminology such as **quality management** and **client satisfaction.** On the other hand, it also emphasized the need for fundamental governance changes that would involve more participation, citizen control, democracy, and responsiveness.

What were the key principles of the NPM? First, as we noted in Chapters 1 and 2, it is critical of traditional bureaucracies. Bureaucracy in this perspective is inflexible, slow, rule bound, and clumsy. Second, a basic question is posed as to whether government should be involved in the policy area in the first place. This seems like much more than a management issue, and it is. But it represents a sea change in thinking that presumes that the lines between state and civil society are drawn in different ways, ways that return substantial responsibilities to nongovernmental actors. Third, if it is determined that a government policy response is appropriate to the problem, the mode of delivery or broad implementation strategy stresses a strong focus on nongovernmental actors (communities, private corporations, citizens) as primary partners in delivery. Fourth, there is greater attention to outcomes and **performance**, with a special emphasis on clear standards of service to which agencies can be held accountable as much as possible. Agencies are encouraged to think of service recipients as customers or clients. Fifth, organizationally, the NPM looks to new hybrid forms of delivery that may have greater flexibility and also to a sharper distinction between policymaking functions in the executive and service functions that can be delivered on a contractual basis by some entity, either at arm's length or in the department.

These principles permit a fairly wide variation in practice, and governments that moved in this direction did so to different degrees and in different configurations, though it is fair to say that the NPM was a broad global movement (Kettl, 2005). Moreover, there are important ideological differences that still surface, whatever the similarities in approach. In Canada, for example, while both provincial NDP and Conservative governments have been interested in decentralization and partnerships, the NDP governments have leaned more in the direction of the nonprofit NGO sector than the private, for-profit sector. It must also be remembered that the NPM itself requires implementation, and government organizations may adopt the rhetoric but not the reality of the approach. However, despite these caveats, governments of all political stripes in Canada came to think about their role and their capacities quite differently, thereby calling into being new forms of policy implementation.

At the federal level, the inauguration of new ways of thinking about management and program delivery came with the 1989 initiative entitled **PS2000**. According to Paul Tellier (1990), who was then the Clerk of the Privy Council and responsible for launching PS2000, the program had three core objectives: better service, improved personnel management, and flexibility. Together, these objectives would shift public sector thinking away from a philosophy of control to a philosophy of empowerment. The process was undertaken through the establishment of ten task forces consisting of deputy and assistant deputy ministers. The Task Force on Service to the Public (PS2000) reviewed "best practices" in the public service with an eye to developing a "template for the model of the ideal service organization" (Rawson, 1991, p. 491). Though it found that individual public servants were keen to provide good service, the system as a whole did not encourage it. Improved service to the public would come only from strong leadership and a commitment to empowering front-line public servants, those who deal directly with clients.

The ten PS2000 Task Force reports submitted over 300 recommendations, many of which dealt with minor administrative changes, and the 1992 progress report on PS2000 showed very thin results across the federal public service. The 1994 federal budget announced the successor to PS2000, the Program Review (though PS2000 was never formally abandoned). Linked to a deficit-reduction strategy, Program Review's "main objective was to review all federal programs in order to bring about the most effective and cost-efficient way of delivering programs and services that are appropriate to the federal government's role in the Canadian federation" (Department of Finance, 1995, p. 33). As described in Chapter 2, ministers were asked to review all their programs in light of the six tests or questions: serving the public, necessity of government involvement, the federal role, scope for partnerships, efficiency, and affordability. Note that the first four of these speak directly to the issue of implementation or how government programs are delivered to the public. Coupled with large budget cuts, the effect of the Program Review was a major downsizing of the federal civil service. In its first sixteen months in office, the Liberal government cut 15 000 full-time-equivalent positions. In the February 27, 1995, budget, the finance minister announced further cuts of 45 000 positions over the next three years (Lee and Hobbs, 1996, pp. 355–56). In terms of program cuts, the average decline in departmental spending between 1994 and 1999 was 20 percent, and while a few programs were increased (senior's benefits and Indian Affairs), a large number saw cuts in the order of 30 percent to 40 percent. Transport Canada saw its budget reduced by almost 70 percent.

Just as important as the financial impact of Program Review, however, was its impact on and reflection of a new way of thinking about government services. The most extensive presentation of the new vision came in the government's blueprint entitled *Getting Government Right: A Progress Report* (Treasury Board of Canada, 1996a). Its strategy had four objectives: (1) clarification of federal roles and responsibilities, (2) better targeting of resources on high priority social and economic issues, (3) better and more accessible government "involving clients more in decision making and using modern and practical service delivery tools," and (4) more affordable government. Overarching these goals was a fundamental rethinking of services and the best ways of delivering them: "A central thrust of the renewal agenda has been to determine where the federal government is best placed to deliver programs or services and where these programs and services are more appropriately delivered by others" (Treasury Board of Canada, 1996a, p. 7)

Program Review officially ended in March 1999, but the management approach outlined in *Getting Government Right* continued, with the result that "the shape, size, and operating practices of the federal public service . . . had been altered dramatically and even irrevocably. . . . From a single focus on deficit reduction, attention has turned to implementing a new type of governance, one that will respond efficaciously to a multiplicity of challenges" such as globalization, demographic shifts, the information society, and eroding citizen trust (Potter, 2000, p. 95). A prime example of fundamental change was Transport Canada: in November 1996 it transferred the Air Navigation System to NAV Canada, a private, not-for-profit corporation that would depend on user charges for its revenues; it transferred 104 of 149 airports to local communities; and it transferred or closed 311 of over 500 harbours and ports (Treasury Board of Canada, 1998). In horizontal terms, the government also launched an **Alternative Service Delivery** (ASD) initiative in 1996, which was then supplemented by a **Quality Services Initiative** and finally an approach that stressed **citizen-centred service delivery** (Treasury Board of Canada, 2000a).

These changes demonstrated an unusually firm commitment not only to deal with the deficit and spending, but also to move more fundamentally and deeply on a public sector reform agenda. *Getting Government Right* was followed four years later with *Results for Canadians,* with a new emphasis on performance and results measurement. *Results for Canadians* made four management commitments:

> First and foremost, the Government of Canada must sharpen its *citizen focus* in designing, delivering, evaluating and reporting on its activities. It must improve service and expand partnerships with other governments, the private sector and voluntary organizations.
>
> Second, management in the public service must be guided by a clear set of *values.* Management must respect and reinforce Canadian institutions of democracy and it must be guided by the highest professional and ethical values.
>
> Third, as an integrating principle, management in all departments, agencies and functions must be focused on the achievement of *results* and on reporting them in simple and understandable ways to elected officials and to Canadians.
>
> Fourth, given the limited nature of public funds, the Government of Canada must ensure *responsible spending.* The costs of initiatives must be linked with results to ensure value for the taxpayer. Existing programs as well as new spending proposals must be systematically assessed and management frameworks must be in place to ensure due diligence and proper stewardship of public funds. Activities critical to the public interest must be resourced sustainably, over the long term. (Treasury Board of Canada, 2000b; emphasis in original)

These commitments were followed up with two other developments. The first was the *Public Sector Modernization Act* (PSMA) of 2003. The act was designed to modernize human resource management in the federal government of Canada by giving deputy heads more flexibility in hiring, redefining the merit principle to again introduce more flexibility, and enhance human resource management and support throughout the government, for example by redesignating the Canadian Centre for Management Development as the Canada School of Public Service, and creating a new agency entitled the Public Service Human Resources Management Agency of Canada (PSHRMAC). That agency was subsequently renamed as the Canada Public Service Agency, and designated as the central agency responsible for human resource management in the government of Canada. Another development in 2005 stemming from the *Results for Canadians* and the PSMA was the Management Accountability Framework (MAF). The MAF was designed to integrate ten key management expectations, bringing together the principal elements of Modern Comptrollership, Human Resources Modernization, Service Improvement and Government On-Line. The MAF is reproduced in Figure 2.4 (p. 91). Each of the elements is accompanied with specific indicators as well as measures for those indicators. These include both process measures (e.g., completed plans or reviews) and improvement measures (e.g., staff and service satisfaction or audit findings).

Another focus has been on expenditure management and control, consistent with the emphasis on rising deficits discussed in Chapter 4. In 2003 an Expenditure Review Committee was launched to lead a program review exercise that was intended to instill a new culture of "continuous reallocation" in the federal government. This was complemented by a refocused TBS and stronger comptrollership functions, projected directly into departments but reporting to the Comptroller General. Within the TBS, the Office of the Comptroller General was strengthened, and each department was to have departmental comptrollers reporting on and approving departmental expenditure plans (no doubt as a response to the criticisms of government spending control). In a move reminiscent of the mid-1990s Program Review, the Expenditure Review process would examine all government programs in terms of seven tests: public interest, role of government, federalism, partnership, value for money, efficiency, and affordability (Treasury Board of Canada, 2004b). The exercise was to focus on departmental reviews of the thirty largest departments, reviews of key horizontal policy areas, and government operation reviews. The goal was to identify $3 billion in savings over four years. There was also to be a review of Crown corporations, and enhancements to public service training. The Harper government launched a revised version of this expenditure review instrument in 2006, again with the aim of finding savings that could be re-allocated to other program areas. This was followed in

2008 with further reallocations and cuts among departments in order to support increased defence spending, particularly for Afghanistan.

As bold as these NPM measures might have seemed in the 1990s, the Canadian approach was somewhat tepid in comparison with other countries: the "style of these reforms was generally moderate, as was the substance" (Gow, 2004, p. 11; also see Cheung, 1997). In the earlier phases of both PS2000 and the subsequent reforms of the cabinet system, for example, there was never the same level of public political commitment and leadership to management change in Canada as there was in the United Kingdom, Australia, or New Zealand. The PS2000 exercise was driven primarily by the mandarinate, with little interest from the executive. Aucoin (1995) cites the Auditor General of Canada's 1993 study to the effect that "Canadian reforms under the Conservatives had met with less than the desired success precisely because the required political and public service leadership had been lacking" (p. 13). In the other Westminster democracies, leadership on management change had come directly from the top, from prime ministers and senior cabinet ministers. The fundamentals of the NPM as experienced in New Zealand and the United Kingdom required a combination of rather radical restructuring around the separation of policy from operations, with a determined focus on service that in turn demands the development and application of performance standards. In Canada, at both federal and provincial levels, restructuring did not go as far, with the main organizational vehicle remaining the department or ministry.

A good example of federal government hesitancy on the re-organizational front comes from the establishment of **Special Operating Agencies** (SOAs), the closest Canadian equivalent to Next Steps agencies (see below). Whereas in the United Kingdom special agencies were central to the government's policy on management because that policy was focused on a single overarching strategy of structural reform, the Canadian approach to SOAs was "part of a larger management improvement complex of strategies" (Armstrong, 1991, p. 6). Remember as well that New Zealand radically separated advice and delivery agencies from ministries. In Canada, five SOAs were created by the end of 1990, and by early 1991 there were fifteen. No new ones were created for another two years, at which point a "stock-taking" exercise was launched that took a year (Seidle, 1995, p. 85). In 1995 the federal Translation Bureau became an SOA, and three others were announced, leading Borins (1995) to note that the "British government, following Sweden, has concluded that over 60 per cent of its activities can be given over to executive agencies while a much more hesitant Canadian federal government has given over to special operating agencies less than 5 per cent of its activities" (p. 125). As of 2004 there were only seventeen federal SOAs (Treasury Board of Canada, 2004a). Six, or less than half, served the "public": the Passport Office, the Canadian Intellectual Property Office, Measurement Canada, the Superintendent of Bankruptcy, Technology Partnerships Canada, and Canadian Investment and Savings. The overall profile of Canadian efforts in this area, therefore, is unimpressive compared to the pace set by some other OECD countries.

In all countries where variants of NPM were implemented, there were moves to change the nature of executive agencies and their relations to service or delivery agencies that went considerably beyond what Canada tried. The logic behind this was that mixing policy development functions with delivery of services in a traditional, hierarchical, civil service bureaucracy would not be conducive to efficiency and flexibility. If the objective is the highest standards of service to the public, then these functions should be clarified and distinguished in some way so that service delivery need not be hobbled by considerations that are more appropriate to policy development and advising the executive.

The clearest and earliest example of this approach to the organization of government functions was the United Kingdom's Next Steps initiative, formally launched in 1988 with the release of the report entitled *Improving Management in Government: The Next Steps* from the Prime Minister's Efficiency Unit. Greer (1994) asserts that the ideas presented in this document were not in themselves radical, addressing age-old questions of how to improve the delivery of public services and what to do about accountability, but that what distinguished Next Steps was that it actually succeeded in implementing these changes (p. 23). The key change was to devolve "the delivery of most public services to *executive,* or *Next Steps agencies,* while policy roles that have traditionally been the role of the senior public service, and related administrative functions, remain the responsibility of departments" (Canadian Centre for Management Development, 1996, p. 33). As we noted in Chapter 2, by 1998 over 377 000 civil servants worked in 138 Next Steps agencies and four departments. That remained relatively steady to 2004 (at about 73 percent of all public servants), though the number of executive agencies at that point was reduced to 9 (Civil Service, 2007).

The Blair government continued these early efforts on public sector reform through its Service First program, which was replaced in 2002 with the Office of Public Services Reform, guided by the Principles into Practice document. The emphasis was on tailored public services to citizens, something continued with the Brown government, though expanded and changed with the revisions to the Charter Mark program (mentioned in Chapter 2) and the introduction of the Customer Service Excellence standard.

> CSE works on four levels—as a driver of continuous improvement, as a tool for developing skills, as an independently assessed means of validating achievement and as a way to capture best

practice and feed lessons back to the centre. Successful organisations will be able to demonstrate:

Personalisation: services must be designed around the needs of the public. Hard-to-reach groups must not be ignored;

Collaboration: Work must be done in partnership with citizens;

Workforce skills: emphasising the link between public service reform and training for staff;

Leadership and commitment: organisations must display customer-focus from the Chief Executive down to frontline staff;

Accountability: to communities and individuals. (Cabinet Office, 2008)

The United Kingdom model restructured government through a division between policy advice (or development) and delivery. The New Zealand model, launched in the mid-1980s, was similar in principle but quite different in design. Launched by Labour governments, the reforms were remarkable for their boldness, rigour, and scope. New Zealand became the poster boy for the NPM around the world, and indeed in 1993 was ranked first by the World Competitiveness Survey for the quality of its government. The objectives and principles behind the reforms were also enunciated with admirable clarity. The objectives were to improve effectiveness, efficiency, and accountability; to reduce expenditures and the size of the public sector; to improve transparency and quality of services. Three key principles in achieving these objectives were that ministers be responsible for selecting outcomes while department executives be responsible for determining inputs (with minimum interference) for achieving those outcomes; that, wherever possible, publicly funded services be open to tender and competition; and that decisionmaking powers be as decentralized and as close to the consumer as possible (Boston et al., 1996, pp. 4–5).

New Zealand, at the time of its reforms, had retained many more commercial and quasi-commercial functions within departmental structures than was characteristic of other Commonwealth countries, and so the first step in the government reorganization was the establishment of "state-owned enterprises" to act as commercially viable providers of government services. A group of these were later privatized in the sale of government assets in 1989 (Seidle, 1995, p. 55). The next stage was the application of a similar model to the provision of operational services within the government itself. This in itself was not unknown in some European countries—Sweden is an example of the "**functional model**" in "which the tasks of policy advice and implementation are generally carried out by separate agencies" (Boston et al., 1996, p. 69). The alternative, which still characterizes most OECD countries, including Canada, is a "**sectoral** model" that vertically integrates advice and delivery within a ministry or department (though this may be changing; see the discussion of Service Canada later in this chapter). In all the cases, the philosophical preference in the New Zealand reforms was to buy these services from commercialized entities, state-owned enterprises, or the public sector. Where that was not possible, however, there was an attempt to divide groups of services and operations into distinct entities. By 1995, fewer than half of government departments had any significant service delivery functions (Boston et al., 1996, p. 78). This model of governance was retained, with modest changes, as part of a "managing for results" framework (State Services Commission, 2004), but has been changed in the most recent public service development plan to 2015 (see discussion later in this chapter on post-NPM developments).

These United Kingdom and New Zealand examples are only part of a larger international trend that in one form or another aimed to restructure the public sector to more sharply define services, agencies that provide them, and accountability relationships both to government and to clients. We addressed this international "policy movement" in Chapter 1. The OECD (2004) highlighted several reform priorities in 2004: budgeting in the public sector, connecting government and citizens, ethics and corruption, human resources management, public sector statistics, regulatory reform, and strategic policymaking. Whereas the emphasis in the mid-1990s seemed to be more on structural reform of governments, recently there has been a shift in attention toward strategic management, particularly of **horizontal issues** that cut across various policy areas, public sector culture (i.e., ethics), human resource management, and continued focus on regulation in the broadest sense of both law and rule-making by other agencies. It reinforced these findings in its 2005 *Modernising Government: The Way Forward*. The highlights of public sector modernizing were: open (transparent) government, enhanced public sector performance, accountability and control, reallocation of expenditures, the use of market-type mechanisms, and improved human resource management.

> In the period under review, many of the assumptions about the extent of direct government responsibility as a service provider have been challenged and, in some countries, radically changed. Governments have progressively withdrawn from commercial activities, ownership of industries and service provision in, for example, communications and energy and water supply. These are explicit governance changes. (OECD, 2005: 16)

Figure 5.1 illustrates the rich range of reforms undertaken by OECD members in the mid-2000s. The data are self-reported, and do not give a sense of magnitude or depth, but they do demonstrate that public sector

Figure 5.1   Management Reform in the OECD

Summary of country recommendations[a]

	Canada	Czech Republic	Denmark	Finland	France	Germany	Greece	Hungary	Iceland	Ireland	Italy	Japan	Korea	Mexico	New Zealand	Norway	Poland	Portugal	Sweden	Switzerland	United Kingdom	Total[b]
Adopting a results-focused budgeting and management approach																						
Move towards results objectives																						
• Improve the quality and encourage the use of performance indicators...	X				X	X	X						X			X	X	X			X	9
... putting more emphasis on outcomes (as opposed to outputs)														X	X						X	3
• Increase commitment to service improvements and client satisfaction	X		X									X										3
• Improve consistency across objectives and co-ordination between agencies															X			X			X	3
• Move to performance-based budgeting...	X							X	X	X						X						5
... extending it to sub-national governments		X		X							X									X		4
Increase managerial autonomy																						
• By giving managers enhanced discretion as to how they reach objectives	X												X	X		X						4
• By increasing the ability of public agencies to carry over unused appropriations												X				X						2
Strengthen accountability frameworks																						
• Develop appropriate instruments to evaluate outcomes						X									X					X		3
• Strengthen performance evaluation and auditing	X				X	X	X	X	X	X	X	X	X			X				X	X	13
• Rely more on activity-based funding systems for public entities[c]...															X		X			X		3
... while safeguarding against cost overruns															X							1
Reforming human resource management																						
Modernize staffing policies																						
• Streamline recruitment procedures...	X												X									2
and use more open recruitment								X									X					2
• Encourage mobility of staff within public service						X				X			X					X				4
• Rely more on fixed-term contracts					X													X				2
Allow wages to reflect market conditions...	X				X							X				X	X					5
... and allow for more functional and regional flexibility in public sector pay schemes						X																1
Rely more on performance-related approaches to personnel management...	X	X	X	X	X	X		X	X	X			X			X	X	X			X	14
... while taking measures to limit wage overruns	X							X														2

a) These policy recommendations are derived from the public spending chapter for individual OECD country reviews published in 2000 for Japan and Mexico; 2001 for Canada and Czech Republic; 2002 for Denmark, Germany, Greece, Hungary, Italy, New Zealand, Norway, Poland, Sweden, Switzerland, and the United Kingdom; 2003 for Finland, France, Iceland, Ireland, Korea, and Portugal.

b) Number of countries for which these recommendations were spelled out among the 21 countries for which in-depth public expenditure chapters in final form are available.

c) In the case of Portugal and Switzerland, this recommendation applies to the hospital sector.

Source: Individual country in-depth chapters on public expenditure.

SOURCE: I. Joumard et al. *Enhancing the effectiveness of public spending: Experience in OECD countries* (2004). Retrieved March 16, 2008, from http://ideas.repec.org/p/oec/ecoaaa/380-en.html.

reform is a global phenomenon. The key question is whether it is still useful to characterize it as an NPM phenomenon, or whether we have moved to a post-NPM stage of reforms. This is tricky, since few governments around the world (at least those in the OECD) have given up on the language of NPM and its emphasis on performance, efficiency, service, and market mechanisms. However, if NPM is not dead, then it has certainly been overshadowed with several new developments in public management reform, none of which amount to a new "paradigm" but which together suggest a substantially changed orientation. Of the OECD's *Modernising Government* priorities (open (transparent) government, enhanced public sector performance, accountability and control, reallocation of expenditures, the use of market-type mechanisms, and improved human resource management), most were dedicated to principles that were not part of the NPM core of the 1980s and 1990s. As well, NPM had been in large part—to be blunt—about downsizing government, reducing expenditures, and making the public sector work more like the private sector. Some large forces in the last five years have upset that agenda, and we mentioned them in previous chapters. One was the impact of 9/11, which revived a sense that strong government, at least on the public security side, was important and necessary. Another was the well-publicized scandals of companies like Enron and Worldcom, and the travails of Canada's own Conrad Black and his company, Hollinger. The financial crash in 2008, with its bail-outs and rescue packages, was another blow. Suddenly, the private sector did not seem like such a paragon of probity and efficiency.

Because Canada did not go as far as other countries in adopting NPM, it did not need to roll back any of its major reforms. In other countries, however, that is exactly what happened. Dunleavy et al. (2005) argue that NPM was marked by three broad themes: disaggregation (splitting up large public sector hierarchies), competition (introducing purchaser/provider separation into public structures), and incentivization (moving to specific performance incentives rather than rewards based on a public sector professional ethos). In terms of our earlier discussion, this only captures part of NPM, but they go on to specify 34 reform components within those three broad themes, and argue that most of these are either stalled or reversed. The disaggregation theme has seen the greatest reversal, particularly with respect to purchaser–provider separation, **agencification,** and growth of quasi-government agencies. Only the following NPM components have continued to spread and enjoy continued support: improved performance measurement, league tables of agency performance, customer-tagged financing, user control, and the introduction of charging technologies. The United States, the United Kingdom, and New Zealand—all early NPM leaders—have recently moved to consolidate or **"re-governmentalize"** certain functions. In the United Kingdom this was trumpeted as **"joined up government"**; the United States example was the creation of the Department of Homeland Security. In the Canadian case, an example is the creation of the Canadian Air Transport Security Authority after 9/11. Previously, airport security had been contracted out to private firms, and the creation of the Authority was part of a five-year, $2.2 billion plan announced in 2001. New Zealand, because it was perhaps one of the most radical innovators in terms of functional differentiation, agencification, and decentralization, is the most interesting. Many of the early NPM enthusiasms have been rolled back and by the early 2000s "combating the vertical siloing of agencies came to be identified by the country's State Services Commission as a key priority" (Dunleavy et al., 2005, 471). Starting in 2005, and building through to 2008 with the latest articulation of its development goals for the public service by 2015, the New Zealand government has increasingly focused on joining up what had once been sundered— networked delivery of services through IT, but also more coordination and integration around horizontal policy themes (Fancy, 2007a, 2007b; State Services Commission 2005, 2007).

While NPM as a movement has either stalled or been reversed, we need to be clear that it has left a strong mark on public sectors around the world—what Hood and Peters referred to as NPM's "aging" and entrance into the "age of paradox" (Hood and Peters, 2004). First, there remains (as the OECD shows) a powerful impulse towards "public sector modernization." There is now, in most countries, a public sector culture of continuous improvement, in part based on the NPM assumption that the public sector should try to be as efficient and as responsive (not always the same thing) as possible. Second, as Dunleavy et al. (2005) point out, some key components of NPM such as a focus on performance, results, client-service, and incentivization, have taken root and continue to be part of public sector practice around the world. Third, some aspects of NPM have been institutionalized and hence are difficult to reverse—in the Canadian context, the **PSMA** is part of the legislative basis of a new human resource management system in the federal government.

At the same time, as we noted above, many countries that introduced strong NPM-inspired changes either in part or in whole have reversed them. Others, like Canada, never went as far and so have not had to roll back as much. For most other countries, as the OECD's 2005 report suggests, the focus of reform has shifted away from decentralization, agencification, and incentivization to preoccupations with openness, accountability, service quality and performance, and improved human resource management. Some argue that this recent focus amounts to a fresh paradigm—either in terms of a search for a new form of post-bureaucratic organization (Kernaghan, Marson, and Borins, 2000), or as "digital-era governance" that is being driven by fundamental information and communications technology changes that are re-shaping the way the government works (Dunleavy et al., 2005). In our view, while reform in most OECD countries is indeed being driven by similar forces, those forces do not amount to a coherent philosophy of the public sector in the same sense that NPM did. We explore at least three of these drivers in the Canadian context in the concluding section to this chapter.

Implementation and a Changing Public Service

We can conclude from the previous section that something indeed has changed about the organization and delivery of public services at every level of government in Canada, first through an extended phase of NPM, and then a more recent focus on post-NPM improvements. Moreover, these changes were part of a global pattern of public sector reform, even though tone and colour differed across different countries. The Canadian experience through the 1990s was, in comparative terms, less far-reaching, radical, or publicly debated than was true of the United Kingdom or New Zealand. In the first half of the 1990s, management reform, while defended in terms of higher standards of service to the public, was driven largely by fiscal constraints at both the federal and provincial levels of government. But the fiscal constraints should be given their due: as we noted in Chapter 4, without those constraints it would have been easy to continue doing business as usual.

Things have changed. Perhaps tellingly, whereas in the 1990s and the early 2000s the federal government and management thinkers used the term "alternative service delivery" to reflect the sort of change they had in mind—alternatives to traditional bureaucracy—the phrase was hardly mentioned by 2008 (the 1996 Treasury Board policy on ASD was replaced in 2002, and then effectively mothballed). The conviction that government services should be delivered imaginatively and with a constant eye to innovation was largely accepted as at least a rhetorical benchmark. One example of how conventional this has become within the profession is the Institute of Public Administration of Canada's (IPAC) Innovation Management Awards, handed out annually since 1990. Box 5.4 lists the annual themes for which IPAC invited applications, and it is striking how the notions of reform, service, collaboration, partnership, performance, and technology dominated over the years.

The examples in Box 5.4 are Canadian, but the **innovation networks** that now appear to bind together public administrators, managers, consultants, and academics have ensured that examples of public sector innovation in program delivery are as widely available as possible—in fact, there is a Global Innovators Network explicitly designed to encourage sharing experiences in innovation. The leading node in this network of innovation is the John F. Kennedy School at Harvard University, which sponsors *Innovations in American Government* (John F. Kennedy School,

BOX 5.4 IPAC INNOVATIVE MANAGEMENT AWARD THEMES, 1990–2007

2007: New Service Breakthroughs with Technology

2006: Sharing Governance: Citizens, Partners and Networks

2005: Public Service without Borders

2004: Pulling Against Gravity: Horizontal Collaboration

2003: In the Know: Knowledge Management

2002: Outside-in: Changing Government to Meet Client Needs

2001: Developing the Public Service of Tomorrow

2000: Collaboration: New Approaches to Policy and Management

1999: Measurement and Recognition

1998: [Not available]

1997: Breakthroughs: Connecting Citizens and Government

1996: Mastering Change

1995: Making Diversity Work

1994: Re-Shaping Government

1993: Better with Less

1992: Partnership Management

1991: Empowerment: Employees, Managers and Organizations

1990: Service to the Public

SOURCE: IPAC. *Innovative Management Award—Themes*. Retrieved March 16, 2008, from http://www.ipac.ca/Award_InnovativeManagementThemes.

2008). The program has recognized innovations in public management since 1986, initially in the United States but then expanding to include Brazil, Chile, China, Mexico, the Philippines, Peru, South Africa, the east African region, and Native American tribes in the United States. In 2003 the program became part of the Kennedy School's Ash Institute for Democratic Governance and Innovation, reflecting a new focus on democratic governance as well as innovative public management. There are now some 400 innovative government innovations that have been recognized through the program. Award winners can be searched in the program's database according to theme: accountability, collaboration, efficiency, participation, pluralism and diversity, social justice, social services, and sustainable development. Whereas a good deal of the academic analyses of NPM innovations have been critical—in part because of its borrowing from private sector models, its emphasis on public sector process constraints over efficiency, and its skepticism about unaccountable public service manager "innovators"—the Kennedy innovations awards program was and is inspired by an optimistic view that public servants can be entrepreneurial in their efforts to create public value, and can achieve "micro-improvements" that collectively add up to substantial and positive changes in governance (Borins, 2008, pp. 5–6).

As we argued above, there are clearly strong traces of NPM themes in these awards programs, and they echo many of the realities of public sector management and reform efforts today. However, that is not the whole story. At least with respect to Canada, several broad developments have occurred that overshadow some of the NPM skepticism of the public sector, even while amplifying some elements of NPM, such as service and performance. We will highlight three major shifts that have occurred in the last five years. The first is a renewed appreciation of the special nature of the public sector, of public sector values, and of how public institutions (government, but the para-public sector as well) serve the public interest. This is in part due to the impact of 9/11 and the 2008 financial crisis, but also has more complicated roots in the realization (discussed in Chapter 2) that in a global, knowledge-based economy, good governance and a well-functioning public service is a key competitive advantage. The second is a new emphasis on accountability and ethics. This is not specific to Canada, though the Federal Accountability Act was a signature policy of the newly elected Conservatives in 1996, and a policy with extraordinarily wide scope. It is not that NPM ignored ethics, it simply did not place it at the centre of its thinking about governance. As the OECD (2005) has noted, accountability and ethics are now central themes, in combination with transparency and openness, in public sector reform.

The third shift is not really a shift at all, but contains the seeds of radical change. A core theme of NPM was enhanced service to citizens. Critics of NPM dismissed this as reducing citizens to clients or customers, but it was more far-reaching than that, and driven by a genuine desire to make government more responsive to public needs. This emphasis on service coincided with the revolution in information and communication technologies, just as governments were moving into the digital age. This is not yet a post-NPM paradigm, but the impact of digital technology on governance is already profound, and promises to have even more dramatic effects in the next decade.

RETHINKING THE VALUE OF THE PUBLIC SERVICE

NPM, despite variations that celebrated the importance of citizen engagement and client service, had a strong undercurrent of skepticism about the public sector. There were good grounds for this in the 1980s and 1990s in terms of practical politics: the public sector had grown for decades without much restraint and public bureaucracies were stereotypically unresponsive and leaden. By the late 1990s, as we noted in Chapter 1, there was a growing realization that the public sector and governance were critical ingredients to economic competitiveness. What some called the "public domain" was being rediscovered as a balancing mechanism for the failure of markets, and a large part of that public domain consisted of government and government services (Drache, 2001). That realization was amplified with the 9/11 attacks, and perhaps even more dramatically with the global meltdown in November 2008. A new sense of the importance of public sector values gradually grew through the early 2000s.

> The public policy dimension is unique to public management as governance. Citizen-centred service requires attention to critical issues of law, rights, and due process not present in the market-place of private service delivery. And managing the public service entails managing in a context of constraints and motivations that are distinct to the public sector. To the degree that privatization and contracting out cannot be extended to all functions of government, public administration, even in a highly devolved management regime, remains subject to political and administrative dynamics that require their own distinctive modes of reform and renewal. (Aucoin, 2002, 50)

Denhardt and Denhardt (2000; 2003), for example, have made the case for a "new civil service" rooted in the responsibility that public servants have to serve and empower citizens. Their seven principles:

1. *Serve, rather than steer.* An increasingly important role of the public servant is to help citizens articulate and meet their shared interests, rather than attempt to control or steer society in new directions.

2. *The public interest is the aim, not the by-product.* Public administrators must contribute to building a collective, shared notion of the public interest. The goal is not to find quick solutions driven by individual choices. Rather, it is the creation of shared interests and shared responsibility.

3. *Think strategically, act democratically.* Policies and programs meeting public needs can be most effectively and responsibly achieved through collective efforts and collaborative processes.

4. *Serve citizens, not customers.* The public interest results from a dialogue about shared values, rather than the aggregation of individual self-interests. Therefore, public servants do not merely respond to the demands of "customers," but focus on building relationships of trust and collaboration with and among citizens.

5. *Accountability isn't simple.* Public servants should be attentive to more than the market; they should also attend to statutory and constitutional law, community values, political norms, professional standards, and citizen interests.

6. *Value people, not just productivity.* Public organizations and the networks in which they participate are more likely to succeed in the long run if they are operated through processes of collaboration and shared leadership based on respect for all people.

7. *Value citizenship and public service above entrepreneurship.* The public interest is better advanced by public servants and citizens committed to making meaningful contributions to society rather than by entrepreneurial managers acting as if public money were their own.

This reflects the idea of a "public service value chain" (Heintzman and Marson, 2005), where trust by citizens is a function of excellence in public service, provided by public servants who are professionally engaged in and proud and confident of their work. It is also a view that public administration and implementation has to be thought of differently. As the Clerk of the Privy Council put it in a 2008 speech:

> For example, in the post 9-11 world, the public service has shifted towards strengthened border security, transportation security, national security, Arctic sovereignty and support for our active military engagement in Afghanistan. In response to pressures of globalization, the public service has helped governments achieve 11 consecutive years of fiscal surpluses, steady and low inflation, corporate taxes that are very competitive with our major trading partners, and infrastructure modernization. Innovations in research funding, long term fiscal support for health care and new, tax-based supports for low income families have re-invigorated university-led research in Canada, strengthened our health care system and made appreciable progress on child poverty alleviation. Service quality standards, with measureable and transparent tracking, have been established in a number of areas and the results are encouraging. And the list goes on, as do the challenges.

> Unfortunately, this reality is not well known. There persists in Canada an all-too-common notion that nothing significant ever changes in public policy, that the public service is more obsessed with process than results, that economically Canada is continually falling behind other nations. But this myth simply does not square with the remarkable transformations in Canada over the last 20 years, and the public service figured importantly in these transformations. This public service is certainly different today, and needs to be, because the times have changed, Canadian

society has changed, the public policy "tool kit" has changed, and public expectations for government have changed including more accountability processes (Privy Council of Canada, 2008a).

The emphasis on public sector renewal since 2006 reflects this new appreciation of both the importance of the public service, and the impending changes due simply to demographic shifts (Privy Council Office, 2007; 2008b). While it might be too much to suggest that this shift entails a "new public administration theory," Bourgon is certainly correct to highlight a change in perspective from NPM's emphasis on markets, productivity, managerialism, and the emulation of "private sector practices in the public sector" (Bourgon, 2007: 13). Her argument is that a new approach to public administration should begin with a focus on citizen-centred services (see below), value for taxpayer's money, and a flexible public service workforce. Its fundamental building blocks would be citizen involvement, the public interest, service to citizens, and collaborative approaches to the development of public policy. Even a critic of her article noted that "the state does not simply provide services, it also carries deep responsibilities for law and order and security, the discharge of which will sometimes bring the public authorities up against the expressed wishes of significant communities or groups, and which will often require the restraining and prevention of individuals from pursuing their preferred courses of action. The re-conceptualization of the 'public interest' that Bourgon refers to needs to accommodate these more coercive and regulatory aspects of the government's role" (Pollitt, 2007: 39). Neither Bourgon nor Pollitt are envisioning the sort of stripped down state imagined in NPM. They are both suggesting, as is the Clerk of the Privy Council, a model of governance where the public service and the public sector are distinct in terms of their values as well as their contributions to society. More evidence for this comes from the recent, renewed emphasis on public service ethics and accountability.

ETHICS AND ACCOUNTABILITY: NEW BENCHMARKS

Heintzman (2007a) notes: "One of the most important things that has taken place in public services right across the country, over the last ten years is a reawakened awareness of the democratic, professional, ethical and people values inherent in public service, and of their importance, both to public service institutions, and to the daily lives of individual public servants." He also argues that the concern for public-service values has been a "prominent feature of public-service reform and renewal in many countries over the past decade" (Heintzman, 2007b: 574). Similar to the point we made above about the rediscovery of the special qualities of the public service, the renewed emphasis on ethics and values was driven by a reaction to NPM and prompted "another careful look at the first principles of public administration . . . a rediscovery of public-service values was intended to address and remedy the confusion resulting from the initial, over-eager embrace of private-sector ideas, ideas that could not be imported indiscriminately into the public sector without great damage to the profession, institutions and practice of public administration" (Heintzman, 2007b: 576).

In the Canadian case, this rediscovery stemmed initially from one of several Deputy Ministers task forces established in 1995 by Jocelyne Bourgon (then Clerk of the Privy Council). The Task Force on Values and Ethics (A Strong Foundation, 2000; originally published in 1996) highlighted the importance of the "the public good, and . . . related values (such as equity and balance), for public service. The notion of the public interest is a touchstone of motivation for public servants. It is for the public service what justice and liberty are for the legal profession, or what healing and mercy are for the medical profession" (A Strong Foundation, 2000: 37). The Task Force report then became the basis for the Values and Ethics Code for the Public Service. The core values of the code are reproduced in Box 5.5. Creation of the code was then followed by a new program linking ethics to democratic reform during the Martin government (Langford and Tupper, 2006).

As a result of the sponsorship scandal and the Gomery Inquiry, discussed earlier, the salience of ethics and accountability only grew in the mid-2000s, and became the centrepiece of the new Conservative government's election campaign in 2006. The Federal Accountability Act was the first piece of legislation introduced by the government, and brought with it a heightened ethics and accountability regime at the federal level. The legislation was extremely complicated, and is too detailed to discuss here, but its highlights included new restrictions on the financing of political parties (e.g., a complete ban on contributions by unions, corporations or other organizations, and a limit of $1000 contribution to parties annually by individuals); a new Conflict of Interest and Ethics Commissioner with enhanced powers, and a new Conflict of Interest Act enshrining codes on conflict of interest and post-employment provisions; tougher rules on lobbyists; a Parliamentary Budget Office; tighter government procurement regulations (e.g., public disclosure of contracts over $10 000); a Public Servants Disclosure Protection Act; and the designation of deputy heads as "accounting officers" (Federal Accountability Act, 2006).

The animus behind this renewed emphasis on ethics and accountability is complicated. In part, as we noted, it stems from a genuine sense of rediscovery of unique public service values and characteristics that hinge on the protection and promotion of the public interest. At the same time, some of it is driven by scandals, distrust, and a suspicion that the public sector needs careful oversight and scrutiny. It has been a strange combination of

BOX 5.5   VALUES AND ETHICS FOR THE PUBLIC SERVICE

PUBLIC SERVICE VALUES

Public servants shall be guided in their work and their professional conduct by a balanced framework of public service values: democratic, professional, ethical and people values. These families of values are not distinct but overlap. They are perspectives from which to observe the universe of Public Service values.

Democratic Values: *Helping Ministers, under law, to serve the public interest.*

- Public servants shall give honest and impartial advice and make all information relevant to a decision available to Ministers.

- Public servants shall loyally implement ministerial decisions, lawfully taken.

- Public servants shall support both individual and collective ministerial accountability and provide Parliament and Canadians with information on the results of their work.

Professional Values: *Serving with competence, excellence, efficiency, objectivity and impartiality.*

- Public servants must work within the laws of Canada and maintain the tradition of the political neutrality of the Public Service.

- Public servants shall endeavour to ensure the proper, effective and efficient use of public money.

- In the Public Service, how ends are achieved should be as important as the achievements themselves.

- Public servants should constantly renew their commitment to serve Canadians by continually improving the quality of service, by adapting to changing needs through innovation, and by improving the efficiency and effectiveness of government programs and services offered in both official languages.

- Public servants should also strive to ensure that the value of transparency in government is upheld while respecting their duties of confidentiality under the law.

Ethical Values: *Acting at all times in such a way as to uphold the public trust.* Public servants shall perform their duties and arrange their private affairs so that public confidence and trust in the

BOX 5.5 (continued)

integrity, objectivity and impartiality of government are conserved and enhanced.

- Public servants shall act at all times in a manner that will bear the closest public scrutiny; an obligation that is not fully discharged by simply acting within the law.
- Public servants, in fulfilling their official duties and responsibilities, shall make decisions in the public interest.
- If a conflict should arise between the private interests and the official duties of a public servant, the conflict shall be resolved in favour of the public interest.

People Values: *Demonstrating respect, fairness and courtesy in their dealings with both citizens and fellow public servants.*

- Respect for human dignity and the value of every person should always inspire the exercise of authority and responsibility.
- People values should reinforce the wider range of Public Service values. Those who are treated with fairness and civility will be motivated to display these values in their own conduct.
- Public Service organizations should be led through participation, openness and communication and with respect for diversity and for the official languages of Canada.
- Appointment decisions in the Public Service shall be based on merit.
- Public Service values should play a key role in recruitment, evaluation and promotion.

SOURCE: Government of Canada, *Values and Ethics Code for the Public Service.* 2003. Retrieved March 17, 2008, from http://www.tbs-sct.gc.ca/pubs_pol/hrpubs/ TB_851/vec-cve1_e.asp#_Toc46202803.

drivers. The first is a genuinely positive commitment to a broader and deeper sense of the value of the public service, exemplified by Bourgon, Tait, the current Clerk (Kevin Lynch), and Heintzman. But this has largely been an internal discourse within the profession. The second driver has tended to overwhelm the first—it is a ramped up distrust of the public service, coupled with a determination to "fix it." The ironic result of this oil and water has been a heightened sense of the importance of public service, its values, its ethical fibre, and its accountability to the public interest. This was muted in NPM, but is loud and clear today.

DIGITAL GOVERNANCE AND QUALITY SERVICE

The mid-1990s was a period of structural reform (however modest in the Canadian case), coupled with a focus on citizen-centred service, satisfaction, and quality. A network of Canadian public servants and policymakers became concerned about the "service gap" or the distance between what citizens expect from their governments and the level of satisfaction that they have with what they actually get. The 1998 Citizens First survey showed that Canadians in fact rated many public services quite highly: "Almost every Canadian survey that has compared public and private sector services has found that citizens rate the performance of government services significantly below that of private sector services." (Canadian Centre for Management Development, 1999, p. 8)

These findings were largely supported in the following two biennial surveys undertaken in 2000 and 2002. The 2002 survey also asked citizens about their priorities for improvement. The findings provide an interesting snapshot of what matters most to people in terms of government services (see Box 5.6 and 5.7 below). The seriousness with which this

---

BOX 5.6   MUNICIPAL AND PROVINCIAL/ TERRITORIAL SERVICES— PRIORITIES FOR IMPROVEMENT

Service	Percent choosing the service as a priority
Visited a physician or medical doctor's office	38
Received hospital services as an outpatient	38
Stayed in a hospital to receive care	36
Roads maintained by your municipality	24
Used municipal public transit (bus, streetcar, subway)	19
Sent one of your children to attend public school	19
Municipal snow removal services	13
Contacted the municipal police force for help	11
Drinking water provided to you at your residence	10

NOTE: *N = 5043; percentages total more than 100% because citizens could select more than one service.*

SOURCE: ICCS & IPAC (2005, Exhibit 3.1, p. 18)

BOX 5.7 — FEDERAL SERVICES—PRIORITIES FOR IMPROVEMENT

Service	Percent choosing the service as a priority
Health Canada: Information on health issues	23
Canada Post	22
Canada Pension Plan (CPP), Old Age Security (OAS)	22
Employment Insurance (EI)	22
Customs and Immigration border services	21
Canada Revenue Agency (CRA)	20
Passports: Get or renew a passport	19
Federal Courts	12
RCMP	12
National Parks	12
National Parole Board, federal prisons	11
Human Resource Centres of Canada, HRCCs	10
Citizenship Services	10
Access to information: 1-800-O-Canada, Canada.gc.ca	10

NOTE: N=4845; percentages total more than 100% because citizens could select more than one service.

SOURCE: ICCS & IPAC (2005, Exhibit 3.2, p. 19)

dimension of implementation is being taken is illustrated by the Service Improvement Initiative that was launched in 2000 and then regalvanized in 2004. A total of forty-seven departments and agencies were required to participate in the initiative, whose target was a minimum 10 percent increase in client satisfaction by 2005. It required measurements of client satisfaction, benchmarks, annual improvement plans, and public progress reports. In describing the initiative, the policy document stated:

> The essence of the *Service Improvement Initiative* is that the continuous and measurable improvement of client satisfaction is the most reliable indicator of improvement in service quality and service performance: it is what quality and continuous improvement should now mean, and how they should be primarily, though not exclusively, measured. Leading-edge service organizations in the public sector, like their counterparts in the private

sector, now use a results-based approach to the continuous improvement of client satisfaction, integrated with the annual business planning cycle. (Treasury Board of Canada, 2000c)

This emphasis on quality and service would be largely empty if there were no way of assessing the success of achieving quality and service goals, and finding out what clients and citizens actually think about the services that they receive. Hence, the emphasis on service is almost inevitably linked to an emphasis on performance assessment, measurement, and results. We will take up the question of performance measurement in Chapter 7, but it can be noted here that there are many ways of assessing outcomes and performance, from actual program impacts on specific targets to levels of satisfaction with services. As we will see in Chapter 7, there is a wide variety of approaches to measuring and reporting on performance; the important thing is that it is being done, and that in comparison with the older tradition of public administration, it is new. In the past, the reporting function focused primarily on the appropriate administration of resources, while policy evaluation took care of cost-benefit analyses of impact analyses. Performance and satisfaction matter now because citizens matter more.

Another clear characteristic of the federal government's approach to public sector reform is the centrality of partnerships. We will discuss this in Chapter 6 in the context of policy communities and networks, and we provided the broader context for this shift in Chapter 2 in terms of shifting governance regimes. Today, implementation is neither primarily about doing it alone nor shifting public responsibilities completely to the private sector. It is about doing it in concert with partners from the voluntary sector, from interest groups and NGOs, from the private and not-for-profit sectors. The range of available modes and partners in service delivery is virtually limitless, with various permutations and combinations of commercialized, voluntary, and purely public services, and every hybrid in between. The main dimensions are commercialization, private/public, and independence from government. Combined with initiatives to improve the quality of services, enhance performance, and publicize results, it is clear that the world of implementation and policy instruments has changed significantly.

This emphasis on service and quality is now more than two decades old. What has stimulated new thinking however is the merging of digital technology and service. As we mentioned earlier, some (Dunleavy et al., 2005) see this as a new public service paradigm. We do not go that far. Many things in government are still delivered in old-fashioned ways, from garbage removal to meals-on-wheels. Moreover, rule-bound bureaucracies are likely to simply shift their rules to be embedded in software as opposed to codes and guidelines in the hierarchy (Fountain, 2001). But, as we noted in Chapter 4, it is undeniable that the "digital state" is a qualitatively different animal from what preceded it, and has certain consequences for the organization of government and the delivery of services. According to Borins, "The most significant change that could flow from IT-enabled government, however, is a reshaping of the public service that consolidates many common functions previously located separately in each department. Three aspects . . . are integrated service delivery organizations, joined-up policy development and knowledge management, and integrated support organizations" (Borins, 2007: 16). From a service provision perspective, this new IT environment—dubbed by some as Web 2.0 governance—adds new channels (web, e-mail) for citizens to register their preferences, and new modes of delivery of services, especially ones that are primarily knowledge based, and new forms of collaboration among public agencies, private and non-profit organizations, and citizens (Williams, 2006). A particularly important development is allowing citizens access to either general information or personal information (e.g., medical records, tax files) that previously would have been available only with great difficulty or not at all. Within governments, Web 2.0's enhanced capabilities are allowing (mostly younger) public servants to organize their own communities using blogs, wikis, and social networking tools analogous to Facebook.

The Service Improvement Initiative described above was what is known in the literature as an "integrated service delivery" (ISD) model that is "multi-channel and multi-jurisdictional" (Flumian et al., 2007: 558). Integrated service delivery "is the result of bringing together related government services so that citizens can access them in a single seamless experience based on their wants and needs. A seamless service delivery system is 'fluid, agile, integrated, transparent, connected'" (Kernaghan, 2007: 103). Service Canada was launched in the 2005 federal budget, building on the successes of the Government On-Line initiative that ran from 1999 to 2006. Service Canada is a single window for federal government services, provided through several channels such as in-person, telephone, Internet and mail delivery. It has over 20 000 employees, operates in over 580 in-person points of service across Canada, and has over 14 million unique website visits per year. Just as importantly, it is "working with a growing number of federal departments, the majority of provinces and community partners to bring services and benefits together in a single service delivery network" (Flumian et al., 2007: 559). Services are available by subject (e.g., education, pensions) but also by categories of citizens (e.g., Aboriginal peoples, newcomers to Canada, people with disabilities). It is clear that ISD of this nature (other examples include Canada's BizPal, which "provides Canadian businesses with one-stop access to permit and licence information for all levels of government," and Australia's Centrelink) does hold important implications both for services and how they are delivered, as well as government organization.

Service Canada's ambition is to provide Canadian citizens and organizations with the bulk of federal as well as provincial and community-based services 24/7 through multiple channels. Just as important, in many instances it lets those citizens and organizations have access to data (e.g., the status of an immigration or passport application) that previously would have been only available to government officials. On the organizational side, Service Canada is becoming the ISD mechanism for the majority of federal departments, who will eventually focus more of their efforts on policy development and program design, and away from implementation of programs and services. This will not be easy:

> Striking a new balance between hierarchy and flexibility, between vertical and horizontal dimensions of accountability, is the nexus of technological and organizational interoperability and innovative leadership. Strengthening the capacities of the public service in this regard, via initiatives such as Service Canada, entails more than incremental modifications to existing structures and processes. A more networked and collaborative mindset must take hold in order to loosen the forces of bureaucratic and political tradition that are intertwined with vertical hierarchy and control. (Roy, 2006, p. 284)

Conclusion

It is easy enough to see what is different about implementation—new organizational forms, clearer standards, use of information technology for ISD, partnerships, a service orientation, and public exposure of plans and performance. Partnering in some format is becoming a critical aspect of governance and service delivery. This poses fresh challenges for public managers and policy analysts, since our traditional paradigms of service delivery have relied on a top-down, centralized control model. When governments act as partners, providing support and frameworks rather than services directly, and when they move to ISD, it changes the nature of the implementation game quite dramatically, for example, through highlighting accountability issues, monitoring, and learning loops. In terms of the theory discussed in the first part of this chapter, modern implementation practices seem to combine strategies of decentralization and integration (the Service Canada model) to reduce blockages in decisionmaking and strategies of interdependency that will actually demand greater attention to communication and cooperation (e.g., partnerships; Savoie, 2004, p. 7).

It should also be clear from this chapter that while the world of policy implementation has changed, the tableaux of those changes are confusing and difficult to trace. The NPM movement dominated public sector and service reform for two decades, with a focus on service quality, results, performance, and fidelity to private sector efficiencies. The post-NPM period has overtaken those initiatives with new stresses on ethics and accountability, and the unique character of public services, but the NPM instinct for change, innovation, service, and quality has not disappeared. Indeed, what is possibly new about the current context is a marriage of NPM and post-NPM philosophies—though whether they can be blended (the web of rules that comes from the Accountability Act is not entirely consistent with a nimble service orientation) is not clear.

We have argued that many of these changes are being driven by deep forces that are difficult, if not impossible, to avoid, and that these changes in governance cut across ideological lines. Certainly the first wave of NPM reforms reflected a combined sense that government could and should be leaner and more efficient, and that it could and should capitalize on emerging information technologies. The human cost was in public sector jobs, with literally thousands of people let go (though in the case of Ottawa, employment increased steadily after 1999 to bring levels back to where they had been in 1995; Statistics Canada, 2004; 2008). Those who remained standing in the rubble of public sector institutions in the late 1990s had little choice but to seek partners and support. A big part of the equation had thus been determined: a smaller public sector, doing fewer things with fewer resources. It was only a matter of time before circumstances demanded innovation, though as we noted the rhetoric of NPM also placed a premium on innovation and service directly.

This initial NPM enthusiasm for disaggregation, competition, and incentivization has, as we argued earlier, been eclipsed for various reasons. Governments post 9/11 have not become smaller, and indeed have continued to grow. There were some policy failures due to NPM ideas (especially in the United Kingdom, the United States, Australia, and New Zealand), and that contributed to rolling back some initiatives (Gregory, 2002). This was accompanied with a new appreciation of the specific qualities of the public sector and the public service, that has led to fresh preoccupations with probity (ethics and accountability) and service (ISD).

We also need to be wary of the interests that are served, and those that are not, by catch phrases like "citizen-centred service delivery," and "partnerships." There is always the danger, for example, that surveys that seem to be searching for citizens' views on services might in the end be used more as legitimizing instruments to support what governments are doing anyway. The same can be said of performance and results reporting. What should be honest attempts at transparency can easily become weapons of government propaganda, skewing the numbers in such a way as to declare perfection. As well, it cannot be lost on many observers that the craze for quality and service exploded just at the time that many services were either being reduced or eliminated. The energy and resources flowing into measurements, benchmarks, surveys, reports, and indicators may serve to persuade the citizenry that governments actually care about what they are doing, when in fact much of government may steam along as usual. Most analyses of quality service initiatives and performance measurement are well aware of these human and political dynamics, and so consequently stress leadership, organizational commitment, and culture change as key ingredients in achieving genuinely different outcomes. This is especially true of ISD, which does pose fundamental organizational challenges for the way government conventionally operates.

We also need to recognize the challenges and problems involved in partnerships, since partnerships (and horizontal coordination) formed such a prominent part of the NPM and continue to be a strong point of emphasis in current public management practice. We raise some of these in Chapter 6, but it is worth addressing them briefly here. The current enthusiasm for partnerships assumes that civil society organizations—these are typically the entities involved in a private/public partnership, though firms are also engaged in some policy areas—have the capacity to take on new responsibilities. Hall and Reed (1998) cautioned over a decade ago that civil society organizations needed considerable capacity-building in order to effectively engage with government in the delivery of services, and more recent reviews had more or less agreed with this early assessment (Phillips, 2006).

It is not merely a matter of weakness or inadequate resources. Nonprofit organizations operate in different ways from government departments, on a different scale, with different values and procedures. The easy assumption that they can step into the breach and immediately partner with government is flawed. We need as well to be cautious about our assumptions about contracting out social services. Most attempts to do so rely on outcome or performance measures, as government departments develop agreements with third parties to provide certain services and give them the flexibility to achieve them as they see fit. However, those same government departments lack a comprehensive assessment of the impacts of their interventions and so have quite imperfect knowledge about how to assess the performance of commercial firms (Panet and Trebilcock, 1998, p. 28). Other types of public-private sector partnerships to deliver different types of goods and services (e.g., infrastructure), have run up against problems in that the private sector actors, as befits commercial entities, often demand confidentiality about key aspects of their agreement or activities, thus short-circuiting important public policy values (Boase, 2000).

The issue is one that has been touched on repeatedly in this chapter, and which has surged in importance in recent years—accountability. The traditional governance model under a parliamentary regime like Canada's assumes that monies are spent by government departments and agencies that are accountable to their ministers, and through them to the government as a whole, and ultimately to the legislature and the people. The new forms of service delivery, either through ISD channels like Service Canada or through horizontal partnerships pose challenges for these conventional practices of democratic accountability. In late 1999, for example, the Auditor General released a report on new governance arrangements that had been developed in the mid-1990s in response to budget cuts and new management thinking. He found seventy-seven such new arrangements that collectively spent $5 billion of taxpayers' money annually. "Under these arrangements, the federal government involves external partners in the planning, design and achievement of federal objectives, replacing delivery by federal employees, contractors or agents. These partners are not accountable to ministers and Parliament" (Auditor General, 1999). The infamous 2003 review of the sponsorship program that eventually led to the Gomery Inquiry also pointed out problems in accountability relationships because of the nature of the program. Even in 2005, the Auditor General found that while there had been improvements, federal central agencies had "not developed enough specialized tools for the governance, accountability, and co-ordination of federal efforts in such initiatives and have made little progress in developing means of funding horizontal programs" (Auditor General, 2005).

In many respects, these are broad questions of governance and not merely technical ones of implementation. Our discussion of ISD and the increasing impact of IT in government showed that there are substantive organizational impacts that go well beyond simply changing delivery channels from in-person to electronic. We will address these larger governance issues in our conclusions in Chapter 9. Chapter 7 will take up the difficult question of asking how we might measure whether all this innovation, alternative service delivery, and quality actually result in efficiencies and positive impact. The next chapter, however, considers the question of the participants in the policy process.

KEY TERMS

agencification—breaking up government departments into quasi-autonomous agencies with more flexible management practices, and usually contractual relationships with political authorities based on performance requirements

alternative service delivery—a term used in the 1990s, but less so now, to describe attempts to deliver government services outside a traditional departmental format, in partnership for example with the private sector or NGOs, or through contracting out

backward mapping—a technique to work out what the policy will look like in terms of delivery of programs at the final point of service, and hence what the implementation needs are at that point

citizen-centred service delivery—ensuring that clients get what they want and that resources are allocated accordingly by focusing on citizens first and assessing their needs and their levels of satisfaction

clearances—the number of agreements required by multiple sets of actors in order for implementation to go forward

client satisfaction—degree to which customers or clients of a service are happy with that service

decentralization—devolution of responsibilities to other government jurisdictions or third parties, and restructuring accountability relationships within government departments

decision chain—the sequence of agreements, decisions, or clearances that have to be surmounted in order for the implementation process to move forward

decision points—a single stage in a decision chain requiring clearances and agreements before movement to the next point is possible

empowerment—the provision of real powers and authorities to the government's other partners in the policy process

forward mapping—the conventional technique of implementation analysis that starts with as clear a statement as possible of the policymaker's intent and proceeds through a sequence of increasingly specific steps to define what is expected of implementers at each level

functional model—the model in which the tasks of policy advice and implementation are generally carried out by separate agencies

horizontal issues—issues that cut across various policy areas

innovation networks—networks that bind together public administrators, managers, consultants, and academics to ensure that examples of public sector innovation in program delivery are as widely available as possible

joined-up government—the UK term for horizontal coordination across government departments and agencies

performance—empirical indicator of how well a program or organization is operating with respect to clearly articulated goals

policy feedback—information about the consequences or impacts of a policy that goes back into its improvement and redesign

PS2000—a 1989–1993 federal public sector reform initiative inaugurated in 1989, which had three core objectives: better service, improved personnel management, and flexibility

Public Service Modernization Act (PSMA)—federal legislation introduced in 2003 to make human resource management in government departments more flexible and decentralized

quality management—managing programs and services with a high priority placed on quality, performance measures, and reporting

Quality Services Initiative—the late 1990s federal initiative that stresses citizen-centred service delivery

re-governmentalize—the opposite of agencification—pulling agencies or activities back into the public sector from the private sector

sectoral model—a model that vertically integrates advice and delivery within a ministry or department

service delivery—procedures and organizational resources devoted to getting services to clients

Special Operating Agency (SOA)—agency that continues to work in the public sector but with special, more relaxed rules that give it more scope to be flexible and service oriented

FURTHER READINGS

Aucoin, P. (1995). *The new public management: Canada in a comparative perspective*. Montreal: Institute for Research on Public Policy.

Bardach, E. (1977). *The implementation game: What happens after a bill becomes a law*. Cambridge, MA: MIT Press.

Borins, S. et al. (2007). *Digital state at the leading edge*. Toronto: IPAC and the University of Toronto Press.

Borins, S. (Ed.) (2008). *Innovations in government: Research, recognition, and replication*. Boston and Washington: Ash Institute for Democratic Governance and Innovation, and Brookings Institution Press.

Hupe, P. L., and Hill, M. (2002). *Implementing public policy: Governance in theory and in practice*. Thousand Oaks, CA: Sage.

Pressman, J. L., and Wildavsky, A. (1984). *Implementation: How great expectations in Washington are dashed in Oakland: Or, why it's amazing that federal programs work at all, this being a saga of the economic development administration as told by two sympathetic observers who seek to build morals on a foundation of ruined hopes* (3rd ed.). Berkeley: University of California Press.

Roy. J. (2006). *E-government in Canada: Transformation for the digital age*. Ottawa: University of Ottawa Press.

REFERENCES

Alexander, E. R. (1989). Improbable implementation: The Pressman-Wildavsky paradox revisited. *Journal of Public Policy, 9*, 451–65.

A Strong Foundation (2000). (Tait Report) *Report of the Task Force on Public Service Values and Ethics*. Ottawa: Canadian Centre for Management Development.

Armstrong, J. (1991). Special operating agencies: Evolution or revolution? *Optimum*, 22(2), 5–12.

Atkinson, M. (1993). Public policy and the new institutionalism. In M. Atkinson (Ed.), *Governing Canada: Institutions and public policy* (pp. 17–45). Toronto: Harcourt Brace Jovanovich.

Aucoin, P. (1995). *The new public management: Canada in a comparative perspective*. Montreal: Institute for Research on Public Policy.

Aucoin, P. (2002). Beyond the "new" in public management reform in Canada: Catching the next wave. In C. Dunn (Ed.), *The handbook of Canadian public administration* (pp. 36–52). Toronto: Oxford University Press.

Auditor General of Canada. (1999). *Report of the Auditor General of Canada*. Chapter 23: Involving others in governing: Accountability at risk. Ottawa.

Auditor General of Canada. (2005). *Report of the Auditor General of Canada*. Chapter 4: Managing horizontal initiatives. Retrieved on March 18, 2008, from http://www.oag-bvg.gc.ca/internet/English/aud_ch_oag_2005_4_e_14942.html#ch4hd3a

Bardach, E. (1977). *The implementation game: What happens after a bill becomes a law*. Cambridge, MA: MIT Press.

Boase, J. P. (2000). Beyond government? The appeal of public-private partnerships. *Canadian Public Administration, 43*(1), 75–92.

Borins, S. (1995, Spring). The new public management is here to stay. *Canadian Public Administration, 38*, 122–32.

Borins, S. (2002). Transformation of the public sector: Canada in comparative perspective. In C. Dunn (Ed.), *The handbook of Canadian public administration* (pp. 3–17). Toronto: Oxford University Press.

Borins, S. (2007). Conceptual framework. In S. Borins et al., *Digital state at the leading edge*. (pp. 14–36). Toronto: IPAC and the University of Toronto Press.

Borins, S. (2008). Introduction. In S. Borins (Ed.), *Innovations in government: Research, recognition, and replication* (1–12). Boston and Washington: Ash Institute for Democratic Governance and Innovation, and Brookings Institution Press.

Boston, J., et al. (1996). *Public management: The New Zealand model.* Auckland: Oxford University Press.

Bourgon, J. (2007). Responsive, responsible and respected government: Towards a new public administration theory. *International Review of Administrative Sciences* 73 (1), 7–26.

Bovens, M., and t'Hart, P. (1996). *Understanding policy fiascoes.* New Brunswick, NJ: Transaction Publishers.

Cabinet Office (United Kingdom). (2008). New standard raises the bar for public services. Retrieved March 10, 2008, from http://www.cabinetoffice.gov.uk/newsroom/news_releases/2008/080310_new_standard.aspx

Canadian Centre for Management Development. (1996). *Key characteristics of departments and executive agencies in the Westminster democracies.* Ottawa: Canadian Centre for Management Development.

Canadian Centre for Management Development. (1999). *Citizen-centred service: Responding to the needs of Canadians.* Retrieved March 16, 2008, from http://www.iccs-isac.org/eng/pubs/CCHandbook.pdf

Cheung, A. (1997). Understanding public sector reforms: Global trends and diverse agendas. *International Review of Administrative Science,* 63 (4), 435–57.

Civil Service (United Kingdom). (2007). *Civil Service Statistics 2004 Annual Report.* Retrieved March 10, 2008, from http://www.civilservice.gov.uk/about/statistics/archive/2004/civil_service.asp

Denhardt, R. B., and Denhardt, J. V. (2000). The new public service: Serving rather than steering. *Public Administration Review* 60 (6), 549–559.

Denhardt, R. B., and Denhardt, J. V. (2003). *The new public service: Serving, not steering.* Armonk, N.Y.: M.E. Sharpe.

Department of Finance (Canada). (1995). *Budget speech.*

Drache, D. (Ed.) (2001). *The market or the public domain: Global governance and the asymmetry of power.* London: Routledge.

Dunleavy, P., et al. (2005). New public management is dead—Long live digital-era governance. *Journal of Public Administration Research and Theory* 16, 467–94.

Edwards III, G. C. (1984). Introduction. In G. C. Edwards III (Ed.), *Public policy implementation* (pp. ix–xv). Greenwich, CT: JAI Press.

Elmore, R. F. (1982). Backward mapping: Implementation research and policy decisions. In W. Williams (Ed.), *Studying implementation: Methodological and administrative issues* (pp. 18–35). Chatham, NJ: Chatham House.

Fancy, H. (2007a). Development Goals for the New Zealand State Services—Draft Milestones for 2015. Retrieved March 11, 2007, from http://www.ssc.govt.nz/display/document.asp?docid=6331&PageType =toc&displaytype=pf

Fancy, H. (2007b). Refresh the Development Goals Milestones project. Discussion paper. Retrieved March 11, 2007, from http:// www.ssc.govt.nz/display/document.asp?docid=6343&PageType=toc& displaytype=pf

Federal Accountability Act. (2006). Retrieved on March 18, 2008, from http://www.faa-lfi.gc.ca/faa-lfi/faa-lfi00_e.asp

Flumian, M., Coe, A., and Kernaghan, K. (2007). Transforming service to Canadians: The Service Canada Model. *International Review of Administrative Sciences, 73* (4), 557–68.

Fountain, J. E. (2001). *Building the virtual state: Information technology and institutional change.* Washington: Brookings Institution.

Goggin, M. L., et al. (1990). *Implementation theory and practice: Toward a third generation.* Glenview, IL: Scott, Foresman/Little, Brown Higher Education.

Good, D. A. (2003). *The politics of public management: The HRDC audit of grants and contributions.* Toronto: University of Toronto Press.

Gow, J. I. (2004). *A Canadian model of public administration?* Ottawa: Canada School of Public Service.

Greer, P. (1994). *Transforming central government: The Next Steps initiative.* Buckingham, UK: Open University Press.

Gregory, R. (2002). Transforming governmental culture: A sceptical view of new public management. In T. Christensen and Per Laegried (Eds.), *New public management: The transformation of ideas and practice* (pp. 231–58). Aldershot: Ashgate.

Hall, M. H., and Reed, P. B. (1998). Shifting the burden: How much can government download to the non-profit sector? *Canadian Public Administration, 41*(1), 1–20.

Heintzman, R. (2007a). Toward a new moral contract: Reclaiming trust in public service. The Vanier Lecture, Regina, May 14. Retrieved on March 17, 2008, from http://www.ipac.ca/saskatchewan/files/ Heintzman_final.pdf

Heintzman, R. (2007b). Public-service values and ethics: Dead end or strong foundation? *Canadian Public Administration, 50* (4), 573–602.

Heintzman, R., and Marson, B. (2005). People, service and trust: Is there a public sector service value chain? *International Review of Administrative Sciences, 71* (4), 549–575.

Hogwood, B. W., and Gunn, L. A. (1984). *Policy analysis for the real world*. Oxford: Oxford University Press.

Hood, C., and Peters, B. G. (2004). The middle aging of new public management: Into the age of paradox? *Journal of Public Administration Research and Theory* 14 (3), 267–82.

Hupe, P. L., and Hill, M. (2002) *Implementing public policy: Governance in theory and in practice*. Thousand Oaks, Calif.: Sage.

John F. Kennedy School of Government. (2008). *Innovations awards programs*. Retrieved March 16, 2008, from http://www.innovations.harvard.edu/award_landing.html

Kernaghan, K. (2007). Beyond bubble gum and good will: Integrating service delivery. In S. Borins et al., *Digital state at the leading edge*. (pp. 102–36). Toronto: IPAC and the University of Toronto Press.

Kernaghan, K., Marson, B., and Borins, S. (2000). *The new public organization*. Toronto: IPAC.

Kettl, D. F. (2005). *The global public management revolution*. 2nd Ed. Washington: Brookings Institution.

Langford, J., and Tupper, A. (2006). How Ottawa does business: Ethics as a government program. In G. B. Doern (Ed.), *How Ottawa spends 2006–2007: In from the cold: The Tory rise and the Liberal demise* (pp. 116–37). Montreal: McGill-Queen's University Press.

Lee, I., and Hobbs, C. (1996). Pink slips and running shoes: The Liberal government's downsizing of the public service. In G. Swimmer (Ed.), *How Ottawa spends, 1996–97: Life under the knife* (pp. 337–78). Ottawa: Carleton University Press.

Linder, S. H., and Peters, B. G. (1990). Research perspectives on the design of public policy: Implementation, formulation, and design. In D. J. Palumbo and D. J. Calista (Eds.), *Implementation and the policy process: Opening up the black box* (pp. 51–66). New York: Greenwood Press.

Majone, G., and Wildavsky, A. (1984). Implementation as evolution. In J. L. Pressman and A. Wildavsky (Eds.), *Implementation: How great expectations in Washington are dashed in Oakland: Or, why it's amazing that federal programs work at all, this being a saga of the economic development administration as told by two sympathetic observers who seek to build morals on a foundation of ruined hopes* (3rd ed.) (pp. 163–80). Berkeley: University of California Press.

OECD. (2004). *Enhancing the effectiveness of public spending: Experience in OECD countries*. Retrieved March 16, 2008, from http://ideas.repec.org/p/oec/ecoaaa/380-en.html

OECD. (2005). *Modernising government: The way forward*. Paris: OECD.

Osborne, D., and Gaebler, T. (1993). *Reinventing government: How the entrepreneurial spirit is transforming the public sector.* New York: Penguin.

Pal, L. A., and Weaver, K. W. (Eds.) (2003). *The government taketh away: The politics of pain in the United States and Canada.* Washington, DC: Georgetown University Press.

Panet, P. de L., and Trebilcock, M. J. (1998). Contracting-out social services. *Canadian Public Administration,* 41(1), 21–50.

Peters, T., and Waterman, R. H. (1982). *In search of excellence.* New York: Harper.

Phillips, S. (2006). *The intersection of governance and citizenship in Canada: Not quite the third way.* Montreal: Institute for Research on Public Policy.

Pollitt, C. (2007). 'Towards a new public administration theory': Some comments on Jocelyne Bourgon's 5th Briabant lecture. *International Review of Administrative Sciences,* 73 (1), 37–41.

Potter, E. H. (2000). Treasury Board as a management board: The re-invention of a central agency. In L. A. Pal (Ed.), *How Ottawa spends 2000–2001: Past imperfect, future tense* (pp. 95–129). Toronto: Oxford University Press.

Pressman, J. L., and Wildavsky, A. (1984). *Implementation: How great expectations in Washington are dashed in Oakland: Or, why it's amazing that federal programs work at all, this being a saga of the economic development administration as told by two sympathetic observers who seek to build morals on a foundation of ruined hopes* (3rd ed.). Berkeley: University of California Press.

Privy Council Office. (2000). Fonctionnaires sans frontières: Operating at the speed of the public interest, Notes for an Address by Mel Cappe. Ottawa.

Privy Council Office (Canada). (2007). *Fourteenth annual report to the Prime Minister on the public service of Canada.* Retrieved February 26, 2008, from http://www.pco-bcp.gc.ca/index.asp?lang=eng&page=clerk-greffier&sub=AnnualReports

Privy Council Office (Canada). (2008a). *The public service of Canada: Too many misperceptions.* Remarks by Kevin Lynch, Clerk of the Privy Council, February 18, 2008. Retrieved February 26, 2008, from http://www.pco-bcp.gc.ca/index.asp?lang=eng&page=clerk-greffier&sub=clerksspeeches&doc=20080218_e.htm

Privy Council Office (Canada). (2008b). *Fifteenth annual report to the Prime Minister on the public service of Canada.* Retrieved February 26, 2008, from http://www.pco-bcp.gc.ca/index.asp?lang=eng&page=clerk-greffier&sub=AnnualReports

Rawson, B. (1991). Public Service 2000 service to the public task force: Findings and implications. *Canadian Public Administration*, 34, 490–500.

Roy. J. (2006). *E-government in Canada: Transformation for the digital age*. Ottawa: University of Ottawa Press.

Sabatier, P. A., and Mazmanian, D. A. (1981). The implementation of public policy: A framework of analysis. In D. A. Mazmanian and P. A. Sabatier (Eds.), *Effective policy implementation* (pp. 3–35). Lexington, MA: Lexington Books.

Savoie, D. J. (1994). *Thatcher, Reagan, Mulroney: In search of a new bureaucracy*. Toronto: University of Toronto Press.

Savoie, D. J. (2004). Searching for accountability in a government without boundaries. *Canadian Public Administration*, 47, 1–26.

Seidle, F. L. (1995). *Rethinking the delivery of public services to citizens*. Montreal: The Institute for Research on Public Policy.

State Services Commission (New Zealand). (2004). Retrieved March 18, 2008, from http://www.ssc.govt.nz/display/home.asp

State Services Commission (New Zealand). (2005). Development Goals for the State Services. Retrieved March 11, 2007, from http://www.ssc.govt.nz/display/document.asp?docid=5439&PageType=toc&displaytype=pf

State Services Commission (New Zealand). (2007d). Transforming the State Services: State of the Development Goals Report 2007. Retrieved March 11, 2007, from http://www.ssc.govt.nz/upload/downloadable_files/Transforming-the-State-Services-SoDG-Report07.pdf

Statistics Canada. (2004). *Employment and average weekly earnings (including overtime), public administration and all industries*. Ottawa: Statistics Canada.

Statistics Canada. (2008). Federal government employment, wages and salaries, by census metropolitan area. Retrieved on March 18, 2008, http://www40.statcan.ca/l01/cst01/govt58a.htm

Tellier, P. M. (1990, Summer). Public Service 2000: The renewal of the public service. *Canadian Public Administration*, 33, 123–32.

Treasury Board of Canada. (1996a, September 30). *Getting government right: A progress report*. Retrieved March 16, 2008, from http://www.tbs-sct.gc.ca/report/govrev/Gfce.asp

Treasury Board of Canada. (1998). *Estimates: 1998–1999 program expenditure detail: A profile of departmental spending*. Retrieved March 18, 2008, from http://www.tbs-sct.gc.ca/tb/estimate/19981999/e98ped.pdf

Treasury Board of Canada. (2000a). *Business plan: 1999–2000 to 2001–2002*. Ottawa.

Treasury Board of Canada. (2000b). *Results for Canadians: A management framework for the government of Canada*. Retrieved on March 16, 2008, from http://www.tbs-sct.gc.ca/report/res_can/rc_1_e.asp#pre

Treasury Board of Canada. (2000c). *A policy framework for service improvement in the Government of Canada*. Ottawa.

Treasury Board of Canada. (2004a). *Population affiliation report*. Retrieved March 16, 2008, from http://www.psagency-agencefp.gc.ca/hr-rh/hrtr-or/hr_tools/Intro_e.asp

Treasury Board of Canada. (2004b). *Strengthening public sector management: An overview of the government action plan and key initiatives*. Retrieved March 16, 2008, from http://www.tbs-sct.gc.ca/spsm-rgsp/spsm-rgsp4_e.asp#Expenditure

Williams, A. D. (2006). *Government 2.0: Wikinomics and the challenge to government*. Networkedgovernment.ca Retrieved June 13, 2008, from http://www.netgov.ca/Government2Williams

Winter, S. (1990). Integrating implementation research. In D. J. Palumbo and D. J. Calista (Eds.), *Implementation and the policy process: Opening up the black box* (pp. 19–38). New York: Greenwood Press.

CHAPTER

6

Policy Communities and Networks

C hapter 1 outlined the foundations of traditional policy analysis, and the major critiques of those foundations. It pointed out that nonetheless, there is a resurgence of interest in making good policy but with a sensitivity to the limitations of the traditional approach and the challenges of contemporary governance. Chapter 2 explored those challenges and their broad consequences for how governments today, in Canada and throughout the world, are changing the way in which they organize their policy thinking, their policy processes, their organizations, and their partners. We developed a detailed understanding of these changes in Chapters 3 to 5. What kind of conceptual lens can we use to understand the more complicated range of players and institutions involved in making policy, and how those players and institutions might change depending on circumstances and the policy issue at hand? In recent years the policy literature has placed great emphasis on policy communities and **policy networks**, two concepts that try to capture the degree to which any policy field or sector is populated by a host of government agencies, interest groups, associations, and social movements, both domestically and globally. It has been argued that the nature of these policy communities and networks is crucial both to policy development and to implementation, especially in a globalized world. On the development side, governments need information that nongovernmental actors possess. On the implementation side, the more coherent the interests and organizations in a sector, the easier it is to implement a decision. In both cases, **global public policy networks** are becoming increasingly important. This chapter reviews the literature on networks, and then shows how contemporary policymaking practice is coming to grips with issues of consultation, citizen engagement, and partnerships.

Politics without interests is an oxymoron, but for many years key strands of the policy literature were prepared to think about policymaking as a rational and largely technical enterprise consisting of priority-setting, options analysis, and careful consideration of costs and benefits. Interests did not enter the picture or, if they did, it was more as a complicating and confusing factor than a constituent component of the process (Nagel, 1988). As we noted in Chapter 1, the origins of policy analysis in the "policy sciences" were steeped in a sense that policy and politics would be immeasurably improved if the messy interplay of political interests could be tamed (if not completely supplanted) by the rational application of technical and expert knowledge:

> Insofar as possible, science and factual information should replace the politics of bargaining and negotiating that characterize pluralist democracy. Decision theorists documented the shortcomings of human judgement and argued that scientific studies could produce decisionmaking models or guidelines that would remove much of the error found in discretionary decisions by bureaucrats, program specialists, and even highly trained professionals such as judges or engineers. Many evaluators, declaring which programs worked and which ones did not, expected public officials to allocate funds accordingly. (Schneider and Ingram, 1997, pp. 30–31)

Chapter 2 described a different world in the making, one where the state is a central but not dominant player in policy processes, where citizens and **interest groups** demand more access to policy development and implementation, and consequently where there is a broader tableau of players and actors. The contemporary study and practice of public policy-making acknowledges this changed reality, and "policy networks" and "policy communities" have emerged as master concepts for conceptualizing new patterns of players and institutions. These are by no means the only frameworks, but they, and a small subset of others, will be examined here in some detail. A sampling of the larger universe of ideas about interests in the policy process is provided in Box 6.1.

Twenty years ago, the idea of policy networks was considered a "new key term" (Marin and Mayntz, 1991, p. 11), one that when joined to policy communities constituted "two of the most important conceptual innovations to emerge" in recent studies of the policy process (Atkinson and Coleman, 1992, p. 158; see Thatcher, 1998 for a detailed intellectual history). Even now policy network theory is "a major approach to the study of public policy making in Canada and elsewhere" (Howlett, 2002, p. 235). For some the concepts are at best "metaphors" (Dowding, 1995), and for others the overlap and confusion of the complementary network concepts (see Box 6.1) leads to little more than a "debate over terminology"

BOX 6.1 CONCEPTUALIZING INTERESTS IN POLICYMAKING: A GLOSSARY

Concept	Definition	Key Source
Advocacy conditions	• A wide range of actors, including government from all levels, officials, interest organizations, research groups, journalists, and even other countries, who share a belief system about a policy area and over time demonstrate some degree of coordinated activity • An important feature is the idea that policy fields are marked by competing advocacy coalitions	• Sabatier and Jenkins-Smith, 1993
Discourse coalitions	• A range of policy actors united by broad ideas about the policy field, ideas that include assumptions, images, rhetoric, linguistic turns • Appears similar to advocacy coalitions but has a stronger emphasis on language and meaning	• Fischer and Forester, 1993
Epistemic community	• Originally developed in the field of international relations, this concept tries to capture the influence of international groups of scientific experts on policy-making, for example, in the environmental field • Emphasis on the power of ideas and expertise, as expressed through professional organizations or individuals	• Haas, 1992

(continued)

BOX 6.1 (continued)

Concept	Definition	Key Source
Global public policy network	• Quasi-official constellations of state actors, international organizations, and non-governmental organizations that do more than advocate, but develop and sometimes even implement policies and assist in global coordination	• Stone, 2004 • Slaughter, 2004 • Reinicke, 1999/2000
Iron triangle	• The stable and cozy relationships among congressional committees, executive agencies (primarily regulatory), and economic interest groups • Implies long-term, stable interactions among a few actors, insulated from the rest of the policy process	• Carter, 1964 • Ripley and Franklin, 1984
Issue network	• Offered as a critique of the "iron triangle" concept in that most policy subsystems were actually quite fluid and changing, with actors coalescing as necessary around issues, not policy sectors	• Heclo and Wildavsky, 1974
Policy community	• The wide set of actors interested and informed about a policy issue, who share at least some common language, but who may be opponents on the issue • Differs from the advocacy coalition approach in that policy communities are presumed to include everyone active in a field	• Wright, 1988 • Coleman and Skogstad, 1990

Policy network	• A subset of actors in the policy community who have a consistently higher level of interest in the policy issue, and interact regularly • The most important feature is the discerning of patterns of relations that have consequences for the development and delivery of policy	• Atkinson and Coleman, 1992 • Van Waarden, 1992
Public interest groups	• Interest groups that advocate on behalf of the public good rather than the direct self-interest of their members • Emphasis is on advocacy for "causes" and the public interest rather than economic lobbying	• Berry, 1977 • Pal, 1993 • Stanbury, 1993 • Phillips, 1993
Social movement organizations	• Interest groups rooted in social transformations of the 1960s that led to new values, new class structures, and new social coalitions (e.g., environmentalism, feminism) • Key feature is the link between organizations and their social foundations, as well as the new dynamics of participation that arise with these organizations	• Offe, 1987 • Zald, 1987 • Klandermans and Tarrow, 1988 • Melucci, 1989
Subgovernment	• A generic concept that expresses the idea that policy does not get made in a single "system" but in subsystems that consist of microcosms of all the relevant political and institutional actors • This concept was developed in the 1950s as part of pluralist analyses of policymaking	• Truman, 1951 • Jordan, 1990 • Pross, 1992

(Lindquist, 1996, p. 219; for additional debates over the utility of the concept, see Marsh and Smith, 2000; Dowding, 2001; Marsh and Smith, 2001; Raab, 2001; Klijn and Skelcher, 2007; Rhodes, 2007). While "**policy community**" and "policy network" are often used interchangeably, the former refers to a wider set of actors who understand the ideas and terminology that define a policy area and have some level of interest in that area, while the latter refers to a subset of those actors whose level of interest is consistently higher and who actually interact with each other. The concerns we will raise in this chapter tap into another issue as well: the degree to which the network concept goes far enough in capturing the realities and contradictions of contemporary policymaking. There has been tremendous pressure in Canada and elsewhere to broaden the policy development process to include more actors such as interest associations, experts, and citizens. Governments today favour alternative modes of program delivery, many of which stress partnerships. **Consultation** and partnering are the order of the day, but managing those relationships is challenging. It becomes even more challenging when we step back and look at networks not simply as domestic players but as internationally and globally engaged. The federal government's Asia-Pacific Gateway and Corridor initiative, for example, engages four western provinces as well as Chinese business and government, with the aim of making Canada the preferred route for entry and distribution of Chinese goods throughout North America. We will return to this example later to show the complexity of modern networked governance.

The next section provides background on the communities and networks literature and then proceeds to analyze the ways in which the realities of policy communities and networks are intruding on the consciousness of policymakers themselves and being addressed through consultation, engagement schemes, and partnership models of implementing public programs. The conclusion returns to the tensions implied by these new pressures. Are our traditional forms of governance up to the challenge?

Communities and Networks: Conceptual Frameworks

APPROACHES AND CONCEPTS

While there has been a harmonic convergence around the ideas of policy networks and communities, that convergence has come from several different directions. It is of more than mere antiquarian interest to explore the various sources of the network idea, since each of the origins suggests a different aspect of the policy process that was inadequately grasped by older theoretical frameworks. This will help us later in the chapter when we examine the contemporary changes in the policy process that are forcing even more radical conceptualizations of networks and webs of interest, cooperation, and conflict.

The broad backdrop to the various origins of network analyses is a concern with understanding the relationship between state and society and, in particular, the organization of interests in society. As banal and obvious as that sounds, the early postwar history of political science and public policy wrestled with the best way of theorizing the connections. While the Marxist literature addressed itself to various ways of thinking about the importance of class, the non-Marxist literature eventually settled on the notion of **"interest group pluralism"** as its master concept (for a broad survey of the literature, see Baumgartner and Leech, 1998). The pioneering postwar book on the subject was David Truman's *The Governmental Process* (1951). Truman, and others in that tradition, conceptualized society as consisting of an almost limitless array of interests that could mobilize around an almost equally limitless range of issues. If people shared interests, they would likely form groups. If issues arose that affected those interests in a policy sense, then the groups would politicize and lobby government. The pluralist tradition as a whole tended to de-emphasize the state or policymaking institutions and stressed the influence of lobbies and interest groups politics (Nordlinger, 1981, Chap. 1; but see Almond, 1990, Chap. 8). While pluralism did not use the contemporary terms of **"interest intermediation"** or **"associational system,"** it drew a distinctive portrait of each. Interest intermediation, or the way in which societal interests interact with state institutions, was sketched as a highly variable, unpredictable, unstable process that depended on the organization of interests and government institutions in each policy sector or **subgovernment**. The associational system—the patterns of groups and organizations—was also depicted as a rather confusing constellation of small, medium, and large groups, competing and cooperating as they felt necessary.

We can identify at least four major sources of inspiration for the broad concept of networks as it has been applied in a variety of different forms. One of the first breaks with pluralism was over its portrait of the associational system and patterns of policymaking. Empirical case studies in the period showed that patterns were much more stable, and relationships far more closed, than pluralists had suggested. Policymaking took place not in the legislature or the executive but in **"iron triangles"** that truly were subgovernments in the sense that they might all be operating according to different principles, with different rhythms and often conflicting outcomes. By the mid-1970s the notion of iron triangles seemed like a caricature too, and Hugh Heclo (1978) crystallized the growing unease by identifying what he called "**issue networks.**" Heclo was not arguing for a new master concept but pointing out that the nature of the (American) policy system had changed. For one thing, the technical complexity of policy issues had increased, demanding the participation of policy experts and researchers rather than just narrow interests. There was a greater fluidity in issue generation as well, as the policy system constantly churned and produced new agenda items. Rather than the stable patterns of control that characterize iron triangles, Heclo saw issue networks as being quite permeable, with a kaleidoscope of changing faces as interest in (not a stake in) the policy issues waxed and waned.

A second important source of work on networks came from comparative research on industrial performance and economic policy. One of the earliest uses of the term "policy network" was in a book edited by Peter Katzenstein (1978a), *Between Power and Plenty*. Katzenstein and his colleagues were interested in the ways in which domestic political structures affected foreign economic policy. Since "the domestic structures in the advanced industrial states differ in important ways, so do the strategies of foreign economic policy which these states pursue" (Katzenstein, 1978b, p. 4). A key conditioning factor of foreign policy was the character of domestic interests and institutions, which could be termed the "policy network." Policy instruments were conditioned by the "character of the policy network spanning both the public and the private sector," and the key factors were the "differentiation of state from society and the centralization within each" (Katzenstein, 1978c, p. 308).

This branch of research had offshoots that remain highly relevant to the work on policy networks today. Work on "state structures" argued that each state had a characteristic pattern of associational and state institutions. This was a search for a single pattern at the broadest or deepest level of a given society that would affect policymaking across all sectors. For example, the work on **corporatism** urged that some countries were characterized by corporatist structures—centralized state agencies and highly centralized associational systems, working in tandem to develop and implement policy—and that, despite variances, corporatist dynamics would be discerned in most policy fields in that polity (Schmitter and Lembruch, 1979). This literature also suggested that corporatist political structures were more effective in the development of economic policy. This helped feed a debate about the nature of the state and its autonomy from social interests (Nordlinger, 1981; Skocpol, 1986), as well as a subsequent interest in political institutions (Weaver and Rockman, 1993). This style of analysis has stressed the structuring effect of state institutions on associational systems (e.g., Baumgartner, 1996; Coleman, 1994). Other work looked more at the relation between state and society in specific (usually economic) sectors and led directly to some of the most important contributions to network analysis.

A third source of inspiration for network analysis was the growing work on "**new social movements**" and "**public interest groups.**" Phillips (1999) defines a social movement as "(a) an informal network of organizations and individuals who, (b) on the basis of a collective identity and shared values, (c) engage in political and/or cultural struggle intended to break or expand the boundaries of the existing system, and (d) undertake collective action designed to affect both state and society" (p. 373; see also Carroll, 1992; Meyer, Jennes, Ingram, 2006). She points out that **social movement organizations** rarely act alone (they are, after all, part of a social movement) and connect through various types of networks. The distinction between the movement and the organizations built upon it is important and gives a clue as to why the network idea spontaneously arose in this field of research. Any movement (e.g., environmental, consumers', women's) is bound to spawn a variety of organizations that address different aspects of its agenda, but those organizations will have a common cause and will seek to cooperate in order to maximize their policy impact.

Public interest groups have been defined as "an organizational entity that purports to represent very broad, diffuse, non-commercial interests which traditionally have received little explicit or direct representation in the processes by which agencies, courts, and legislatures make public policy" (Schuck, 1977, p. 133). Broadly speaking, these are citizens' organizations and typically are either very similar, or identical, to social movement organizations such as consumers' groups and environmental organizations. Both public interest groups and social movement organizations have a penchant for "expressive politics" or a political agenda that does not focus exclusively on material issues, and certainly not on direct political gain. While some skepticism is warranted regarding their altruism, it remains true that in structure and strategy, public interest groups differ markedly from traditional types of organizations. But as champions of what Chapter 2 called "**postmaterialist values**" these interest groups have had success in promoting their policy agendas and mobilizing their resources. Berry's (1999) empirical analysis of the impact of these groups in the American congressional system in 205 cases between 1963 and 1991 concluded that "citizens groups have become prolific and enduring participants in legislative policymaking" (p. 32). He also concluded that the most numerous and effective groups had been "liberal" ones (or postmaterialist in the pursuit of lifestyle, environmental, consumer, and moral issues) and that they had been able to "get Congress to consider policies that are obnoxious to business and energetically fought by corporations and trade groups" (p. 83). No equivalent studies have been done in Canada, but evidence from citizens' organizations around the Free Trade Agreement and the North American Free Trade Agreement suggests that the Canadian political system became more impervious to citizen lobbying in the 1990s, even while the networks of groups expanded considerably in the face of policies designed to support globalization (Ayres, 1998, p. 144).

A final source of inspiration for the network concept has been the changing nature of political reality, some elements of which are reflected in the sources described above and some of which were addressed in Chapter 2. Kenis and Schneider (1991, pp. 34–36) captured these changes almost two decades ago, but they resonate well with the current sense of what has changed on the governance landscape:

1. *Emergence of organized society*: more and more of our social and political life is controlled by "organized collectivities," and as their importance and number increase, so will their interdependencies.

2. *Sectoralization*: the functional differentiation of policies, programs, and agencies.

3. *Crowded policy domains*: more organized collectivities and corporate actors means more intervention and participation within a given policy space.

4. *Scope of policy-making*: growth both in the number of policy domains and degree of intervention in them.

5. *Decentralization and fragmentation of the state*: the state increasingly consists of a host of discrete and loosely coordinated institutional entities.

6. *Blurring of boundaries between the public and private*: governments are increasingly involved at the interstices of civil society in implementing informal relationships (e.g., speech codes).

7. *Rise of private governments*: many political tasks can no longer be accomplished without the help of private organizations.

8. *Transnationalization of domestic politics*: policy issues are affected by factors at the international level and governments increasingly pursue policy objectives through international forums.

9. *The importance of information*: increased complexity demands better information and scientific expertise.

The result?

> Increasingly unable to mobilize all necessary policy resources within their own realm, governments consequently become dependent upon the cooperation and joint resource mobilization of policy actors outside their hierarchical control. Policy networks should therefore be understood as those webs of relatively stable and ongoing relationships which mobilize dispersed resources so that collective (or parallel) action can be orchestrated toward the solution of a common policy problem. (Kenis and Schneider, 1991, p. 36)

We will return to the question of how these new realities affect the policy process and generate network dynamics. At this point, it should be clear why the network/community concept is as important as it is: it has filtered through both policy studies and the broader study of government and politics because it reflects some important shifts in our forms of governance. The increasing complexity of both society and government; the importance of information and its associated technologies; the reliance of government on nongovernmental actors to both formulate and implement policy; shifts in class structure, values, and social groups: these are some of the forces that underpin an interest in networks and communities. All of these changes continue to exercise an important influence on modern policymaking, but they have been supplemented and reinforced by the broader factors described in Chapter 2.

In all the variants of network analysis, the central questions are, first, how to conceptualize the relationships between civil society and the state, and second, what difference certain patterns of relations make to policy outcomes. A third question of more relevance to the practitioner is rarely raised in this scholarly work but will be the focus for the second half of this chapter: how to manage and nurture relations between government agencies and their policy constituencies. But first, we will briefly examine the state of the art in conceptualizing policy networks.

Policy Network/Community Analysis

It is one thing to say that policy networks and communities are important; it is another thing to conceptualize those networks. Paul Pross (1995) offered an early definition as well as a diagrammatic portrait of policy communities. Policy communities are "groupings of government agencies, pressure groups, media people, and individuals, including academics, who, for various reasons, have an interest in a particular policy field and attempt to influence it" (p. 265). Figure 6.1 displays what Pross calls his "bubble diagram" of policy communities. Note that it divides the policy community in any given policy field into the "subgovernment" and the "**attentive public.**" Actual decisionmaking takes place in the subgovernment, which is dominated by large institutions, groups, and core government agencies. Players in the subgovernment, Pross argues, work to limit participation from outsiders. The attentive public are the outsiders whose main influence on the process is to generate ideas and discussion through conferences, publications, and occasional lobbying. In Pross's view, the policy community is actually an insulating device to keep a grip on the process; indeed, he argues that most of the inside players in a policy community try to keep debate within the realm of the technical and routine. Figure 6.1 shows a policy community in which the federal

Chapter 6   Policy Communities and Networks   **265**

Figure 6.1 Policy Community "Bubble Diagram"

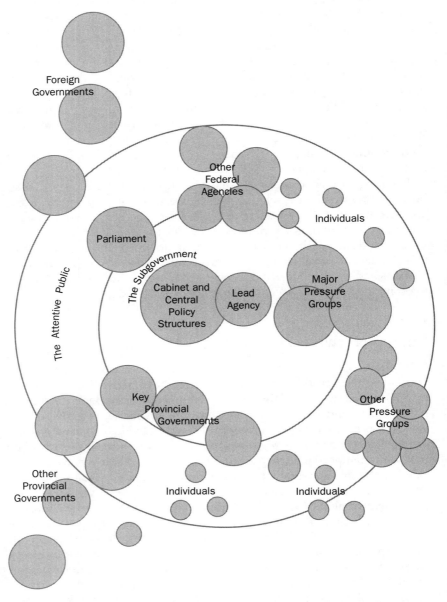

SOURCE: Pross, A.P. (1995). Pressure groups: Talking chameleons. In M.S. Whittington and G. Williams (Eds.), *Canadian Politics in the 1990s* (p. 267). Toronto: Nelson Canada.

government is dominant, but the basic structure of core agencies in the subgovernment surrounded by other groups and agencies is generic.

There are several limitations to this way of thinking about policy communities. For one thing, it is largely static (though Pross was careful to argue that, in fact, policy communities are constantly in flux). For another, it does not travel well across policy fields. Some areas are indeed dominated by government agencies, and largely insulated from outside pressures—fiscal policy comes to mind. But many others are increasingly open to pressures from the attentive public, and that public is not prepared to be polite and keep policymaking at the level of routine. In social and educational policy, and increasingly in municipal policy, for example, fundamental assumptions about the role of governments are constantly being posed. Another problem is that in this model, foreign governments and foreign pressure groups are relegated to the margins. This metaphor is increasingly obsolete in a globalized and post-9/11 world. Finally, the model does not capture varying relations among the actors. The bubbles are large or small, but the figure as a whole gives no idea of the connections (or lack thereof) among the players.

Some of these limitations have been addressed in more refined models of policy networks (to which Pross's work is an important contribution). In a tradition that descends directly from Katzenstein's framework, this approach focuses on two variables: the nature of centralization in the state and the centralization or organization of the associational system. This is often termed a "structural approach" to network analysis because it focuses on patterns of relations among actors, patterns that can be mapped and are to some degree distinct from the beliefs or ideas that the actors themselves carry in the policy process. If we take a simple dichotomy of high organization/low organization, then we have a straightforward group of four categories to start with. In his excellent survey of the policy network literature, Lindquist (1992) draws on work by Atkinson and Coleman (1989a; 1989b) and Coleman and Skogstad (1990) to neatly summarize the network types in a chart, reproduced as Figure 6.2 (with five types). The degree of organization here means things like analytic capacity, access to important data and information, ability to act unilaterally, coordination, focus on long-term or short-term issues, and a reactive or anticipatory policy stance (Lindquist, 1992, p. 134). Figure 6.3 (page 269) offers another graphic representation of these networks, accompanied by brief definitions.

This depiction of policy network types has the advantage of variety. It is clear that there will be variation in policy networks across policy fields (though why that is, and if there are any underlying patterns to network organization in a specific political system, is a tougher question). Governments, or more precisely, the core agencies in the subgovernment, can be either well organized, strong, and policy capable or weakly organized

Figure 6.2 Policy Network Categories

SOURCE: Lindquist, E.A. (1992). Public managers and policy communities: Learning to meet new challenges. *Canadian Public Administration*, 35, 135.

without much policy capacity. Atkinson and Coleman (1989a, pp. 80–81) identify four conditions for what they call "state autonomy at the sectoral level": the bureau should have (1) a clear conception of its role and a value system that supports its mandate, as well as support from the minister, (2) a professional ethos distinct from that of its clients, (3) a body of law and regulation that it firmly administers, and (4) the capacity to generate its own information related to its mandate. In addition, the authors argue that state agencies are distinguished by their degree of concentration, by which they mean strong, informal alliances between the political executive and officials. By the same token, associational systems can be weak or strong. Atkinson and Coleman (1989a, pp. 82–83) identify six conditions for a "highly mobilized sector." Business groups (their focus) should have (1) separate associations representing different products and producers, without overlap or competition, (2) only one association that speaks for the sector as a whole, (3) a high proportion of firms represented in the sector's associations, (4) large firms that demonstrate leadership in the sector, (5) in-house capacity to generate information among firms and associations, and (6) associations that can strike deals with government and make them stick with members.

The Atkinson and Coleman schema actually yields eight categories of networks. The more criteria one adds, of course, the more types of networks one can generate. Van Waarden (1992), for example, argues that the major dimensions of policy networks are "(1) actors, (2) function, (3) structure, (4) institutionalization, (5) rules of conduct, (6) power relations, and (7) actor strategies" (p. 32). He further subdivides each of these dimensions to arrive at a list of thirty-eight criteria defining thirteen

Figure 6.3 Definitions of Policy Networks

TYPE	CHARACTERISTICS
Pressure Pluralist Network	State agency is autonomous; associational system is dispersed and weak. Many groups compete for state agency's attention. Groups advocate policies rather than participate in policy-making.
Clientele Pluralist Network	State agencies are both weak and dispersed, as are associational systems. Agencies rely on associations for information and support and allow them to participate in policy-making.
Corporatist Network	State agency is strong and autonomous; associational system comprises a few large and powerful groups, usually representing consumer and producer interests. Groups and agency both participate in policy formulation and implementation.
Concertation Network	State agency is strong and autonomous; associational system is dominated by one organization that represents it. Agency and organization are equal partners in long-term planning and policy-making.
State-Directed Network 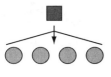	State agency is strong and autonomous; associational system is weak and dispersed. State dominates policy sector and associational system.

■ = State Agencies   ⬤ = Organizations

SOURCE: Pal, L. (1992). *Public Policy Analysis: An Introduction*, 2nd ed. Toronto: Nelson, p. 112.

different types of policy networks! Recognizing that this is unmanageable, Van Waarden recommends concentrating on three criteria: the number and type of societal actors involved, the major functions of networks (e.g., negotiation, consultation, coordination, cooperation in policy formation, or implementation), and the balance of power between state and societal interests.

Apart from pretty diagrams, what do policy networks tell us about policymaking? Most of this network literature has been applied to economic policy fields and assumes that concentration plus organization equals policy-capable systems. While this makes some intuitive sense, it needs to be treated cautiously. For one thing, it has a vaguely undemocratic flavour. The more hierarchical, coordinated, and tidy the policy sector, the fewer opportunities there will be for the "attentive public" to get into the act. Current policy thinking is that the wider the networks and the more competition among players, the better policy outcomes will be. For another, as policy sectors get more complex and more globalized, the demands for information from all sectors and connections among the players rise exponentially. The tightly coordinated policy networks recommended in this literature may not be adequate to the new dynamics of modern policy process. Howlett (2002) zeroes in on this issue by attempting to correlate the nature of policy change with the nature of the policy networks associated with the policy field. He hypothesized that the more closed the subsystem of actors to new ideas and to new actors, the more difficult it would be to make radical changes in policy. His empirical findings demonstrated that

> [S]ubsystem structure is important because when the same core sets of policy actors are involved in defining policy options, the common understanding of a policy problem and the solutions they develop from shared experiences, combined with the durability of subsystem members' interests, promotes "incremental" change. Paradigmatic policy changes representing a significant, though not necessarily total, break from the past policy goals and programme specifications, on the other hand, was [sic] found to have occurred only when new ideas and interests could penetrate policy subsystems. (pp. 259–60)

In addition to the structure of networks, some approaches argue that the tactics and skills of actors in those networks are an important factor in explaining outcomes (Marsh and Smith, 2000). This is essentially an attempt to make the concept more dynamic, and to understand policy networks as both structures and processes. At any given point, a network can be mapped or visualized in terms of its characteristics (Raab, 2002) or the actual processes over time that give rise to those characteristics, and that have feedback loops from outcomes that in turn affect the network and its behaviour. For example, it's one thing to know that a soccer team is "structurally" weak because of the quality of its players and how they interact on the field. It's quite another thing to observe the same team in action, watching the flow of play, how they react to each other and their opponents. This latter, more dynamic way of viewing networks allows us to bring in both communication/interaction and learning or reacting to the results of that interaction (Pemberton, 2000).

ADVOCACY COALITIONS

The **advocacy coalition** framework (ACF) shares many of the insights of the policy community/subgovernment literature but approaches networks completely differently from the work discussed above. As Paul Sabatier (1993) describes it,

> The advocacy coalition framework (ACF) has at least four basic premises: (1) that understanding the process of policy change—and the role of policy-oriented learning therein—requires a time perspective of a decade or more; (2) that the most useful way to think about policy change over such a time span is through a focus on "policy subsystems," that is, the interaction of actors from different institutions who follow and seek to influence governmental decisions in a policy area; (3) that those subsystems must include an intergovernmental dimension, that is, they must involve all levels of government (at least for domestic policy); and, (4) that public policies (or programs) can be conceptualized in the same manner as belief systems, that is, as sets of value priorities and causal assumptions about how to realize them. (p. 16)

A distinctive feature of the ACF is its emphasis on the role of ideas and values in the policy process. The ACF assumes that both policy actors and policies themselves can be understood in terms of the structure of their belief systems. These systems have three key elements. The first is the deep or normative core, which consists of fundamental axioms about human nature, justice, and priorities among values such as security, health, and life. These ideas are very difficult to change through policy arguments. The second set of ideas is the near (policy) core, and it comprises notions about the proper scope of government activity, distributions of power and authority, orientations on substantive policy conflicts, and basic choices about policy instruments. These are difficult to change but can be altered if experience seriously differs from theory. The final set contains secondary aspects and consists of instrumental decisions needed to implement the policy core such as decisions about administrative rules, budgetary allocations, and statutory interpretation. These are comparatively easy to shift or change and constitute the bulk of technical policy argumentation.

Figure 6.4　The Advocacy Coalition Framework

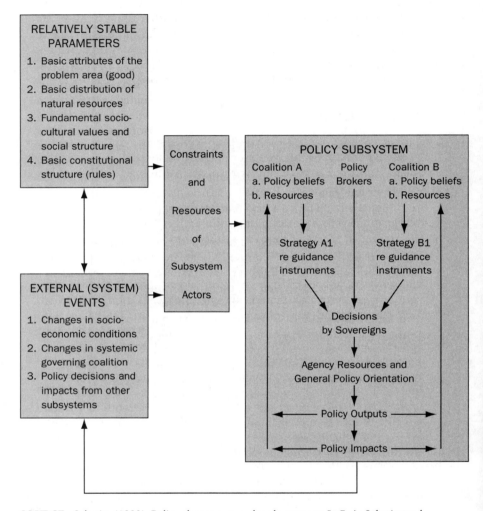

SOURCE: Sabatier (1993). Policy change over a decade or more. In P. A. Sabatier and H. Jenkins-Smith (Eds.). *Policy Change and Learning: An Advocacy Coalition Approach*. Boulder, CO: Westview, p. 18. See also Sabatier and Jenkins-Smith (1999).

Figure 6.4 illustrates the main elements of the ACF. Note that it has both a strong dynamic quality as well as a contextual dimension that places policy subsystems into the larger socioeconomic and political situation of the polity. The relatively stable parameters are system variables that change only slowly over time but set the stage in terms of institutions as well as resources for policy actors. The external events embrace both unpredictable shocks to the subsystem as well as the interaction effects with other subsystems. Together, these provide constraints, resources, and opportunities for the policy subsystem, which, in the ACF, is dominated by a number of advocacy coalitions, "composed of people from various governmental and private organizations who share a set of normative and causal beliefs and who often act in concert" (Sabatier, 1993, p. 18). These coalitions pursue competing strategies to achieve their policy objectives, a conflict that is usually mediated by policy brokers interested in compromise. At any given time, the policy sector will be dominated by a winning coalition. The framework is interested in what it calls "policy-oriented learning" or "relatively enduring alterations of thought or behavioral intentions that result from experience and are concerned with the attainment (or revision) of policy objectives" (Sabatier, 1993, p. 19). Most change in policy subsystems occurs because of external shocks, but instrumental learning is important, especially if the goal is better public policy.

The ACF also has several distinct hypotheses about how policy subsystems operate. Among them are (1) in any subsystem, the lineup of allies and opponents is stable over periods of a decade or so, (2) there is more consensus within coalitions on core beliefs than on secondary ones, (3) government policies rarely change if the original sponsoring coalition is still in power, (4) policies for which there are quantitative data are more amenable to policy learning than areas distinguished by qualitative data, and (5) policy learning across belief systems is more likely when there exists a prestigious forum that forces professionals from all sides to participate.

The ACF is a useful framework for mapping out, in a dynamic fashion, the players, issues, and debates in a policy subsystem. Its incorporation of ideas and values, as well as the impact (usually limited) of expertise and scientific professionals, is welcome. Also, the idea of a coalition gets around the more rigid and insular conceptualization in the network literature that divides subsystems into decisionmakers and attentive, but impotent, publics. Unlike the structural approach to policy networks, however, it does not provide any *a priori* typologies. Indeed, it is relatively weak in describing patterns of relationships either among the coalitions themselves or among brokers.

Policy Communities and Policy Management

The various approaches to policy networks discussed above give us the ability to map actors, understand their relationships, and possibly make some predictions about policy processes characterized by different types of networks or coalitions. But do these theories go far enough in capturing the contemporary complexities of the policy process? As we argued, the network idea itself can be seen as a response to changing political realities. If the realities continue to change, should the concept of networks be refined as well?

THE CONTEMPORARY IMPORTANCE OF POLICY NETWORKS

It is no coincidence that the concepts related to policy communities and networks began to multiply and develop just around the time that associational systems were becoming more complex. We saw earlier that Heclo's idea of "issue networks" was explicitly designed to capture the idea of a more fluid, information-based policy system in which government departments and industry players (what Pross calls the subgovernment) were no longer entirely dominant. Both Canada and the United States saw a surge in the growth of various social movements and public interest groups in the 1970s (Paltiel, 1982; Walker, 1991; Baumgartner and Mahoney, 2005). While there are no reliable data on broad trends in the last decade, there is no doubt that groups continue to multiply across most sectors, though not likely at the same pace that marked the 1970s and early 1980s. The complexity, intensity, and importance of the associational system and policy networks/communities for policymaking continues to be affected by the various factors outlined in Chapter 2, along with several other factors that define the new mode of governance that is emerging in Canada and elsewhere.

Globalization and increasingly sophisticated forms of communications also continue to change the nature of policy networks. With the early exception of the notion of **epistemic communities** (see Box 6.1)—which draws explicitly on international connections among experts—much of the communities/networks and associational literature still presume a national or domestic framework. As policy issues increasingly get driven upward to the international level, and as government officials and NGOs increasingly respond by connecting to counterparts everywhere around the globe, the idea that policy networks are primarily domestic is being re-thought. Domestic human rights groups, for example, now are routinely connected to international networks (Keck and Sikkink, 1998), as are groups organized around population issues, economic development, and the environment. Chapter 1 pointed to the emergence of a "global civil society," something that has been anticipated as an aspect of a new world order for some time (Falk, 1987; Walker, 1988; for a recent snapshot see Messner, 2002; Glasius, Kaldor and Anheier, 2003; Scholte, 2004). Statistics Canada estimates that in 2003 there were over 161 000 nonprofit and voluntary organizations in Canada, drawing on 19 million Canadian volunteers (Statistics Canada, 2005). Leading domestic organizations have complex and wide-ranging contacts with counterparts around the world, particularly if they have mandates that encourage cross-border collaboration, such as in environment, trade, or human rights (*Canadian Development Report*, 1999). As we noted in Chapter 2, this emergence, while not entirely new (think of the global Anti-Slavery Society of the 1800s), has benefited greatly from modern information and communications technologies. Technology makes it easier for both domestic and international networks to mobilize. While technology is important, conscious choices also have been made to bring nongovernmental actors into the global policy process. International agencies such as the UN, for example, particularly in the 1990s, "accelerated the global associational revolution by affirming the right of nongovernmental actors to participate in shaping national and global policies on the environment, population, human rights, economic development, and women" (Batliwala, 2002, p. 394). International UN conferences on the environment (Rio in 1992), human rights (Vienna in 1993), population (Cairo in 1994), social policy (Copenhagen in 1995), women (Beijing in 1995), and housing and cities (Istanbul in 1996) became platforms for the development of international networks of activists.

Globalization of policy networks and the impact of technology continues apace in the 2000s. Stone (2008, 22) vividly describes what she calls the "global agora" of policy making.

> In the Athenian agora, the mint, shrines and statuary, shops and law courts, the market hall and the council house, and the Assembly were all in physical proximity even if women, slaves, or resident foreigners had little participation in these forums. In the global agora, the international institutions are dispersed between Washington, DC, the Hague, Geneva, and Paris. The nodes of global finance are found in exclusive venues in New York, London, Tokyo, and a few other global cities such as Basle or Davos. . . . policy networks and self-regulation privatize decision making. Consequently, the institutional locations are dispersed and the boundaries of the global agora are indeterminate and opaque. Policy activity is as likely to take place inside private associations among nonstate actors as in intergovernmental conferences.

The range of global policy actors is increasing exponentially. The most obvious and visible are international governmental organizations such as the UN, the OECD, and the WTO. As we mentioned in previous chapters, this tier has now been supplemented with disaggregated global coordination among state officials, dealing with specific policy sectors such as finance, criminal activity, or corruption. Yet another layer consists of NGOs active on the global level, but connected to domestic concerns (the environment, human rights). The result is a diffuse system of transnational networks of loosely coordinated governance, as well of course of networks of protest and opposition to that governance. These global social movements of protest are organized in ways that do not necessarily reflect common identity or even common interest—they articulate "experiences of displacement" (Mcdonald, 2006, p. 18).

Technology makes these networks possible—the technology of travel, of communications, or the transfer and circulation of information. A little more than ten years ago, NGO activists attending UN conferences would have had to queue at the phones to make long-distance calls to their colleagues at home. Cell phones, laptops, PDAs, Google, and e-mail were unknown. That has all obviously changed, and the next wave will build on these platforms and create even more empowered network capabilities. The explosion of "social networking" technologies in the mid-2000s shows the potential. In addition to organizational knowledge management systems such as Microsoft's SharePoint, there are tools like Facebook that allow almost instant social networks to arise, share information, and even mobilize. In 2007 for example, Michael Geist, an Ottawa law professor who was concerned about impending copyright legislation, established a Facebook group entitled "Fair Copyright for Canada." He sent the first notice about the group to about 100 people, and within a week there were 10 000 members, and two weeks later 25 000. The group is home to (at time of writing) 38 000 members, and over 500 wall posts, photos, and discussion groups. It was not a purely virtual space—some 50 people linked to the site protested at Industry Minister Jim Prentice's open house in Calgary (Geist, 2008). The same was true of protests in Colombia against the terrorist group FARC. The Facebook site declared "No More Kidnapping, No More Lies, No More Murders, No More FARC." On February 4, 2008, over 1 million people took to the streets of Bogota to protest the group's holding of hostages. They were supported by thousands around the world (Economist, 2008).

An early illustration shows how the ground has shifted in global policy networks. The 1997 Land Mines Convention hinged on a massive international campaign to ban the use, production, and stockpiling of antipersonnel (AP) mines throughout the world. The specific problem with AP mines is that they remain in place well after military conflicts between belligerents are over and thereby become a threat to innocent civilians traversing the area (they remain in the hills overlooking Sarajevo, for example). It was estimated that there were 26 000 casualties per year due to AP mines, casualties that leave their victims—if they live—with shattered or severed limbs. The movement to ban production and use of AP mines, and eventually to put existing ones out of commission, was led by the International Campaign to Ban Landmines (ICBL). The ICBL consisted of over 1000 NGOs from over 60 countries. "It is a loosely organized and unstructured network—with only a handful of key full-time and paid activists—that draws on the resources, both financial and human, of a broad spectrum of member organizations interconnected by fax machines, the Internet, periodic conferences, and a common goal" (Cameron, Lawson, and Tomlin, 1998, p. 5). The Canadian government played a major role in 1996 in sponsoring two key conferences of states, international agencies, and NGOs to accelerate the progress toward a global ban, and eventually to negotiate a treaty. However, it was the ICBL (along with the International Red Cross) that really propelled the issue forward and provided the broad support and prodding governments needed. The ICBL was formed in 1992 from a cluster of six NGOs active in the AP mines issue and in human rights. One of the most interesting aspects of the ICBL was its lack of conventional organization and coordination. It operated without a secretariat, a central office, bureaucracy, or an overarching media strategy, and individual NGO members were free to pursue their own means of lobbying and campaigning as they saw fit within their local circumstances (Williams and Goose, 1998, pp. 22–23). Coordination was achieved largely through frequent exchanges of information and face-to-face contacts, in which fax, e-mail, and telephone played an important, but not determining role. It was all the more remarkable, therefore, that by the October 1996 Ottawa conference, the ICBL was given a seat at the table of governments and was actively engaged in drafting language that would feed into the December 1997 conference that produced the treaty. Significantly, the United States was opposed to the ban but in the end could not pressure governments to abandon it, and so remained a nonsignatory. The ICBL and Jody Williams, its coordinator, received the 1997 Nobel Peace Prize for their work.

Along with these dynamics of globalization and technology, science and science-related issues are increasingly important in policymaking. The greater the scientific dimension of a policy issue, the greater the importance of scientific or specialized information and those who possess it. The concept of epistemic communities captures both the new prominence of scientific specializations and their international connections. Scientific expertise in this context means more than the physical sciences; it embraces the growing importance of such social science disciplines as economics, psychology, criminology, social welfare, and management. The burgeoning field of environmental policy depends on scientific assessments, many of which are not much more than "guesstimates" but that are crucial nonetheless for coming to terms with problems such as ozone depletion and the impact of toxic substances. A case in point is the current debate over the effect of pesticides on humans and the environment. In May 2000 the House of Commons Standing Committee on Environment and Sustainable Development released its report entitled *Pesticides: Making the Right Choice for the Protection of Health and the Environment*. It noted that there were some 7000 registered pesticides in

Canada with over 500 active ingredients but that many of these substances had not been re-evaluated for years. While recommending a "precautionary principle" that would call for an absolute priority for the protection of human health and the environment, the Committee also acknowledged the need for large amounts of new scientific research to clear up many ambiguities and uncertainties about the actual and potential impact of pesticides. In 2007, the same Committee was reviewing the 1999 Canadian Environmental Protection Act, and noted that "the government has, until now, had the responsibility of identifying each substance of concern from amongst the 23 000 substances on the Domestic Substance List (DSL). Thus the onus has been on government to collect and analyze the data to show toxicity. It has done this through the Priority Substance List (PSL) process and through examination of international decisions. The PSL in particular has been a very slow and onerous route" (Standing Committee on Environment and Sustainable Development, 2007).

A knowledge-dependent policy process poses several challenges for policymakers. One is the need to somehow balance expertise with democracy. Scientists and experts make claims and recommendations based on notions of truth, not majority wishes. The fear is that an overly rational policy process will be driven more by small cliques of experts than by the democratic desires and participation of the public. The problem is even more acute when an issue is highly contentious and disputed. A case in point is genetically modified (GM) foods. The Canadian Biotechnology Advisory Committee submitted a report in 2002 recommending an improved regulatory regime, and its first two recommendations concerned governance and transparency, and public involvement (Canadian Biotechnology Advisory Committee, 2002).

Another aspect of communities and networks that is changing in the current policy climate is their alignment with levels of government. This involves two interesting dynamics. The first is the more obvious one of the last few years: as governments devolve more of their policy responsibilities to jurisdictions that are closer to the people or closer to the policy problem (even as they shift some responsibilities upward), policy communities change to reflect the new "core" in the subgovernment. Municipal restructuring in Ontario, for example, compelled amalgamation in cities like Toronto and Ottawa. Services that were once dispersed are now part of single regional or consolidated governments in both cases, and local policy communities that previously would have been fragmented in terms of different communities now have to re-organize and focus their efforts on a new "core" government. The other dynamic reflects some of the forces cited in Chapter 2, wherein the lines between policy fields get increasingly blurred, thereby encouraging governments to "migrate" into new areas to meet their policy objectives. A good example was the

Government of Canada–Voluntary Sector Initiative announced in June 2000 (Phillips, 2003). Ottawa recognized the importance of the "third sector" for the quality of life for Canadians and for the quality of service delivery in many areas, and the initiative was designed to build capacity in the sector.

Finally, governments are increasingly attracted to the ideas of partnerships and **framework policies** (setting parameters but letting others deliver programs). Partly this is due to resource constraints, and shifting responsibilities onto third parties is a way of offloading expenses. However, the broad consensus that appears to be emerging about the limitations of governments, and the virtues of setting frameworks within which private actors can pursue their interests, places greater emphasis on partnerships between the public and private/nonprofit sectors. Policy communities and networks are important today not only because they represent interests that have to be integrated into the policy process, or information that is crucial to analysis, but because they are important sinews for implementation and delivery. The concept of working partnerships for the development and delivery of services implies a very different set of relationships than is typically envisaged in the communities/networks literature. That literature focuses more on the political dynamics of interest representation, whereas the challenges of partnerships focus more on the logistics of joint action to achieve common goals.

The preceding suggests a somewhat confusing array of forces that serve to make policy communities and networks—domestic and global—even more important than they have been in the past, but also perhaps more challenging to integrate into the policy process. The associational system shows no signs of shrinking, and some elements of it, such as those involved in the delivery of public services, may face considerable pressures to expand. Information technologies make possible even wider, global connections of interests and communities. Movements like human rights, environment, and women's issues are truly global in scope. At the same time, some policy issues get driven further down, and so some networks that would have had their centre of gravity at the national level now become truly local or regional. Finally, the information and organizational capacities of policy communities are being viewed in a different light by policymakers; these are resources they need, and they have to think of new ways to develop linkages.

We can conclude then that contemporary importance of policy networks and communities has not diminished; indeed, it has grown. However, the realities of the policy process continue to change the nature and dynamic of those communities, posing substantial challenges for policymakers. Lindquist (1992; 1996) offered the concept of "stewardship" to capture what these challenges entail. More recently, the same theme has been taken up by Goldsmith and Eggers (2004) with their notion of networked government: "The hierarchical model of government persists, but its influence is steadily waning . . . government by network bears less resemblance to a traditional organizational chart than it does to a more dynamic web of computer networks that can organize or reorganize, expand or contract, depending on the problem at hand" (Goldsmith and Eggers, 2004, p. 8). Assuming that policy communities and networks are crucial components in the development and implementation of public policy, a core responsibility for any public manager is the improvement of learning and adaptive capacities, leading to higher levels of policy debate and relevant policy expertise. What this entails in practice depends on the type of policy community or network in question and its specific needs. Capacity-building for intellectual communities may mean enhancing informational resources and communication abilities. For communities involved in policy delivery, it may mean development of organizational capacity through training. The governance dynamics of small, dense networks will be different from networks with larger numbers of members, and so the way in which government interacts with those networks will differ as well (Provan and Kenis, 2008). Whatever it means, thinking about the policy networks and communities relevant to one's policy mandate is a key responsibility for the public manager in 2009 and beyond.

CONSULTING, ENGAGING, AND PARTNERING

The two big trends in policy community relations or management have been public consultations/citizen engagement and partnerships. Both of these can be viewed cynically. Consultations and citizen engagement can be seen as empty theatrics where interest groups rant predictably while decisionmakers watch the clock, waiting for it all to be over so that they can then go and make the decisions they were going to make anyway. Both also keep everyone busy in a ritualistic way, ultimately validating what decisionmakers wanted to do in the first place (Cooke and Kothari, 2001). Partnerships can be viewed as an attempt to get out of key areas of government responsibility by shifting delivery (but not adequate financial or logistical support) over to the private/nonprofit sector. More subtly, civil society associations can be roped into monitoring performance and results, apparently playing an important role in the policy process, but more or less watching the horse's back end, and not contributing to what goes into the front (Laforest and Phillips, 2007). There is a strong element of truth in these critiques, but they capture, at best, only half of the reality. Policymakers realize the limitations of these strategies (and sometimes manipulate those limitations to their own ends), but they also genuinely believe that consultation in policy design and partnership in policy delivery are important aspects of their jobs. They may not always like it, but they will undertake it, often willingly but also because some form of consultation with the public is increasingly mandated as an aspect of public policy development. There are real puzzles in this engagement, however—challenges that have to be recognized and addressed if governance is to evolve into the next decade. With consultations, the challenge is balancing public demands with the realities of hard decisions. With partnerships, the challenge is balancing accountability with autonomy.

CONSULTATION AND ENGAGEMENT

The dictionary definition of consultation is simply to ask for advice or opinion, or a type of communication between two or more parties. Any government that purports to be democratic, one would think, is intrinsically a government that consults. The recent emphasis on consultation therefore seems a bit puzzling from this perspective. If governments have not been consulting when making and implementing policy, then what have they been doing? In fact, there is a more specific meaning to consultation in the current context, one that reflects the forces described in Chapter 2. Almost any form of communication can be seen as a consultation, if by that term we mean only the exchange of information or views. Government polling, for example, might be seen as a form of consultation since it probes for the views of citizens on a wide variety of subjects. The same might be true of task forces, royal commissions, parliamentary committees, referenda, and even elections, all of which are often described as consultations with the public. Using the term this broadly, however, wrings out almost any of its usefulness.

Consultation is different. First, it is usually focused on the operational and programmatic level, as opposed to broad values or directions for policy development. One can still consult about broad values, but these should be clearly connected to specific issues and programs. The interlocutors, therefore, are the agencies responsible for program design and delivery, and direct clients or stakeholders in the relevant policy community or network. This distinguishes consultation as a policy management activity from broader forms of political representation, such as parliamentary committee hearings on a piece of legislation, for example. The objective is ongoing development and management of the policy or program in question, not the establishment of parameters for political discussion and debate.

The emphasis on consultation with stakeholders at the federal level goes back to the early 1990s, for example, with the report of the PS2000 Task Force on Service to the Public, which argued that consultation should become a routine aspect of public policymaking (Privy Council Office, 1993). Consultation practices vary quite widely across departments, depending on the issues and the preferences of ministers and senior officials. Ever since 1992, federal departments and agencies have been formally urged to consider public consultation a key part of the development of policy. The 2003 federal Guide to Making Federal Acts and Regulations noted that consultation in instrument choice is "essential" to making good choices, and includes public consultation under the rubric of "good governance guidelines" (Privy Council Office, 2003). The 2004 federal guide to drafting a **Memorandum to Cabinet,** the policy document outlining the rationale for any proposed bill, required a statement of a consultation strategy (Privy Council Office, 2004). The rules of strict confidentiality of draft legislation have also been relaxed somewhat, so that consultations can now be undertaken around proposed legislation. The only federal policy area in which consultations are mandated is in the creation of new regulations. The Cabinet Directive on Streamlining Regulation states that "Departments and agencies are responsible for identifying interested and affected parties, and for providing them with opportunities to take part in open, meaningful, and balanced consultations at all stages of the regulatory process (Government of Canada, 2007). The guidelines go on to say that:

When undertaking consultations, departments and agencies are to:

- inform and engage Canadians on the nature and implications of the public policy issue based on available evidence, science, or knowledge;

- include Canadians in developing policy objectives;

- set out the process and timelines in a clear manner so that affected parties can organize and provide input; and

- provide timely feedback to Canadians and affected parties on the outcome of the consultations and on the priorities considered in decision making.

As we noted above, and as these guidelines make clear, the focus of consultations is largely programmatic and practical—it is intended to improve policy development, design, and implementation processes. It is not usually understood to entail a broad discussion and exchange of values that underpin policy proposals. The term for this sort of communication is "citizen engagement."

The shift to "engagement" from "consultation" seems to have occurred, in part, because of the continued lack of trust that citizens have toward government and dissatisfaction with the connotations of consultation—a process that suggests a fairly passive communication of views from "stakeholders" to government officials who will ultimately make the key decisions. With a decline in trust has come a decline in citizen participation in politics and public deliberation. Voter turnout in the 2004 and 2006 elections was 60.9 percent and 64.7 percent respectively (Elections Canada), but plummeted to 59.1 percent in the October 2008 election. There has been much discussion in recent years of declining public trust in the public service and the public sector, fed by sensationalism around reputed scandals and on-going exposures such as the Gomery Inquiry. Rebuilding that trust requires better engagement between the public sector and the public (Green and Côté, 2007). One can trace the earliest emergence of the idea of public participation in Canada at the level of local government in the 1970s, linked in part to trying to get citizens involved in increasingly complex land-use planning issues (Graham and Phillips, 1998, p. 5) but also because of civil activism and municipal reform movements (Thomas, 1995). But the concern is now part of the wider "policy movement" discussed in Chapter 1. The OECD, for example, as early as 1999, launched a survey on "Strengthening Government-Citizen Connections" with the participation of twenty-one member countries and the European Commission:

> OECD countries clearly view the issue of government-citizen relations with growing concern. Several countries cited low or declining confidence in public institutions as one motivation for recent initiatives to strengthen government-citizen connections. A related trend cited by many of these countries was declining participation in political parties. Many others cited pressures created by increased citizen demands for information and expectations that government provide more responsive and better quality service. There is a growing perception in the OECD countries that representative democracy is not working as well as it has in the past. Thus, governments are looking to new or improved models and approaches for better informing and involving citizens in the policy-making process. (OECD, 2000, p. 1; also see OECD, 2001)

This was followed up with a study in 2003 that argued that "active participation is the new frontier" of governance (OECD, 2003). The concern to engage citizens is also in part a reflection of a deeper concern about the eroding democratic foundation of contemporary politics and policymaking. Citizen engagement thus has both an instrumental dimension—trying to tap into the knowledge and perspectives of citizens themselves, unfiltered by media or interest groups—and a legitimating dimension—to try to shore up the public's support for policy initiatives by bringing the public more actively into the process. Building open government has become a major project for OECD members. Almost all to date have Freedom of Information Acts and an Ombudsman's office (OECD, 2005). In line with the argument we made in the previous chapter about new trends in public management, the emphasis on consultation and engagement has deepened into a new concept of "social accountability." The range of efforts is wide, and includes binding legal strictures on information exposure, support for specific target groups, the use of ICTs, and engagement with media or advocacy groups (Caddy et al., 2006).

The European Union maintains a web site entitled "Your Voice in Europe" that is a one-stop shop for all EU wide consultations on all policy issues. Citizens can participate in internet-based consultations by accessing discussion papers and other documents on the web site through a knowledge base, and then answer questionnaires. Live chat with policymakers is also available (European Commission, 2008).

The key challenge in citizen engagement is developing techniques to actually engage citizens. Consultations, as we described them above, can naturally be assumed to attract stakeholders and interest groups, but even in that context it is a challenge to go beyond simple tabling of inflexible views and to move to a more deliberative process. Seasoned policymakers wince at the idea of consultation that simply collects together "the usual suspects" who have a particular axe to grind. Citizen engagement is exactly what it says—somehow getting ordinary citizens to come forward and thoughtfully engage on a policy question. Various innovative techniques have been suggested to genuinely bring citizens into an informed dialogue and exchange with government. Some, like **study circles,** are designed to facilitate decisionmaking at the community level. Study circles are championed by the Study Circles Resource Center in Pomfret, Connecticut and the model entails bringing people from all over a neighbourhood, town, or city together in small groups of eight to twelve who work through the same issue for a period of time and then all come together to share ideas and develop plans. The technique has been used in over 500 communities in the United States to address citizens' concerns about schools, youth, violence, and other issues. The Center changed its name to "Everyday Democracy" in 2008, but continues to work at stimulating community level dialogue and engagement around issues such as racism, education, and immigration (Everyday Democracy, 2008).

Another technique is **citizens' juries** or panels, originally developed by the Jefferson Center in Minneapolis, Minnesota. A randomly selected jury of about eighteen individuals hears from a variety of expert witnesses and deliberates together on a given issue. The jury then presents its recommendations to the public. The technique has been used in the United States to address issues such as national health care reform, budget priorities, environmental issues, and local school needs, as well as by organizations in Great Britain, Germany, Denmark, Spain, Australia, and other countries. Prime Minister Gordon Brown decided to use the technique in 2007 to introduce a "new politics," more consultative and engaged directly with citizens. Juries were used to discuss school safety and National Health Service reforms (Jefferson Center, 2007). This small-scale consultation stands in contrast to **deliberative polling,** a technique pioneered by the American social scientist James Fishkin (1991; Fishkin and Laslett, 2003). It involves between 250 and 600 people who form a representative sample of the community, and who are polled for their preliminary views on an issue. They then engage in small group discussions and pose questions to experts and politicians, and are once again polled at the end of the process once they have had the opportunity to reflect and deliberate. Similar techniques include standing panels, community issue groups, and consensus conferences. Fishkin has even suggested a national version—"deliberation day"—to be held every presidential election day (Ackerman and Fishkin, 2004). An innovative Canadian variant is "citizens' dialogue," developed by the Canadian Policy Research Networks. The technique involves a carefully selected representative panel of citizens (usually several hundred) across Canada, or if it is a provincial issue, in that province, who meet and have a structured dialogue on important issues. The dialogue usually lasts for a day and is steered by a professional facilitator. A sounding is taken at the beginning of the dialogue, and then again at the end, to see where and how opinions have changed. The technique was used, for example, in the Commission on the Future of Health Care in Canada (the Romanow Commission; see Box 6.2), as well as in the run-up to Ontario's 2007 referendum on a proportional election system.

It is easier to list principles and techniques than to put them into practice, particularly by governments; most of the techniques cited above were pioneered and are used by nonprofit organizations. Whereas consultation and engagement at all levels of government has become a sort of policy mantra, the realities and challenges are more complex. For one thing, consultations are only one stream of information and advice into the policy process, but those who are consulted naturally want to see their efforts reflected in policy outputs. As well, the openness demanded by consultation can run against the organizational grain of government, which sometimes requires a high degree of confidentiality (e.g., sensitive information about third parties) or strong executive action (e.g., responding to an emergency).

PARTNERSHIPS AND HORIZONTAL MANAGEMENT

There is some overlap between the concept of consultation and of partnership. Indeed, Kernaghan's (1993) classification of partnerships has consultation as one end of a continuum of power sharing over decisions and implementation: (1) consultative partnerships: exchanging advice and information, (2) contributory partnerships: money or other forms of support for projects managed by a third party, (3) operational partnerships: sharing work in achieving goals, but the main decisions are still made by one partner, usually government, and (4) collaborative partnerships: sharing both work and decisionmaking (pp. 62–65). While it seems puzzling that public officials would willingly relinquish some of their autonomy, there has been a rising interest in collaborative partnerships,

BOX 6.2   CITIZEN'S DIALOGUE ON HEALTH CARE

The Commission partnered with the Canadian Policy Research Networks, a not-for-profit policy think-tank, to organize 12 regional one-day "deliberative dialogue" sessions across the country. Each session brought together some 40 randomly selected Canadians. At the outset of the process, participants completed a questionnaire probing their perceptions of the challenges confronting Canada's health care system and their preferred solutions for addressing them. They were subsequently provided with a workbook outlining four scenarios for revitalizing the health care system that included arguments for and against each scenario. (An analysis of historical public opinion research data indicated that each of the scenarios enjoyed a relatively high level of public support—despite the seemingly irreconcilable values-base implicit among them. The purpose of the "deliberative dialogue" sessions was to oblige Canadians to make difficult choices between the competing scenarios.)

Working with professional facilitators, participants spent the balance of the day discussing the four scenarios and their likely consequences. At the end of the day, participants were asked to complete a second questionnaire to assess whether their initial perceptions had changed and if so, why. The results of the 12 sessions were analyzed and common themes and directions noted. A national public opinion survey was then undertaken to assess whether the results of the "deliberative dialogue" process would be validated. The four scenarios were:

- More public investment—The first scenario was to add more resources (such as doctors, nurses, and equipment) to deal with medicare's current problems by increasing public spending, either through a tax increase or by re-allocating funds from other government programs.
- Share the costs and responsibilities—The second scenario was to add more resources to deal with current problems not by increasing public spending but through a system of user co-payments for health care services that would provide an incentive for people not to over-use the system as well as needed funds.
- Increase private choice—The third scenario was to give Canadians increased choice in accessing private providers for health care services. Side-by-side with the public system, Canadians also could access health care services from a private sector provider

(either for-profit or not-for profit) and pay for it from their own resources or private insurance.

- Reorganize service delivery—The fourth scenario was to reorganize service delivery in order to provide more integrated care, realize efficiencies and expand coverage. Under this scenario, each Canadian would sign up with a health care provider network that would work as a team to provide more co-ordinated, cost-effective services and improved access to care.

SOURCE: Commission on the Future of Health Care in Canada. (2002). *Building on values: The future of health care in Canada*, pp. 271–72.

both with private sector entities and nonprofit, noncommercial organizations such as those in the social services sector. And partnerships can also involve different government departments, either at the same level or across jurisdictions. The reasons for partnering reflect our earlier arguments in this chapter. Governments want to save money, and partnerships with firms or nonprofit organizations can be a way of offloading services. But governments also recognize some of their own limitations in directly delivering services, and so partnerships can be a means of improving service delivery, getting better feedback, and encouraging civic engagement.

There is a great variety of partnership forms (Rosenau, 2000), but as a general mode of implementation (and of policymaking), it is seen as a major departure as well as a major challenge. This is because traditional governance is hierarchical, and sees government authorities as having the core responsibility for delivering services. True partnerships imply a degree of equality and shared responsibility. From a management perspective, that means that new skills of collaboration and coordination will be required as partnerships become more pervasive. This type of management is called "horizontal" management and has attracted a great deal of attention recently:

> Horizontal management can be defined as the coordination and management of a set of activities between two or more organizational units, where the units in question do not have hierarchical control over each other and where the aim is to generate outcomes that cannot be achieved by units working in isolation. (Bakvis and Juillet, 2004, 9)

Governments around the world are increasingly concerned with policy coherence and developing "horizontality." In a sense, any government is itself an example of horizontal management; cabinets are, for example, mechanisms to develop collective decisionmaking across portfolios. Central agencies like the Privy Council Office or the Treasury Board are also mechanisms of coordination. What is new is that this interest in horizontality is extending to all levels of government bureaucracy, with the growing expectation that government departments will work more closely and collaboratively with each other to solve problems that cut across bureaucratic jurisdictions, that they will work more closely and collaboratively with other departments in other jurisdictions, and that they will increasingly partner with nongovernmental actors. While horizontal management is not necessarily the best way to approach every policy issue, at the federal level there is a sense that it is a reality that is here to stay.

It is best to think of horizontal management as a continuum running from a minimalist to a maximalist level of coordination (Peters, 1998). The minimal level entails nothing more than mutual recognition of activities and an effort not to duplicate or interfere. At the maximalist end of the continuum, one will find partnerships based on formal agreements about objectives, resource sharing, and coordinating procedures. Partnering arrangements can be of various types: consultative (sharing information), operational (sharing work), or truly collaborative (sharing decisionmaking).

There is sufficient experience and interest in horizontal management to have developed a set of best practices. According to the Auditor General of Canada (2000), the key success factors are:

- Identifying an effective co-ordination structure (establishing roles and responsibilities and promoting co-ordination through levers and incentives);
- Agreeing on common objectives, results, and strategies (this includes defining performance expectations and how departments will contribute);
- Measuring results to track performance;
- Using information to improve performance; and
- Effectively reporting performance.

According to Canadian Centre for Management Development (CCMD)—now the Canada School of Public Service—Roundtable discussions and research on horizontality, the key themes were:

- Leadership that marshals the powers of influence and persuasion is the key driver. It is best exercised through dialogue, with an emphasis on active listening.
- A culture that values collaboration and trust among partners is essential.

- Horizontal initiatives have a life cycle that makes timing crucial.
- Continual reflection and adjustment are required to maintain momentum.
- Managers of horizontal initiatives need to maintain contact with vertical structures for the sake of securing accountability, authority, and resources.
- Support systems (knowledge bases, resource allocations, and the like) too often work against horizontal management and need to be adapted. (Fitzpatrick, 2000)

The Canada School argued that the key dimensions of horizontal management are mobilizing teams and networks, developing shared frameworks, building supportive structures, and maintaining momentum (Hopkins, Couture, and Moore, 2001). As with the best practices above, these call for different skill sets from public managers. They also pose important organizational challenges. Perhaps the pre-eminent one is accountability. When governments enter into partnerships, by necessity they relinquish power and control. In cases of substantial loss of control, however, the government agency is still in some measure responsible for the expenditure of public funds and for outcomes, yet those expenditures and outcomes may be determined more by the partner than by the government agency. Government organizations are used to operating in a hierarchical, top-down fashion, but partnering implies spheres of autonomy as well as coordination for the different partners. How to combine that autonomy, the prime contribution of the partnership agreement, with accountability for performance and results? As Langford put it: "As part of this move, contemporary managers must develop the relationship-building, negotiating, contract management, risk assessment, and performance measurement skills required to work effectively in a partnership world" (Langford, 1999, p. 108).

A good example of the challenge is Canada's Asia-Pacific Gateway and Corridor Initiative. Launched in 2005, it aims to make Canada and the west coast the main conduit for goods, services, and cultural exchanges between Asia and North America. Since it means moving goods from Asia through British Columbia, and then through rail and highway transport to Ontario and the United States, several provinces are involved, as are municipalities and private companies and of course Asian governments such as China, Hong Kong, and Singapore. The initiative refers to partnerships as a component of "21st century governance":

Since various issues directly impacting Gateway and Corridor effectiveness and exploitation interact with each other in important ways, they are best addressed in an integrated fashion rather than in isolation. Partnership is essential. The Gateway approach offers a coherent framework for joint leadership and focused collaboration among the different public and private sector actors who control or influence the key issues.

New approaches to governance, reflecting an outward-looking perspective on global commerce, are necessary to ensure maximum efficiency of existing assets. For the Government of Canada, there is an internal dimension as well. Various federal departments have responsibilities that directly impact the Gateway. The immediate measures identified under this Initiative include activities led by Transport Canada, the Department of Foreign Affairs and International Trade, Western Economic Diversification Canada, the Canada Border Services Agency, Parks Canada and Human Resources and Social Development Canada. An ongoing element of the Initiative will be a policy renewal agenda that aims in part to work across the "silos" to advance the long-term development and exploitation of the Gateway and Corridor. (Transport Canada, 2008)

A specific variant of the more generic notion of partnering is **public-private partnerships,** or PPP (or P3). The Canadian Council for Public-Private Partnerships defines them as: "A cooperative venture between the public and private sectors, built on the expertise of each partner, that best meets clearly defined public needs through the appropriate allocation of resources, risks and rewards" (2008). There are various models of PPPs that combine risk and resources in different ways:

Design-Build (DB): The private sector designs and builds infrastructure to meet public sector performance specifications, often for a fixed price, so the risk of cost overruns is transferred to the private sector. (Many do not consider DBs to be within the spectrum of PPPs).

Operation & Maintenance Contract (O & M): A private operator, under contract, operates a publicly-owned asset for a specified term. Ownership of the asset remains with the public entity.

Design-Build-Finance-Operate (DBFO): The private sector designs, finances and constructs a new facility under a long-term lease, and operates the facility during the term of the lease. The private partner transfers the new facility to the public sector at the end of the lease term.

Build-Own-Operate (BOO): The private sector finances, builds, owns and operates a facility or service in perpetuity. The public constraints are stated in the original agreement and through ongoing regulatory authority.

Build-Own-Operate-Transfer (BOOT): A private entity receives a franchise to finance, design, build and operate a facility (and to charge user fees) for a specified period, after which ownership is transferred back to the public sector.

Buy-Build-Operate (BBO): Transfer of a public asset to a private or quasi-public entity usually under contract that the assets are to be upgraded and operated for a specified period of time. Public control is exercised through the contract at the time of transfer.

Operation License: A private operator receives a license or rights to operate a public service, usually for a specified term. This is often used in IT projects.

Finance Only: A private entity, usually a financial services company, funds a project directly or uses various mechanisms such as a long-term lease or bond issue. (Canadian Council for Public-Private Partnerships, 2008)

Some prominent Canadian examples include: Confederation Bridge, Highway 407 Electronic Toll Route, Moncton Water Treatment Plant, St. Lawrence Seaway Commercialization, Kelowna Skyreach Place and the Bruce Nuclear Power Plant lease. A measure of the seriousness which all levels of government now take PPP, Ottawa in its 2007 budget pledged $1.2 billion to a Public-Private Partnerships Fund to increase opportunities for infrastructure development. Nonetheless, as a collaborative strategy, PPPs are still opposed by some as "hybrids" of incompatible private-sector and public sector logics. The ingredients of success seem to be clear communication and buy-in from all partners, credible evaluations, fair sharing of risks, strong management, effective and continuous external evaluation, and good dispute resolution mechanisms (Hubbard and Paquet, 2007).

Conclusion

This chapter has examined the two sides of policy communities and networks: (1) the academic side with its emphasis on the explanation and description of patterns of associational-state linkages in policy domains, and (2) the public management approach to consultation and partnerships. The two overlap in important ways but are also distinct. They share the insight that contemporary governance entails a substantial degree of private/nonprofit/public cooperation and interaction at every phase of the policy process, and that the quality of policy outcomes often depends on the nature of these interactions. However, the emphasis in the policy communities and networks literature has been on describing the actors and evaluating the implications of the broad character of their relationships in terms of associational and organizational cohesion. The work on consultation/engagement and partnerships has had a more microscopic and management orientation: how do we get these things to work at the level of a specific program or policy issue?

In keeping with the theme of this book, both streams converge on the same idea: modern policymaking cannot be directed by government and simply supplemented by representations from the public or interest groups (Goldsmith and Eggers, 2004). That model died years ago, as analysts and practitioners realized the importance of new social movements, public interest groups, more complex national and global associational systems, and the strategic value of information. As we argued in this chapter, networks are, if anything, more important now than before, even as their fundamental characteristics have changed in light of globalization and other forces. Government has a more sober assessment of its own capacities. It cannot monopolize information anymore, and, in many policy areas, is heavily dependent on the specialized expertise or experience of its partners. Even with what appears as a resurgence of the role of government in 2009, it will still be more of a maestro than a master. The key point about networks is that they are systems of mutual interdependence where no one actor—including government—can dominate the rest. The government's policy role remains crucial, but it shifts its focus to network management strategies. "Network management provides a way for actors to cooperate without solutions being forcibly imposed or cooperation becoming redundant as a result of decentralization or privatization" (Kickert and Koppenjan, 1997, p. 43).

Does that mean that government is necessarily weaker? In some ways, yes. In other ways, however, network management actually suggests a broadening and deepening of government influence through its leverage in policy networks and partnerships. The crucial question is the degree to which government remains a leader in these networks and partnerships. Also, we sometimes forget the other powers and instruments that governments have at their disposal to encourage private/public partnerships. This is what some analysts have referred to as "**strategic governance**" (de Bruijn and ten Heuvelhof, 1995; Rethemeyer, 2005). Policy networks, for example, are characterized by the interdependency of actors, the complexity of coalitions and organizational players, the reluctance to cooperate because of uncertainties about real interests and ultimate outcomes, and instability in that players shift constantly. Government can facilitate the effectiveness of networks by addressing these characteristics; for example, by distributing information, by helping organizations and interests coalesce and participate, and by developing novel proposals for exchange and cooperation.

If policy communities and networks are as important to the policy process as we suspect, then policy analysis and policy management have to change considerably. Analysis has to come to terms with the fact that policy outcomes depend crucially on the actors in the community and the nature of the network. Policy management has to shift its attention to new organizational forms of public sector and private sector cooperation and interaction. As we noted earlier, there is a host of challenges that come with this new importance of networks. One such challenge is the ability to balance the more traditional forms of governance (which do not go away entirely) with network practices: "The complex and diverse universe of organizations and processes involved with the governing processes today cannot be easily divided into two categories: public versus private or networks versus bureaucracies. It makes more sense to think in terms of hybrids and on-going transitions, not pure types and overnight transformations" (Thomas, 2006). Another one is ensuring that the participation of citizens is real, influential, and reinforces and supports democratic practice (Laforest and Phillips, 2007; Klijn and Skelcher, 2007).

KEY TERMS

advocacy coalition—a wide range of actors, including government from all levels, officials, interest organizations, research groups, journalists, and even other countries, who share a belief system about a policy area and over time demonstrate some degree of coordinated activities

associational system—constellation of small, medium, and large groups, competing and cooperating as they feel necessary

attentive public—the outsiders whose main influence on the process is to generate ideas and discussion through conferences, publications, and occasional lobbying

citizens' juries—a randomly selected jury of about eighteen individuals that hears from a variety of expert witnesses and deliberates together on a given issue

consultation—process whereby government gauges the views and opinions of nongovernmental organizations, citizen groups, and associations

corporatism—a system wherein centralized state agencies and centralized associational systems work closely to develop and implement policy

deliberative polling—a technique that usually involves between 250 and 600 people who form a representative sample of the community and who are first polled on their views on an issue, informed in some depth on that issue, and then polled again

epistemic community—originally developed in the field of international relations, this concept tries to capture the influence of international groups of scientific experts on policymaking; for example, in the environmental field

framework policies—a technique whereby government sets the broad parameters for policy outcomes but lets others deliver programs

global public policy networks—quasi-official constellations of state actors, international organizations, and nongovernmental organizations that do more than advocate, but develop and sometimes even implement policies and assist in global coordination

interest group—a voluntary, membership-based organization that lobbies governments on issues of concern to its members

interest group pluralism—a system in which a wide variety of interests succeed in getting themselves heard throughout government

interest intermediation—the process whereby societal interests interact with state institutions

iron triangle—the stable and cozy relationships among congressional committees, executive agencies (primarily regulatory), and economic interest groups

issue network—offered as a critique of the "iron triangle" concept in that most policy subsystems were actually quite fluid and changing, with actors coalescing as necessary around issues, not policy sectors

Memorandum to Cabinet—the policy document outlining the rationale for any proposed bill, which now must state what consultations the Minister has undertaken or plans to undertake

policy community—the actors in a policy network, presumably those who share at least some common language and conceptual reference points but who may be opponents on the issue

policy network—the patterns of relations among members of the policy community

postmaterialist values—term used to describe the amalgam of conditions consisting of the rise of postmaterialism, the increased salience of rights, and the new emphasis on "difference"

public interest group—interest groups whose emphasis is on advocacy for "causes" and the public interest rather than economic lobbying

public-private partnership—a cooperative venture between the public and private sectors, built on the expertise of each partner, that meets well-defined public needs through the appropriate allocation of resources, risks, and rewards

social movement—an informal network of organizations and individuals who, on the basis of a collective identity and shared values, engage in political and/or cultural struggle intended to break or expand the boundaries of the existing system, and undertake collective action designed to affect both state and society

social movement organization—interest groups rooted in social trans-formations of the 1960s that led to new values, new class structures, and new social coalitions (e.g., environmentalism, feminism)

strategic governance—the use of the powers and instruments that governments have at their disposal to encourage private/public partner-ships, networks, framework agreements, and broad direction for the policy system as a whole

study circles—a consultation technique designed to facilitate broadly based, grassroots decisionmaking at the community level

subgovernment—a generic concept that expresses the idea that policy does not get made in a single "system" but in subsystems that consist of microcosms of all the relevant political and institutional actors

FURTHER READINGS

Caddy, J., Peixoto, T., and McNeil, M. (2007). Beyond public scrutiny: Stocktaking of social accountability in OECD countries. World Bank Institute Working Paper. Retrieved on March 18, 2008, from http://www.oecd.org/dataoecd/43/3/38983242.pdf

Goldsmith, S., and Eggers, W. (2004). *Governing by network: The new shape of the public sector*. Washington, D.C.: Brookings Institution.

Keck, M. E., and Sikkink, K. (1998). *Activists beyond borders: Advocacy networks in international politics*. Ithaca: Cornell University Press.

Kickert, W. J. M., Klijn, E.-H., and Koppenjan, J. F. M. (Eds.) (1997). *Managing complex networks: Strategies for the public sector*. London: Sage.

Sabatier, P. A., and Jenkins-Smith, H. (Eds.). (1993). *Policy change and learning: An advocacy coalition approach*. Boulder, CO: Westview.

Stone, D. (2008). Global public policy, transnational policy communities, and their networks. *The Policy Studies Journal, 36* (1), 19–38.

REFERENCES

Ackerman, B., and Fishkin, F. S. (2004). *Deliberation day*. New Haven: Yale University Press.

Almond, G. (1990). *A discipline divided: Schools and sects in political science*. Newbury Park, CA: Sage.

Atkinson, M. M., and Coleman, W. D. (1989a). *The state, business, and industrial change in Canada*. Toronto: University of Toronto Press.

Atkinson, M. M., and Coleman, W. D. (1989b). Strong states and weak states: Sectoral policy networks in advanced capitalist economies. *British Journal of Political Science, 19*, 47–67.

Atkinson, M. M., and Coleman, W. D. (1992, April). Policy networks, policy communities and the problems of governance. *Governance, 5*, 154–80.

Auditor General of Canada. (2000). *Managing departments for results and managing horizontal issues for results*. Retrieved on March 24, 2008, from http://www.oag-bvg.gc.ca/internet/English/att_0020xe11_e_10954.html

Ayres, J. M. (1998). *Defying conventional wisdom: Political movements and popular contention against North American free trade*. Toronto: University of Toronto Press.

Bakvis, H., and Juillet, L. (2004) *The horizontal challenge: Line departments, central agencies, and leadership*. Ottawa: Canadian School of Public Service.

Batliwala, S. (2002, December). Grassroots movements as transnational actors: Implications for global civil society. *Voluntas: International Journal of Voluntary and Nonprofit Organizations, 13*, 393–408.

Baumgartner, F. R. (1996, January). Public interest groups in France and the United States. *Governance, 9*, 1–22.

Baumgartner, F. R., and Leech, B. L. (1998). *Basic interests: The importance of groups in politics and in political science*. Princeton: Princeton University Press.

Baumgartner, F. R. and Mahoney, C. (2005). Social movements, the rise of new issues, and the public agenda. In D. S. Meyer, V. Jenness, and H. Ingram (Eds.), *Routing the opposition: Social movements, public policy, and democracy* (pp. 65–86). Minneapolis: University of Minnesota Press.

Berry, J. M. (1977). *Lobbying for the people: The political behavior of public interest groups*. Princeton: Princeton University Press.

Berry, J. M. (1999). *The new Liberalism: The rising power of citizen groups*. Washington, DC: Brookings Institution Press.

Caddy, J., Peixoto, T., and McNeil, M. (2007). Beyond public scrutiny: Stocktaking of social accountability in OECD countries. World Bank Institute Working Paper. Retrieved on March 18, 2008, from http://www.oecd.org/dataoecd/43/3/38983242.pdf

Cameron, M., Lawson, R. J., and Tomlin, B. W. (1998). To walk without fear. In M. A. Cameron, R. J. Lawson, and B. W. Tomlin (Eds.), *To walk without fear: The global movement to ban landmines* (pp. 1–17). Toronto: Oxford University Press.

Canadian Centre for Philanthropy. (2000). *Federal/voluntary sector initiative*. Retrieved March 24, 2008, from http://www.imaginecanada.ca/

Canadian Council for Public-Private Partnerships. (2008). Definitions. Retrieved on March 24, 2008, from http://www.pppcouncil.ca/aboutPPP_definition.asp

Canadian Development Report 1999. (2000). Ottawa: North-South Institute.

Carroll, W. K. (Ed.). (1992). *Organizing dissent*. Toronto: Garamond.

Carter, D. (1964). *Power in Washington: A critical look at today's struggle in the nation's capital*. New York: Random House.

Coleman, W. D. (1994, July). Banking, interest intermediation and political power. *European Journal of Political Research, 26,* 31–58.

Coleman, W. D., and Skogstad, G. (1990). Policy communities and policy networks: A structural approach. In W. D. Coleman and G. Skogstad (Eds.), *Organized interests and public policy* (pp. 14–33). Toronto: Copp-Clark.

Cooke, B., and Kothari, U. (Eds.). (2001). *Participation: The new tyranny*. London: Zed Books.

de Bruijn, J. A., and ven Heuvelhof, E. F. (1995). Policy networks and governance. In D. Weimer (Ed.), *Institutional design* (pp. 161–79). Boston: Kluwer Academic Publishers.

Dowding, K. (1995). Model or metaphor? A critical review of the policy network approach. *Political Studies, 43,* 136–58.

Dowding, K. (2001, March). There must be end to confusion: Policy networks, intellectual fatigue, and the need for political science methods courses in British universities. *Political Studies, 49,* 89–105.

Economist. (2008). Facing down the FARC. February 7. Retrieved on March 22, 2008, from http://www.economist.com/world/la/displaystory.cfm?story_id=10650741

Elections Canada. (2007). Voter turnout at federal elections and referendums, 1867–2006. Retrieved on March 15, 2008, from http://www.elections.ca/content.asp?section=pas&document=turnout&lang=e&textonly=false

European Commission. (2008). Your voice in Europe. Retrieved on March 24, 2008, from http://ec.europa.eu/yourvoice/consultations/index_en.htm

Everyday Democracy. (2008). *Ideas and tools for community change*. Retrieved on March 24, 2008, from http://www.everyday-democracy.org//en/Index.aspx

Falk, R. (1987). The global promise of social movements: Explorations at the edge of time. *Alternatives, 7,* 173–96.

Fischer, F., and Forester, J. (Eds.). (1993). *The argumentative turn in policy analysis and planning.* Durham, NC: Duke University Press.

Fishkin, J. S. (1991). *Democracy and deliberation: New directions for democratic reform.* New Haven, CT: Yale University Press.

Fishkin, J. S., and Laslett, P. (Eds.) (2003). *Debating deliberative democracy.* Malden, MA.: Blackwell.

Fitzpatrick, T. (2000). *Horizontal management: Trends in governance and accountability.* Action-Research Roundtable on the Management of Horizontal Issues. Ottawa: Canadian Centre for Management Development. Retrieved on March 24, 2008, from http://www.myschool-monecole.gc.ca/research/publications/pdfs/Horiz-Trends-rev.pdf

Geist, M. (2008). Fair copyright for Canada. Retrieved on March 22, 2008 from http://www.facebook.com/group.php?gid=6315846683

Glasius, M., Kaldor, M., and Anheier, H. (2003). *Global civil society 2002.* Oxford: Oxford University Press.

Goldsmith, S., and Eggers, W. D. (2004). *Governing by network: The new shape of the public sector.* Washington, D.C.: Brookings Institution.

Government of Canada. (2007). *Cabinet directive on streamlining regulation.* Retrieved on March 22, 2008, from http://www.regulation.gc.ca/directive/directive-eng.pdf

Graham, K. A., and Phillips, S. D. (1998). Making public participation more effective: Issues for local government. In K. A. Graham and S. D. Phillips (Eds.), *Citizen engagement: Lessons in participation from local government* (pp. 1–24). Toronto: Institute of Public Administration of Canada.

Green, I., and Côté, A. (2007). *Leading by example.* Ottawa: Public Policy Forum.

Haas, P. M. (1992, Winter). Introduction: Epistemic communities and international policy coordination. *International Organization, 46,* 1–35.

Heclo, H. (1978). Issue networks and the executive establishment. In A. King (Ed.), *The new American political system* (pp. 87–124). Washington, DC: American Enterprise Institute for Public Policy Research.

Heclo, H., and Wildavsky, A. (1974). *The private government of public money.* London: Macmillan.

Hopkins, M., Couture, C., and Moore, E. (2001). *Moving from the heroic to the everyday: Lessons learned from leading horizontal projects.* Roundtable on the Management of Horizontal Initiatives. Ottawa: Canadian Centre for Management Development. Retrieved March 24,

2008, from http://www.csps-efpc.gc.ca/Research/publications/html/horinz_rt/horinz_rt_1_e.html

Howlett, M. (2002, June). Do networks matter? Linking policy network structure to policy outcomes: Evidence from four Canadian policy sectors 1990–2000. *Canadian Journal of Political Science, 35,* 235–67.

Hubbard, R. and Paquet, G. (2007). Public-private partnerships: P3 and the "porcupine problem." In G. B. Doern (Ed.), *How Ottawa spends, 2007–2008: The Harper Conservatives—Climate of change,* (pp. 254–72). Montreal and Kingston: McGill-Queen's University Press.

Jefferson Center. (2007). "British Prime Minister Gordon Brown uses citizen juries." Retrieved March 16, 2008, from http://www.jefferson-center.org/index.asp?Type=B_LIST&SEC={FE67AE78-C3E6-4A12-94E1-A2CF75FB82B9}#{6BED07AE-E48E-4481-9B77-7F79E70815C5}

Jordan, G. (1990). Subgovernments, policy communities and networks: Refilling the old bottles? *Journal of Theoretical Politics, 2,* 319–38.

Katzenstein, P. J. (1978a). *Between power and plenty: Foreign economic policies of advanced industrial states.* Madison: University of Wisconsin Press.

Katzenstein, P. J. (1978b). Introduction: Domestic and international forces and strategies of foreign economic policy. In P. J. Katzenstein (Ed.), *Between power and plenty: Foreign economic policies of advanced industrial states* (pp. 3–22). Madison: University of Wisconsin Press.

Katzenstein, P. J. (1978c). Conclusion: Domestic structures and strategies of foreign economic policy. In P. J. Katzenstein (Ed.), *Between power and plenty: Foreign economic policies of advanced industrial states* (pp. 295–336). Madison: University of Wisconsin Press.

Keck, M. E., and Sikkink, K. (1998). *Activists beyond borders: Advocacy networks in international politics.* Ithaca: Cornell University Press.

Kenis, P., and Schneider, V. (1991). Policy networks and policy analysis: Scrutinizing a new analytical toolbox. In B. Marin and R. Mayntz (Eds.), *Policy networks: Empirical evidence and theoretical considerations* (pp. 25–59). Boulder, CO: Westview Press.

Kernaghan, K. (1993, Spring). Partnership and public administration: Conceptual and practical considerations. *Canadian Public Administration, 36,* 57–76.

Kickert, W. J. M., and Koppenjan, J. F. M. (1997). Public management and network management: An overview. In W. J. M. Kickert, E.-H. Klijn, and J. F. M. Koppenjan (Eds.), *Managing complex networks: Strategies for the public sector* (pp. 35–61). London: Sage.

Klandermans, B., and Tarrow, S. (1988). Mobilization into social movements: Synthesizing European and American approaches. *International Social Movement Research*, 1, 1–38.

Klijn, E.-H., and Skelcher, C. (2007). Democracy and governance networks: Compatible or not? *Public Administration*, 85 (3), 587–608.

Laforest, R., and Phillips, S. (2007). Citizen engagement: Rewiring the policy process. In M. Orsini and M. Smith (Eds.), *Critical policy studies* (pp. 67–90). Vancouver: UBC Press.

Langford, J. (1999). Governance challenges of public-private partnerships. In S. Delacourt and D. G. Lenihan (Eds.), *Collaborative government: Is there a Canadian way?* (pp. 105–11). Toronto: Institute of Public Administration of Canada.

Lindquist, E. A. (1992, Summer). Public managers and policy communities: Learning to meet new challenges. *Canadian Public Administration*, 35, 127–59.

Lindquist, E. A. (1996). New agendas for research on policy communities: Policy analysis, administration, and governance. In L. Dobuzinskis, M. Howlett, and D. Laycock (Eds.), *Policy studies in Canada: The state of the art* (pp. 219–41). Toronto: University of Toronto Press.

McDonald, K. (2006). *Global movements: Action and culture*. Oxford: Blackwell.

Marin, B., and Mayntz, R. (1991). Introduction: Studying policy networks. In B. Marin and R. Mayntz (Eds.), *Policy networks: Empirical evidence and theoretical considerations* (pp. 11–23). Boulder, CO: Westview Press.

Marsh, D., and Smith, M. (2000, March). Understanding policy networks: Towards a dialectical approach. *Political Studies*, 48, 4–21.

Marsh, D., and Smith, M. J. (2001, August). There is more than one way to do political science: On different ways to study policy networks. *Political Studies*, 49, 528–41.

Melucci, A. (1989). *Nomads of the present: Social movements and individual needs in contemporary society*. Philadelphia: Temple University Press.

Messner, D. (2002). World society—structures and trends. In P. Kennedy, D. Messner, and F. Nuscheler (Eds.), *Global trends and global governance* (pp. 22–64). London: Pluto Press.

Meyer, D. S., Jenness, V., and Ingram, H. (Eds.) (2006). *Routing the opposition: Social movements, public policy, and democracy*. Minneapolis, MS.: University of Minnesota Press.

Nagel, S. (1988). *Policy studies: Integration and evaluation*. New York: Praeger.

Nordlinger, E. A. (1981). *On the autonomy of the democratic state.* Cambridge, MA: Harvard University Press.

OECD. (2000, December–February). *Focus: Public Management Newsletter,* no. 15.

OECD. (2001). *Engaging citizens in policy-making: Information, consultation and public participation.* PUMA Policy Brief No. 10. Retrieved March 24, 2008, from http://www.oecd.org/dataoecd/24/34/2384040.pdf

OECD. (2003). *Open Government: Fostering dialogue with civil society.* Paris: OECD.

OECD. (2005b). *Public sector modernisation: Open government.* Policy Brief Feb 16, 2005. Retrieved March 18, 2008, from http://www.oecd.org/dataoecd/1/35/34455306.pdf

Offe, C. (1987). Challenging the boundaries of institutional politics. In C. S. Maier (Ed.), *Changing boundaries of the political: Essays on the evolving balance between the state and society, public and private in Europe* (pp. 63–105). Cambridge, UK: Cambridge University Press.

Pal, L. A. (1992). *Public policy analysis: An introduction,* 2nd ed. Toronto: Nelson.

Pal, L. A. (1993). *Interests of state: The politics of language, multiculturalism and feminism in Canada.* Montreal: McGill-Queen's University Press.

Paltiel, K. Z. (1982). The changing environment and role of special interest groups. *Canadian Public Administration, 25,* 198–210.

Pemberton, H. (2000, December). Policy networks and policy learning: UK economic policy in the 1960s and 1970s. *Public Administration, 78,* 771–92.

Peters, B. G. (1998). *Managing horizontal government: The politics of coordination.* Ottawa: Canadian Centre for Management Development. Research Paper No. 21, 1998.

Phillips, S. D. (1993, Winter). Of public interest groups and sceptics: A realist's reply to Professor Stanbury. *Canadian Public Administration, 36,* 606–16.

Phillips, S. D. (1999). New social movements in Canadian politics: Past their apex? In J. P. Bickerton and A. G. Gagnon (Eds.), *Canadian politics* (3rd ed.) (pp. 371–91). Peterborough, ON: Broadview Press.

Phillips, S. D. (2003). In accordance: Canada's voluntary sector accord from idea to implementation. In K. L. Brock (Ed.), *Delicate dances: Public policy and the nonprofit sector* (pp. 17–62). Montreal and Kingston: McGill-Queen's University Press.

Privy Council Office (Canada). (1993). *Task force report: Service to the public.* Ottawa: Minister of Supply and Services.

Privy Council Office (Canada). (2003). *Guide to making federal acts and regulations.* 2nd ed. Retrieved March 24, 2008, from http://www.pco-bcp.gc.ca/index.asp?lang=eng&page=information& sub=publications&doc=legislation/lmgtoc_e.htm

Privy Council Office (Canada). (2004). *Memorandum to Cabinet.* Retrieved March 24, 2008, from http://www.tbs-sct.gc.ca/asd-dmps/ db/mcdg_s_e.asp

Pross, A. P. (1992). *Group politics and public policy* (2nd ed.). Toronto: Oxford University Press.

Pross, A. P. (1995). Pressure groups: Talking chameleons. In M. S. Whittington and G. Williams (Eds.), *Canadian politics in the 1990s* (pp. 252–75). Toronto: Nelson Canada.

Provan, K. G. and Kenis, P. (2008). Modes of networked governance: Structure, management, and effectiveness. *Journal of Public Administration Research and Theory,* 18, 2, 229–52.

Raab, C. (2001, August). Understanding policy networks: A comment on Marsh and Smith. *Political Studies,* 49, 551–56.

Raab, C. (2002, October). Where do policy networks come from? *Journal of Public Administration Research and Theory,* 12, 581–622.

Reinicke, W. H. (1999/2000). The other world wide web: Global public policy networks. *Foreign Policy,* 117, 44–57.

Rethemeyer, R. K. (2005). Conceptualizing and measuring complex networks. *Public Administration Review,* 65 (1), 117–21.

Rhodes, R. A. W. (2007). Understanding governance: Ten years on. *Organization Studies,* 28 (8), 1243–64.

Ripley, R. B., and Franklin, G. A. (1984). *Congress, the bureaucracy and public policy* (2nd ed.). Homewood, IL: Dorsey.

Rosenau, P. V. (Ed.). (2000). *Public-private policy partnerships.* Cambridge: MIT Press.

Sabatier, P. A. (1993). Policy change over a decade or more. In P. A. Sabatier and H. Jenkins-Smith (Eds.), *Policy change and learning: An advocacy coalition approach* (pp. 13–39). Boulder, CO: Westview.

Sabatier, P. A., and Jenkins-Smith, H. (Eds.). (1993). *Policy change and learning: An advocacy coalition approach.* Boulder, CO: Westview.

Sabatier, P. A., and Jenkins-Smith, H. (1999). The advocacy coalition framework: An assessment. In P. A. Sabatier (Ed.), *Theories of the policy process* (pp. 117–66). Boulder, CO: Westview.

Schmitter, P. C., and Lembruch, G. (Eds.). (1979). *Trends towards corporatist intermediation.* Beverly Hills, CA: Sage.

Schneider, A. L., and Ingram, H. (1997). *Policy design for democracy.* Lawrence: University Press of Kansas.

Scholte, J. A. (2004). Civil society and democratically accountable global governance. *Government and Opposition, 39,* 211–33.

Schuck, P. H. (1977, March/April). Public interest groups and the policy process. *Public Administration Review, 37,* 132–40.

Skocpol, T. (1986). Rediscovering the state: Strategies of analysis in current research. In P. B. Evans, D. Reuschemeyer, and T. Skocpol (Eds.), *Bringing the state back in* (pp. 3–37). Cambridge, UK: Cambridge University Press.

Slaughter, A.-M. (2004). *A new world order.* Princeton: Princeton University Press.

Standing Committee on Environment and Sustainable Development. (2007). Fifth report. Retrieved on March 2, 2008, from http://cmte .parl.gc.ca/Content/HOC/committee/391/envi/reports/rp2614246/ envirp05/03-honour-e.htm

Statistics Canada (2005). Cornerstones of community: Highlights of the national survey of nonprofit and voluntary organizations – 2003 revised. Catalogue no. 61-533-XPE. Retrieved March 18, 2008, from http://www.statcan.ca/english/freepub/61-533-SIE/61-533-SIE2005001.pdf

Stone, D. (2004). Transfer agents and global networks in the 'transnationalization' of policy. *Journal of European Public Policy* 11 (3), 545–66.

Stone, D. (2008). Global public policy, transnational policy communities, and their networks. *Policy Studies Journal, 36* (1), 19–38.

Thatcher, M. (1998, October). The development of policy network analyses: From modest origins to overarching frameworks. *Journal of Theoretical Politics, 10,* 389–416.

Thomas, P. (2006). Are networks the wave of the future? *Networkedgovernment.ca.* Retrieved on March 24, 2008, from http://www .networkedgovernment.ca/DoubtingThomas

Thomas, T. (1995). When "they" is "we": Movements, municipal parties, and participatory politics. In J. Lightbody (Ed.), *Canadian metropolitics: Governing our cities* (pp. 115–36). Toronto: Copp Clark.

Transport Canada. (2008). 21st century governance. Retrieved on March 24, 2008, from http://www.tc.gc.ca/majorissues/APGCI/ governance.htm

Truman, D. (1951). *The governmental process: Political interests and public opinion.* New York: Alfred A. Knopf.

Van Waarden, F. (1992). Dimensions and types of policy networks. *European Journal of Political Research, 21,* 29–52.

Walker, J. (1991). *Mobilizing interest groups in America: Patrons, professions and social movements.* Ann Arbor: University of Michigan Press.

Walker, R. B. J. (1988). *One world, many worlds: Struggles for a just world peace.* Boulder, CO: Lynne Rienner Publishers.

Weaver, R. K., and Rockman, B. A. (1993). Assessing the effects of institutions. In R. K. Weaver and B. A. Rockman (Eds.), *Do institutions matter? Government capabilities in the United States and abroad* (pp. 1–41). Washington, DC: The Brookings Institution.

Williams, J., and Goose, S. (1998). The international campaign to ban landmines. In M. A. Cameron, R. J. Lawson, and B. W. Tomlin (Eds.), *To walk without fear: The global movement to ban landmines* (pp. 20–47). Toronto: Oxford University Press.

Wright, M. (1988). Policy community, policy network, and comparative industrial policies. *Political Studies, 36,* 593–614.

Zald, M. N. (1987). *Social movements in an organizational society: Collected essays.* New Brunswick, NJ: Transaction.

7 Evaluation

Consult any text on policy analysis and you will find passages extolling the indispensability of policy and program evaluation. It could hardly be otherwise, given that program evaluation is primarily about trying to figure out how successful a policy has been, whether it met its objectives, how far it fell short, and what might be done to improve its impact. The same passages that extol evaluation, however, are usually complemented by ones that say that it is expensive, difficult, rarely conclusive, and politically unpopular. Precisely because evaluation is so potentially crucial to the fortunes of a policy or program, opponents and supporters work hard to get the evaluation results they need to strengthen their case. That is, if evaluation takes place at all. Not only is it politically sensitive (who wants to hear bad news?), it can seem secondary to the really important job of designing and implementing solutions to public problems. Policy evaluation therefore has enjoyed more theoretical than practical popularity, and in Canada at least, has not been enthusiastically supported either as a government or a third-party (i.e., foundation or think tank) activity. This is changing. The new emphasis on results, accountability, and performance, coupled with a shift to public-private partnerships and networks of collaboration, increases the need for evaluation because it places new pressures on governments to demonstrate value for money. Not only does evaluation have a higher profile, but also different forms of evaluation (such as client satisfaction and overall program performance) are becoming increasingly important. Thus, what is happening in this field directly reflects developments described in Chapters 3 to 6.

Policy analysis, defined as the disciplined application of intellect to public problems, encompasses everything from reading a newspaper to careful scientific research. In practice, much of what passes for professional policy analysis is called policy evaluation. It is conducted by governments as well as private firms, assumes a mastery of certain quantitative and qualitative techniques, and is aimed at the improvement or betterment of public policies and programs. Its central questions are: Does this program do what it is supposed to be doing? If not, why not? What should be done? Policy analysis is openly prescriptive, and serves to monitor government activities. Policies attempt to solve or manage public problems; at some point governments (and citizens) need to know whether interventions are making a difference and are worthwhile. Since most government services are on a not-for-profit basis, there are no clear market signals (i.e., profit, loss, increase or decrease in demand) to measure performance.

The improvement of programs is the core function or purpose of evaluation as it is conducted in governments, but there are other purposes as well. Rossi, Lipsey, and Freeman (2004) highlight four (pp. 34–38). The first is the one we have already mentioned and will develop further below—program improvement. Typically this means working with program managers as the program is being implemented, or what is called **formative evaluation.** Another purpose is for **accountability**—in this instance, the objective is oversight once the program is close to completion, or what is called **summative evaluation.** Evaluations can also be done to generate more general knowledge that may or may not be directly relevant to the program but that might cast light on a social issue or casual questions. Finally, evaluations can be done as a political ruse or for public relations—either to produce data to support a program or justify a decision that has already been made. In this chapter, we will concentrate on evaluation with the first objective.

Policy evaluation seems deceptively simple, but determining whether a program has its intended effect, in a world in which every effect has multiple causes, and every cause a vast stream of effects, is always difficult, and sometimes impossible. This is the core of what is termed the **attribution problem**—what was the contribution of a given policy intervention to resolving a given issue? Information is sometimes faulty or nonexistent, people uncooperative, policies' objectives vague, or measuring instruments weak. As well, evaluation is by its nature unpopular. Who wants to be told their program is a failure? Evaluation often delivers unpleasant truths, creating great temptations to shoot, or at least ignore, the messenger. However, despite these built-in limitations and liabilities, as well as a history of, at best, tepid support from most policy managers, evaluation experienced a renewed popularity in the mid-1990s. The 1995 OECD update on public management developments in twenty-five countries, for example, noted: "A wide range of performance-oriented initiatives has been reported in 1994 as the shift of management focus from processes to results gains momentum. Those mentioned here cover two main aspects: a drive for better reporting of performance; and increased emphasis on setting targets for service quality levels and measuring results against them" (p. 10). A decade later the emphasis was just as strong if not stronger. *Modernising Government* observed that the clearest trend in performance across OECD members was "the introduction of performance-oriented budgeting and performance management" (OECD, 2005, 58). Curristine's survey of OECD countries noted:

> In the majority of OECD countries, efforts to assess the performance of programmes and ministries are now an accepted normal part of government. Countries follow a variety of different methods to assess performance, including performance measures, evaluations, and benchmarking. Twenty-six out of the 28 responding countries stated that they use both performance measures and evaluations to assess performance. There is also a growing interest in benchmarking, with 12 countries adopting this approach. In the past 15 years, there has been a renewed emphasis on performance measures (principally of outputs and outcomes) in budgeting and management; however it is clear that despite this trend, governments continue to make equal use of evaluations. While both methods provide information on performance, they provide different types of information. Performance measures deal with outcomes, outputs and/or process indicators. Evaluations often include a more detailed review of attributes and causality issues. Evaluation typically includes recommendations on changes to activities or programmes to improve performance. (Curristine, 2005, 89)

There are several reasons for this resurgence. First, evaluation is typically championed by the management consulting industry, since that is where a great deal of its claims to expertise lie (Saint-Martin, 2000). As governments in recent years have tried to borrow more management practices from the private sector, they have also tended to import a greater profile for evaluation. Second, fiscal pressures from the 1990s have created a mindset—through program reviews and reallocation exercises—that at least in principle no program is sacred and everything should be evaluated for best results and monies redirected as necessary. A third related reason is that many of the new techniques of governance discussed in Chapters 3 to 6 on design, implementation, and policy communities demand better accountability mechanisms. That, therefore, means evaluation or assessment. When public agencies used to be largely responsible for the delivery of public programs, public managers assumed that accountability for performance was built into the organization of delivery. Once delivery and design are severed, or once policies and programs are coproduced with the private and nonprofit sectors, government is primarily either writing cheques or setting frameworks. If government is not to do this blindly, it needs to clarify what it wants out of a relationship, and how the results will be monitored and measured. A fourth reason is entangled with the sense that citizens have declining levels of trust in public authorities and public policies. Rigorous evaluation of the performance of public agencies, and the communication of that evaluation to the wider public, is one means for re-establishing support for public institutions. "Today, global and domestic forces demand more effective management and higher levels of organizational performance. Leaders and managers in public and non-profit organizations face demanding constituencies, higher public expectations, and aggressive media scrutiny" (Wholey, 2003, p. 44).

This chapter has two primary objectives. The first is to introduce some of the main techniques used in evaluation research, as well as some of the benchmarks and rules of thumb for successful evaluations. This section is merely an overview of the logic of the techniques, and does not pretend to be comprehensive. The second objective is to review the history of federal government evaluation efforts in the last twenty years, and provide a sense of context about the state of evaluation in this country and the potential for its new and enhanced status. To date, Canadian practice has restricted evaluation to more of a management tool than a real challenge to government programs. The chapter closes with a discussion of the place of evaluation both in policy analysis and in democratic governance.

Types of Evaluation

Michael Patton (1997) argues that "**program evaluation** is the systematic collection of information about the activities, characteristics, and outcomes of programs to make judgments about the program, improve program effectiveness, and/or inform decisions about future programming" (p. 23). Weiss defines evaluation as "the *systematic assessment* of the *operations* and/or the *outcomes* of a program or policy, compared to a set of *explicit* or *implicit standards,* as a means of contributing to the *improvement* of the program or policy" (1998, p. 4; emphasis in original). Rossi, Lipsey, and Freeman (2004) define program evaluation as "the use of social research procedures to systematically investigate the effectiveness of social intervention programs in ways that are adapted to their political and organizational environments and are designed to inform social action to improve social conditions" (p. 16).

Several features of these definitions should be noted. First, they refer to "practice" and "application" of techniques. Second, they identify "improvement" of public policy decisionmaking processes as the ultimate goal of evaluation. Third, they highlight the "systematic" character of evaluation research. Evaluation presents itself, in short, as a scientific, systematic, empirically oriented, applied discipline or set of disciplines that analyzes current programs in order to generate intelligent information that can be used to improve those programs or the decision processes that produced them. The creative and intuitive aspect of evaluation should not be understated: Patton (1987) lists 100 different types of evaluation and argues persuasively that each one demands creativity (pp. 98–205). As we mentioned in Chapter 1, one of the most deceptively simple things about a policy is stating its goals. Before a program can be evaluated, its underlying problem definition and its goals must be understood, and so evaluators spend a good deal of time in what is usually termed the pre-evaluation phase, talking to program administrators and piecing together what people think they are doing. This is closer to cultural anthropology than regression analysis. Nonetheless, it is fair to say that of all the subfields within policy analysis, evaluation has remained closest to the traditional empiricist model. Evaluators are the accountants of the policy profession and, like balance sheets, their reports on effectiveness and impact can sometimes be received with glum resignation. Indeed, because the traditional empirical techniques used in most conventional evaluations are fairly standardized (even though they vary in their application case by case), and because evaluation results are supposed to be neutral and unbiased, there has been a greater momentum behind the professionalization of evaluation than other fields of policy analysis. The American Evaluation Association (formed in 1986), for example, adopted guiding principles in 1994 and slightly updated them in 2004:

1. Systematic Inquiry: Evaluators conduct systematic, data-based inquiries.

2. Competence: Evaluators provide competent performance to stakeholders.

3. Integrity/Honesty: Evaluators display honesty and integrity in their own behavior, and attempt to ensure the honesty and integrity of the entire evaluation process.

4. Respect for People: Evaluators respect the security, dignity and self-worth of respondents, program participants, clients, and other evaluation stakeholders.

5. Responsibilities for General and Public Welfare: Evaluators articulate and take into account the diversity of general and public interests and values that may be related to the evaluation. (American Evaluation Society, 2008)

The Canadian Evaluation Society has similar guidelines that emphasize competence, integrity, and accountability (Canadian Evaluation Society, 2008). Evaluators must be aware that while they are engaged in providing information to improve programs, ultimately those programs are delivered by people and for people, and moreover their assessments inevitably will be coloured to some degree by choices and values.

While these definitions appear to give evaluation a wide scope of application in policymaking, indeed to the point that it seems synonymous with policy analysis itself, it is worth keeping some fundamental distinctions in mind between policy analysis and evaluation (Geva-May and Pal, 1999). A careful reading shows that evaluation is almost always linked to existing programs, either through the analysis of those programs themselves or of information relevant to them. Because of their expertise, evaluators are also often involved in generating and analyzing data that are relevant to problem definition, trend forecasting, and program design aspects such as target populations. Rossi, Lipsey, and Freeman (2004) term these **"diagnostic procedures"** that entail, for example, the use of census data, existing **social indicators** such as literacy or crime rates, and surveys to determine the nature and scope of a problem (pp. 110–11). **Needs assessment** can be even more specific, for example, the health needs of a small rural community, and would depend on specially designed surveys and reviews of existing data. This is certainly a respectable and important component of evaluation (but, as we shall see below, a fairly small part of what evaluators and policy analysts actually do) but is not its core. The core of program evaluation "includes the measurement of program performance—resource expenditures, program activities, and program outcomes—and the testing of causal assumptions linking these three elements" (Wholey, 1994, p. 15). Figure 7.1 illustrates these three categories with some illustrative questions.

Figure 7.1   Core Categories of Program Evaluation

Process Evaluation (Program Activities)

What are the components of the program?

How is the program delivered?

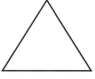

Impact Evaluation (Outcomes)

Did the program have the intended effects?

If not, why not?

Efficiency Evaluation (Costs/Benefits)

What was the ratio of benefits to costs in this program?

Given what we spent, did we get the most out of it?

Before program evaluation can be conducted, therefore, we normally have programs in place—evaluation typically is *ex post* analysis, or after the launch of a program. As obvious as this seems, it reminds us that the very first step in any policy evaluation is trying to understand the policy and its programs, primarily in terms described in Chapter 1—what is the problem, what are the goals, and how are programs designed to address that problem? As Weiss points out, there are many cases where programs are quite unambiguous—changing highway speeds, increasing benefits in some income support program, or introducing a new medical testing program such as mammograms for a target population. However, many other programs, and often the most interesting or controversial ones, combine resources, people, and practices in complex ways. "In most social programs, it takes effort to understand the content of the program, what actually goes on. Operations often differ markedly from day to day and from staff member to staff member" (1998, p. 49). Regional development programs, sweeping changes in curriculum, or new gun control regulations are not easy to describe, nor is it self-evident what the program "really is." This is because the program on the ground may be different—in the way that its administrators understand it and implement it—from what the program is on paper. An evaluator who measured the "paper program" might be evaluating something that in fact does not exist. By the same token, not knowing the "real" program means that the evaluator may not be asking the right questions or gathering the right data.

Before conducting an evaluation, therefore, evaluators should learn about the program as it really is as well as what it was designed to be. They can review previous evaluations, published literature, and program materials, and conduct both formal and information interviews with a variety of program and policy personnel as well as clients to put the puzzle together. They can then develop two related models to help them map out what the program is and how it tries to accomplish its objectives. The first guide is **program theory**, or hypotheses and explanations about the "causal links that tie program inputs to expected program outputs" (Weiss, 1998, p. 55). We discuss this in detail below in connection with **impact evaluation**, but it is a theory about how the program will exercise its ultimate effect or outcome. For example, a training program for unemployed youth has a target of increasing the numbers of youth who get jobs. The program theory might be that the reason the youth are unemployed is because of lack of skills, and so by providing training, the program provides the skills and makes the youth more attractive to employers. However, it might be that the program offers young people the opportunity to widen their circle of contacts, and thereby learn about more job opportunities. In both instances, the program and the outcomes are the same, but the "mechanisms" (what Weiss terms not the activities themselves but the responses to these activities) are different.

Figure 7.2 Program Theory and Implementation Theory (Example)

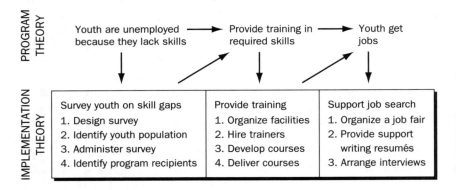

The second guide or map that is crucial for evaluators (especially when they conduct **process evaluations**) is the **implementation theory** that lies behind the program. These are the specific activities and resources that are mobilized in connection with each of the links in the program's **causal chain** or **logic model**. To use the youth training program once again as an example, the implementation theory would detail steps such as publicizing the program among targeted youth groups and arranging the counselling and the content of the training, the rooms, and other forms of support. For program administrators, the assumption—since their job is to implement the program as it was designed in the belief that it is supposed to work— is that if all the steps in the implementation theory are fulfilled, the program will achieve its results. The relationship between program theory and implementation theory is illustrated in Figure 7.2.

Logic models are another way of mapping programs, and bring together program theory and implementation theory. "A logic model is a plausible and sensible model of how the program will work under certain environmental conditions to solve identified problems" (McLaughlin and Jordan, 2004, 7). While usually depicted as a chart or diagram, the essence of a logic model is a narrative of what the program is targeting, how it works, and what it is trying to achieve. Figure 7.3 illustrates the key elements of a logic model, though these can be extended considerably. As an example, we could take the needle exchange program that has been in place in Ottawa since 1991 (City of Ottawa, 2008). The policy targets people at risk or infected with either or both HIV and hepatitis. These include those who use and inject drugs, have sexual partners who use drugs, or who are sex industry workers. The policy is that

> Needle exchange services operate on the principle of providing
> clients with an adequate amount of sterile needles to meet their

Figure 7.3 Key Elements of a Logic Model

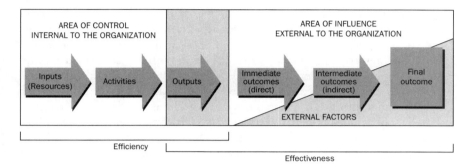

SOURCE: Treasury Board of Canada, 2002.

requirements for safe injecting while maximizing the return of used needles to the program. No client will be refused sterile needles on the basis that they do not have any used needles to exchange.

Based on Figure 7.3, what would a logic model of this program look like?

Resources: Financial, materiel, human resources that are marshalled for a program. Staff, exchange sites, needles, disposal facilities, biohazard containers, finances. It could include partners such as pharmacies that will accept used needles.

Activities: All of the actions necessary to produce the output and eventually the outcomes. Even in a small program like this one, the range is enormous, from training staff, to inspections, to site establishment, to logs of returned needles, to reporting.

Outputs: Products, goods and services actually provided through the program. Needles made available for exchange, sites available for those exchanges.

Immediate Outcomes: The short-term changes or benefits that are "caused" by the program. The number of needles exchanged and the number of people served.

Intermediate Outcomes: Usually defined as behavioural changes that occur as a result of immediate outcomes. People exchanging needles instead of re-using them.

Final Outcome: The ultimate objective of the program. Reduction of harm to needle users and reduction of the incidence of the spread of HIV and hepatitis.

There are several points to note about logic models. Figure 7.3 makes it clear that the "area of control" for an organization in this chain of cause and effect is between inputs and outputs. As one moves to outcomes, and especially to final outcomes, external factors have a greater role to play, and bring back the attribution issue mentioned earlier. It also illustrates the two dimensions of efficiency and effectiveness that will be discussed in greater detail below. Efficiency is about the allocation of resources within organizations to meet stated goals. Effectiveness is about whether that allocation meets those goals and has the desired outcomes. Finally, the model is deceptively simple. Ottawa's policy statement on needle exchange is somewhat vague on whether it is aimed purely at harm reduction for needle users or for a wider social benefit of reducing the incidence of disease. Developing an accurate logic model of a program requires careful analysis and consultation to determine what is actually intended, what is actually going on, and what is actually achieved.

IMPACT EVALUATION

A central evaluative question is whether a policy or program has an impact. Evaluating outcomes is critical to determining whether a program is successful or not in terms of its intended effects. Impact evaluation takes the program as the independent or causal variable and tries to isolate its effect from other influences in the environment. This assumes that goals are clear, but sometimes they are not. As we noted above, in addition to trying to understand the goals, the evaluator should also develop a map of the causal theory that underpins the program, along with mechanisms of change. Logic models help do this, since they explicitly connect resources and activities to outputs and outcomes. The arrows or connections between the elements of a logic model are the causal mechanisms. This not only helps in determining what data to gather and which indicators to highlight but also provides alternative path explanations that might be examined if the evaluation turns up ambiguous results. In the training example, if the employment rate for youth who complete the program is lower than expected, this might be because the skill enhancement occurred only for those youth who had certain background characteristics (e.g., finished secondary school, had had at least one other training program, etc.). If the needle exchange program had low take-up, it might be because of where the sites were located.

Having determined a program theory, impact evaluation goes on to look at actual causal chains by examining the program's effects. Impact evaluation tries to isolate causes and effects, but this is no easy task since any single cause or effect is (or may be seen to be) intimately bound to numerous other causes and effects. A single effect may conceivably have several causes, and the policy intervention is only one of them. Figure 7.4

Figure 7.4 Causal Model of Program Impact

A. Simple Model of Program Impact

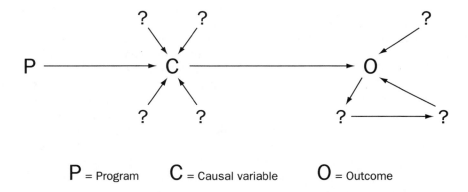

B. Complex Model of Program Impact

P = Program   C = Causal variable   O = Outcome

provides a schematic diagram of the assumption and the problem. It helps to begin with a simple model of policy impact: here, some policy *P* is intended to affect some casual variable *C*, which will then have a desired effect on some outcome O. Note that a policy or program never has a direct influence on behaviour; it is always targeted on some factor that is assumed to influence behaviour, and by influencing that factor yields desired outcomes. Speed limits, for example, assume that accidents are in part caused by driving too quickly. Accident rates are the O or outcome, while speeding is *C*. A program to either set lower limits or enforce them more rigorously could be two examples of interventions. But now consider the more complex model in Figure 7.4. It adds variables to the *C* and the O categories. Speeding itself can be regarded as a **dependent variable,** something caused by other factors. Speeding is affected by such things as weather conditions, road congestion, safety quality of cars, and so on. If an anti-speeding campaign were found to be associated with lower accident rates, would that mean that the program was successful? Not at all, since it may be that there were fewer speeders about, or that other conditions were responsible for the diminution of accident rates.

Various strategies have been developed to deal with this problem. They all rely on statistical techniques to a greater or lesser degree, and all strive to control or neutralize the extraneous causal variables that might have produced the effect. In cases where these preferred strategies are unavailable, too expensive, or time consuming, a technique called "**meta-analysis**" is sometimes used (Boruch and Petrosino, 2004). Instead of gathering new data, evaluators review the existing literature on a specific program, treating each evaluation study as a single case. This "pooling" of evaluations requires a fairly large set, however, sometimes in the hundreds, in order to be valid. One advantage of meta-analysis, on the other hand, is that this pooling increases the number of "observations" of the effects of a particular intervention in a variety of settings and thereby can increase the confidence level of any assertions about its effects. Weiss points out, for example, that meta-analysis has in some instances shown that many kinds of social programs that were once thought to have little effect in fact have statistically significant cumulative outcomes (1998, p. 242).

The ideal method to try to empirically isolate cause and effect is the classic **experimental design**. In this design, people are randomly assigned to one of two groups; measures are taken of target variables before the program is introduced and again afterward. The program is applied to only one group, the **experimental group**. The second group is the **control group**. If there is a sufficiently large difference in post-program scores, then the program or intervention is deemed to have caused it. The **random assignment** of individuals to the two groups controls for alternative explanations or causes, since the odds of being in either group are the same. In aggregate, the groups are identical in every respect except for the policy intervention (Weiss, 1998, p. 215). Experimental designs are frequently used in the educational policy field, where, for example, a new reading program might be tested on two groups of students. Pre-program reading scores for the experimental group and the control group would be gathered, the program administered, and post-program scores compared to see if they are statistically different.

Despite their statistical superiority as a measure of impact, experimental designs are rarely used in policy evaluation in Canada, though more widely in the United States, especially in the education policy field (St. Pierre, 2004). They are costly and usually time consuming; decision-makers frequently want quick answers. There are also political and ethical problems with separating people into experimental and control groups. Many public programs deliver benefits to the populace, and from a political perspective it might be imprudent to deliberately withhold a benefit from some group simply to meet testing requirements. As Rossi, Lipsey, and Freeman (2004) point out, randomized experiments run into major ethical dilemmas, as in the controversy over withholding potentially beneficial AIDS drugs. In the medical field, for example, there are periodic debates about the efficacy of new, expensive drugs until they have been thoroughly tested. They appear to assist some patients, but do they have an appreciable impact on national health? Finally, some important policy variables cannot be disaggregated to observe differential effects on separate groups. Interest rates, the value of the dollar, and budget deficits are examples of policy variables that apply nationally or not at all. Classic experimental designs are useless in trying to determine their impact.

Nonetheless, while rare in comparison with other techniques, program evaluation based on experimental design does take place. In Canada the leading exponent is the nonprofit Social Research and Development Corporation (SRDC)—modelled after the Manpower Demonstration Research Corporation started over twenty-five years ago in the United States. SRDC brings together researchers around the analysis and evaluation of social programs in multiple locales and over extended time periods to see what actually works and what does not. As the SRDC puts it,

> What makes SRDC unique in Canada is its experience in designing, implementing, and evaluating large-scale demonstration projects using random assignment evaluation designs. This pioneering work involves combining rigorous quantitative analysis with innovative qualitative research techniques in order to be able to tell what works, for whom it works, and why it works. . . . SRDC's core research activities are focused on rigorous impact and benefit-cost evaluations of new program models. However, we also conduct implementation research and formative evaluations designed to study the process by which new programs are introduced, and to identify obstacles to implementation and bottlenecks in service delivery. (SRDC, 2008)

The SRDC's six main projects are the Self-Sufficiency Project (SSP), the Earnings Supplement Project (ESP), the Community Employment Innovation Program (CEIP), learn$ave, the Child Care Pilot Project (CCPP), and Access to Post-Secondary Education Pilot Projects. All six are test programs supported and funded by Human Resources and Social Development Canada. SSP was started in 1992 by New Brunswick and British Columbia and is an earnings supplement to poor, single parents on welfare that tries to increase household income and encourage work. Almost 9000 people voluntarily participated in the project. The ESP provided a supplement to recipients of Employment Insurance (EI) to help them choose work, even at lower than their previous wages, rather than long-term attachment to EI. It had over 11 000 participants. CEIP is targeted at individuals who are eligible for EI or on social assistance and gives them the opportunity to volunteer for community service employment.

Those who take up the offer will stop receiving EI or social assistance benefits and receive a weekly $300 stipend instead. learn$ave is a program that revolves around a matched savings program entitled Individual Development Accounts. Low-income Canadians receive $3 for each dollar they deposit in the account, for a total of up to $6000 over three years. The accounts can be used only for training, education, and small-business start-ups. Once the experiment is concluded, SRDC will conduct an evaluation of whether the scheme actually induced participants to save and invest more in education. CCPP is studying the impacts of a pre-school program for children in six minority Francophone communities across Canada, using quasi-experimental techniques rather than pure randomized groups. The Access to Post-Secondary project is an evaluation of several programs geared to increase participation in post-secondary institutions by students in high schools in New Brunswick and British Columbia. In this case, a pure social experiment model was used by randomized assignment of schools.

In all six cases, the fundamental question is whether people, if given the proper incentives, would prefer work over income support, whether once they get jobs they keep them or find other employment, and whether they are prepared to invest in themselves. Income assistance like welfare or EI is considered by many to be "passive" in that it does not encourage people back into the labour force, and worse, induces dependency after long periods of time. But EI and social assistance are both designed in ways that impose penalties on people when they find jobs—their benefits are cut or reduced significantly—and it is difficult to know what the effect of earnings supplement programs might be. In both the SSP and ESP, the SRDC conducted long-term evaluations based on experimental design—they divided the participants into control and program groups and tried to compare the impact of the two programs over time. Box 7.1 provides some details on the methodology behind evaluating the CEIP.

Experimental designs of the type engineered by the SRDC are time consuming and expensive, as well as technically challenging. In the face of these difficulties, rigorous experimental design often gives way to other, **quasi-experimental** forms of impact evaluation. One technique is to use time-series data to establish **pre-program and post-program** comparisons. Another, weaker form of impact evaluation is the **single observation** or pre-experimental design. In this method, a program or policy is implemented and then measurements are taken of outcomes. Assume, for example, that a government job creation program allocates $300 million for employment in depressed regions. Within a year it is found that 80 percent of program participants are regularly employed. This actually says little about the real program impact, however, because the participants might have been self-selecting (i.e., only motivated individuals participated) or because the economy might have improved generally.

BOX 7.1

SOCIAL RESEARCH AND DEMONSTRATION PROJECT

EVALUATING THE COMMUNITY EMPLOYMENT INNOVATION PROJECT (CEIP) [EXCERPTS]

CEIP is not a traditional job creation project. Although the program does address a short-term need for employment, it is first and foremost a research study that is testing an active re-employment strategy as an alternative to the passive receipt of Employment Insurance (EI) or Income Assistance (IA). Designers of CEIP also sought to build upon lessons learned from earlier approaches in developing the program model.

One of the most important features of CEIP, and one that sets it apart from earlier community employment initiatives, is its evaluation design. Under SRDC, CEIP has been set up as a demonstration project using a multiple methods approach to evaluate its effects on both individuals and communities. The evaluation strategy for CEIP includes four main components: implementation research, individual impact studies, a community effects study, and a cost–benefit analysis. *Implementation research* to carefully document how the project was implemented, to assess how closely the program in the field matched the original design, to evaluate potential participants' understanding of the CEIP offer, and to identify delivery issues that can aid in better understanding how and why the program worked (or failed to work). *Individual impact studies* use a random assignment design—widely accepted as the most reliable way to estimate a program's impacts—to compare the experiences of those in CEIP's program group with the experiences of a control group who were not eligible to work on community-based projects. Three impact studies are produced at different phases of the project: (1) an early impact report at 18 months after enrolment of participants; (2) an interim report at 40 months covering the full period of program eligibility, and (3) a final report at 54 months post-enrolment focusing on post-program actions. *A community effects study* using both a "theory of change" approach and a quasi-experimental comparison community design to evaluate the effects on the communities that participated in CEIP. *A benefit–cost analysis* to compare the economic benefits that accrue to both the participating individuals and the communities with the cost of producing those benefits.

BOX 7.1 (continued)

The first component, implementation research, has been completed and published. The latter two, a community effects study is the subject of a separate report, and a benefit–cost analysis is forthcoming. The goal of this second individual impact analysis is to measure the changes in outcomes that CEIP produces for the individuals who take part. The methodology being used to conduct the analysis is a random assignment evaluation design. Simply looking at the outcomes of those who take part in a program in isolation would overstate the program's achievements because all positive developments would be attributed to the program—this would not identify the extent to which the observed outcomes simply reflect what people would have done on their own. The challenge in an impact evaluation is to determine the difference that the program makes—the changes in outcomes that result from the program. The process of random assignment ensures that there are no systematic pre-existing differences between the program and control groups. They differ only in that one group is eligible for the program and the other is not. Therefore, any differences that are observed over time in the experiences of the two groups can be attributed with confidence to the program.

During the enrolment phase, 5980 eligible EI beneficiaries and 804 eligible IA recipients were randomly selected and mailed letters of invitation to an information session where they learned about CEIP and were given the opportunity to volunteer. The vast majority of those who showed up also enrolled in CEIP: of the 1620 EI beneficiaries that attended, 62 percent signed the enrolment form. In the IA sample, 93 percent of attendees enrolled in the program (516 out of 557 people). Half of the enrollees from both the EI and IA samples were then randomly assigned to the program group, who were eligible for CEIP, and the other half to the control group, who were not.

There are four data sources being used for the impact study in this report. Each source is described in more detail below. First, a *Baseline Survey* was administered to all CEIP volunteers at the point of enrolment in the study. The survey collected information on a range of demographic characteristics, household composition, income, and employment history. Beyond being useful to describe the population involved in the study, the baseline survey provides data to support the impact analysis. Second, the primary data sources used for this impact study are the *18- and 40-month*

Follow-up Surveys. Statistics Canada administered these as telephone surveys to program and control group members approximately 18 and 40 months after their enrolment in the study. Modules covered all of the key outcomes of interest, which could not be analyzed through administrative data sources, including employment history, personal and household income, social capital, employability skills, household composition, attitudes, and health and well-being. Third, EI and IA *Administrative Records* are used to determine the amounts and duration of transfer receipt by sample members. And fourth, a *Project Management Information System* was implemented in the CEIP program office to support operations and service delivery while also collecting critical research data including participation rates in CEIP, types of community jobs, duration of work, and amounts of community wages received. This information is used in conjunction with survey and administrative data to derive the employment and earnings outcomes.

SOURCES: Gyarmati et al. (2007a, pp. 2, 6, 9–11) and Gyarmati et al. (2007b, p. 7)

A variation of the single observation technique is the pre-program/post-program scheme, which does try to compare scores before and after an intervention, but only for a single group. Without a control group, it is impossible to tell whether any differences in the scores are due to the program intervention or some other cause. A final, widely used, but not very powerful, design for determining impact is **contrasted groups.** In this design, program recipients are compared to nonrecipients, and the differences are ascribed to the program.

PROCESS/IMPLEMENTATION EVALUATION

Process or implementation evaluation monitors an existing program to assess the effort put into it (Posvac and Carey, 1980, p. 12). This is not the same as measuring success. As Patton (2002) puts it, process evaluation involves looking at "how something happens rather than or in addition to examining outputs and outcomes" (p. 159). Typically, reporting systems are developed to provide agencies with information about target populations, extent of coverage, and delivery mechanisms. Process evaluation can review program guidelines, the organization of field offices, staff training, communications systems, and even staff morale to improve organizational performance. It takes the program for granted and aims at improving the process whereby goals are met. This may sound routine, but is both conceptually important and, in practical terms, accounts for a great deal of what actually passes for program evaluation:

> Process evaluations aim at elucidating and understanding the internal dynamics of how a program, organization, or relationship operates. Process studies focus on the following kinds of questions: What are the things people experience that makes this program what it is? How are clients brought into the program, and how do they move through the program once they are participants? How is what people do related to what they're trying to (or actually do) accomplish? What are the strengths and weaknesses of the program from the perspective of participants and staff? What is the nature of staff-client interactions? . . . Process data permit judgments about the extent to which the program or organization is operating the way it is supposed to be operating, revealing areas in which relationships can be improved as well as highlighting strengths of the program that should be preserved. (Patton, 2002, pp. 159–60)

Process evaluation is clearly linked to implementation and can be thought of as the evaluation of implementation procedures. This helps clarify the importance of process evaluation to program evaluation as a whole, as well as its link to impact analysis. In Chapter 5 we pointed out that the quality of implementation is quite distinct from the quality of a program—bad programs can be well implemented, and vice versa. Process evaluation is a natural complement to impact evaluation, since we need to know whether observed outcomes are the result of the program intervention as it was planned or are due to quirks in the delivery. In other words, program theory and design (the causal links and interventions sketched in Figure 7.4) may be fine, but the execution is flawed. If we can assure ourselves that execution is as planned, then any failures will be due to program design. This, of course, makes it sound as though implementation and impact can be neatly severed, and they cannot. But they do represent different orientations in evaluative work.

Scheirer (1994, p. 45) points out that the full description of "**program components**" is the foundation of process analysis, though the concept of "**program logic**" is sometimes used to sketch out the causal links for impact evaluation (Framst, 1995). Scheirer defines program components as "strategies, activities, behaviors, media products, and technologies needed to deliver the program, along with a specification of the intended recipients and delivery situations" (p. 45). This is tougher than it sounds and requires extended interviews with both program administrators and clients to see what the components are and how well they are being implemented. The next trick is to determine what good or effective implementation entails. It is not directly linked to desired outcomes, which is the realm of impact evaluation. Rather, it tries to determine what the desired outcome is, and then asks what steps or mechanisms the program itself envisions in delivering the intervention to achieve that outcome. A training program for middle-aged unemployed workers, for example, assumes that better training will lead to jobs. This is questionable in many cases, but the process evaluator takes it as given. She then asks what program components go into the delivery of that training: classrooms, syllabus, materials, staff, and equipment. It should be possible to develop criteria that let us measure whether a training program is being delivered well or badly (e.g., rundown facilities, disorganization, unqualified instructors, broken equipment). If delivery quality varies, then assuming that the program is properly designed, the path to improvement is to work on better implementation. If the quality of implementation is generally high across a range of sites, but outcomes are still poor, then the problem would seem to be in program design.

As we will see in the next section of this chapter, the general field of process and implementation evaluation has grown dramatically in the last twenty years. Evaluation as a whole has become more important as governments are under pressure to be more results oriented and accountable. Impact evaluation, the analysis of results, is not easy or cheap, and there is a natural inclination to assume the design is fine, and that disappointing outcomes must be due to inadequate effort. At the same time, governments are looking more to consumer or client satisfaction as a key program outcome, and this often has more to do with delivery parameters than with the causal modelling underlying program design. Delivery parameters are more commonly referred to as "benchmarks," and typically focus on performance rather than process, though the two are related. Performance measures or benchmarks for concrete services are usually based on measures of workload, efficiency, effectiveness, or productivity. Finally, as more and more programs are delivered by nongovernmental organizations, and as more of their financial and organizational support comes from groups of partners (firms, government, foundations), these partners want to monitor how well things are proceeding. Monitoring tends to be more casual and less systematic than process evaluation, but they are "similar kinds of inquiry" (Weiss, 1998, p. 181). These, and other forces, have conspired in recent years to raise the profile of process and implementation analysis quite significantly.

A type of process evaluation known as performance reporting or managing for results, has become quite important in Canada, the United States, and many other OECD countries. In fact, in the United States, as a result of the 1993 Government Performance and Results Act, all federal government agencies must submit to the Director of the Office of

Management and Budget and to Congress strategic plans on performance goals and evaluation plans to measure that performance. These have to include an agency mission statement, one or more strategic goals, means to achieve those goals, the link between annual goals and long-term outcomes, identification of key factors that could affect achievement of strategic goals, and a description of program evaluations used in preparing the plan and a schedule for future evaluations (Office of Management and Budget, 2007).

Performance reporting and management depends on the distinction between inputs, outputs, outcomes, and indicators (Schacter, 1999). Inputs are the resources allocated to programs and organizations. Outputs are the activities government agencies undertake, such as the provision of services. Outcomes are the eventual results of those activities in terms of the public good. Indicators are the empirical measures of inputs, outputs, and outcomes. The thrust of performance measurement is to train attention on outcomes—what ultimately matters the most—and link them to a logical model that connects inputs (resources) with activities, outputs, and outcomes. Looked at in this way, performance measurement is about much more than simply measuring things—it entails a management regime that requires a public organization to have a clear idea of what its objectives are, and a regular means of reporting on its success in achieving those objectives. Performance reporting is thus different from policy or program evaluation, which typically takes place near the end of a program's life and is more of a one-time analysis of program impacts. Performance measurement should be viewed as part of a larger management regime, which should try to link results with strategic planning and budgeting and resource allocation.

It is important to get several key factors right in order to do performance measurement properly and successfully (*The Performance Based Management Handbook*, 2001).

- *Clarity about the program*: Since performance measurement is about measuring the success of a program, it is vital to know what that program is about and what its intended objectives are. This is more difficult than it seems, since different people in an organization may have different ideas about what their program is actually about. "Profile—a concise description of the policy, program or initiative, including a discussion of the background, need, target population, delivery approach, resources, governance structure and planned results" (Treasury Board of Canada, 2001a)

- *Logic model*: As discussed above, at the heart of any process of performance reporting is a "logic model" that ties inputs to activities, to short-term, intermediate, and final or ultimate outcomes. Part of the challenge of performance measurement is coming up with indicators for these different levels of outcomes, and coming to judgments about the specific contribution of an agency and its activities to eventual outcomes. A logic model is an illustration of the results chain or how the activities of a policy, program, or initiative are expected to lead to the achievement of the final outcomes. (Treasury Board of Canada, 2001a)

- *Judgment*: The paradox of performance measurement is that while it is driven by a desire for precision and a clear assessment of the contribution of government programs to specific outcomes, the literature acknowledges that there are huge technical problems associated with disentangling the specific effect of those programs from all of the other factors that might contribute to those outcomes. This means that successful performance measurement has to acknowledge that there is always an element of judgment. That judgment can be disciplined and careful, but it still is judgment. It is important to acknowledge the limits of both the indicators one chooses and the evidence for those indicators. This in turn has consequences for the presentation of the performance report. Rather than try to come up with hard, conclusive links between inputs, activities, and outcomes, evaluators are encouraged to tell a **"performance story"** that provides a credible portrait in narrative form of results and expectations, mentioning both anticipated as well as unanticipated outcomes (Mayne, 2003, pp. 13–14).

- *Attribution*: A key challenge in performance measurement is attribution, or determining what a program's contribution has been to a specific outcome. The more difficult question is usually determining just what contribution the specific program in question made to the outcome. How much of the success (or failure) can we attribute to the program? What has been the contribution made by the program? Despite the measurement difficulty, attribution is a problem that cannot be ignored when trying to assess the performance of government programs. Without an answer to this question, little can be said about the worth of the program, nor can advice be provided about future directions (Mayne, 2001).

- *Credible indicators*: Performance can be measured only if there are indicators of both outputs and outcomes. Selecting indicators is not automatic, even if a program is explicit about what its intended outcomes are supposed to be. Successful performance measurement depends in part on finding credible indicators that tell you something important about a program, and that can be successfully measured.

- *Linking resources to results*: Performance measurement is not an end in itself. It should contribute to the wider process of governmental resource allocation. In principle, if programs are found to be underperforming, resources should be moved out of them to other programs that are achieving deeper public benefits. Moreover, linking resources to results is a mechanism for supporting transparency in government decisions as well as stronger accountability to citizens.

- *Sustainability—part of a strategy*: Performance measurement needs to be part of a broader, ongoing strategy of performance assessment. It cannot be episodic or occasional. This feature touches quite closely on the issue of organizational culture, since it highlights the fact that proponents of performance measurement are not simply looking for a new tool of governance, but at changing the way in which governance operates. The ultimate goal is government that continually tries to do better, to be more responsive, and to assess its activities against standards and benchmarks. This is a strategic focus, not simply a technical one.

Getting these factors right is a critical ingredient in the successful establishment of a performance measurement regime. At one level, most of these factors reflect technical considerations and methodological issues—this is clear, for example, for the design of a logic model that links inputs to ultimate outcomes, the selection of indicators, and dealing with the attribution problem. But at another level, performance measurement requires organizational change—this is clear, for example, for linking resources to results, and sustainability. But it is also implied in the more technical success factors. "Know the program" means development of consensus on program objectives. The same is true for designing a logic model. The exercise of judgment and allocation of attribution requires reflection on an organization's environment—the organization has to be outward looking.

What then does performance measurement demand of organizations and the people who work in them? The literature highlights four organizational implications of performance measurement. The first is that if a true performance measurement regime is established, it means a focus on performance and outcomes rather than on process or outputs. The latter are clearly easier and safer to deal with. The second is a willingness to be evaluated at both an organizational and a personal level (at minimum through the performance of programs for which one is responsible). The third is a focus on continuous improvement; if performance measurement is to mean anything, it needs to be linked both to the development and adjustment of new programs and to resource allocation. The fourth is greater transparency and accountability; performance measurement means reporting both to the public and to senior managers and political managers.

Combined, these implications can make life in public organizations quite uncomfortable. Assuming that there are sufficient resources in place to establish an effective performance measurement regime, the critical success factor boils down to people thinking and behaving differently in their organizations.

EFFICIENCY EVALUATION

Even if a policy achieves all its objectives and impacts, this might be at an exorbitant cost. Having the desired impact means a policy is effective, but if it is achieved only at great cost, it may not be efficient. Two major techniques are typically used to address this sort of concern: cost-benefit and **cost-effectiveness analysis** (for a detailed overview, see Rossi, Lipsey, and Freeman (2004), Chap. 11). Both techniques focus on the problem of resource allocation, since the issue of efficiency in public programs is really the issue of alternative and superior allocations of scarce resources.

Cost-Benefit Analysis

The logic of **cost-benefit analysis** is quite simple. The question is not only whether a policy or program has an impact but also at what cost. Policy-makers want to relate costs and benefits in some way. Private businesses do this by measuring profits, though they also monitor other indicators such as productivity. Profit equals income minus expenses, both of which are calculated in monetary terms. As well, business firms measure income (or benefits) from their own perspective, not from the perspective of the consumer using a given product. Government services rarely yield revenue, and since they are services to the community, what counts as "income" is the benefit from the point of view of the community. The translation of these **social benefits** into purely monetary terms is sometimes difficult compared to a private firm, which simply bases its calculations on a market price. The challenge for government is to go beyond the bottom line (which is either impossible or inappropriate for public programs), and calculate the net social benefit by calculating the difference between total benefits and total costs associated with a program. Thus the basic steps in cost-benefit analysis are logically quite clear (these are explained in more detail below): decide on the accounting unit (whose costs and benefits are to be calculated); catalogue all costs and all benefits over time; monetize (attach a monetary value) to those costs and benefits; discount those costs and benefits over the period of time that the project or program will be operating; and determine the net social benefit.

Table 7.1 gives a simplified example of three policy choices for which costs and benefits have been calculated. Both choices A and B have higher net benefits than choice C, but each of them is less efficient in terms of the ratio of benefits to costs. In other words, each dollar of expenditure in choice C purchases $2 of benefits, while choices A and B purchase only $1.50 of benefits. The table also illustrates some of the problems of program choice. Alternative C is clearly the most efficient and would be chosen on that basis. But it also delivers the least net benefit, $1 million

Table 7.1
NET BENEFIT AND COST-BENEFIT CALCULATIONS

Alternative	Benefits	Costs	Benefits – Costs	Benefit/Cost Ratio
A	$9 000 000	$6 000 000	$3 000 000	1.50
B	$6 000 000	$4 000 000	$2 000 000	1.50
C	$2 000 000	$1 000 000	$1 000 000	2.00

compared to $3 million and $2 million for alternatives A and B respectively. One technique is to try to combine net benefit and ratio measures in some way, for example, by comparing the gain in net benefits to the loss in efficiency. The proportional loss in efficiency by moving from C to A (25 percent) is outweighed by the gain in net benefits (200 percent) so that from this perspective, A might be the preferred alternative. A is also preferred over B since, while the ratios of benefits to costs are the same, the net benefits of A are greater than those of B. These examples show that the selection of alternatives is not a mechanical process that follows easily once costs and benefits have been determined. While in the abstract it may seem easy to choose efficiency over net benefits, in the real world, decision criteria are less sharp.

It may appear that a cost-benefit ratio greater than one is self-evidently good, since there is some net gain for an investment of resources. But benefits and costs affect different categories of people, and thus may involve equity considerations or the proportional distribution of benefits and losses equally to similar groups. Cost-benefit analysis, however, is not concerned with distributional or equity issues; it relies on a social welfare criterion known as **Pareto optimality.** This criterion states that a change is worthwhile if at least one person is made better off while no one else is worse off. It is not the same as an increase in total benefits, if that increase depends on someone else's loss. For example, consider a string of ten rural homes, nine of which have barely adequate road access and the tenth none at all. A tax levy on all ten homes to build a new road connecting them could possibly be Pareto optimal, as long as the benefits of improved access for the nine homes equalled the levy. The tenth home would of course be much better off. In this example, everyone is at least as well off as before, and one person may be much better off. Few policy decisions are this clear. The limitations of the Pareto criterion led economists to develop another, more flexible one: the **Kaldor-Hicks criterion,** which identifies potential Pareto improvements as those that, assuming that net gainers could compensate losers, would leave at least one person better off without anyone else worse off. The redistribution is hypothetical, and so in effect the Kaldor-Hicks version of Pareto optimality is a criterion of net benefits. Potential Pareto improvements, it is argued, will increase total societal benefits (for both winners and losers) over time.

Practising evaluators normally leave these arcane matters of social welfare functions to academic economists. From a practical perspective, the tough issues in cost-benefit analysis are the determination and quantification of costs and benefits. Two such general problems are the selection of the **accounting unit** and the issue of **intangibles.** The accounting unit problem is about whose costs and benefits are to be measured. Three basic choices are the individual, the government, and society. Consider an employment agency decision on whether to provide counselling services to its clients. One way of assessing costs and benefits is to focus on the individual program participants: costs might include less time for leisure or job search, while benefits might be increased job skills. From the governmental or agency perspective, costs would be the budgetary ones of mounting the program, while benefits might be increased hiring rates and tax revenues as former clients get jobs. The societal perspective is the most comprehensive, weighing costs and benefits for total national income. Benefits, for instance, might include the value to the national economy of the jobs that clients get. The estimates of benefits and costs will differ depending on the accounting unit chosen.

The problem of intangibles concerns the difficulty of placing monetary values on some costs and benefits. Aesthetic considerations in town planning, the value people place on leisure, the sense of security provided by universal health care: all are presumably important in determining costs and benefits but are difficult to quantify. It is arguable that cost-benefit analyses of public programs tend to estimate costs (program or budget costs) more accurately than benefits, many of which are intangible. Educational policy evaluation, for example, has trouble measuring such benefits as civility and cultural breadth and tends by default to concentrate on job-related benefits. Cost-benefit calculations usually avoid quantifying intangibles, preferring instead to simply mention them as considerations. A related issue is that even if costs and benefits can be monetized, not all of them have an equal chance of occurring. Evaluations thus sometimes attach probabilities to costs and benefits.

The careful classification and treatment of different types of costs is the first step in competent cost-benefit analysis. One important category is **opportunity cost** or the foregone benefits of doing one thing and not another. Assuming scarce resources, doing one thing always means foregoing something else. Cost-benefit analysis, insofar as it tries to facilitate comparisons across alternatives, tries to address the issue of opportunity cost. Other common distinctions are made in determining costs. External versus internal costs and benefits refer to indirect or unintended spillovers from a program. For example, polluting industries sometimes create jobs at home (internal benefit) while generating environmental costs elsewhere (external costs). Incremental versus **sunk costs** is another important distinction. Sunk costs are those incurred in the past; incremental costs are additional or future costs expended to mount or continue a program. A final distinction is between total and **marginal costs.** The total costs of a new counselling program for unwed mothers, for example, would include the proportion of total costs of the agency (e.g., clerical services, furniture, building, heat, light, etc.) accounted for by the program. But since these costs would occur anyway, the marginal cost of the program would be the additional resources devoted to it.

Costs and benefits usually do not occur immediately, and each may flow in different streams. In the case of capital projects or pensions, it may take many years before benefits are realized. This raises a problem of measurement, since most people prefer their benefits to come now and their costs to come later. The element of time therefore has to be assessed in estimates of future costs and benefits. The usual procedure is to apply a **discount rate** to the present value of costs and benefits incurred in a project, to arrive at a measure of net present value (Boardman et al., 2001, Chaps. 6, 10). The trick is in selecting an appropriate rate. The predominant method assesses the opportunity costs of capital, meaning the rate of return if program sums were invested in the private sector. If the economy were uncluttered by monopolies or by taxation regimes that alter pretax rates of return and restrictive foreign trade, then market rate of interest could be taken as the discount rate. Because rates of return are affected by these institutional features, economists make numerous and contentious adjustments to arrive at estimates of the real discount rate.

Cost-Effectiveness Analysis
Cost-effectiveness analysis is closely related to cost-benefit analysis and shares many of its concepts. It is a somewhat simpler and more limited technique, but one that acknowledges the shortcomings of cost-benefit approaches. Cost-effectiveness analysis restricts itself to comparing different program alternatives for achieving a given set of goals. It thus differs from cost-benefit analysis, which purports to compare programs with different goals in terms of a common denominator of benefits. Cost-effectiveness analysis refrains from efforts to monetize benefits. It simply takes program goals or outcomes as given, and then assesses different cost strategies for achieving those goals. It assumes that the least-cost strategy is the preferred alternative. Cost-effectiveness techniques can also be applied in reverse by assuming a fixed budget and choosing alternatives that provide the highest rate of goal achievement—the "biggest bang for the buck." So, "cost-effectiveness analysis is most appropriately used

where there is already general agreement on the nature of the program outcomes and where the outcomes of the alternatives being compared are the same or very similar" (Guess and Farnham, 2000, p. 251).

Typical cost-effectiveness analysis relates the monetized costs of a program to a nonmonetized measure of effects. A fisheries department, for example, may want to increase the fish stock in a lake by 30 percent over five years, or by 100 000 fish. It can choose between restricting fishing licences and stocking the lake. Restricting licences would require greater surveillance expenditures in the amount of $30 000 per year, while restocking the lake might incur a one-time expenditure of $100 000. Over five years, the first alternative yields a cost-effectiveness ratio of $1.50 per fish, while the second costs $1.00 per fish. It would appear that the second alternative would be more efficient or cost-effective.

Cost-effectiveness analysis poses the same problems as cost-benefit analysis. Which costs to consider? In the fisheries case, only departmental costs were counted, but the first alternative should also include foregone fishing by those excluded from licences. Defining the different types of costs and their relationship would also be necessary as would discounting for the project over the implementation period. But cost-effectiveness analysis makes no judgments of relative benefits; it passes these considerations on to decisionmakers, who apply other criteria. A cost-effectiveness analysis may help determine the cheapest way to build a fighter jet but is incapable of showing whether other uses of those funds would be of greater benefit to society.

Policy Evaluation in Canada

The tone of the first part of this chapter certainly conveys the impression that program evaluation is an essential part of any reasonable approach to policymaking: how could we presume to make policies and programs, trying to solve policy problems, if we had no idea of impact or efficacy? As odd as it may sound, however, evaluation as it is currently understood and practised is a relatively recent development in governance. Its first golden age was in the 1970s, after which it went into slight decline, though another golden (or at least, silver) age may be dawning. This relatively late start, however, coincides with the rise of the policy analysis movement itself. Both, as Chapter 1 showed, were postwar phenomena associated with the rise of more activist government, particularly in the 1960s. Program evaluation, for example, depends on the application of social science tools that themselves were developed only in this period. More subtly, program evaluation depends on viewing what government does in program terms. We do that now, because after a quarter century of public policy development and the assumption that governments have a wide horizon of responsibilities to deal with social problems, we simply take it for granted that government activity can be understood in terms of numerous clusters of programs, which, after all, are interventions to solve social issues. There was a time when the scope of government was considerably narrower, and its activities could be understood more simply in terms of activities like building roads or bridges, or providing relatively uncomplicated services like basic education. If everyone gets the same basic education, and the presumption is that the content of that education should adhere to well-established guidelines (e.g., the three Rs, the literary canon), then there is not much point in talking about programs. The type of policy evaluation that goes on within this framework is typically a financial audit, to ensure that monies are spent appropriately. When, however, the different needs of different students (e.g., recent immigrants, people with disabilities, gifted children, girls, boys, adults, illiterate people) have to be addressed, and when different educational goals are targeted (e.g., occupational, academic, life skills), or linked to developing a knowledge economy, then suddenly what once passed as simply education now needs to be understood in terms of a range of specialized education *programs*. The type of evaluation that goes on in this context shifts from financial audits to program evaluation of outcomes and efficiency.

The term "program" first came into formal use in the Canadian federal government's estimates of expenditure only after 1971 (Sutherland, 1990, 140). Previously, a program "could be anything from the whole effort and apparatus of unemployment insurance to a regrouping of activities to realize a short-term special project" (p. 140). The change was due to the introduction and implementation of the **planning-programming-budgeting system** (PPBS), pioneered in the United States (and ironically, abandoned the same year that the Canadian federal government succeeded in applying it across all departments and in the expenditure budget process). PPBS was foreshadowed in 1969 with the Treasury Board's release of its PPBS Guide (Government of Canada, 1969). The idea was that PPBS would be gradually introduced into the Canadian budgetary process, eventually encouraging all departments to state their activities in programmatic terms, that is, in terms of goals and objectives, specific costs associated with programs designed to achieve those goals, and resources devoted to each program. Ideally, this would permit comparisons across all government agencies of related goals and their related programs. Moreover, the 1969 Guide presumed that once goals and associated programs and resources were identified, then the work of evaluation (principally cost-benefit) could go forward almost automatically. Again, to quote Sutherland (1990): "It was thought that both alternative ways of delivering the same program and different programs could be compared with one another in productivity terms—output per input unit. Analysts would be able to compare strategies for reaching given goals within a given program, but also to compare programs/goals with one another in terms of their expensiveness" (p. 143).

As Savoie (1990) notes, at the time, PPBS was thought by most practitioners and observers to hold "great promise, and few dissident voices were heard" (p. 57). Some provincial governments swiftly followed suit, most notably New Brunswick, which introduced PPBS in 1970. However, by the mid-1970s, the bloom was off the PPBS rose. Some of the wilting had to do with the failure of PPBS to help manage expenditures. In the Canadian context, PPBS had been introduced as part of the budget system, on the assumption that rigorous analysis and comparison of objectives and programs would automatically generate information that would clarify planning as well as facilitate reallocations of resources to more efficient and effective programs. That did not happen, in part because the logic of PPBS was entangled with another agenda at the time to reduce central agency control over departments. Given that PPBS did not produce a lot of good analysis, the result was less overview and more spending (Savoie, 1990, pp. 60–61). The second problem was that, even with substantially new resources being devoted to analysis, evaluation, and consulting, the results of cost-benefit and performance analysis "could generate only a drop in the ocean of analysis that would be required if every identified purpose-oriented spending entity was to be tracked" (Sutherland, 1990, p. 144).

There were two responses to this. The first was from the Treasury Board and consisted of an odd blend of both extending and limiting the scope of program evaluation. In 1977 it issued Treasury Board Policy Circular 1977–47, which for the first time formally stated the requirement that all federal government programs periodically undergo an evaluation (Leclerc, 1992, p. 51). The 1977 circular was followed in 1981 with a formal guide to evaluation that remained in place for a decade (Treasury Board of Canada, Office of the Comptroller General, 1981). However, whereas the earlier PPBS framework had implicitly assumed that evaluations would take place automatically, rely principally on cost-benefit analysis, and generate comparative information across programs, the new policy left the evaluation cycle (three to five years) and the selection of programs to be reviewed up to administrators; it did not recommend any specific form of evaluation, and eschewed comparison (Sutherland, 1990, pp. 144–45). Thus, with a kind of logic that would delight Lewis Carroll, program evaluation became both universally mandated for all federal government programs over time and yet was left up to the discretion of departmental managers as to targets and techniques of evaluation. We will come to some assessments of the scope and impact of program evaluation in the federal government as a result of these policies, but it should be clear that the context had been set for *ad hoc,* politically inspired, and relatively insipid evaluation. Evaluation as it came to be understood and institutionalized in

Canada evolved into a "strategic management tool for departments and agencies" (Segsworth, 1992, p. 305). Program evaluation sank into the soft folds of the bureaucratic underbelly and became an information source for managers to improve programs rather than a real tool of accountability and comparison. In itself, there is nothing objectionable in the use of program evaluation for management purposes, but its almost exclusive dedication to this end falls far short of its potential.

The second response to the failure of PPBS came from the Auditor General of Canada. J. J. Macdonnell was appointed Auditor General in 1973 and began to press for the establishment of a comptroller general for the government of Canada. (A position by that name had existed previously but had been abolished in the mid-1960s.) Macdonnell was a private sector accountant and wanted to establish private sector accounting practices in the government. He tried to persuade senior cabinet ministers of the idea, but they balked at the duplication of existing Treasury Board functions. Macdonnell then dropped a verbal bombshell in his 1976 report when he stated that "I am deeply concerned that Parliament—and indeed the Government—has lost, or is close to losing, effective control of the public purse" (Auditor General of Canada, 1976, p. 9). The media seized on this, and the government was forced to announce a Royal Commission on Financial Management and Accountability as well as negotiate with Macdonnell on the establishment of the Office of Comptroller General. The office was indeed established, with "full responsibility for the coordination of evaluation planning, for policy guidance, and for assessing the quality of evaluation findings in studies carried out by departments" (Savoie, 1990, p. 114). However, it was more a political sop than an indication of commitment to evaluation. Nonetheless, it happened that "program evaluation did indeed develop into a growth industry and that it grew around the Office of the Comptroller General" (Savoie, 1990, p. 114). The special link through program evaluation was thus established between the comptroller general, the Auditor General, and departments. The comptroller general provides guidelines and advice on evaluation, but evaluations themselves are conducted by departments. The Auditor General cannot independently conduct evaluations but reports on the success or failure of evaluation across the government. Nonetheless, as a result of these changes, "the scope of the 'audit' of government spending in federal Canada has undergone a more significant transformation than in any other Westminster system . . . from reporting on the ledgers of expenditure to contesting . . . the legitimacy of policy conceived by election Governments" (Sutherland, 1999, p. 112).

The 1981 evaluation guide was updated and altered in 1991 as a result of a policy shift to reflect the logic of PS2000. This change, and the 1994 amendment discussed below, both illustrate the degree to which evaluation is a reflection of the institutional and policy environment and not simply a bundle of techniques that can be generically applied. The key change was a new emphasis on evaluations that would focus on quality of service to the public. In a document entitled *Into the 90s: Government Program Evaluation Perspectives,* the comptroller general explained the new approach:

> PS2000 is about reorienting the Public Service. One of the reforms it calls for is the restoration of the preeminence of service to the public when carrying out the functions of government. Establishing a consultative, client-centred corporate culture requires research, and program evaluation offers a unique range of skills and experience to improve the delivery and cost-effectiveness of programs. A sample of recent evaluations shows that a variety of service issues were addressed and that some of them led to better quality of service to the public.
>
> But, program evaluation offers more than just balanced, analytic methods and a digest of lessons learned. Many evaluators employ client-based consultations to carry out and market their studies. With a little broadening and some deepening of the stakeholder base, this approach could become an effective conduit for program managers not only to assess the quality of their service to the public but also to create a receptive environment for change. (Treasury Board of Canada, Office of the Comptroller General, 1991, pp. 1–2)

What did this new evaluation industry achieve between 1977 and the early 1990s? First, the quantity of evaluations began to rise dramatically. In 1980 there were only seven program evaluations in the government of Canada that met the definition in the guidelines. By 1984–85, thirty-seven federal departments were conducting them and there were over 100 studies (Savoie, 1990, p. 114). The Auditor General reported that in 1991–92 there were eighty evaluations conducted across the federal government, compared with ninety-nine in 1987–88 (Auditor General of Canada, 1993, p. 247). The Auditor General conducted wide-ranging reviews of the evaluation function in the federal government in his annual reports in 1983 and 1986 and was generally critical of their quality. The 1993 report, based on data from forty-two program evaluation units, noted that both the annual number of evaluations and the resources devoted to them were in decline (pp. 244–45). Examining a sample of these, the report noted that "in only about half of the programs did evaluation deal with program relevance and cost-effectiveness" (p. 230):

> Evaluation managers attached the greatest importance to helping management resolve operational issues and improve programs. They placed a much lower priority on the role of evaluation in

challenging existing programs to support resource allocation decisions, and on evaluating large program units to support accountability to Parliament. (p. 245)

The 1996 annual report of the Auditor General, while noting that the context for evaluation in the federal government had changed quite dramatically in three years since its last review of evaluation, still found the government's efforts wanting (Auditor General of Canada, 1996, Chap. 3). In examining four departments in detail, the Auditor General found that evaluations still focused on smaller operational details of greater interest to administrators than to Parliament or the public. On balance, there had been some improvements, but the Auditor General's conclusions were still mixed: "We still see weaknesses in planning, in monitoring action in response to the findings of evaluation studies, and in implementing systematic approaches to assessing the performance of evaluation units" (Auditor General of Canada, 1996, Chap. 3).

The emphasis on the evaluation function was renewed in the late 1990s, partly as a result of the Auditor General's critique, but also other forces. It began, as we outlined earlier, with the 1995 budget and the new framework introduced in Program Review. It brought together guidelines for program review, internal audit, and evaluation under one roof. Program Review goals set the parameters for the other functions, all of which were harnessed to "support the principles of managing by results" (Treasury Board of Canada, 1994, p. 1-1-2). Another key feature was the attempt to integrate the evaluative function more closely with management. In characteristic Canadian fashion, evaluation still remained a management tool, and the 1994 policy urged a "productive alliance between managers and review professionals that will link review more visibly to management decision-making and innovation, as well as accountability" (Treasury Board of Canada, 1994, p. 1-1-2).

The 1994 policy was superseded by a new one in 2001. The focus remained on linking evaluation to management: "Managing for results is the prime responsibility of public service managers. As outlined in the management framework for the federal government, *Results for Canadians*, public service managers are expected to define anticipated results, continually focus attention towards results achievement, measure performance regularly and objectively, and learn and adjust to improve efficiency and effectiveness" (Treasury Board of Canada, 2001b)

Supporting the new *Results for Canadians* management framework and the new evaluation policy was the development of a template for a Results-based Management and Accountability Framework (RMAF). Departments were required, in addition to the normal reporting functions (consisting of annual **departmental performance reports (DPRs)**, and **reports on plans and priorities (RPP)**, to develop RMAFs for all policies and programs. This signaled, as we noted in Chapter 2, a new public management focus on **results orientation**. The key components of an RMAF are

1. *Profile*—a concise description of the policy, program or initiative, including a discussion of the background, need, target population, delivery approach, resources, governance structure and planned results.

2. *Logic model*—an illustration of the results chain or how the activities of a policy, program or initiative are expected to lead to the achievement of the final . . . outcomes.

3. *Ongoing performance measurement strategy*—a plan for the ongoing measurement of performance, including the identification of indicators for the outputs and outcomes in the logic model and a measurement strategy describing how these indicators will be collected, how often and at what cost.

4. *Evaluation strategy*—a plan for the evaluation of the policy, program or initiative, including the identification of formative and summative evaluation issues and questions, the identification of associated data requirements, and a data collection strategy which will serve as the foundation for subsequent evaluation activities.

5. *Reporting strategy*—a plan to ensure the systematic reporting on the results of ongoing performance measurement as well as evaluation, to ensure that all reporting requirements are met. (Treasury Board of Canada, 2001a)

In 2003, the Treasury Board conducted an interim evaluation of its evaluation policy (Treasury Board of Canada, 2003). The policy had been in existence for only eighteen months, but continued funding for initiatives under the policy was contingent on an evaluation. The results were mixed. Implementation of the policy varied significantly among departments, and smaller agencies reported limited or nonexistent evaluation functions. While departments were making improvements, there was still a "capacity gap" of roughly one-third in terms of personnel needs to staff evaluation positions. More worryingly, the report noted that "Projected workloads are forecast to increase at a rate of approximately 200% over the upcoming two years while the number of evaluation staff is expected to increase by only 20–30% over the same time period." The general evaluation capacity in both large and small (but especially small) departments was considered "minimal," and it was not clear whether RMAFs were being effectively implemented.

Another factor propelling the new emphasis on evaluation was the announcement in 2003 of an Action Plan for Democratic Reform. The plan reinforced the importance of RMAFs and the expectation that there would be a strong evaluation function within departments (Treasury Board of Canada, 2005). With the adoption in 2006 of the requirement that each department develop and report on its Program Activity Architecture (PAA), there was an additional stress on linking activities to strategic outcomes. Finally, the Federal Accountability Act of 2006 introduced new requirements that departments evaluate the relevance and effectiveness of their grants and contributions programs each year. The result was that by that year, 97 percent of departments and large agencies had evaluation committees (Treasury Board of Canada, 2006). Problems remained however. Most evaluations focused on program improvement, not on cost-effectiveness. This once again demonstrated the continuing bias in the federal government's evaluation function towards program management (Aucoin, 2005). Half of all evaluations were of programs that had budgets of less than $4 million, and 12 percent covered programs with budgets of less than $500 000 (Treasury Board of Canada, 2006). Some important, though small agencies, had virtually no evaluative capacity at all: e.g., Office of the Commissioner of Official Languages, Canadian Nuclear Safety Commission, and the National Energy Board. Most damning, perhaps, was that 23 percent of evaluations in 2004–05 were deemed to be of poor quality (Treasury Board of Canada, 2007).

These shortcomings, in addition to new pressures from the Accountability Act, had the government considering a new evaluation policy in mid-2007 to replace the existing 2001 framework (at time of writing that new policy has not been implemented). The policy was to re-focus evaluation on value-for-money and strengthen accountability for performance of the function, expand evaluation coverage, strengthen governance and usage, develop appropriate evaluation competencies and standards for evaluators, improve the Treasury Board's capacity to monitor and use evaluation results, and address small agency evaluation needs (Treasury Board of Canada, 2007). Evaluation information would be more closely integrated with departmental performance reporting and program activity architecture.

Performance evaluation and reporting has been a perennial focus for the Canadian government since the 1970s, and clearly became even more important during the 1990s with Program Review and budget cutting exercises. That importance has only grown with continued efforts at tighter expenditure management and new, tighter accountability regimes and a stronger emphasis on performance. But there can be no avoiding the conclusion that performance evaluation and reporting has not made as much headway in the federal government as one would think studying the policy documents, though the 2007 initiative may take evaluation to a new level. There are several possible reasons for this. First, as we noted, the Canadian approach has been to avoid strong external evaluation functions, and integrate evaluation with management. There is nothing wrong with this, but it does leave the fox guarding the chicken coop. Second, it has to be recognized that performance evaluation takes place in specific institutional contexts. De Bruijn (2002) talks about the "perverse effects" of performance measurement: among other things, it can stimulate strategic behaviour where organizations focus on performance indicators only (in order to score points); it can stifle innovation if organizations decide that innovation is too risky (and hence will lose performance points); and good performance may even sometimes lead to punishment (for example, when a well-performing organization gets its budget cut because "it's doing so well it can probably do as well with less"). Introducing a performance regime without addressing these perversities means that it might become more a charade than a viable management tool.

Conclusion

Program evaluation has always enjoyed support, in principle, from policymakers. The logic of policy analysis, as described in Chapter 1, emphasizes careful definition of policy problems, consideration of options, and interventions that lead to amelioration or improvement. Policy as intervention depends on some idea of causal connections. In this sense, every policy or program is a guess, a hypothesis about social problems. Evaluation serves the vital function of providing empirical feedback on those hypotheses in action: did they work, what impact did the intervention have, at what cost? It is for this reason that public policy theory urges the integration of policy evaluation into every stage of the policy process; since evaluation in a sense is the collective memory of what worked and what did not, integration of that information can save errors and effort.

But just as evaluation has been granted this pivotal role in theory, in practice it has been viewed skeptically and often marginalized in the policy process. The reasons are not hard to understand. Even the strongest partisans of evaluation acknowledge the often severe methodological limitations of answering impact and efficiency questions (Radin, 2006). More art than science, it is always possible to find reasons why positive or negative evaluation results are flawed. These very limitations, as well as the sheer expense of doing thorough evaluations, have usually limited evaluation to routine monitoring or process studies. Also, as we noted, there is the paradox that while evaluation seems essential in theory, in practice it can appear to be a frill when compared to direct program responsibilities and delivery. Thus, traditionally, evaluation has been the poor cousin of the policy process, often relegated to small policy analysis units divorced from direct policy management responsibilities

(Hollander and Prince, 1993). Insofar as evaluation tends to be the dismal science of policy analysis—showing that impacts are weak or dubious, and often much more expensive than first anticipated—nobody really appreciates the bad news. Again, this seems to have changed somewhat, with the requirement of audit and evaluation committees within departments and agencies, and the integration of evaluation into the RMAF as a key management function.

To these generic reasons for the limited impact of evaluation (noted even as recently as 2006) should be added some specific Canadian twists. First, as we noted in the brief history of the Office of Comptroller General, the establishment of evaluation guidelines and institutions in the Canadian federal government in the early 1980s was done partly to placate the Auditor General and was implemented without much enthusiasm. The drivers for enhanced evaluation seem to continue to be external, and an evaluation culture is only gradually taking hold in the federal government. That said, it should also be noted that the institutional scaffolding supporting the evaluation function has been considerably strengthened in recent years. Second, the Canadian practice, and this is true of the provincial level of government as well, has been to use evaluation as a management tool. Evaluation units have been embedded in departments, and departmental managers have been responsible for the evaluation function, governed by loose central agency guidelines. This contrasts with the United States, where congressional committees aggressively sponsor evaluation of programs within their policy fields as a challenge to the executive and where independent **think tanks** and policy groups abound. The parliamentary system tends to be more closed to outside influences than the U.S. congressional system, and so the "evaluation climate" created by vibrant and vocal think tanks is not as rich in Canada as it is in the United States. To this must be added cultural (Canada seems to encourage less policy entrepreneurship) and economic (Canada's philanthropists have not channelled as much money into think tanks and foundations) influences (Abelson and Carberry, 1998; Abelson and Lindquist, 2000; Abelson, 2002). The best estimate is that there are only about 100 think tanks in Canada and, among them, fewer than ten major nongovernmental, noncommercial policy institutes (e.g., C. D. Howe Research Institute, Canada West Foundation, Conference Board of Canada, Canadian Tax Foundation, Fraser Institute, Institute for Research on Public Policy, Canadian Institute for Economic Policy, and Canadian Energy Research Institute). Despite the high visibility of some think tanks and policy institutes in the media and at specific points in the policy cycle (Abelson, 1999), and the occasionally headline-grabbing report (e.g., the Fraser Institute's 2004 report on legalizing and taxing marijuana), most think tanks generate relatively bland publications.

Despite this gloomy assessment of evaluation and its potential to influence policymaking, this chapter has shown that evaluation may be enjoying a fitful renaissance of sorts. Evaluation may not only be getting marginally more important in government, but also the nature of evaluation itself may be changing. For example, the new emphasis on accountability and performance results means that the goals or outcomes of policy and programs are defined more broadly than ever before. A focus on results will encourage more impact-oriented evaluations. However, current policy paradigms also stress client satisfaction and a service orientation as outcomes. This means that the old division between process and impact analysis might be blurring, and increasingly the key impacts sought by policymakers are satisfaction and support of the process and program itself. The heightened importance of evaluation has generated discussions about better training for evaluators, possibly through newly created certificate programs at Canadian universities (Gussman, 2006). Others have gone further, and argued that the roughly 80 separate offices for program evaluation spread out across the federal government do not create a critical central authority for evaluation excellence. The suggestion is that a new position be created, the office of the Evaluator General, to oversee the evaluation function as a third-party champion, encouraging excellence and making the evaluation function throughout government more visible and accountable (D'Aloisio et al., 2007).

There is a great deal to be skeptical about in policy and program evaluation, in performance measurement and results, but we prefer to end on an optimistic and uplifting note. Yes, in practice, evaluation studies can seem so insipid, qualified, and immersed in murky politics as to appear useless. Some critics dismiss evaluation as a policy sideshow, a carnival of dubious methodological handsprings and somersaults that rarely yields serious results (Radin, 2006). For other critics, insofar as evaluation is dominated by expert discourse, it threatens democracy by drawing debate away from ordinary citizens and entrapping it in a closed universe of language only a few can speak. This fear is surely overdrawn, particularly given the limited role that evaluation has played in Canadian policymaking and the new emphasis on making performance and results measurement accessible to citizens. We are tempted to make the opposite argument, though well aware that it holds certain dangers as well. The basic questions that form the foundations of program evaluation are vital to any democratic discussion of public policy—what works and at what cost? These are not the only questions that one can pose about policy, but they are important ones, which if seriously addressed can only benefit policy discussion. Canadian efforts should continue to emphasize the importance of broad evaluation of policy, as well as the wider exposure and dissemination of evaluation results.

KEY TERMS

accountability—the quality of being accountable to another for one's actions; entailing an obligation to respond to questions and regularly report

accounting unit—in doing cost-benefit analysis, the unit or jurisdiction in which costs and benefits will be ascribed

attribution problem—the difficulty of determining what the specific contribution of a policy or program intervention has been to outcomes, in contrast to all other possible factors that might have affected those outcomes

causal chain—the link of various causes and effects in producing outcomes in the implementation process

contrasted group design—an experimental evaluation design where recipients are compared to nonrecipients, and the differences are ascribed to the program

control group—in experimental designs, the randomly assigned group that will not be the recipient of the intervention or program and that will form the basis of comparison with the experimental group

cost-benefit analysis—evaluation of a program in terms of its total costs compared to its total benefits, expressed in monetary terms

cost-effectiveness analysis—compares different program alternatives for achieving a given set of goals; it is also applied by considering a fixed budget and choosing alternatives that provide the highest rate of goal achievement

departmental performance report (DPR)—annual report on performance of each federal department for the previous fiscal year

dependent variable—the variable that is being explained

diagnostic procedures—procedures in which the evaluators are often involved in generating and analyzing data that are relevant to problem definition, trend forecasting, and program design aspects

discount rate—the rate chosen to discount future benefits, usually assessed as the opportunity costs of capital, meaning the rate of return if program sums were invested in the private sector

experimental design—the evaluation of impact based on randomly assigned experimental and control groups

experimental group—the randomly assigned group to which the program or intervention is applied in an experimental design

formative evaluation—evaluation designed to support development and improvement of a program as it is being implemented

impact evaluation—analysis of the actual effect or impact of a program on its intended target, along with unintended consequences

implementation theory—the specific activities and resources that need to be mobilized in connection with each of the links in the program's causal chain to achieve the desired outcome

intangibles—the costs and benefits of a program for which it is difficult to place monetary values

Kaldor-Hicks criterion—identifies potential Pareto improvements as those that, assuming that net gainers could compensate losers, would leave at least one person better off without anyone else worse off

logic model—usually a graphical representation of the links between program inputs, activities, outputs, immediate outcomes, and long-term results

marginal cost—the additional unit of cost of doing something

meta-analysis—a technique where evaluators review the existing literature on a specific program, treating each evaluation study as a single case and building statistical conclusions based on these observations

needs assessment—a review of the service and support needs of a particular agency or group

opportunity cost—the foregone benefits of doing one thing and not another

Pareto optimality—the criterion of optimization that states that a change is worthwhile if at least one person is made better off while no one else is worse off

performance story—reporting of program results in such a way as to highlight both successes and shortcomings, the challenges faced by the organization, and what it might do in the future to improve results

planning-programming-budgeting system (PPBS)—encourages departments to state their activities in programmatic terms, that is, in terms of goals and objectives, specific costs associated with programs designed to achieve those goals, and resources devoted to each program

pre-program/post-program design—an evaluation technique that uses time-series data for the period before program implementation and after to draw conclusions about the likely impact of the intervention

process evaluation—monitors an existing program to assess the effort and organizational resources put into it

program components—typically, the strategies, activities, behaviours, media products, and technologies needed to deliver the program, along with a specification of the intended recipients and delivery situations

program evaluation—an essential part of any reasonable approach to policymaking that assesses, in some sense, how well programs are doing in terms of their stated objectives

program logic—sketches out the assumed causal links that will yield specified outcomes in order to conduct impact evaluation

program theory—the hypotheses and explanations about the causal links that tie program inputs to expected program outputs

RPPs (reports on plans and priorities)—annual report required from each federal government department and agency about their plans and priorities for the coming fiscal year

quasi-experimental design—all contrasted or comparing group designs that fall short of the demand for completely random assignment of the groups

random assignment of groups—a method used in experimental design where the odds of being in either the experimental or control group are the same

results orientation—a management focus on new forms of review, audit, and evaluation based on results

single observation design—a method of evaluation that relies on a measure of impact only after the program is introduced

social benefits—the benefits obtained from the point of view of the community of the services provided by government

social indicators—data that represent important characteristics of society such as crime, literacy, health; contrasted to the usual economic indicators such as inflation and unemployment

summative evaluation—an evaluation undertaken at the end of a program to gauge its success

sunk cost—costs that have incurred in the past and that are not recoverable

think tanks—nongovernmental, sometimes for-profit and sometimes nonprofit, organizations dedicated to research and discussion of policy issues with the wider public and decisionmakers

FURTHER READINGS

Boardman, A. E., Greenberg, D. H., Vining, A., and Weimer, D. L. (2001). *Cost-benefit analysis: Concepts and practice.* Upper Saddle River, NJ: Prentice-Hall.

de Bruijn, H. (2002). *Managing performance in the public sector.* London: Routledge.

Mayne, J. (2003). *Reporting on outcomes: Setting performance expectations and telling performance stories.* Ottawa: Office of the Auditor General of Canada. Retrieved March 30, 2008, from http://www.oag-bvg.gc.ca/internet/English/oag-bvg_e_10189.html

Patton, M. Q. (2002). *Qualitative research and evaluation methods* (3rd ed.). Thousand Oaks, CA: Sage.

Rossi, P. H., Lipsey, M. W., and Freeman, H. E. (2004). *Evaluation: A systematic approach* (7th ed.). Thousand Oaks, CA: Sage Publications.

Treasury Board of Canada. (2005). *The health of the evaluation function in the government of Canada: Report for the fiscal year 2004–05.* Retrieved on March 30, 2008, from http://www.tbs-sct.gc.ca/eval/dev/health-santé/pdf/hefgc-sfegc_e.pdf

Wholey, J. S., Hatry, H. P., and Newcomer, K. E. (Eds.) (2004). *Handbook of practical program evaluation,* 2nd Ed. San Francisco, CA: Jossey-Bass.

REFERENCES

Abelson, D. E. (1999). Public visibility and policy relevance: Assessing the impact and influence of Canadian policy institutes. *Canadian Public Administration,* 42(2), 240–70.

Abelson, D. E. (2002). *Do think tanks matter?: Assessing the impact of public policy institutes.* Montreal: McGill-Queen's University Press.

Abelson, D. E., and Carberry, C. M. (1998). Following suit or falling behind?: A comparative analysis of think tanks in Canada and the United States. *Canadian Journal of Political Science,* 31(3), 525–56.

Abelson, D. E., and Lindquist, E. A. (2000). Think tanks in North America. In J. G. McGann and R. K. Weaver (Eds.), *Think tanks and civil society: Catalysts for ideas and action* (pp. 37–66). New Brunswick, NJ: Transaction Publishers.

American Evaluation Society. (2008). *Guiding principles for evaluators.* Retrieved March 20, 2008, from http://www.eval.org/Publications/GuidingPrinciples.asp

Aucoin, P. (2005). *Decision-making in government: The role of program evaluation.* Discussion Paper. Treasury Board of Canada. Retrieved on March 30, 2008, from http://www.tbs-sct.gc.ca/eval/tools_outils/Aucoin/Aucoin_e.asp

Auditor General of Canada. (1976). *Annual report 1976.* Retrieved March 30, 2008, from http://www.oag-bvg.gc.ca/internet/English/aud_fs_e_925.html

Auditor General of Canada. (1993). *Annual report 1993*. Retrieved March 30, 2008, from http://www.oag-bvg.gc.ca/internet/English/aud_fs_e_925.html

Auditor General of Canada. (1996). *Annual report 1996*. Retrieved March 30, 2008, from http://www.oag-bvg.gc.ca/internet/English/aud_fs_e_925.html

Boardman, A. E., Greenberg, D. H., Vining, A., and Weimer, D. L. (2001). *Cost-benefit analysis: Concepts and practice.* Upper Saddle River, NJ: Prentice-Hall.

Boruch, R. F., and Petrosino, A. (2004). In J. S. Wholey, H. P. Hatry, and K. E. Newcomer (Eds.), *Handbook of practical program evaluation,* 2nd Ed. (pp. 176–203). San Francisco, CA: Jossey-Bass.

Canadian Evaluation Society (2008). *CES Guidelines for ethical conduct.* Retrieved March 20, 2008, from http://www.evaluationcanada.ca/site.cgi?s=5&ss=4&_lang=an

City of Ottawa. (2008). *Needle exchange policy.* Retrieved on March 29, 2008, from http://www.ottawa.ca/residents/health/living/harm/site/policy_en.html

Curristine, T. (2005). Program information in the budget process: Results of the OECD 2005 Questionnaire. *OECD Journal on Budgeting, 5* (2), pp. 87–132. Retrieved March 20, 2008, from http://www.oecd.org/dataoecd/13/2/37714836.pdf

D'Aloisio, G., et al. (2007). An evaluator general for Canada—A solution for filling the accountability void? *Networked Government* Issue 7. Retrieved on March 31, 2008, from http://www.networkedgovernment.ca/2007Issue7

de Bruijn, H. (2002). *Managing performance in the public sector.* London: Routledge.

Framst, G. (1995, October/November). Application of program logic model to agricultural technology transfer programs. *Canadian Journal of Program Evaluation,* 10, 123–32.

Geva-May, I., and Pal, L. A. (1999). Good fences make good neighbours: Policy evaluation and policy analysis—exploring the differences. *Evaluation,* 5(3), 259–77.

Government of Canada. (1969). *Planning, programming and budgeting guide.* Ottawa: Information Canada.

Guess, G. M., and Farnham, P. G. (2000). *Cases in public policy analysis.* Washington: Georgetown University Press.

Gussman, T. (2006). Improving the profession of evaluation. *Canadian Evaluation Society.* Retrieved on March 31, 2008, from http://www.evaluationcanada.ca/site.cgi?s=1&ss=1&_lang=en&num=00627

Gyarmati, D., de Raaf, S., Nicholson,C., Palameta, B., Hui, T., and MacInnis, M. (2007a). *Improving skills, networks, and livelihoods through community-based work: Three-year impacts of the community employment innovation project.* Ottawa: Social Research and Demonstration Corporation. Retrieved March 21, 2008, from http://www.srdc.org/uploads/CEIP_Improving_Skills_EN.pdf

Gyarmati, D., de Raaf, S., Nicholson, C., Palameta, B., Hui, T., and MacInnis, M. (2007b). *Improving skills, networks, and livelihoods through community-based work: Three-year impacts of the community employment innovation project.* Executive Summary. Ottawa: Social Research and Demonstration Corporation. Retrieved March 21, 2008, from http://www.srdc.org/uploads/CEIP_executive_summary_EN.pdf

Hollander, M. J., and Prince, M. J. (1993, Summer). Analytical units in federal and provincial governments: Origins, functions and suggestions for effectiveness. *Canadian Public Administration, 36,* 190–224.

Mayne, J. (2001, Spring). Addressing attribution through contribution analysis: Using performance measures sensibly. *The Canadian Journal of Program Evaluation, 16,* 1–24.

Mayne, J. (2003). *Reporting on outcomes: Setting performance expectations and telling performance stories.* Ottawa: Office of the Auditor General of Canada. Retrieved March 30, 2008, from http://www.oag-bvg.gc.ca/internet/English/oag-bvg_e_10189.html

McLaughlin, J. A., and Jordan, G. B. (2004). Using logic models. In J. S. Wholey, H. P. Hatry, and K. E. Newcomer (Eds.), *Handbook of practical program evaluation,* 2nd Ed. (pp. 7–32). San Francisco, CA: Jossey-Bass.

OECD. (1995). *Public management developments: Update 1995.* Paris: OECD.

OECD. (2005). *Modernising government: The way forward.* Paris: OECD.

Office of Management and Budget (United States) (2007). *Circular no. A-11: Preparation, submission and execution of the budget.* Retrieved March 20, 2008, from http://www.whitehouse.gov/omb/circulars/a11/current_year/s210.pdf

Patton, M. Q. (1987). *Creative evaluation* (2nd ed.). Newbury Park, CA: Sage.

Patton, M. Q. (1997). *Utilization-focused evaluation: The new century text* (3rd ed.). Thousand Oaks, CA: Sage Publications.

Patton, M. Q. (2002). *Qualitative research and evaluation methods* (3rd ed.). Thousand Oaks, CA: Sage.

Posvac, E. J., and Carey, R. G. (1980). *Program evaluation: Methods and case studies*. Englewood Cliffs, NJ: Prentice-Hall.

Radin, B. A. (2006). *Challenging the performance movement: Accountability, complexity, and democratic values*. Washington, D. C.: Georgetown University Press.

Rossi, P. H., Lipsey, M. W., and Freeman, H. E. (2004). *Evaluation: A systematic approach* (7th ed.). Thousand Oaks, CA: Sage Publications.

Saint-Martin, D. (2000). *Building the new managerialist state: Consultants and the politics of public sector reform in comparative perspective*. Oxford: Oxford University Press.

Savoie, D. J. (1990). *The politics of public spending in Canada*. Toronto: University of Toronto Press.

Schacter, M. (1999). *Means . . . ends . . . indicators: Performance measurement in the public sector*. Ottawa: Institute on Governance.

Scheirer, M. A. (1994). Designing and using process evaluation. In J. S. Wholey, H. P. Hatry, and K. E. Newcomer (Eds.), *Handbook of practical program evaluation* (pp. 40–68). San Francisco: Jossey-Bass.

SRDC. (2008a). "About SRDC." Retrieved March 21, 2008, from http://www.srdc.org/en_about_us.asp?categoryId=514

St. Pierre, R. G. (2004). In J. S. Wholey, H. P. Hatry, and K. E. Newcomer (Eds.), *Handbook of practical program evaluation*, 2nd Ed. (pp. 150–75). San Francisco, CA: Jossey-Bass.

Sutherland, S. L. (1990, Summer). The evolution of program budget ideas in Canada: Does parliament benefit from estimates reform? *Canadian Public Administration, 33*, 133–64.

Sutherland, S. L. (1999). Bossing democracy: The value-for-money audit and the electorate's loss of political power to the auditor general. In R. M. Bird, M. J. Trebilcock, and T. A. Wilson (Eds.), *Rationality in public policy: Retrospect and prospect, a tribute to Douglas Hartle* (pp. 109–40). Toronto: Canadian Tax Foundation, Canadian Tax Paper No. 104.

The performance-based management handbook: A six-volume compilation of techniques and tools for implementing the Government Performance and Results Act of 1993. (2001). Washington: Training Resources and Data Exchange, Performance-Based Management Special Interest Group for the Office of Strategic Planning and Program Evaluation, 2001. Retrieved March 30, 2008, from http://www.orau.gov/pbm/pbmhandbook/pbmhandbook.html

Treasury Board of Canada. (1981). *Guide on the program evaluation function*. Ottawa: Minister of Supply and Services.

Treasury Board of Canada. (1991). *Into the 90s: Government program evaluation perspectives.* Ottawa: Office of the Comptroller General.

Treasury Board of Canada. (1994, July). *Treasury Board manual— Review, internal audit and evaluation* (Amendment RIE/94-1). Ottawa: Treasury Board of Canada.

Treasury Board of Canada. (2000). *Results for Canadians: A management framework for the government of Canada.* Retrieved March 30, 2008, from http://www.tbs-sct.gc.ca/res_can/rc_e.html

Treasury Board of Canada. (2001a). *Guide for the development of results-based management and accountability frameworks.* Retrieved March 30, 2008, from http://www.tbs-sct.gc.ca/eval/pubs/RMAF-CGRR/rmaf-cgrr-01-e.asp

Treasury Board of Canada. (2001b). *Evaluation policy.* Retrieved March 30, 2008, from http://www.tbs-sct.gc.ca/pubs_pol/dcgpubs/TBM_161/ep-pe_e.asp

Treasury Board of Canada. (2003). *Interim evaluation of the Treasury Board's evaluation policy.* Retrieved March 30, 2008, from http://www.tbs-sct.gc.ca/eval/tools_outils/int-prov_e.asp#exsum

Treasury Board of Canada. (2005). *The health of the evaluation function in the government of Canada: Report for the fiscal year 2004–05.* Retrieved on March 30, 2008, from http://www.tbs-sct.gc.ca/eval/dev/health-santé/pdf/hefgc-sfegc_e.pdf

Treasury Board of Canada. (2006). *Valuing the evaluation function: Problems and perspectives.* Retrieved on March 30, 2008, from http://www.tbs-sct.gc.ca/eval/ppt/jun06-001/vef-vfe_e.asp

Treasury Board of Canada. (2007). *Evaluation policy renewal—overview.* Retrieved on March 30, 2008, from http://www.tbs-sct.gc.ca/presentations/rma-dpr/overview-apercu/overview-apercu_e.pdf

Weiss, C. H. (1998). *Evaluation* (2nd ed.). Upper Saddle River, NJ: Prentice Hall.

Wholey, J. S. (1994). Assessing the feasibility and likely usefulness of evaluation. In J. S. Wholey, H. P. Hatry, and K. E. Newcomer (Eds.), *Handbook of practical program evaluation* (pp. 15–39). San Francisco: Jossey-Bass.

Wholey, J. S. (2003). Improving performance and accountability: Responding to emerging management challenges. In S. I. Donaldson and Michael Scriven (Eds.), *Evaluating social programs and problems* (pp. 43–61). Mahwah, NJ: Lawrence Erlbaum Associates.

8

Policymaking under Pressure

This book is based on the idea that the context for policymaking has changed significantly in recent years, and that we consequently need to rethink our tools and the way that we do policy analysis. One major and relatively new change seems to be the degree to which policymaking increasingly takes place under pressure, in circumstances of adversity and uncertainty, dealing with crises, disasters, and emergencies. The most obvious are terrorist threats and bombings, environmental and weather threats, epidemics such as SARS and avian flu, Mad Cow disease, the global financial crisis. There are several reasons for this: the increasing interdependency of complex systems such as the Internet, pan-continental energy grids, or global financial markets; the rapid transmission of disease because of global markets for food products and enhanced ability of individuals to travel around the world; the possibility that environmental changes are inducing new natural disasters (e.g., flooding, climate change, erosion); the ability of modern media to both instantly magnify events and broadcast them in real time; conflict zones that drive refugees to seek safety; increasing involvement in low-intensity warfare such as in Afghanistan, and its unpredictable twists and turns. Whatever the reasons, the modern reality of policymaking is marked increasingly by dealing with crisis. The problem is that most of the models of decisionmaking used in the policy literature are models predicated on the normal, the everyday, the linear, and the expected. What happens when policymakers are confronted with the abnormal, the unusual, the uncertain, and the unexpected? This chapter provides an overview of some themes in an increasingly important area of policymaking and public management: handling crisis and emergency.

Conventional policy theory and practice is strongly influenced by the rational model described in Chapter 1. The model assumes a series of logical steps and processes to come to decisions about public policy. We mentioned some of the assumptions that underpin the model, and some of the challenges. But we can go a little deeper. The model tends to assume a relatively small number of decisionmakers, perhaps even only one. It assumes, if not complete information, at least reasonably high levels of information and data to inform decisions, a high degree of certainty in short. In order for the sequence to take place at all, the model assumes that there is sufficient time for that sequence to unfold. And finally, coupled to the assumption that there is sufficient information to make choices, is the notion that problems are reasonably well defined.

There are many instances of public policy in which these assumptions, or at least approximations to these assumptions, hold reasonably well. Routine or "normal" policy analysis therefore can be undertaken more or less within the broad framework of the rational model: problems are defined, models of causal variables developed, data gathered, options or alternatives generated, and choices made based on some set of criteria. But we also know that the real world of public policy is marked at times—and seems increasingly to be marked—by emergencies and crises. Policy decisions have to be made under pressure, and all the assumptions of the rational model are stretched if not broken. Most crises and emergencies involve multiple actors, with overlapping authorities. Instead of single decisionmakers there are many, and they have to be coordinated. Instead of reasonably high levels of information and data, crisis and emergency is marked by randomness and uncertainty. Time seems to be truncated, and major decisions have to be made quickly. Finally, as we noted with the SARS crisis and problem definition in Chapter 3, the policy problem is often ill defined or so complex that it defies easy categorization and analysis. All of these characteristics marked the global financial crisis of October 2008.

While we commonly think of crisis and emergency as the same thing, there is distinction between them that affects the way we think about them and the way we react to them. An **emergency** is an abnormal and unexpected threat event that requires immediate action. A **crisis** is a turning point or moment of danger that threatens the survival of an entire system. A house fire, for example, would usually be considered an emergency rather than a family crisis. The latter would be some event or development that threatens the existence of the family as such (the death of a member). Something can be a crisis and an emergency at the same time, from different perspectives. A forest fire or a flood that threatens to destroy a community is evidently a crisis for that community since it threatens its very existence. From the government's perspective, it is an emergency since it does not threaten the government's existence. As well, emergencies can quickly evolve into crises. The 9/11 attack on the World Trade Center was a massive emergency, but for a short time it looked as well as if it might be a crisis for all the United States (in case this was the first phase of an attack on the country) and the government (in case leading members of the administration were killed). There is somewhat less scope for interpretation in the cases of emergency, though naturally there can be differences in point of view. But most emergencies by definition are abnormalities with severe consequences occurring in a short space of time. We can mistake some unwanted events as emergencies (e.g., someone faints, but others think it is a heart attack), but generally emergencies are defined in terms of significant and immediate threat, usually to physical property or life. A crisis, since it is a threat event that affects the integrity of the system, is more debatable precisely because a judgment has to be made about what the system is, what its component elements are, how they work together to maintain that system, and why the threat event might undermine those elements. A "cabinet crisis" requires a judgment about whether a threat event (e.g., the resignation of a prominent minister) might bring down the government as a whole. What kind of threat event could undermine the integrity of the entire United Nations system, and thereby be a crisis?

There is obviously a relationship between emergency and crisis, but they call forth different types of responses and different forms of public management. These will be explored later in the chapter. For the moment, it is worth trying to discern the generic elements of a substantial threat event, whether it falls into one category or another. Substantial threat events seem to be determined by four factors: randomness, severity, uniqueness, and time compression. Figure 8.1 charts the variances as running from low to high, and carves out four quadrants with different configurations. Events that are highly random (not expected), severe in terms of consequences, unique or previously not encountered

Figure 8.1 Categorizing Threat Events

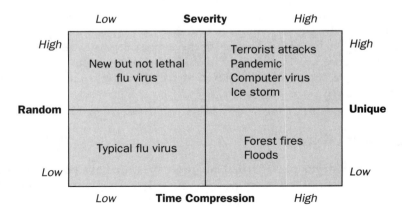

and hence without an information base, and compressed in time (moving rapidly; requiring rapid response), pose the greatest type of threat. Events that are low on all four dimensions pose the least threat and are the easiest to manage. The other two categories are mixed. Events like some floods and forest fires are predictable to a degree, but still pose severe threats and need a quick response. Since they have happened before and have typical configurations, there are routines in place to deal with them. In the other category, at the top left quadrant, severity is low, but the event is unexpected or difficult to predict, and largely unknown. Types of events can migrate into different quadrants as more is known about them. A flu virus that is unknown in one year, even while it is predictable that it will move through the population in the fall and winter, is unique. Once the strain has been determined, a vaccine can be prepared the next year.

Severity is a key factor in every scenario, and can be defined in terms of scope and intensity of negative impact. The wider the scope of a threat event, and the greater its intensity or negative impact, the more pressure there will be for a rapid response. Time compression is to some extent, though not exclusively, a function of severity. SARS was a greater threat than Mad Cow disease because of its potential severity (an immediate life-threatening pandemic versus a threat of longer duration), and time compression was a function of that severity but also because how easily and quickly the disease spread.

The challenge for contemporary policymakers is that crisis and emergency threat events that promise severe negative impacts with wide scope seem to be increasingly common. While a good deal of policymaking is still "normal" in the sense that while difficult, threat events can be handled through normal political processes, more and more seem to fall into the category of emergency or crisis. By definition, crises and emergencies are events that strain a policymaking system and perhaps even cause it to collapse. Too many emergencies—indeed sometimes only one—that are not handled well can pose a crisis for the system. The question is what techniques of analysis and of management can be drawn upon to deal with these types of challenges. The rest of the chapter begins by reviewing some of the theoretical foundations of crisis management and policymaking under pressure, and then moves to risk assessment, emergency preparedness, and crisis management.

Modelling Chaos

Some of the ingredients of policymaking under pressure have been mentioned above, but are there more precise ways of conceptualizing those elements? One of the first attempts in the policy literature to come to grips with this problem was Ira Sharkansky's (1986) notion of "policy-making under adversity":

> Shifts and time-compressed turns in the nature of issues make traditional policy paradigms, policy assumptions, policy habits, policy "grammars," and grand policies increasingly doubtful. Recent, present, and foreseeable shifts and jumps in policy issues include transformations in expectations, aspirations, and beliefs; inflections of the internal dynamics of policies, which make their linear continuation with only incremental changes impossible or counterproductive; jumps in the material features of policy issues; and emergence of new and unprecedented problems. (Sharkansky, 1986, p. 23)

It is the discontinuities, the "jumps" that create challenges. As we noted above, if normal policymaking may be seen as incremental, with each step more or less predictably or controllably emanating from the last, then what is nonincremental, unpredictable to a certain degree, and not immediately controllable has the potential to create crisis. On August 14, 2003, for example, parts of the northeastern United States and Ontario experienced a power blackout. It lasted for four days in some parts of the United States, and Ontario saw rolling blackouts for more than a week before power was restored (U.S.–Canada Power System Outage Taskforce, 2004). The outage was estimated to have cost the United States upward of US$10 billion, and as much as $2.3 billion in lost manufacturing shipments from Ontario. This was a shift and jump with vengeance. The linear continuity of power at a flip of a switch is taken for granted by citizens, and while there are peaks and surges in demand, these can normally be managed. Ironically, that day was considered normal, without unusually heavy power demands in and around Ohio, where the first system collapse occurred. Due to a combination of human and software error, failures in that region's power grid were not noticed in time, and because of the integration of the North American power grid system, a failure in Ohio rippled through and hit Ontario and several other U.S. states. We will discuss the nature of causation in chaotic events in a moment, but the point here is the shift and jump that Sharkansky mentions. In terms of Figure 8.1, this was a high threat event or emergency, because it scored high on severity, unexpectedness, and uniqueness and time compression, much like the US sub-prime mortgage crisis.

Shifts and jumps indicate a break from a linear routine. Every threat event contains a large element of surprise that makes it different from normal. People who live in earthquake zones, for example, know that there is likely to be an earthquake sometime, but not exactly when. In some instances, like SARS, the event is a total surprise since it literally has never happened before. Beyond the element of surprise, however, crises or emergencies as nonlinear *policy* problems are collective action problems.

Comfort (1999), for example, looks at what she calls "shared risk" problems—crises or emergencies that affect large communities—as **nonlinear policy problems.** Her 1999 classic study reviewed examples of earthquakes and emergency response to them:

> Shared risk is nonlinear in that small differences in initial conditions, repeated in actions over time, lead to unpredictable outcomes. It is also dynamic, in that a change in the performance of one sub-unit of the affected system may directly influence that of other units in its immediate vicinity, creating a ripple effect of failure throughout the system. Problems of shared risk are not easily amenable to control strategies, particularly if the control is externally imposed. They appear to be more problems of collective learning, involving multiple groups at different levels of understanding, commitment, and skill, as well as requiring different types of knowledge, authority, and action for effective resolution. . . . Methods for addressing problems of shared risk differ from those used in traditional policy analysis. Since the problems are nonlinear and dynamic, the assumptions underlying this inquiry are those related to discovery rather than control. Traditional means of bounding the problem are ineffective, since the boundaries between the environment and the participants are open. The threat may affect different groups within the subsystem differently, and these differences, iterated over time, lead to different consequences for the whole system. (pp. 4–5)

The idea of nonlinearity in policy problems of emergency situations poses more than an incidental challenge to policy analysis. As we noted in Chapter 1, the conventional discipline is based on a rational model, which in turn owes its core assumptions to deeply embedded assumptions in what constitutes knowledge and techniques to generate knowledge, as well as how that knowledge is used—essentially as information through communication. "Breakdowns" occur through communication or informational failures. Comfort (2007) argues that in a case like Hurricane Katrina, information about the impending storm and its communication were remarkably accurate; the underlying problem was "cognition" or developing a shared picture of the likely threat among a very heterogeneous group of actors (multiple jurisdictions at multiple levels, with private sector and nonprofit organizations as well). The rational model of decision-making assumes linearity—reasoning from information to decisions. In emergencies, whether floods or fires, that process is too slow. "Emergency managers using cognition do not review the entire set of rules of operation for the system but rather scan the margins for discrepancies or malfunctions. It is the discrepancy between what they view as normal performance and the change in status of key indicators that alerts them to potential danger"

(Comfort, 2007, 193). Klein, for example, shows that actors involved in providing emergency services (e.g., firefighters, crisis ward nurses) rely on "recognition-primed decisionmaking" that draws rapidly and almost intuitively on analogies of previous experiences (Klein, 1998).

Another strand in this critique of linear reasoning is to base the challenge on new scientific theories that break with Newtonian mechanics and deterministic science. The theories include quantum mechanics, complexity theory, chaos theory, and cognitive science (Morçöl, 2002). The difference is between seeing the world as a clock or as a cloud. A clock has deterministic mechanisms, the system works on the basis of clear causality and connections, and the clock as a whole is stably configured as a clock and nothing else. Imagine a cloud, either of vapour or of thousands of tiny insects. Its boundary is constantly shifting and changing, its shape elongates and contracts, and yet it is still recognizably a cloud. The mechanisms of interaction are much more challenging to explain—there are no pulleys or gears, only what appear to be random interactions of particles or insects that constantly ripple through the system. And yet the system, with all of its disparate elements, manages to maintain an equilibrium, is self-correcting and adaptive.

As Comfort (2006) notes, the "effective mobilization of response to extreme events on a large scale is one of the least understood problems in public management. This process requires the rapid search, exchange and absorption of valid information regarding sudden, damaging events transmitted through a network of organizations that crosses disciplinary, organizational and jurisdictional boundaries" (p. 312). Normal policymaking and normal responses can be organized hierarchically, but in emergencies with high stress, high uncertainty, and multiple actors, hierarchy breaks down very quickly. What is needed instead is dynamic, complex, nonlinear systems of adaptive self-organization. As an example, Comfort (1999, pp. 8–9) has drawn eight key concepts from the scientific literature on complexity and chaos that describes elements of these types of systems. First, the evolution and dynamics of these communities, like all complex systems, depend greatly on initial conditions and characteristics of the system. Even small differences among systems in these initial conditions can have far-reaching consequences. Second, random events occurring outside the system can have great effects on the system itself, and take it into unpredicted directions. Third, these random events are irreversible within the system in the sense that whatever impacts they have become part of the system itself. Comfort's example is how an unexpected earthquake led to revisions in building codes that significantly altered construction in seismic zones in California. Fourth, feedback loops of communication and coordination lead to adaptation by mutual adjustment (our cloud example above, or a school of fish). Fifth, because multiple actors create constraints for action through the need for coordination, centres of energy and influence crop up in these systems (leaders or "strange attractors") that move the system forward. Sixth, this forward motion in a complex system can involve a transition to a new equilibrium of a substantially changed system. Seventh, the behaviour of the system often yields unpredictable results, and, finally, these systems can develop recurring patterns of behaviour in different contexts to achieve similar system-wide goals. Later in this chapter we will examine the implications for policy and in particular for emergency preparedness and response from these ideas.

A final illustration of thinking differently about complex systems and change that casts light on shifts and jumps is the idea of the **tipping point.** Gladwell (2000) argues that the world is full of instances—from fashion to crime rates to drug use—of often abrupt, dramatic, and inexplicable changes. Certain books and clothing styles appear out of nowhere and become social phenomena. Inner-city crime can suddenly leap up, or decline precipitously. These phenomena are equivalent to systems that undergo a sudden transition. Gladwell is focusing on social systems and rapid transitions, and argues that these tipping points are analogous to epidemics and function with similar mechanisms. "Epidemics are a function of the people who transmit infectious agents, the infectious agent itself, and the environment in which the infectious agent is operating. And when an epidemic tips, when it is jolted out of equilibrium, it tips because something has happened, some change has occurred in one (or two or three) of those areas" (pp. 18–19). He somewhat dramatically calls these three agents of change the Law of the Few, the Stickiness Factor, and the Power of Context.

The Law of the Few builds on the simple insight that epidemics typically are spread by just a tiny subset of everyone who gets infected. The most jarring example is of Gaetan Dugas, the Canadian flight attendant who claimed to have had 2500 sexual partners all over North America and who was linked to 40 of the earliest AIDS cases in New York and California. In social dynamics, the idea is that a small number of unique individuals spread the word. Not just any individual, however. Gladwell identifies three types of individuals whose unique gifts make a huge difference in the social distribution of information: connectors, mavens (a Yiddish word that means collectors of knowledge), and salesmen. Connectors are those types of persons with lots of social connections, and moreover, social connections to the right people—others who themselves are influential in their circle. Connectors are people who span various social worlds and who can effectively "market" an idea or a product. Mavens on the other hand are basically information brokers who know a great amount of detail about something, and pass that information along to connectors, who in turn distribute it more widely. Salesmen are another select group of people "with the skills to persuade us when we are unconvinced of what we are hearing" (Gladwell, 2000, p. 70).

If social epidemics depend on the nature of the messenger, they also depend on the nature of the message, or what Gladwell calls the stickiness factor, or how memorable something is, which in turn depends on small cues and small aspects of the message that appeal to people. Finally, the power of context is analogous to the conditions in which a medical epidemic takes place—the same communicable disease in a context of poverty and crowding versus sanitation and space. Gladwell cites the well-known "broken windows" theory of crime contagion (Kelling and Coles, 1996). The idea is that broken windows in a community signal to passersby that no one cares about that community, and soon more windows get broken. All sorts of small disorders like this—graffiti, for example—encourage an epidemic of crime because criminals are encouraged to believe that no one cares enough to challenge their behaviour. The classic illustration of this was the condition of the New York subway system in the mid-1980s—inefficient and overrun by petty crime. A consultant at the time encouraged the city to focus on the lurid graffiti that graced almost every subway car, because it was a visible symbol of the system's decay. The city established cleaning stations and ensured that any car with graffiti was cleaned immediately. It took six years. At the same time, in the face of serious crimes on the subway, the authorities bore down on fare cheating, on the same principle that a small expression (it was estimated there were 170 000 people a day using the system without paying) of disorder sent a clear message that any other criminal act was fine.

In a striking similarity to complexity and chaos theory, the idea of a tipping point at which something changes dramatically and exponentially also argues that small changes in small aspects of initial conditions can have large effects:

> Merely by manipulating the size of the group, we can dramatically improve its receptivity to new ideas. By tinkering with the presentation of information, we can significantly improve its stickiness. Simply by finding and reaching those few special people who hold so much social power, we can shape the course of social epidemics. In the end, Tipping Points are a reaffirmation of the potential for change and the power of intelligent action. (Gladwell, 2000, p. 259)

Tipping points, chaos theory, complexity theory—all seem far removed from practical policymaking. But in fact, they are conceptual schemes and approaches that try in some measure to capture reality in ways superior to a more linear, rationalist, positivist model. What are some of the practical implications of these types of more dynamic models for the way we think about public policy? For one thing, initial conditions make a difference in how systems evolve. Coupled with this is an emphasis on a system of interactions, and not a single problem. Conventional policy analysis, as explained in Chapter 3, begins with problem structuring. Even though we alluded to the fact that problems are complex and that they come in clusters, it is still largely an analysis that focuses on one vector of issues or challenges. And it presumes that one can make an intervention along that vector and change causal relations and thus change outcomes. An example might be an inner-city community-based program to counsel teenagers on sexuality and drugs. A conventional approach would see the "problem" in terms of negative outcomes from unsafe sexual practices and dependency on drugs. Obviously, the analysis would highlight the role of schools and families, but it would target youth themselves as "clients" of the program and seek interventions—probably on a large scale in order to produce results on a large scale. A complex systems approach would look at teenagers within the community context, and at "systems" embedded in teenage groups (peer pressure, social bonding, what is considered "cool") and take that as a point of departure. It might also be sensitive to the fact that the same program might have very different results depending on what community and what groups of youths were being supported—the initial conditions of each system would make a big difference in outcomes. A real-world example is Canada's program on fetal alcohol syndrome and fetal alcohol effects for First Nations. As the program documentation notes, the earlier approaches to this problem tended to focus on individuals who came to be "isolated from their families and communities, and the communities' men, pregnant women, and mothers have been impacted by shame, guilt, and grief" (Health Canada, 2007). Now, people are "beginning to realize that FAS/FAE are community issues that need to be addressed on an individual, family, and community level, utilizing partnerships at the regional and national level."

A second implication is the importance and indeed the inevitability of random events that can shock a system and change its trajectory dramatically. "Planning for the unexpected" is of course difficult to do, but this mindset encourages a mentality of monitoring the environment as well as internal processes regularly. It might also encourage deliberate redundancy in systems that are fragile or whose failure will have far-reaching consequences. Redundant information systems in the financial sector, for example, are routine in order to avoid the possibility of breakdown due to external events. A third implication is that large changes can come from small interventions. This is the insight embedded in the idea of tipping points, but it is a feature as well of other complex systems theories. From a policy point of view, it implies that significant change can be generated from small, focused interventions that take system characteristics seriously. Fourth, in line with the notion that complex systems have internal mechanisms of modest equilibrium, there is an emphasis on feedback loops of communication and information. When a school of fish is observed in motion, it seems almost like a single organism, even while it is made up of hundreds of actors mutually adjusting to the myriad of each other's actions. Complex social systems—from loose coalitions to formal organizations—also require inordinate amounts of communication and information exchange to work. This is a lesson from the implementation literature, of course, but it takes on a new angle in the context of complex systems theory. In traditional implementation thinking, the problem is communication from above down the line, to ensure that the original policy idea unfolds as planned and that everyone is more or less operating in the same framework. From a complex systems perspective, the communication has to be 360 degrees in three dimensions. It is about information moving up as well as sideways and from top to down. It is about information and communication as the loose glue that ties the system together, but also makes it possible to adapt and adjust. In the real world, of course, we increasingly see instances of this kind of complex system behaviour. The 2004 federal election was called the first Blackberry election, after the ubiquitous device that allows anywhere-anytime e-mail and telephone communications. In this case, political parties were able to behave like schools of piranhas, with each member mutually adjusting through immediate communication to everyone else in the school. Barack Obama's presidential campaign took electronic campaigning to an entirely new level.

The final implication is about adaptation. The conventional approach to policy analysis and implementation sees it as a linear unfolding. But bring in randomness, unpredictability, and the influence of small events, and it is likely that at any given point the system (an organization, a political party) will need to respond to shocks and either regroup or transform itself in the light of that external shock. This means adaptation that maintains the integrity of the system in some fashion. This requires communication and, more importantly, system learning. There needs to be a capacity to build on experiences, incorporate them into practice, and embed them into some sort of collective memory. Conventional theory also presumes a fairly flat organization. Learning does not happen as well in systems that are grounded in command-and-control frameworks. Interestingly, Sharkansky assumed that policymaking under adversity would require "power concentration" (Sharkansky, 1986, p. 123). More contemporary complex systems theory argues that what is required in fact for resilience is distributed and shared responsibility so that lessons can be learned quickly and moved through the system. Well-functioning organizations do this all the time; they do not merely monitor, they absorb and try to learn from experiences. This is not as easy as it sounds, and an organization truly devoted to learning and adaptation requires a host of mechanisms to make it work.

Having looked through some theoretical lenses on the issues of emergency and crisis, we can now turn to real-world examples. The next sections address three important areas that fall under the rubric of policymaking under pressure: risk assessment, emergency management, and crisis management.

Risk Assessment

From a policy perspective, **risk** is increasingly an important component about thinking through policy issues and managing policy organizations. This is due in part to the events of 9/11, which sensitized all organizations, private and public, to threats and risks. In this sense, risk is associated with threats to government assets and personnel, and can arise from cataclysmic terrorist acts or simple accidents in the field. A second factor is the rise in insurance costs, which makes risk management more than a matter of taking out a policy; it becomes a matter of actively mitigating or avoiding risks. Finally, the public is less tolerant of even small errors made by private and public organizations, and is more ready to litigate in a climate where courts are prepared to hand out increasingly punitive damages.

The federal government has had a **risk management** policy in place since 2001. Box 8.1 provides a flavour of what is required by departments and agencies. The policy states

> The importance of risk management has been growing steadily during the last several years. There is increasing awareness and expectation in Canada and abroad of the need to manage risks, rather than leaving them solely to insurance.

BOX 8.1 — GOVERNMENT OF CANADA RISK MANAGEMENT POLICY

POLICY REQUIREMENTS

IDENTIFICATION

1. Departments must identify the potential perils, factors and types of risk to which their assets, program activities and interests are exposed.

MINIMIZATION

2. Departments must analyze and assess the risks identified, and design and implement cost-effective risk prevention, reduction or avoidance control measures.

3. Departments must:
   (a) select underwriting options;
   (b) self-underwrite the risks to which the government alone is exposed and over which it generally has control, and provide for and absorb, through their annual appropriations, any cost that may arise from self-underwriting;

(c) ensure that contractors do not procure insurance on risks that are clearly the responsibility of the government, and that contractors are not indemnified by the government against the risks to which only the contractors are exposed.

4. Departments must plan and budget for containment, compensation, restoration and disaster recovery.

CONTAINMENT

5. Departments must activate emergency organizations, systems, and contingency plans, and initiate recovery measures.

COMPENSATION, RESTORATION AND RECOVERY

6. Departments must:
   (a) investigate incidents to determine their causes;
   (b) assess the extent and value of damages and determine potential legal liability; and
   (c) make incident reports.

7. Departments must settle and pay claims by or against the Crown and against its servants in an adequate and timely manner, and generally refer cases involving legal proceedings, and claims associated with a contract, to the Department of Justice.

8. Departments must repair or replace damaged assets and operating systems to return operations to normal as soon as possible.

9. Departments must:
   (a) report each fiscal year in the Public Accounts: all payments of claims against the Crown; all ex gratia payments; court awards; and all losses of $1,000 or more including accidental destruction of, damage to, or theft of, assets that would normally be covered by insurance had insurance existed;
   (b) report to the appropriate law enforcement agencies losses over $1,000 which are due to suspected illegal activity; and
   (c) maintain their own data-base as part of the feedback system of management information.

10. Departments must establish new or improved measures to prevent the recurrence of incidents, and to recover from disasters.

SOURCE: Treasury Board of Canada. (2001). *Risk management policy.* Retrieved March 31, 2008, from http://www.tbs-sct.gc.ca/pubs_pol/dcgpubs/RiskManagement/riskmanagpol1_e.asp#_Toc457619040.

The risk environment has been evolving rapidly, as advancing technological and social developments bring forth new or hitherto dormant risks associated with such phenomena as hijacking, hazardous materials, pollution, electronic data, and exposure to legal and political liability. The government has an obligation to be fully aware of the state of the art in risk management, and to prevent losses and unnecessary expenditures. (Treasury Board of Canada, 2001a)

Risk, of course, is to some large extent a subjective assessment at both the individual and the cultural level. Some people see no risks in activities that make others quail. Societies define risk differently as well. For example, there is a case to be made that contemporary industrial societies have elevated "safety" to almost a religious level (Beck, 1992, 1999; Furedi, 2002). On almost any conceivable measure, from life expectancy to the likelihood of suffering accidents, people generally today (in developed countries, to be sure) are safer than ever before. Paradoxically, that very condition of relative safety may inflate people's expectations about how safe things should be, and hence lower their tolerance to risk. Nonetheless, there are internationally recognized definitions of risk. The International Organization for Standards defines risk as a "combination of the probability of an event and its consequences." The Canadian Standards Association defines risk as "the chance of injury or loss as defined as a measure of the probability and severity of an adverse effect to health, property, the environment or other things of value." These and a myriad of other definitions highlight two key points about risk: chance or probability, and severity of consequences. This is exactly the logic behind auto insurance. Companies calibrate their insurance premiums to age, sex, type of car, driving environment, and use. These are all measure of probability. Young male drivers of sports cars in urban centres who will use their cars a lot are a greater risk (i.e., the probability of a car accident is higher) than middle-aged, rural drivers who go out only to church on Sunday in the family sedan. The other dimension is the severity of the consequence. If the consequence, usually defined in negative terms (there can be outcomes of risk that are positive: "take a chance on love") is slight, even if the probability is high, then the risk factor would be considered negligible. However, a low probability of a severe consequence (a nuclear plant explosion) can give one pause, simply because the result might be so awful. In normal language, the concept of risk is associated with probabilities that negatively valued events or outcomes will occur. We don't think it a "risk" to possibly encounter an old dear friend on the street; it is more of a chance or an opportunity. However, it makes perfect sense to view meeting up with someone you dislike as a "risk." The other common language feature of risk is that it should be a probability of not just something severe happening, but something severe that is relevant to the core mission of the risk-assessing organization. From a policy point of view, this means assessing risks that would impede program development and delivery, and risks that would challenge the organizational mission as a whole.

What does risk management entail? Clearly, it requires the assessment of risk in the first instance, and developing strategies to deal with the risk. Assessing risk is part and parcel of developing a risk profile for the organization (Treasury Board of Canada, 2001b). The first step in that process is conducting an internal and external **environmental scan**. The internal risk factors typically are organizational: personnel, resources, information technology, and so on. A standard way of assessing the external environment is in terms of the PEST schema (also known as the STEP schema): political (federal–provincial relations, turf wars with other agencies, other governments, international bodies, international and domestic social movements, and stakeholders that may take adverse positions to policy); economic (local and national markets, price fluctuations, currency fluctuations, labour force movements, competition in one's target markets); social (demographic trends, current social debates and fashions); and technological (new technologies on the horizon and how they will be integrated into operations, scientific discoveries, new uses for old technologies, adequacy of internal technologies in the face of changing external technological environment). The next step is the consideration of the types and nature of risk facing the organization:

The environmental scan increases the organization's awareness of the key characteristics and attributes of the risks it faces. These include

- *Type of risk*: technological, financial, human resources (capacity, intellectual property), health, safety;
- *Source of risk*: external (political, economic, natural disasters); internal (reputation, security, knowledge management, information for decision making);
- *What is at risk*: area of impact/type of exposure (people, reputation, program results, matériel, real property); and
- *Level of ability to control the risk*: high (operational); moderate (reputation); low (natural disasters). (Treasury Board of Canada, 2001b)

As we noted earlier, risk is to some extent in the eye of the beholder. It is linked to the notion of probability, but distinct from it nonetheless. For example, it might be possible to mathematically calculate the probability of some accident at 80 percent. Some would see that figure and consider it too high. Others—less "risk averse"—would look at it and consider the 20 percent probability of it not occurring as being quite comforting.

Security and stock markets work in exactly the same way, offering products with different risks attached that appeal to different segments of the market. This is to underline the point that an organization's risk profile is only the classification of the types and probabilities of risks it faces. It is not an assessment of how seriously to take those risks. This is a more difficult process, and ultimately depends on the judgment of management, based in turn on the risk aversion of key stakeholders. For private firms this is a matter of checking with stakeholders; for public organizations it is trickier since the potential stakeholder base is quite large, and in any event, the organization is supposed to be motivated by the public interest (Pal and Maxwell, 2004).

Public organizations face a special problem in developing risk profiles because of the risk aversion of most clients. Most public services are monopoly services not provided in the same degree in the private sector—education, health, and the myriad of social services are prime examples. With few or no alternatives, clients of these services demonstrate a strong negativity bias—the risk of any change or withdrawal of benefit is considered very serious. This is a standard problem that all democratic governments face when they inflict pain or losses on their citizens (Pal and Weaver, 2003). On the other hand, risk analysis can become a smokescreen for bad policy. If there is a "risk," for example, that the media will learn about a grants and contributions scheme that is not running well, and that risk is "managed"—the net effect in terms of democracy is probably negative. A risk that truth will be told, that abuses will be exposed, that malfeasance might see the light of day—these are indeed risks, but "managing" them so they do not cause problems is the antithesis of good public service. Managing risk always has to be put in the broader context of ethical government behaviour. A risk by definition is the probability of bad news—but what counts as bad has to be measured against the yardstick of ethics.

Emergency Management

Managing emergencies might at first blush appear to be a contradiction. In times of emergency or disaster, public (and it has to be admitted, private) authorities are put to the ultimate test. The public interest always appears abstract and distant when discussed in terms of broad policy or hypotheticals. However, when a bridge crumples, when forest fires rage, when buildings collapse, terrorists strike, or financial markets collapse, there is a clear and present imperative for governments to act. They need to show that in some way they were prepared, that they can deal with the emergency, and that they will manage the aftermath.

Emergency management has been defined as the "process of developing and implementing policies and programs to avoid and cope with the risks to people and property from natural and man-made hazards" (Cigler, 1988, p. 5). Obviously, there has been a response function in government as long as government has been around—to fires, medical services, disaster relief, and crime. But the field of emergency management has emerged only in the last twenty years as a distinct area of public administration. It has taken on even greater importance since 9/11 and subsequent terrorist attacks in Madrid and London. The possibility of deliberate and calamitous damage to life and property has increased exponentially in the last few years. Emergency and crisis are now much more closely aligned—something that at one time might have been a mere emergency, if the result of a terrorist attack—could become a crisis that challenges the entire political and economic system. Yet the issues are similar to those discussed above—shared risk, uncertainty, response under conditions of incomplete knowledge with severe time pressures. An emergency by definition is something that happens unexpectedly, and requires immediate response. The question is how to frame that response, and how to prepare.

There have been several challenges to emergency management in the past. One is that most emergencies conventionally occur "on the ground"—that is, they require a response from local governments and communities. This places a huge burden on levels of government that are not usually well endowed with funds and personnel. The second traditional problem is that many emergencies are low-probability events. In the normal course of things, people try to avoid the hazards that lead to emergencies. However, while the probability is low, the consequences can be severe. So there is a compulsion on the part of governments to prepare for possible emergencies, but not much of a public constituency pushing for that response or lobbying for it. There is also a psychological bias to underestimate broadly based risk, and a commensurate reluctance to pay the taxes required to deal with it. This has changed completely since 9/11. There is a much heightened sense of the possibilities of deliberate danger, and the pummelling that Canada and other countries have received through emergencies such as Mad Cow and SARS (see Box 8.2 and Box 8.3 on pages 369 and 376) has driven home the importance of preparation and the importance of having the capacity to deal with threats.

The standard framework for emergency management has four phases or elements (see Figure 8.2 on page 368). The first is **mitigation.** This includes some of the steps discussed above under the heading of Risk Assessment. A government agency has to scan its internal procedures and its external environment, assess the probabilities of disaster, and take steps

Figure 8.2 The Process of Crisis and Emergency Management

SOURCE: Canadian Centre for Management Development. (2004). *Crisis and Emergency Management: A guide for managers of the public service of Canada*. Table 2 at p. 9. Retrieved April 2, 2008, from http://www.csps-efpc.gc.ca/Research/publications/pdfs/crisis_e.pdf.

to mitigate or reduce those probabilities. The reason this is part of a management framework is that risk assessment and mitigation is an ongoing process that should be woven into daily organizational practices. The second step or phase is preparedness. Whereas mitigation involves the active attempt to prevent or avoid disasters, preparedness is about being ready for the inevitable but unpredictable accidents that will occur. This

BOX 8.2

STATE AND LOCAL HEALTH OFFICIAL EPIDEMIC SARS CHECKLIST

ARE YOU AND YOUR JURISDICTION READY FOR EPIDEMIC SEVERE ACUTE RESPIRATORY SYNDROME (SARS)?

This checklist, developed in collaboration with the Centers for Disease Control and Prevention, has been modeled on a previous Association of State and Territorial Health Officials (ASTHO) checklist for pandemic influenza preparedness (*Preparedness Planning for State Health Officials: Nature's Terrorist Attack—Pandemic Influenza* www.astho.org/pubs/PandemicInfluenza.pdf). Preparations made to respond to other public health emergencies, including bioterror events, will generally be applicable to epidemic SARS planning.

The items on this checklist are intended for use by health officers at all levels—state, regional, district and local. The division of responsibilities between state and local levels varies among states, and often within states, according to the size of the population served by local health agencies. The items on this checklist should be interpreted in the context of the responsibilities of your public health agency and the division of responsibilities within your community, regardless of level of government. For some local public health agencies, for example, the capabilities needed for certain items may be available from a state health department but are not present locally.

Every locality should plan for the possibility of a local public health crisis such as widespread SARS-CoV transmission, in which help from other public health agencies is not available because they are facing similar crises. At the same time, there are advantages to coordinating response plans on a regional and statewide basis, partly so that isolation and quarantine procedures are applied uniformly and equitably.

SARS would be considered to be widespread in the United States if and when cases occur throughout the nation, in multiple locations, in persons without known epidemiologic links to places with community transmission of SARS-CoV or to known SARS cases. Local, district, and state public health agencies should be prepared to address all of the following items when the disease is present

BOX 8.2 (continued)

elsewhere in the world and to implement those preparations when widespread disease occurs in the United States.

LEGAL AND POLICY ISSUES

❑ 1. My jurisdiction has a draft or formally adopted epidemic SARS plan.

❑ 2. Agreements have been obtained with my state's healthcare insurers, Medicaid program, and healthcare product and service providers for cooperation with public health recommendations during an epidemic.

❑ 3. I have reviewed with legal counsel my jurisdiction's laws and procedures on quarantine, isolation, closing premises and suspending public meetings and know how to implement them to help control an epidemic.

❑ 4. I am familiar with my state's medical volunteer licensure, liability, and compensation laws for in-state, out-of-state, returning retired, and non-medical volunteers.

❑ 5. I know whether my state allows hospitals and other licensed healthcare institutions to use temporary facilities for provision of medical care in the event of a public health emergency.

❑ 6. My jurisdiction's epidemic plan addresses Worker's Compensation and Unemployment Compensation issues related to health care and other workers missing work because of isolation or quarantine.

❑ 7. I have identified any deficiencies in my jurisdiction's laws and procedures on quarantine, isolation and related capacities and initiated steps to have those deficiencies corrected.

❑ 8. I know what provisions are in place, if any, for compensation of persons with economic or health injury resulting from needed SARS control measures and for limitation of liability of health care providers and agencies.

AUTHORITY

❑ 9. My state has an executive SARS epidemic planning committee that oversees the planning process, in cooperation with local health agencies.

❑ 10. My state has identified the authority responsible for declaration of a public health emergency and for officially activating our plan during a SARS epidemic.

❑ 11. My jurisdiction has identified key stakeholders responsible for development and implementation of specific components of the SARS epidemic plan, including enforcement of isolation, quarantine, and closure and decontamination of premises.

❑ 12. My jurisdiction's elected officials, appointed officials, and other agency heads know their respective responsibilities in the event of an epidemic.

❑ 13. My jurisdiction has a command system in place (e.g., the Incident Command System) to govern roles and responsibilities during a multi-agency, multi-jurisdictional event.

❑ 14. I am familiar with the controlling authority over intrastate and interstate modes of transportation, should these need to be curtailed during an epidemic (e.g., airplanes, trains, ships, highways).

❑ 15. My staff has relationships with health authorities of adjoining counties or states and with federal agencies to ensure effective communication during a public health emergency.

❑ 16. My jurisdiction has identified an overall authority in charge of coordinating different medical personnel groups during an epidemic.

❑ 17. I know personally the key individuals from the state and local authorities who will assist in maintaining public order and enforcing control measures, if needed, during an epidemic.

❑ 18. I am familiar with the procedure for enlisting the National Guard's assistance during a public health emergency.

SURGE CAPACITY

❑ 19. I know how to access current recommendations on treatment of cases and prevention of transmission in the hospital, long-term care and home care settings.

❑ 20. My jurisdiction's emergency response planning has involved health care product and service providers to determine how to best prevent and control disease spread and manage the health care of the population during an epidemic.

BOX 8.2 (continued)

☐ 21. I am familiar with the required protocol for securing needed emergency healthcare services and supplies during a public health emergency.

☐ 22. My jurisdiction has identified ways to augment medical, nursing, and other health care staffing to maintain appropriate standards of care during an epidemic.

☐ 23. My jurisdiction has identified ways to augment public health laboratory, epidemiology and disease control staffing to meet emergency needs and in the event public health workers are affected by an epidemic.

☐ 24. My jurisdiction has a process to recruit and train medical volunteers for provision of care and vaccine administration during a public health emergency.

☐ 25. My jurisdiction has identified alternate facilities where overflow cases from hospitals and well persons needing quarantine away from home can be cared for and has developed processes with Emergency Medical Services to assess, communicate, and direct patients to available beds.

☐ 26. My jurisdiction has identified facilities for outpatient and inpatient care of children with SARS and their families.

☐ 27. My jurisdiction's epidemic plan addresses the mechanics of how isolation and quarantine will be carried out, such as providing support services for people who are isolated or quarantined to their homes or temporary infirmary facilities and protection for workers providing these services.

☐ 28. My jurisdiction has a plan for ensuring that appropriate personal protective equipment, including N-95 or higher level respirators, is made available for persons whose job requires exposure to people with SARS, and that needed training and fit-testing are provided.

☐ 29. My jurisdiction has a plan for dealing with mass mortality, including transportation and burial of bodies.

☐ 30. My jurisdiction has a plan for providing mental health services to mitigate the impact of a SARS epidemic.

COMMUNICATIONS AND EDUCATION

☐ 31. I have conveyed the importance of epidemic preparedness, and its overlap with bioterrorism preparedness, to my jurisdiction's chief executive and to other state and local law and policy makers.

☐ 32. I know personally the key individuals from public health agencies, the medical community, and the political community with whom I will need to communicate during an epidemic.

☐ 33. My jurisdiction has begun educating the public on epidemic SARS to instill acceptance of the epidemic response (including quarantine and isolation) and to optimize public assistance during an epidemic.

☐ 34. My jurisdiction has opened a regular channel of communication and begun educating health care providers (including first responders) and their organizations and unions on epidemic SARS (including diagnosis, treatment, and management of cases and contacts to prevent transmission).

☐ 35. My jurisdiction has opened a regular channel of communication and begun educating chief executive officers of health care organizations on epidemic SARS (including management of patients in health care settings, health care worker protection, physical facility needs, voluntary or forced furloughs of exposed workers, etc.).

☐ 36. My jurisdiction has established a multi-component communications network and plan for sharing of timely and accurate information among public health and other officials, medical providers, first responders, the media and the general public.

☐ 37. My jurisdiction has begun identifying and planning to produce and provide education and information materials for media, providers, the public, and occupational groups whose duties may expose them to SARS, in appropriate languages and in forms suitable for limited literacy populations.

☐ 38. Whoever is selected as the primary public spokesperson for my jurisdiction during an epidemic is ready to clearly and consistently answer the following types of questions:

☐ How is the SARS-associated coronavirus (SARS-CoV) transmitted?

☐ How long are people infectious after they have SARS?

☐ What is isolation? What is quarantine?

☐ What is the justification for isolation of cases and quarantine of contacts?

BOX 8.2 (continued)

❑ What is the legal authority for isolation of cases and quarantine of contacts?

❑ What is the difference between a probable and a suspected SARS case?

❑ Who should be tested for the SARS-associated coronavirus?

❑ What can members of the public do to protect themselves?

❑ In the event a vaccine or antiviral treatment become available, what specific priority groups might be vaccinated or treated first?

❑ 39. My jurisdiction has identified the most effective media to get messages out to the public during an epidemic (e.g., TV, radio, print media, internet, Web sites, hotlines).

❑ 40. My jurisdiction has planned how to coordinate state, local, and federal public messages and ensure they are consistent and timely.

LABORATORY AND SURVEILLANCE

❑ 41. In the event of a SARS epidemic, I will have available daily counts of key community health indicators, such as numbers of emergency department visits, hospital admissions, deaths, available hospital beds and staff, facility closings, numbers of contacts being traced and numbers under quarantine.

❑ 42. The public health laboratory that serves my jurisdiction can test for the SARS-associated coronavirus by serology and/or PCR.

❑ 43. My state has identified those labs that can test for the SARS-associated coronavirus.

❑ 44. The public health laboratory that serves my jurisdiction has linked to clinical laboratories and provided training on the use of SARS tests, biosafety, specimen collection, packing and shipping, and rule-out testing.

❑ 45. Public health laboratories in my state have computerized record-keeping to help with data transmission, tracking, reporting of results to patients and facilities, and analysis during an epidemic.

□ 46. My jurisdiction has determined how to assess and document the spread and impact of disease throughout the population, including special populations at risk (such as health care workers and first responders), during a SARS epidemic, including enhancements to routine surveillance.

□ 47. My jurisdiction has computerized record-keeping for cases, suspected cases, contacts, and persons under public health isolation or quarantine orders to help with data transmission, tracking and analysis during an epidemic.

□ 48. My jurisdiction's epidemiology staff, in cooperation with other public health agencies, has the capacity to investigate clusters of SARS cases, to determine how disease is being transmitted, to trace and monitor contacts, to implement and monitor quarantine measures, and to determine whether control measures are working.

□ 49. My jurisdiction has plans for educating health care providers about recognition and reporting of SARS, about the current case definition, and about sources of current information on all aspects of SARS.

PREPAREDNESS IN OTHER AGENCIES

□ 50. The emergency response system is ready to deal with epidemic SARS as called for in an all-hazards or epidemic plan.

□ 51. My jurisdiction has carried out a community-wide epidemic SARS table-top or field exercise, to train on and evaluate its epidemic plan.

□ 52. Community partners such as hospitals, EMS services, law enforcement agencies, health care practitioners, environmental hygiene/remediation services, news media, schools, and colleges know what part they are expected to play during an epidemic and are prepared to do so.

□ 53. The law enforcement and court system in this jurisdiction are prepared to enforce isolation and quarantine orders and to promptly adjudicate appeals to public health orders, as provided by statute.

SOURCE: Centers for Disease Control and Prevention. (2004). *Public Health guidance for community-level preparedness and response to severe acute respiratory syndrome (SARS) Version 2 Supplement A: Command and control, Appendix A1, State and local health official epidemic SARS checklist.* Retrieved March 28, 2008 from http://www.cdc.gov/ncidod/sars/guidance/A/app1.htm

BOX 8.3   MAD COW IN CANADA

In August 2006, the Canadian Food Inspection Agency, the federal regulator responsible for monitoring the safety of Canadian cattle, confirmed a case of mad cow disease in an older cow in Alberta. It was the fifth case in 2006 and the eighth since 2003. The agency said locating the cow shows the success of its monitoring program. Brad Wildeman, vice-president of the Canadian Cattlemen's Association, took the same line. More infected animals have been found because of the extent of the testing, he said. "We probably have the most aggressive, safest beef supply of any country in the world."

For years, Canada had been virtually free of mad cow disease. But in May 2003, veterinary officials in Alberta confirmed that a sick cow sent to a slaughterhouse in January of that year had been inspected, found to be substandard, and removed so that it would not end up as food for humans or other animals. The carcass was, however, sent to a processing plant for rendering into oils. Its head was kept for testing. Samples were sent to the world testing laboratories in the U.K., which confirmed the case of mad cow.

"What is important is that the system worked," said Shirley McClellan, Alberta's agriculture minister at the time. "We have a very thorough and respected inspection system." She was insistent to remind the public that the disease is not contagious within a herd.

But McClellan's assurances didn't stop the U.S., Japan, South Korea, Australia and other countries from imposing temporary import bans of Canadian beef.

Several ranches in Alberta, B.C. and Saskatchewan were quarantined as a precaution, including the infected cow's home ranch.

In an investigation into the source of the infection, 1,400 cows were slaughtered and tested for the disease. No other cows were found to have BSE until late December, 2004.

Western premiers demanded $360 million compensation from the federal government for losses to the beef industry because of the mad cow scare. Ottawa would later offer $190 million.

Over the summer of 2003, cattle ranchers held barbeques across Canada to help promote Canadian beef.

In August, the U.S. reopened its borders to some Canadian beef, but the border was still closed to live cattle. By this time, a cow that would have normally sold for $1,300 was selling for $15. Canadian beef producers asked Ottawa to approve a mass slaughter of 620,000 cattle to reduce the size of the herd and prevent further damage to the industry.

In October, CBC News reported that the border would reopen to live cattle in December 2003. But on Dec. 23, 2003, the U.S. announced that it had discovered its first apparent case of BSE in a cow in Washington state.

Several countries banned beef from the U.S. soon after the announcement, but Canada restricted imports only on some products made from cattle and other ruminants. It still allowed the import of cattle destined for immediate slaughter, boneless beef from cattle under 30 months of age and dairy products.

DNA evidence later revealed that the cow was born in Canada, and the U.S. kept its border shut to live Canadian cattle.

It took a little more than a year for the United States to announce that it would reopen its border to live Canadian cattle younger than 30 months.

On Dec. 29, 2004, The USDA announced that it recognized Canada as a "minimal-risk region" for BSE and imports of young Canadian cattle would resume March 7, 2005.

The new classification means the U.S. will not again close its borders to Canadian beef unless there are two or more cases of BSE per one million cattle older than 24 months of age in each of four consecutive years. Simply put, Canada can have up to 11 cases of BSE and still be considered a safe country for cattle exports.

The move came less than a month after U.S. President George W. Bush made his first official visit to Canada and said the process for reopening the border was underway.

However, five days before the ban was to be lifted, a U.S. judge granted a temporary injunction to stop the reopening of the border. The ban came at the request of a group of American ranchers called R-CALF, who filed a lawsuit saying reopening the border would cause irreparable damage to the U.S. beef market.

In June 2005, the U.S. Department of Agriculture confirmed the country's second known case of BSE, in a Texas-born cow.

And on July 14, 2005, a three-judge panel of the U.S. Ninth Circuit Court of Appeals overturned a temporary injunction that banned importation of Canadian cattle. U.S. Agriculture Secretary Mike Johanns announced that day that the U.S. border was "immediately" open to live Canadian cattle.

THE BRITISH CONNECTION

Previously, Canada had only one case of a cow infected with BSE. The animal, reported on a farm near Red Deer, Alta., in December

BOX 8.3 (continued)

of 1993, was imported from Britain. Agriculture Canada opted to destroy the animal and its five herd mates.

Mexico, one of the largest importers of Canadian beef at the time, temporarily banned imports of Canadian cattle after the incident. The United States, another major consumer of Canadian beef, sent observers to Canada to see how the incident was handled.

As a result, and because of the rumours of possible human health implications circulating in Britain, the Ministry of Agriculture decided to destroy any animal imported from Britain between 1982 and 1990, the year a ban was placed on British beef imports to Canada. This slaughter also included the offspring of any of those animals.

All told, 363 animals were destroyed and their owners compensated. Some said the destruction was unnecessary, especially the farmers whose cattle were killed, but the ministry said it was better to err on the side of caution after seeing what was happening in Britain. As of January 2005, 148 Britons had died of CJD and five others were infected but still living.

During the summer of 1995, the disease surfaced again. The Canadian Red Cross Society revealed two of its donors had died of Creutzfeldt-Jakob disease, CJD. Two years later, concern over blood was raised again after a man was found to be a carrier of a gene linked to a hereditary form of CJD.

In August 2002, doctors confirmed a man in Saskatchewan died from new variant CJD—the human counterpart to mad cow disease. He had spent some time in the United Kingdom and it appeared he acquired the disease while he was there, doctors said.

The man had an endoscopic examination before he died and that equipment was then used on other patients. However, because of disinfection and cleaning procedures, the risk of cross contamination is minute. Public health officials phoned patients who had received examinations with the endoscope to inform them.

It's still not known if the disease can be transmitted through blood products.

In 1996, the Canadian government suspended imports of British beef embryos and semen. Agriculture Canada also began a review of the practice of using meat meal and bone meal as a protein source in beef cattle feed. In 1997, changes designed to keep animal parts out of animal feeds were implemented. Among them, Ottawa made it illegal to give beef herds products made from rendered cattle. However, rendered cattle could be used in feed for pigs and poultry.

A month after Canada's first case of BSE, a panel of experts recommended that the parts of the cow that can pass on BSE, such as the brain and spine should be kept out of all animal feed. That's policy in most European countries.

It's a recommendation that has met stiff resistance in the beef industry. Including rendered cattle parts in feed means disposing of heads and intestines can make money for cattle farmers instead of costing them money.

Meanwhile, documents obtained by CBC News through the Access to Information Act show that in the weeks after that first case of BSE, cattle were allowed to eat feed meant for chicken and pigs. Some of the feed was likely made from the original diseased cow.

The federal agriculture minister at the time, Andy Mitchell, said the government is moving to ban the use of cattle remains in all feed. The regulations were due to be in place by the middle of 2005.

In fact, the CFIA got the right in July 2005 to make violators of its rules pay penalties; before that, it had been limited to warnings, seizure of products that broke the rules, suspension or cancellation of permits and prosecutions.

In June 2006, the agency said that effective July 2007, it "is banning cattle tissues capable of transmitting bovine spongiform encephalopathy from all animal feeds, pet foods and fertilizers."

But small establishments will get additional time to comply. The government said it had allocated $80 million to help the industry implement the new rules.

QUICK FACTS

- Canada has close to 13.5 million cows and calves. About 5.7 million (or 42 per cent) are in Alberta.
- Canada's total beef exports amount to $2.2 billion annually, and have risen sharply in recent years. Since 1991, beef exports have risen from 100,000 tonnes to about 500,000 tonnes. Growth in exports has been greatest to Japan, South Korea and Mexico. Alberta's share of total beef exports is 39 per cent (worth about $860 million a year).

SOURCE: CBC News (August 24, 2006). *Mad Cow in Canada: The science and the story.* Retrieved March 29, 2008, from http://www.cbc.ca/news/background/madcow/.

requires planning, and indeed the establishment of some sort of emergency response plan that outlines who is in charge, what kind of coordination will take place, and the distribution of resources and responses. Part of being prepared is simulating an actual emergency and going through the steps. This can sometimes seem silly to the public at large, but trained emergency professionals know that an effective response to disaster depends on calm threat assessment and reaction. It helps if people have gone through something similar before. The third step or phase is response—what one does when the emergency actually occurs. In part this involves following the plans made during the preparation phase, but every situation is unique. Moreover, there has to be an element of innovation and creativity in responding to a particular situation, so plans need to be supple enough that they provide guidance without tying people to the specifics. The final phase is recovery—reviewing what happened, how well the response went, and what lessons there are to be learned for the next event.

There is a temptation to think of emergency response in terms of elaborate plans and clear command and control organization. Obviously plans are important, as are drills and preparation. Some central authority and clear lines of responsibility are important as well. But the nature of disaster and emergency ultimately requires supple responses by interacting systems: local governments, communities, provinces, national authorities, and sometimes even international actors. As discussed in the theoretical section of this chapter, disaster and emergency response needs to be thought of in terms of complex systems made up of multiple actors who in the end do not have ultimate authority over anyone else. Mobilizing a complex system to respond to disaster involves an enormous amount of information processing and communication. Comfort, in discussing different models of these types of networks, notes that

> . . . the objective is to critique actual performance against a prior model of organizational structure in order to improve performance in a continuous process of collective learning. The decision makers use their experience to identify gaps in the organizational system model in order to correct performance for the next event. The logic of these approaches is to identify what the organization does not know in changing environments or new situations and to devise better means of coping with unknown conditions. Acknowledgment of error is not a negative action but rather serves as the basis for learning and contributes to improved future performance. The major resource in each of these models is the capacity of individuals to learn and to transmit that knowledge to other participants in the system. Each approach acknowledges the need to design organizational structures and processes

that facilitate individual and organizational learning as well as to identify and correct potential errors on a timely basis. (Comfort, 2005, p. 347)

Since 9/11, organizing for emergency response to security threats has become a priority for both Canada and the United States. Shortly after the terrorist attacks, President Bush reorganized his administration by forming the Department of Homeland Security (DHS) to coordinate a host of functions that previously were scattered through the federal government. The DHS is massive; it employs 208 000 people throughout the country from twenty-two former government agencies such as the Immigration and Naturalization Service, the Federal Emergency Management Agency (FEMA), the Secret Service, and the Coast Guard. DHS is organized into three directorates, four offices, and a host of agencies. The Directorates and Offices comprise: The Directorate for National Protection and Programs; The Directorate for Science and Technology; The Directorate for Management; The Office of Policy; The Office of Health Affairs; The Office of Intelligence and Analysis; and The Office of Operations Coordination. The DHS is responsible for a bewildering array of security initiatives, of which the following is just a sample:

- Fencing the US [Mexico] border, with the ambition of eventually creating 670 miles of fencing by the end of 2008.

- Implementation in January 2008 of the Western Hemisphere Travel Initiative requiring secure documents (passports or special documents) for all air travelers entering the United States.

- US Immigration and Customs Enforcement removed about 240 000 illegal aliens and made 850 arrests in 2007.

- A Comprehensive Radiation Detection program that deploys over 1000 radiation detection devices at land and sea ports of entry. 100 percent of cargo containers crossing the southern border are scanned for radiation.

- Establishment of the Computer Emergency Readiness Team, or US-CERT, providing a 24-hour watch center, which in 2007 issued over 200 alerts on cyber security vulnerabilities or incidents. (Department of Homeland Security, 2007)

These are only a few examples, but they illustrate the scope and depth of the American concerns with terror. They also demonstrate the point that emergency response in most instances happens on the ground where the emergency is first declared. The federal government can do a lot of coordination and interoperability of communications equipment, but ultimately the first line of response to any emergency is at the community level and among businesses and firms. This means that the DHS is interacting with and coordinating a vast network of governmental and nongovernmental actors to effectively deal with terrorist threats. The sad irony is that the protection of liberty and democratic government requires a highly centralized and some would say intrusive agency.

Canada has been compelled to match American efforts in emergency preparedness and security. The constant flow of trade and travel between the two countries made it imperative that Canada demonstrate to the United States that it too would take terrorist threats seriously, even though the likelihood of a terrorist attack in Canada is remote. In December 2003 a new department was created to integrate all aspects of emergency preparedness and wider threats, Public Safety and Emergency Preparedness, headed then by the deputy prime minister to highlight its importance. It now is named Public Safety Canada, and is responsible for emergency management (which includes critical infrastructure protection, cyber security, disaster mitigation, and emergency preparedness), national security, crime prevention, law enforcement, and corrections policy. While Public Safety Canada is the lead department for public safety, it works closely with five agencies: Canada Border Services Agency; Canadian Security Intelligence Service; Correctional Service of Canada; National Parole Board; and Royal Canadian Mounted Police) and three review bodies (Commission for Public Complaints against the RCMP; Office of the Correctional Investigator; and RCMP External Review Committee). They are united in a single portfolio and report to the same minister. Together, these agencies have an annual budget of $6 billion and more than 52 000 employees working in every part of the country (Public Safety Canada, 2007).

As well, in May 2004, the federal government issued its first comprehensive statement on national security entitled *Securing an Open Society*. The document is revealing in several ways. First, the fact that it represented Canada's first comprehensive policy statement on security suggests both the new priority that security issues have and the heightened threat environment in which Canada finds itself. Second, threats that at one time were parcelled out among different departments and agencies are now coordinated under one umbrella—security or safety. This includes natural disasters and emergencies, transportation, intelligence, public health, and border security. The policy promised to put more money into security and intelligence gathering, and proposed to create a new parliamentary committee on National Security as well as a Government Operations Centre to coordinate key national players in the event of national emergencies. It also proposed the creation of a national Public Health Agency and a Chief Public Health Officer for Canada. Finally, it pledged to create an external advisory body on National Security (Privy Council Office, 2004). All of these promises were kept (Government of Canada, 2005).

Canada's counterterrorism activities are governed by the National Counter-Terrorism policy, which was significantly updated in 2001 with the passage of the Anti-Terrorism Act in the wake of the 9/11 attacks (the act was passed December 2001). It contained amendments to the Criminal Code, the Official Secrets Act, the Canada Evidence Act, and the Proceeds of Crime (Money Laundering) Act, all intended to deal with terrorist acts as well as activities (i.e., raising money) in support of terrorism. With the act, it became a criminal offence to knowingly collect or provide funds to carry out terrorist activities, be a member of a terrorist group or facilitate its activities, or knowingly harbour or conceal a terrorist. It also increased police investigatory powers. A key element of the legislation, of course, is the definition of a terrorist group or entity. The law allows the authorities to maintain a public "list of entities" (a person, group, trust, partnership or fund, or an unincorporated association or organization) if there are reasonable grounds that that entity "has knowingly carried out, attempted to carry out, participated in or facilitated a terrorist activity; or is knowingly acting on behalf of, at the direction of or in association with an entity that has knowingly carried out, attempted to carry out, participated in or facilitated a terrorist activity." The listing is a public statement that the government believes that entity to be involved in terrorist activities, and it also freezes the entity's assets. As of September 2007, the list consisted of forty entities. The first ten entities on the list are described in Box 8.4 on page 384.

Emergency preparedness and counterterrorism are now part of a single continuum of policy responses, since of course the great fear now is that terrorist groups will induce emergencies as part of their campaigns. The Madrid subway bombings in March 2004, for instance, were likely an Al-Qaeda attack that resulted in 201 dead and 1500 injured. A year later, the London tube bombings occurred, killing fifty-five people and injuring 700. The 2003 blackout in Ontario and the northeastern United States could just as easily have been caused by a terrorist attack, and would have had the same effect of paralyzing a good part of the continent. Natural disasters still occur, of course, and there are routine ways of preparing and responding to them. The new and alarming connection between emergency preparedness and security concerns is forcing a radical rethinking across a range of policy areas that at one time would have been in separate organizational silos. The visible organizational evidence of this is the creation of agencies like Homeland Security in the United States and Public Safety Canada. Legislation on terrorism, charitable donations, security and intelligence gathering, customs and border control—all have changed in the last five years and become much more closely connected to each other.

There are several significant policy challenges that flow from these changes. The first and most obvious is the threat to civil liberties. This

Chapter 8 Policymaking under Pressure **383**

BOX 8.4   LISTED ENTITIES UNDER CANADA'S ANTI-TERRORISM ACT (A SELECTION)

1. AL QAIDA

Al Qaida is the central component of a network of Sunni Islamic extremist groups associated with Osama bin Laden, which functions as an umbrella organization, with branches in the Middle East, Africa, Central Asia, and North America. Al Qaida is committed to overthrowing secular governments in Islamic countries and using force to eliminate all Western influences in such countries. Bin Laden, and those within his network, believe that the only way these goals can be achieved is through violence and terrorist activities up to and including martyrdom. The Bin Laden network has been directly or indirectly associated with the 1998 bombings of two US embassies; the 2000 bombing of the USS Cole; and the 2001 World Trade Center and Pentagon attacks.

2. AUM SHINRIKYO

Aum Shinrikyo / Aleph is a religious terrorist organization that was founded by Shoko Asahara in Japan in 1987. Apart from the teachings of Asahara, the sect's beliefs are based on an eclectic selection of Tibetan Buddhism, the apocalyptic aspects of Shiva, the Hindu god of destruction, the Zen masters, Isaac Asimov's science fiction, and the Judeo-Christian concept of Armageddon. Its organizational structure mimics that of the nation state and its 2001 membership was estimated at 1,500 to 2000, most of whom were located in Japan. Despite its status as a religious organization, Aum Shinrikyo/ Aleph was run like a business, and at one point, the Japanese government estimated its net worth at approximately $1 billion. Aum Shinrikyo / Aleph was responsible for 12 deaths and the hospitalization of over 5000 persons as a result of its sarin gas attack on the Tokyo subway system on March 20, 1995. It was also responsible for several other mysterious chemical incidents in Japan in 1994, and has been accused of detaining members against their will, extortion, kidnapping members who decided to leave, and even murdering members who either refused to turn over all their possessions or to return to the sect. Despite the arrest and convictions of many of its members, in March 2002 the Japanese Justice Minister was quoted as saying that "the cult group still maintains its essential dangerousness and we need to keep watching its moves."

3. Ejército de Liberación Nacional (ELN)

The Ejército de Liberación Nacional (ELN), founded in 1964, is the second-largest leftist rebel group in Colombia, after FARC. The group strongly opposes foreign involvement in Colombia's oil industry, saying it violates the country's sovereignty and that foreign companies are unfairly exploiting Colombia's natural resources. The ELN's principal aim is to 'seize power for the people' and establish a revolutionary government. For the ELN, guerrilla warfare is the indispensable means with which to solve all of Colombia's problems. It is estimated to have between 3,000 and 5,000 active members. There are close ties between the ELN and FARC. One of the more important links is common membership in the Simon Bolivar Guerrilla Coordination Board. The ELN is known for kidnapping, hijacking, bombing, extortion and guerrilla warfare. The ELN hits strategic economic targets, particularly the oil pipeline owned by the Colombian Petroleum Enterprise (Ecopetrol), causing disruption and loss of revenue to the state oil company. While its activities have been limited to Colombia, it has acted against Canadian interests by kidnapping a Canadian employee of Occidental Petroleum and attempting to assassinate the Canadian manager of a Texas oil company in Bogota.

4. Euskadi Ta Askatasuna (ETA)

The Euskadi Ta Askatasuna (ETA) is the most powerful of the Basque terrorist groups and has been called the most dangerous terrorist organization in Europe. It is said to have killed over 800 people and carried out about 1,600 terrorist attacks since it was formed. It is headquartered in the Basque provinces of Spain and France, but has bombed Spanish and French interests elsewhere. Its stated goal is the creation of an independent Basque state that would contain the six Basque provinces of Spain and France, as well as the Navarra province of Spain. It has further demonstrated a muted commitment to Marxism such that its created state would likely be based on Marxist principles. The ETA has engaged in bombings, assassinations and kidnappings to further its political and ideological goals. These activities are intended to intimidate the public (or a segment of the public) and force the Spanish government to accede to its demands.

5. Gulbuddin Hekmatyar

Gulbuddin Hekmatyar, leader of the group Hezb-e Islami Gulbuddin (HIG) espouse an Islamist anti-Western ideology whose political or

BOX 8.4 (continued)

religious objective is the overthrow of the administration of Afghan President Hamid Karzai, the elimination of all Western influence in Afghanistan and the creation of an Islamist fundamentalist state. On July 23, 2002, Al Qaida became a listed entity pursuant to section 83.05 of the *Criminal Code*. Since late 2002, and to achieve its political and religious objectives, Hekmatyar has joined forces with Al Qaida and the Taliban to form an anti-Western, anti-US, anti-Afghan government alliance which would continue targeted *jihad* against the "anti-Islam and anti-Muslim elements." Since 2002, Hekmatyar has reportedly established a base, recruited new members and initiated mobile training camps with Al Qaida and the Taliban in Afghanistan and Pakistan, with the goal of carrying out terrorist activity in Afghanistan.

6. JEMAAH ISLAMIYYAH (JI)

The Jemaah Islamiyyah (JI) is an Islamist terrorist organization that has developed economic and military assets, through the use of cells (fiahs) operating throughout Southeast Asia. Guided by its objective of creating an Islamic state ruled by sharia'h (Islamic law), the JI wishes to create an Islamist theocracy (JI's conception of Dawlah Islamiyyah or Islamic state) that would unify Muslims in Thailand, Malaysia, Indonesia, Brunei and the Southern Philippines. Sharing a common philosophy with the groups in the Al Qaida network, the JI and its leadership have been linked to Al Qaida, both before and after the attacks of September 11, 2001. The JI has emerged as the most extensive transnational radical Islamist group in Southeast Asia. Since its inception, the JI has been responsible for a series of bank robberies, hijackings and the bombing of civilian targets.

7. KAHANE CHAI (KACH)

The Kahane Chai (Kach) is a group of right-wing, politico-religious, anti-Arab, Jewish terrorists, whose overall aim is to restore the biblical state of Israel, i.e. to expand the borders of Israel to include the occupied territories and parts of Jordan. To this end, the group aims to intimidate and threaten Palestinian families and mount sustained political pressure on the Israeli government. In the past, Jewish extremist groups, like Kahane Chai (Kach), have been willing to engage in terrorism to derail the Arab-Israeli peace process. The Kahane Chai (Kach) is known to have links both to other members of the "Kahanist Movement" and to other Jewish extremist splinter groups. The Kahane Chai (Kach) organizes protests against the Israeli government, and harasses, threatens and assaults Arabs and Palestinians in the West Bank. Its tactics include shouting down opponents, disturbing public speeches and engaging in physical confrontations with law enforcement officials. It has also threatened to attack Israeli government officials. Like the approach taken by the Jewish Defence League (JDL), the targets of the Kach Party (KP) and Kahane Chai (KC) have also included leading figures in Israel, as well as Jews and Jewish organizations that support policies of the Israeli government, or those who disagree with their violent tactics and philosophy. Kahanists have shot, stabbed and thrown grenades at Palestinians in Jerusalem and the West Bank. In instances where the KP and KC have not themselves claimed responsibility for anti-Arab attacks, they have declined to condemn such violence and have often glorified it.

8. LIBERATION TIGERS OF TAMIL EELAM (LTTE)

The Liberation Tigers of Tamil Eelam (LTTE) is a Sri Lankan-based organization which advocates the creation of an independent homeland in the north and northeastern part of Sri Lanka which it has called "Tamil Eelam". Its war against the government of Sri Lanka has been fought on three fronts: a political campaign, guerrilla warfare, and a terrorist campaign. The LTTE is committed to using a variety of terror tactics in order to achieve its objectives, including attacking political, economic, religious and cultural targets, as well as targeting civilians. The LTTE's campaign has included plans to create Tamil-only northern and eastern provinces, and to this end it has aggressively expelled non-Tamils from these regions. The LTTE also endeavours to eliminate moderate Tamils and other Tamil militant groups that compete with it for influence and power within the Sri Lankan Tamil community.

9. MUJAHEDIN E KHALQ (MEK)

The Mujhedin-e-Khalq (MEK) is an Iranian terrorist organization that was based in Iraq until recently. It subscribes to an eclectic ideology that combines its own interpretation of Shiite Islamism with Marxist principles. The group aspires to overthrow the current regime in Iran and to establish a democratic, socialist Islamic republic. This Islamic socialism can only be attained through the destruction of the existing regime and the elimination of Western

BOX 8.4 (continued)

influence, described as "Westoxication". To achieve this Islamic ideology, the use of physical force, armed struggle or jihad is necessary. Besides having had an alliance with Saddam Hussein, the organization has or had ties with: Amal, the Kurdish Democratic Party of Iran (KDPI), the Palestine Liberation Organization (PLO), Al Fatah, and other Palestinian factions. The MEK is even suspected of past collusion with the regime of the Taliban in Afghanistan.

10. SENDERO LUMINOSO (SL)

Sendero Luminoso (SL) has been stated to be among the world's most ruthless guerrilla organizations whose goal it is to destroy existing Peruvian institutions and replace them with a communist peasant revolutionary regime which would rid the country of foreign influences. Its area of operations is limited to Peru, with most of its activities in rural areas, but some of its attacks have taken place in the capital, Lima. It is estimated that over 30,000 people have died by political violence in Peru since SL took up arms in 1980 and that their activities have caused $20 billion (US) in property damage. SL was founded by Abimael Guzman, a university professor, in the late 1960s but began its armed struggle, or "People's War", on or about May 1980. SL is known for its indiscriminate bombing campaigns, selective assassinations and its killing of innocents. While none of its activities have taken place in Canada, the group has targeted some Canadian citizens and interests such as the bombing of a Bata shoe warehouse in Lima, the bombing of the Canadian Embassy, an ambush of trucks associated with a Canadian alpaca operation that killed eight people and the murder of a Canadian aid worker.

SOURCE: Public Safety Canada (2007). *Currently Listed Entities*. Retrieved March 30, 2008, from http://www.publicsafety.gc.ca/prg/ns/le/cle-eng.aspx.

has been a mounting concern in all countries where security measures have been strengthened. Intelligence services have been given strengthened mandates and new powers; new border security measures are considerably more invasive than in the past, and there have been reported instances of racial profiling. Finding the right balance between the protection of civil liberties and public safety will be an ongoing test of public authorities. A second challenge is less philosophical than it is organizational—the challenge of coordination and implementation. As we discussed in Chapter 5, all public policy faces the problem of implementation. That challenge is more acute in the emergency and security area than in most others. The sheer size of the organizations being created—as noted above, Homeland Security employs 208 000 people—means that there will be problems in internal coordination and communication. But it is in the nature of emergencies to require widely dispersed response, which is inherently difficult to manage. In the ice storm of 1998, for example, over 4 million people in Ontario, Quebec, and New Brunswick lost power, and 600 000 had to evacuate their homes. A disaster of this magnitude cannot be responded to simply by government alone, even though Ottawa, the provinces, and local municipalities all had to work together. Nongovernmental organizations, charities, international agencies, and volunteers have to come together to respond, and all somehow have to be coordinated in a system of "shared governance" (May and Williams, 1986). And of course, the context of an emergency means that by definition time pressures are high, as are the stakes in terms of human life and property. Since most emergencies are new in some sense, relying exclusively on prepared plans can introduce inflexibilities in response. An extreme example of this comes from the initial responses by American aviation and defence authorities in the 9/11 events—they relied on protocols developed in the 1970s for airplane hijackings. For all these reasons, Comfort emphasizes the importance of adaptive systems of response that rely on self-organization: "Sustaining the process of self-organization in a continuing way requires access to communication for all the participants to support the exchange of information, stored memory for actions taken that allow reflection and redesign, and evaluation and feedback from the other participants in the group" (Comfort, 1999, p. 271). This places the emphasis on the *system* of response, including the wide availability and exchange of information among members of that response community.

Crisis Management

We distinguished earlier between crisis and emergency. Emergencies are typically physical events (though not exclusively) that threaten human life and property. From a "system" perspective—the political system, the economic system, even the social system—an emergency is a threat event, but not one so severe that it will cause the system to collapse. A crisis is usually considered to fall in that category; we might think of it as an emergency that is so extreme that it threatens system integrity. Also, as we noted, an emergency can evolve into a crisis is if is handled badly and people lose faith in the authorities or managers. The tainted blood scandal, one of Canada's worst health crises, arose first as an emergency around the safety of Canadian blood products, but became an organizational crisis for the Red Cross, which eventually had to close its doors in Canada (see Box 8.5, page 393).

This is more than just semantics. When we are looking at crises, we are looking at specific types of events that require specific management and policy responses that are different from the responses and preparation for emergencies. And while it is difficult to find conclusive evidence on this, it seems that crisis (a threat to organizational integrity) is becoming a more important and indeed routine part of the context for developing and implementing public policy. There are several reasons this might be true. First, information about what governments are doing is much more widely available than ever before thanks to the Internet and access-to-information legislation. And information flows more rapidly and easily because of a 24/7 media environment and communications technology. For example, when SARS broke out on the Chinese mainland in 2002, the authorities initially forbade any public discussion of the disease. Despite this, almost half the urban population in Guangzhou received news of it through unofficial means, principally text messaging over mobile phones (Huang, 2003, p. 12). Second, in a news- and media-saturated policy environment, it is easily possible for "master narratives" to be formed by the press that then feed on themselves and are very difficult to revise or rebut. Good, for example, highlights the role the media played in the 1999 HRDC scandal. Initial reports were that $1 billion in HRDC grants and contributions had gone missing, a "billion-dollar boondoggle." Once that impression was made in the public mind, it was almost impossible to shake:

> After the immediate release of the HRDC grants and contributions audit on 19 January, and for the rest of the week, the media used a simple and dramatic storyline: "One billion dollars lost." The expression, however distorted, was dramatic and the image vivid. A seemingly dull internal administrative audit was 'recontextualized' into a newsworthy sound-bite and a catchy headline. In fact, no money was lost. After months of individually reviewing 17,000 grants and contributions files across all programs in the department, representing some $1.6 billion, HRDC officials concluded that the amount of outstanding debts owing to the government was $85,000. . . . [T]he media developed a preformed storyline that the grants were used for political purposes and, as a consequence, corruption was inevitable. (Good, 2003, p. 64)

Third, as we have noted in previous chapters, there is a pervasive mood of cynicism and distrust of government. Bad news—any type of bad news—can very easily and quickly be framed in that mental context and seen as evidence of rank incompetence, malfeasance, or corruption. A crisis can grow out of a simple error if that error gets magnified to the point where it becomes emblematic of systemic problems. The HRDC scandal—such as it was—did in the end lead to the demotion of a minister who at the time had been widely touted as a possible future prime minister, and to the splitting of the department into two.

From a policy and management perspective, the key thing about crisis is responding to it and managing it as effectively as possible. Indeed the response itself—if badly coordinated—can become the crisis once the initial triggering event is over. In the case of HRDC, the triggering event was the release of an audit of grants and contributions that appeared to suggest that the monies were badly handled. Once the media framed the story in those terms, the actual crisis was a crisis of not being able to effectively respond and get the facts of the case on the public record. A crisis gets resolved when it is handled well and overcome. Of course, the problem is that crises are typically unexpected, take place under strong time constraints and uncertainty, and usually have enough new elements that one cannot rely exclusively on prepared plans. Nonetheless, in reviewing experiences in dealing with crises and emergencies, it is possible to distill some useful lessons (Canadian Centre for Management Development, 2003a; 2003b).

Perhaps the most obvious first step is to be mentally prepared to acknowledge the existence of a possible crisis. Managers should assume that crises will occur and that they can arise from almost any possible event, however innocuous. As Good states of his own response to the HRDC stories in the press, "I believed that the matter would 'blow over.' In retrospect, I should have read the media reports in a more pessimistic manner to prepare myself, and my staff, for what lay ahead" (Good, 2003, p. 211). He goes on to say that public servants should be accustomed to expecting the unexpected and to be "overly prepared for the expected"—in this case, paying close attention to the external environment and how it might respond to information about grants and contributions. A second step involves ensuring the ability to respond quickly and accurately to the crisis and, most importantly, to the way the media handles the crisis. "Once the crisis has been confirmed, it is important to immediately establish a management team to oversee the response. The designated members of the response team and spokespersons must suspend their normal activities and devote themselves fully to the crisis. It is essential to ensure that team members are prepared to assume the responsibilities assigned to them" (Canadian Centre for Management Development, 2003a, p. 26).

A third lesson is that those who are tasked with dealing with the crisis know their respective roles and the lines of accountability and leadership. This is important for a number of reasons. In government, there are usually several departments and agencies that can plausibly take a lead role, and not coordinating them can be disastrous—conflicting messages and contradictory communications are sure to make a bad situation worse. Another dimension is that in crisis situations it is often necessary to make difficult decisions, and without clear lines of accountability those necessary decisions may be delayed or confused. However, as discussed earlier, coordination should not be confused with hierarchy. To some extent there must be vertical command and control systems, but they have to be matched with adaptive horizontal networks (Farazmand, 2007, p. 156).

A fourth key step, possibly the most important of the list, is developing a good communications strategy. This has several elements. The right spokespersons should be designated early in the crisis, properly briefed, and properly trained to deal with media. It is often the case that the first messages that get out to the public as a crisis is developing set the frame for much of what follows, and are difficult to change or shift. Information has to be circulated within the organization responsible for dealing with the crisis, in order to facilitate learning and organizational coordination. To the extent possible, responses to the media and other external audiences should be complete and honest, and if information is missing or unavailable, it should be produced as quickly as is feasible.

The fifth step, once the crisis has been resolved, is to draw lessons from the event and try to prevent a similar thing happening in the future. Mitigation and prevention strategies have their limits of course, like generals always fighting the last war. But they are essential for organizational development and for at least having a chance of dealing with the next potential crisis that comes along, as one inevitably will.

We have defined crisis as a threat event that can undermine the integrity of a system. This can mean a government, a department, or even a policy or program. It is for this reason that crises eventually have to be addressed by leaders who have key responsibilities for those organizations or programs. Crisis management is not normal, routine management, and coordinating the response to a crisis may be the single most important thing that organizational managers do. That is why crisis management, while it requires collective and coordinated response, is a severe test for those at the top of the organization. While decisive action is often required, that has to be balanced against communications, information-sharing, and teamwork.

BOX 8.5   THE TAINTED BLOOD CRISIS (1998)

BACKGROUND

The Red Cross has a history in Canada almost as old as the country itself. It can be traced back to 1885, to the battlefield of Louis Riel's North West Rebellion, where a surgeon general made a Red Cross flag out of white cloth and two torn strips of red artillery cotton so he could distinguish a horse-drawn wagon being used to transport the wounded. Eleven years after the rebellion, Dr. George Sterling Ryerson, the same man who flew the makeshift flag, won approval from Britain to form a Canadian Branch of the Red Cross in Toronto. The organization grew quickly and in 1909 the federal government adopted the Canadian Red Cross Society Act. In 1927, the International Committee of the Red Cross recognized the society as an autonomous group. It went on to become the preeminent not-for-profit organization in the country.

On February 3, 1947, the Canadian Red Cross opened its first civilian blood donor clinic in Vancouver with the goal of providing free blood to anyone who needed it. Before that, patients had to pay for or replace the blood they were given in hospitals. In the late 1970s and early 1980s, Canada's blood system infected approximately 1,200 people with the HIV virus and it has been estimated that another 12,000 people were infected with hepatitis C. Many of the victims were hemophiliacs and people who had received blood during routine operations. At that time we had less knowledge than we do now about these viruses. Many of those who had been infected did not know they had received contaminated blood. Some people unknowingly passed on the viruses to their spouses and family members. As a result by the 1990s it was estimated that the number of infected people had increased substantially and exponentially. The staggering number of victims illustrated that the blood system had failed the very people it was supposed to protect. In response many people began calling for a judicial inquiry into Canada's blood system.

In 1993 Justice Horace Krever was appointed to head a Commission of Inquiry with the mandate to investigate the management and operation and contamination of the blood system in Canada. After nearly four years of a public judicial inquiry, Justice Krever issued his much-awaited final report on November 26, 1997.

Krever's report stopped short of finding the Canadian government liable for the contaminated blood or singling out individuals for blame. But he criticized federal and local authorities for their roles in distributing the tainted blood. The report also criticized the Canadian Red Cross for failing to put into place an adequate screening program for high-risk blood donors. After the report was issued the Red Cross (through Gene Durnin) apologized. "While we cannot know your suffering, we will weep with you. While we cannot feel your loss we grieve with you. We are very sorry."

Krever also recommended that the thousands of people infected with hepatitis C should be entitled to automatic compensation. He did not set an amount. The 1,200 people infected with HIV through tainted blood products had already been compensated by the federal government. Further, the Red Cross and its insurers together with the provinces contributed to a second compensation program for HIV victims—the Multi-Provincial/Territorial Assistance Program. There had been no requirement for court proceedings or legal negotiations in an overwhelming numbers of these cases.

But federal and provincial health ministers decided not to compensate hepatitis C victims at all, leaving the Red Cross with billions of dollars in claims. This led to massive complications. By the time the issue had been sorted out the Canadian Red Cross had been forced to seek bankruptcy protection under the Companies' Creditors Arrangement Act. It shook the organization to its foundation and nearly brought it tumbling down.

SOURCE: Canadian Centre for Management Development. (2003). *The federal experience: Case studies on crisis and emergency management.* Ottawa: Canadian Centre for Management Development (now known as the Canada School of Public Service). Retrieved March 31, 2008, from http://www.csps-efpc.gc.ca/Research/publications/pdfs/crisis_case_e.pdf

Conclusion

Emergency, crisis, and pressure have attracted more attention as themes in the private sector management literature than in the public sector, until recently. Corporations face competitors, and so something like a product recall or losing a top executive can threaten the viability of a corporation. Public sector organizations, at least traditionally, enjoyed some insulation from these types of pressures, but of course political crises arise all the time. However, they do not typically pose the same kind of threat to the entire viability of a program or the existence of a public sector agency.

The ground has shifted in many ways, and public policymaking under pressure is an increasingly important feature of doing policy work. The intensification of international terrorism in recent years is one obvious example, but is not the whole story. Dealing with natural disasters such as floods and forest fires has always been part of the government's responsibility, but it may be that as a result of climate change the incidence of these events is increasing (Briceno, 2004; James, 2007). And the scale can be devastating, as when Hurricane Katrina flattened New Orleans (Brinkley, 2006). The combination of interdependencies in things like trade (Mad Cow) and technology (Internet) mean that emergencies and threat events can spread rapidly and paralyze whole populations, if not industries and economic processes, as the economic crisis in late 2008 showed. Pandemics and public health risks appear to be on the rise; the listeriosis crisis in late 2008 almost destroyed Maple Leaf foods. And finally, the public mood, while perhaps more supportive of governments that are addressing emergencies or attacks, is still suspicious. Coupled with a media bias towards "gotcha journalism," this can make for a volatile environment in which to deal with emergencies. If things are badly handled, even to a modest degree, there is a new potential for expansion into full-blown crisis:

> The modern crisis is the product of several modernization processes—globalization, deregulation, information and communication technology, developments and technological advances, to name but a few. These advances promote a close-knit world that is nonetheless susceptible to infestation by a single crisis. Comparatively slight mishaps within these massive and intricate infrastructures can rapidly escalate in unforeseen ways. A prime example can be found in the European food and agriculture sector. One animal was diagnosed with foot and mouth disease in a remote English farm and, within days, the disease had affected all of Europe. Farmers, slaughterhouses, distributors, butcheries, consumers, inspection agencies, policy makers, and politicians endured enormous economic and social-psychological costs. (Boin and t'Hart, 2003, p. 546)

It is important to remember the actual, political context of crisis and policymaking under pressure. Crises and emergencies are difficult to handle at the best of times, but if they are becoming both more frequent and with wider-reaching consequences, we should not be surprised that crisis management as a real process will sometimes look different than what we might hope from a "lessons learned" approach that does not take into account the real dynamics to which decisionmakers are exposed. Boin and t'Hart's (2003) review of the literature points out six broad public expectations about crisis that are not borne out by research. To begin with, there is a public expectation that leaders should put public safety first. In fact, policy leaders always have to balance the costs and benefits of mitigation and prevention. It is simply too costly to have absolute, 100 percent safety. Rather, it is a question of how much risk can be reasonably tolerated. As well, the public is somewhat schizophrenic on risk and safety issues. On the one hand it often complains about excessive regulation that stifles individual choice (e.g., pharmaceutical regulations that prevent access to experimental drugs) but on the other it expects that drugs available on the market have been tested to be safe. As well, mitigation and prevention of nonevents do not attract political credit. There is little political incentive to invest heavily in safety.

A second public expectation is that leaders should prepare themselves for worst-case scenarios, a recommendation that we made earlier. In fact, the evidence from both private and public sector organizations seems to be that, unless one has experienced crisis in the past, or is operating in a community with similar experiences, the organizational and leadership reflex is to place a low priority on continual crisis preparation. In part this is due to a rational calculation that there may be zero benefit from investing time in preparation for an event that may never occur. As well, less rationally, organizational leaders may be reluctant to confront weaknesses in their organizations. A third expectation is that leaders should heed warnings about future crises. The reality is that many crises take time to build, and in practice all kinds of warning signals are misinterpreted or ignored, usually because the crisis by definition is a "new" event and does not fit the frame of reference of authorities. In June 2004 the National Commission on Terrorist Attacks upon the United States concluded that there had been several intelligence failures in the run-up to the 9/11 attacks. The CIA in particular missed clues that suggested the crisis was looming:

> The problems that prevent leaders from heeding warnings are manifold and fundamental. Leaders are routinely engulfed in oceans of information and advice. Moreover, they face ambiguous and contradictory signals. Warnings do not come with flashing lights; they are hidden in expert reports, advisory memos, or a colleague's casual remark. The warnings have to be distilled from a series of seemingly minor and insignificant indications. An additional problem is that information passageways to leaders often are obscured. Bad news, in particular, faces formidable obstacles on its way to the top of the organization, especially in bureaucratic organizations. These barriers are fundamentally social. Nobody wants to alarm his boss unnecessarily, and nobody wants to acquire the reputation of a troublemaker. In the absence of these signals, leaders run a big risk of becoming the victim of "silences" in the organizational communication pattern. (Boin and t'Hart, 2003, p. 547)

A fourth expectation is that during a crisis leaders take charge and directly oversee the crisis management activities. In reality, crises are much more fluid and dynamic events than this would allow, and in practice it is systems or networks of responses from many agencies, NGOs, and other actors that deal with the multiple facets of a crisis. As we noted earlier, coordination is definitely required in crisis response, but it is important to have realistic expectations of how tightly that can be managed and directed from above. A fifth public expectation is that leaders show tangible sympathy for victims of a crisis or emergency. This extends from public expressions of grief and support to financial compensation and assistance. The problem is that in the heat of the moment, leaders can make promises that they subsequently cannot keep, or raise expectations so high that they inevitably disappoint. (This was a factor in the early responses to the global financial crisis in October 2008.) The final public expectation that Boin and t'Hart identify is that leaders strive to learn the lessons of the crisis. Again, the political context in the aftermath of a crisis almost actively militates against that. A normal reaction after a crisis has been dealt with is to find its causes, and this rapidly degenerates (especially with the media) into a blame game. Leaders know that they are a target, and so instead of dispassionately "learning lessons," they focus on spin control and plausible deniability.

Chaos, risk, emergency, and crisis: these take us to the outer limits of the "normal" policy process, and yet they are themselves becoming normal aspects and challenges of doing policy work. This is the turbulence mentioned in the subtitle to this book: effective public management requires the skills and capacities to manage policy processes in conditions of great and perhaps even increasing turbulence.

KEY TERMS

crisis—a turning point or moment of danger that threatens the integrity of an entire system

emergency—an abnormal and unexpected threat event that requires immediate action

emergency management—the process of developing and implementing policies and programs to avoid and cope with the risks to people and property from natural and man-made hazards

environmental scan—an assessment of both internal and external risks, usually in terms of strengths and weaknesses, and threats and opportunities

mitigation—actions taken based on a risk assessment to lower those risks and prevent them from happening

nonlinear policy problems—problems where small changes in initial conditions can have large consequences, where uncertainty is high, and where there are discontinuities in normal events and shared responsibilities for action

risk—probability of an event with negative consequences; key dimensions are level of probability and severity of risk

risk management—a management framework that encourages the identification and assessment of risk, and its mitigation or prevention as part of a medium- to long-term strategy

tipping point—dramatic moment in an epidemic when everything can change; a sudden, unexpected change in what to that point has been a stable system

FURTHER READINGS

Boin, A., and t'Hart, P. (2003, September–October). Public leadership in times of crisis: 'Mission Impossible'? *Public Administration Review*, 63, 544–52.

Canadian Centre for Management Development. (2003). *The federal experience: Case studies on crisis and emergency management*. (CCMD is now called the Canada School of Public Service). Retrieved March 31, 2008, from http://www.csps-efpc.gc.ca/Research/publications/pdfs/crisis_case_e.pdf

Comfort, L. K. (1999). *Shared risk: Complex systems in seismic response*. Amsterdam: Pergamon.

Giuliani, R. W. (2002). *Leadership*. New York: Hyperion.

Gladwell, M. (2000). *The tipping point: How little things can make a big difference*. Boston: Little, Brown and Company.

Klein, G. A. (1998). *Sources of power: How people make decisions*. Cambridge, Mass.: MIT Press.

REFERENCES

Beck, U. (1992). *The risk society: Towards a new modernity*. Newbury Park, CA: Sage.

Beck, W. (1999). *World risk society*. London: Polity.

Boin, A., and t'Hart, P. (2003, September–October). Public leadership in times of crisis: 'Mission Impossible'? *Public Administration Review*, 63, 544–52.

Briceno, S. (2004, March). Global challenges in disaster reduction. *The Australian Journal of Emergency Management*, 19, 3–5.

Brinkley, D. (2006). *The great deluge: Hurricane Katrina, New Orleans, and the Mississippi Gold Coast.* New York: Morrow.

Canadian Centre for Management Development. (2003a). *Crisis and emergency management: A guide for managers.* Ottawa: Canadian Centre for Management Development (now known as the Canada School of Public Service). Retrieved March 31, 2008, from http://www.csps-efpc.gc.ca/Research/publications/pdfs/crisis_e.pdf

Canadian Centre for Management Development. (2003b). *The federal experience: Case studies on crisis and emergency management.* Ottawa: Canadian Centre for Management Development (now known as the Canada School of Public Service). Retrieved March 31, 2008, from http://www.csps-efpc.gc.ca/Research/publications/pdfs/crisis_case_e.pdf

Cigler, B. A. (1988). Emergency management and public administration. In M. T. Charles and J. C. K. Kim (Eds.). *Crisis management: A casebook,* (pp. 5–19). Springfield, IL: Charles C. Thomas.

Comfort, L. K. (1999). *Shared risk: Complex systems in seismic response.* Amsterdam: Pergamon.

Comfort, L. K. (2005). Risk, security, and disaster management. *Annual Review of Political Science,* 8, 335–356.

Comfort, L. K. (2006). Inter-organizational coordination in extreme events: The World Trade Center attacks, September 11, 2001. *Natural Hazards,* 39 (2), 309–27.

Comfort, L. K. (2007). Crisis management in hindsight: Cognition, communication, coordination, and control. *Public Administration Review,* 67 (s.1), 189–97.

Department of Homeland Security (United States). (2007). *Fact sheet: Select Department of Homeland Security 2007 achievements.* Retrieved March 29, 2008, from http://www.dhs.gov/xnews/releases/pr_1197477138027.shtm

Farazmand, A. (2007). Learning from the Katrina crisis: A global and international perspective with implications for future crisis management. *Public Administration Review,* 67 (1), 149–59.

Furedi, F. (2002). *Culture of fear: Risk-taking and the morality of low expectation.* 2nd ed. London: Continuum International Publishing.

Gladwell, M. (2000). *The tipping point: How little things can make a big difference.* Boston: Little, Brown and Company.

Good, D. A. (2003). *The politics of public management: The HRDC audit of grants and contributions.* Toronto: University of Toronto Press.

Government of Canada. (2005). *Securing an open society: One year later—Progress report on the implementation of Canada's national security policy.* Retrieved March 30, 2008, from http://www.pco-bcp.gc.ca/docs/information/Publications/secure/secure_e.pdf

Health Canada. (2007). *Fetal alcohol syndrome/Fetal alcohol effects.* Retrieved March 27, 2008, from http://www.hc-sc.gc.ca/fnih-spni/famil/preg-gros/intro_e.html

Huang, Y. (2003, Fall). The politics of China's SARS crisis. *Harvard Asia Quarterly,* 7, 9–16.

James, M. (2007). The permanent-emergency compensation state: A "postsocialist" tale of political dystopia. In M. Orsini and M. Smith (Eds.), *Critical policy studies* (pp. 321–46). Vancouver: UBC Press.

Kelling, G. L., and Coles, C. M. (1996). *Fixing broken windows.* New York: Touchstone.

Klein, G. A. (1998). *Sources of power: How people make decisions.* Cambridge, Mass.: MIT Press.

May, P. J., and Williams, W. (1986). *Disaster policy implementation: Managing programs under shared governance.* New York: Plenum Press.

Morçöl, G. (2002). *A new mind for policy analysis: Towards a post-Newtonian and postpositivist epistemology and methodology.* Westport, CN: Praeger.

Pal, L. A., and Maxwell, J. (2004). *Assessing the public interest in the 21st century: A framework.* Background study for the External Advisory Committee on Smart Regulation. Retrieved March 31, 2008, from http://www.cprn.org/doc.cfm?doc=508&l=en

Pal, L. A., and Weaver, R. K. (Eds.). (2003) *The government taketh away: The politics of pain in the United States and Canada.* Washington: Georgetown University Press.

Privy Council Office (Canada). (2004). *Securing an open society: Canada's national security policy.* Retrieved March 31, 2008, from http://www.bcp-pco.gc.ca/docs/information/Publications/natsec-secnat/natsec-secnat_e.pdf

Public Safety Canada. (2007). About us. Retrieved March 30, 2008, from http://www.publicsafety.gc.ca/abt/index-eng.aspx

Sharkansky, I. (1986). *Policymaking under adversity.* New Brunswick, NJ: Transaction Books.

Treasury Board of Canada. (2001a). Risk management policy. Retrieved March 31, 2008, from http://www.tbs-sct.gc.ca/pubs_pol/dcgpubs/RiskManagement/riskmanagpol1_e.asp#_Toc457619040

Treasury Board of Canada. (2001b). *Integrated risk management framework.* Retrieved March 31, 2008, from http://www.tbs-sct.gc.ca/pubs_pol/dcgpubs/RiskManagement/rmf-cgr_e.asp

U.S.–Canada Power System Outage Taskforce. (2004). *Final report on the August 14, 2003 blackout in the United States and Canada: Causes and Recommendations.* Retrieved March 31, 2008, from https://reports.energy.gov/BlackoutFinal-Web.pdf

CHAPTER

9 Conclusions

R eaders who made it this far will probably have a mixed reaction to the arguments in this book. Some of you will be impressed at the deep changes that governments and the policy process are undergoing and generally supportive of a more quality-centred, client-focused policymaking system. Others (perhaps even the same ones who are impressed!) will be dismayed or at least uneasy with the portrait drawn in this book. Governments are becoming more businesslike, and policy is arguably more responsive to clients and stakeholders. But is businesslike government the zenith of democratic aspiration? Decentralization seems fine, but how far can it go before we lose a sense of common standards and shared community? Client satisfaction is laudable, as is responsiveness to stakeholders. But are we merely customers and interests, or is there a richer role that we play in the public sphere as citizens? All of these questions should have occurred to you as you considered the previous chapters. They raise the issue of the quality of the policy process as well as its ultimate ends. In the panic of November 2008, almost all antigovernment sentiment evaporated, as banks and car companies lined up for handouts, and the US government contemplated a deficit of $1 trillion, due in part to a possible $700 billion stimulus package. We expect governments to be more accountable and transparent, and we also increasingly expect government to be a key guarantor against major risks such as climate change, the collapse of financial markets, pandemics, or terrorists. But that acknowledgment is still tempered by a stronger sense of the limits of the state, both in terms of its capacities and its procedures. For various reasons that are rooted in the factors discussed in Chapter 2, we expect government not merely to be efficient but to be "good" in some ethical sense as well. This chapter briefly summarizes the main arguments and findings from previous chapters, and then addresses these deeper questions of policy and democratic governance.

Policy Analysis: Rethinking the Tool Kit

Policy analysis is a relatively new discipline in the modern sense, though of course thinking about what governments do goes back as far as the invention of state structures and stable social organizations as early as the Mesopotamian period around 350 BC. As Chapter 1 pointed out, the modern roots of the policy analysis movement lie in the 1950s and particularly in the 1960s' expansion of American government programs in education and social assistance. Most of what passes today for professional policy analysis and evaluation has its foundations in the application of rational models and techniques drawn from the social sciences. There was great hope in the early years that these techniques would squeeze some if not all of the politics out of decisionmaking—perhaps relegating it to higher-order value choices—and lead to improvements not only in the way that policies were made but of course in the results as well. Chapter 1 touched on some of the debates that grew up around implementation and evaluation in the 1970s and 1980s, and that ultimately contributed to the malaise in policy studies and analytical work.

The 1990s was a decade of ascendancy for new theories of public management and their application in the form of reorganizations of major agencies and programs, along with often deep expenditure cuts and steep increases in taxes. Canada was close to the middle of the OECD pack in this regard, with countries like New Zealand and Britain going much further in changing the structure and practice of government. The changes at the federal level in Canada were nonetheless profound—50 000 civil servants were either let go or retired; departments like Transport Canada were virtually eviscerated; assets such as airports and harbours were divested to local authorities; major income support programs such as unemployment insurance and major transfer programs for health and social assistance were radically altered. The changes at the provincial level were no less profound: hospitals were closed, school boards abolished, cities and regions reorganized. The Harris and Klein governments were the vanguard in tax cuts, program reductions, and re-organizations, all of which invited massive illegal strikes by public sector workers in both provinces.

After a period of surpluses at both provincial and federal levels, we are now seeing large deficits generated by economic downturn and attempts to stimulate the economy. The effect of the last decade lingers, however, even in a period when governments will accumulate more debt. The dreaded "d" word is treated cautiously; the federal government has alluded to "temporary" and not "structural" deficits. The UK government in November 2008 introduced a "temporary" cut to its value-added tax (the equivalent to the Canadian GST). Gloomier predictions are that Canada and the rest of the world could be facing two or more years of recession, if not outright deflation. Around the world, there has been a growing understanding that governments—however much they might be downsized or reduced in scope and influence—have a tremendous impact on their societies. But that impact is not merely instrumental in the sense of providing basic services or bailouts, but includes systemic effects on the economy, the environment, and social structures themselves. While good governance does not necessarily result in strong economies and robust societies, bad governance will yield nothing but misery. This has stimulated a resurgence of interest in good governance and good policymaking.

However, the modern policy movement bears the scars and the lessons of the last decade. For one thing, there is more humility about the practice of policy analysis itself. We will return to this in a moment, but the primary point is that the limits of the rational model and social science techniques are now widely acknowledged—after all, almost no one anticipated the financial crash in late 2008. Outside evaluation studies, which retain a strong empiricist and technical orientation, most other types of policy work recognize the inevitably value-laden character of policy choice, design, and implementation. For another thing, the new public management (NPM) movement of the 1990s left an indelible impression on thinking about the state and the public sector. Some of this has involved the transfer of business practices to the public sector, a transfer that is not always beneficial or appropriate. NPM introduced a more careful posture on the possibilities of state action, as well as a willingness to think about a variety of tools to attack policy problems. Despite appearances, this was not jettisoned in the global governmental response to the economic downturn in late 2008. The final major difference in the current policy revival is the sensitivity to how the world seems to be changing fundamentally and hence altering both the nature of policy problems and their responses. Those changes are summarized in Chapter 2, but subsequent chapters demonstrated their impact across the full spectrum of the policy process. The traditional categories of problem definition, design, implementation, and evaluation certainly continue to apply and continue to be applied by policymakers themselves to make sense of what they do. But the content of those categories has shifted in important ways in order to respond to the impact of globalization, culture shifts, and management theory.

Chapter 3 showed how the nature of problem definition has shifted in recent years. Problem definition remains central to thinking about policy, but the sources and the nature of the problems governments face have changed profoundly. We noted how globalization is now at the centre of the policy research agenda being discussed and debated around the country. The question of technology and productivity is entangled in the concept of the knowledge-based economy and pressures on innovation, both artifacts of globalization and the new phase of industrial or post-industrial development. These forces are generating new challenges in the areas of economic growth, human development, and social cohesion. The chapter also argued that ideas in good currency—the bedrock for the social and political process of agenda-setting—have changed as well. The key change here has been in the perceptions of the fiscal capacity of governments. While those perceptions have changed as governments are called upon to spend unprecedented amounts of money to keep the economy afloat, there is still caution about simple bailouts in favour of "investments."

Chapter 4 carried this analysis forward to look at instrument choice and policy design. The new context, at least before the financial crisis, was that spending instruments were to be used cautiously and often in the form of "boutique" programs without major expenditure commitments; regulatory practices are being redesigned as well as being held more accountable. Governments around the world had a preference to design policies around self-regulative instruments or set framework regulations that look to results rather than micro-management of behaviour. There was more reliance on individual responsibility. Governments continue to experiment with partnerships and the use of information technology for new forms of delivery of programs and services, especially through the Internet. At the same time, however, there are signs that there is a new interest in government as a social regulator and protector. Concerns about the economy, crime video violence, and the environment are driving governments to be more, not less, robust in their interventions. The impact of globalization on jobs and communities is also forcing governments, even very conservative ones, to bridle their enthusiasm for market mechanisms in favour of economic and social policies that try to insulate their populations to some degree. On other fronts, as Chapter 2 outlined, profound value shifts in Western countries have also contributed to demands that governments address broad issues like the environment.

Chapters 5, 6, and 7 expressed the same themes. Implementation of public policy is changing everywhere to be less top-down and more explicitly designed around partnerships, with a clearer division between policy design and delivery. Policy communities have accordingly become more important in the policy mix. Governments depend more on their partners both for policy advice and implementation. Modern policy cannot be directed by government or merely supplemented by other actors in respective policy communities. Chapter 6 provided a good illustration of how this changed context alters the way in which we think about players in the policy process. Today, the emphasis is on "governance" as opposed to government—that is, on nonhierarchical, multiple-stakeholder, diffuse systems of negotiation and compromise in which government is a player and an occasional leader but more rarely the dominant actor (Rhodes, 1997, 2007). The notion of policy communities and policy networks flows directly from this appreciation. But why are governments limited to being players in networks? They remain undeniably large institutions, but the impact of globalization and technology on government practice and power has been profound. We pointed out in Chapter 2 that this diminution of power should not be exaggerated, but it has nonetheless occurred. Western governments no longer have monopolies of knowledge or expertise, nor do they have the capacity to tackle all the really important—but huge—problems that face the country. Take the question of productivity through mobilizing science and technology. Even if one accepts that governments have a strong policy role here, for example in setting tax incentives for investments and in supporting research, it is clear that the key players are going to be business, labour, and the research and innovation sectors. Governments today increasingly have to work in networks to design and implement policy solutions. The 2008 financial crisis demonstrated that governments do have one important tool at their disposal—money—but any economic stimulus they offered still had to be brokered with communities, businesses, civil society, provinces, and foreign governments and financial institutions.

Chapter 7 showed how evaluation has changed as well. It has enjoyed a renaissance of sorts as governments have emphasized results, accountability, performance, and client satisfaction. With the new focus on results and clients, however, have come new emphases in evaluative techniques, harnessing them more closely to continuous program review and the use of innovative implementation techniques. Chapter 8 picked up on themes that were adumbrated in earlier chapters and in the third edition. Security threats—from terrorism to computer viruses to pandemics—are connected to globalization. Some of the natural disasters that loom may be connected to industrial development and climate change. Whereas risk assessment and emergency and crisis management were on the fringes of public policy and public administration studies two decades ago, they are increasingly central to the tool kit, especially after the economic meltdown in fall 2008.

Normally, it is useful to be skeptical of the cult of the "new." Not everything changes radically all the time, whatever advertisers and politicians may tell us. However, in the case of policymaking and public management, it does not seem hyperbolic to talk about a substantially new context and the need for new responses. The evidence of change in society and economy is all around us, as is the evidence of change in the ways that governments behave and public servants think about the nature of governance. While some of the new thinking in policy and management may indeed be a response to fads, or driven by the interests of international agencies such as the OECD or international consultants, it is undeniable that the changes are substantial and real. Going "beyond policy analysis" has involved trying to think about the applicability of old tools to these new circumstances and problems.

There is yet another sense in which we may go "beyond policy analysis" or the traditional orientations of the discipline. As we noted in Chapter 1, the roots of policy analysis and evaluation were in a social science tradition of rationalism and **instrumentalism**. The latter means a problem-solving orientation that thinks in terms of a solid distinction between means and ends. Policy and the programs that flow from it are technical solutions as insulated as possible from values, ethics, and concepts of higher purpose. In practice, of course, policymaking is shot through with values, even though dealing with values raises substantial practical difficulties. As Peters notes,

> Despite these practical difficulties, it is important for citizens and policymakers to think about policy in ethical terms. Perhaps too much policymaking has been conducted without attention to anything but the political and economic consequences. Of course, such utilitarian values are important bases for evaluating a program, but they may not be the only relevant criteria. Both the policymaker and the citizen must be concerned also with matters of justice and trust in government. Indeed, it may be that justice and social trust ultimately make the best policies—and even the best politics. (Peters, 2006, p. 466)

The remainder of this chapter will go beyond an instrumental perspective on public policy and policy analysis and address three key issues: the nature and purpose of modern governance, the role of ethics and values in policy and public management, and benchmarks for the policymaking process.

Nature and Purpose of Modern Governance

In the end, what's it all about? What is the purpose of public policy and public policy analysis? The conventional, formulaic answer of course is the improvement of the lives of the population or the maximization of the public interest. These are formulaic answers because they have no content—everything depends on the definitions of "improvement" and of "public interest." Nonetheless, it seems that modern governments are being prodded in some new directions in terms of purpose and policy, purposes that are driven to a large extent by the changed circumstances we have discussed throughout this volume. Before we address them, however, we need once again to emphasize that the changes in governance we have seen in the last decade do not necessarily imply smaller and weaker governments. We argued in previous chapters that characterizing these changes as smaller government was simplistic. Indeed, there are some areas (e.g., climate change, financial markets, innovation) where demands for government activity have increased substantially, and there has also been a rethinking of the nature of what government does. The following list of issues or themes is obviously idiosyncratic but does touch on some contemporary concerns and debates about what governments, in the end, are all about and the major new challenges they face, both in Canada and throughout the world.

THE STATE, BUSINESS, AND CITIZENS

One interesting development that touches on the nature of government is a rethinking of the idea popular in the 1990s that governments should be more like businesses and treat citizens more like customers and clients. The backlash against this started almost at the same time as the recommendation itself, particularly in the academic community. It has gathered force over the years, however, with an increasing emphasis on the differences between governments and businesses and the importance of treating citizens as citizens and not just customers. It was probably magnified in late 2008 with the apparent collapse and inefficiency of private markets and even the biggest business operations.

The NPM, and a lot of the new policy thinking described in this book, is dedicated to making government more businesslike. There is nothing wrong with this, and in some instances, such as quality services and client satisfaction, it is long overdue. However, there is a difference between making government more businesslike and treating government just like another business, particularly in a post-Wall Street bail-out world where business practices have been severely criticized as not only foolish but venal and even immoral. The crisis was unprecedented, as was government action around the world, from Washington to Dublin. Capitalism was on the ropes, national economies teetered, and the only entity that could ride to the rescue of the masters of the universe was the state. As inglorious as the whole affair was, it reinforced a sense that governments and markets were different if interconnected worlds. Of course, the best businesses recognize that they have public responsibilities, as well as governance responsibilities to their customers, competitors, and employees. But that does not make them governments. The two spheres of government and business are quite distinct, and each should function in ways that are appropriate to its sphere. Government is vital for any civilized society, not simply as an instrument to get things done but as a public space wherein we fulfill and enjoy our responsibilities and privileges as citizens.

Even during its zenith, several observers pointed out that NPM's emphasis on service-client relations, while helpful, was too limited a vision of the full range of responsibilities and rationales of the public sector. Gow (1995), for example, pointed out, "In considering citizens as clients of the administration, one must wonder about the nature of the relationship as it concerns those who fall under the disciplinary authority of the state, be they prisoners, people in regulated industries or dependents of the state" (p. 558). Doern (1994) made a similar case: "Bureaucracy seen abstractly as an 'it' serving the customer, 'us' or 'me,' in a new form of franchised 'McState' is not all or even *most* of what democratic governance is about" (p. 92). Mintzberg (1996) argued that we actually wear four hats in relation to government: customer, client, citizen, and subject. Governments do relatively few things for us as customers, that is, as consumers of goods and services that probably could just as easily be provided through the market. A larger proportion of the services we get from government, such as health care or education, are professional services for which we are clients. But we also relate to government as subjects, in the sense of the duties and obligations that we have to obey, and that, if we do not, will incur the discipline of state authority. Our relationship as citizens is more complex still, embracing both obligations as well as rights. Respecting the integrity of government does not mean that government should do all things and be all things. What it does mean is respecting the specific nature of government as well as its importance to the exercise of our democratic citizenship. It means preserving the dignity of the public square in the knowledge that if we characterize government as just another form of business, we risk losing our own character as citizens. A world of customers and clients might be a paradise of consumption and service, but it would not be a democratic commonwealth.

As we mentioned earlier, the NPM movement left several important legacies that still affect governments around the world, including Canada's, even if public sector management thinking is now going in different directions (e.g., digital state, accountability, personalization of services, re-governmentalizing services and agencies that had been spun off). Being treated like a valued customer who might be able to take his or her business elsewhere is a marked improvement over being treated as a faceless and powerless citizen waiting in an endless and dreary queue for the next available official. Receiving basic services more efficiently and responsively is a good thing. Certainly, as we noted in Chapters 5 and 7, governments across the world are continuing to emphasize quality services, as well as citizen-centred service, and we noted the more robust version under Prime Ministers Blair and Brown, which sees performance (to the extent of individualizing services) as key to good governance. This will not go away, but it is being complemented by a growing sensibility to an arena wherein people engage as citizens and not just as customers. Chapter 6 explored the burgeoning interest in citizen engagement and its growing role in the policy process. Sometimes this is done to tap into reservoirs of expertise and policy-relevant information, but often it is done with an eye to shoring up a sense of legitimacy for the system as a whole and bringing people more directly into the policy process. The regular calls for parliamentary reform that would enhance the relationship between MPs and the constituents reflect this concern, as do various schemes to revise the electoral system. As early as 2000, for example, the Institute for Research on Public Policy's report *Strengthening Canadian Democracy* explicitly grounded its proposal for electoral reform on opinion surveys that showed that Canadians "continue to feel that they do not have much say over what government does and that their elected representatives are not in touch with the people" (Howe and Northrup, 2000, p. 52). The constant references to citizens and enhanced citizenship in government policy documents from all levels is another canary in the coal mine on this issue. The sponsorship scandal and the Gomery Inquiry fed a public appetite for institutional change, with the Martin government introducing a new cabinet position of Minister in charge of Democratic Reform, a position that Prime Minister Harper maintained. Part of the Federal Accountability Act took aim at party financing and lobbyists, and the Prime Minister announced measures such as fixed federal election dates (which he reneged upon in order to hold the October 2008 federal election at a time to his advantage) and Senate reform (which died on the order paper). Both British Columbia and Ontario established citizens' assemblies to examine proportional representation, and both made positive recommendations that were, however, defeated.

CLIMATE CHANGE

The modern environmental movement was born in the late 1960s and over time has become a powerful policy driver around issues like clean air and clean water, pollution, and forms of economic production and technology. About twenty years ago a new dimension of environmental policy began to take shape—the concern with climate change and greenhouse gas emissions. Scientists were debating whether the earth's overall climate (not simply day-to-day weather patterns) was changing fundamentally, and in fact warming rapidly by historical standards. Initially there was a great deal of skepticism about the data, but over time the weight of evidence seemed to support the climate change hypothesis. More importantly, the primary *cause* of this change in the earth's climate was human activity, specifically the emission of "greenhouse gases" (water vapour, carbon dioxide, methane and some others) through development and economic production. Carbon dioxide (CO_2) accounts for about 80 percent of greenhouse gases, and its principal source is the burning of fossil fuels. As discussed in Chapter 2, this causal matrix puts human economic activity, and specific types of activities that emit more of these gases than others, front and centre in the policy debate. It is this connection that has led to international treaties such as the Kyoto Protocol, the search for "sustainable production" or green technologies, and debates over cap-and-trade systems of emissions control versus carbon taxes. In little over a decade, Canadians, and indeed other citizens around the world, have focused on climate change as a key policy challenge and key worry for the future. Because the challenge is so substantial, and because the solution seems to be a reduction in emissions (especially carbon) linked to virtually every dimension of economic activity, dealing with climate change has the potential to become the policy driver for most governments in the first half of the 21st century. The international prominence of the issue is underscored by the fact that the 2007 Nobel Peace Prize went to Al Gore, who tirelessly raised awareness over the years (and made a film *An Inconvenient Truth*, which won an Oscar), and the Intergovernmental Panel on Climate Change (IPCC), a scientific body established under the auspices of the World Meteorological Organization and the United Nations Environmental Program, that provides neutral and objective assessments of current international scientific opinion and research on the subject.

Climate change is caused by greenhouse gases that accumulate in the atmosphere and which trap heat that would otherwise radiate out into space. As the gases accumulate, the amount of trapped heat increases, and the earth's temperature rises. The IPCC's fourth report, released in 2007, noted that "Eleven of the last twelve years (1995–2006) rank among the twelve warmest years in the instrumental record of global surface temperature (since 1850). The 100-year linear trend (1906–2005) of 0.74 [0.56 to 0.92] °C is larger than the corresponding trend of 0.6 [0.4 to 0.8] °C (1901–2000) given in the Third Assessment Report (TAR). . . . The temperature increase is widespread over the globe and is greater at higher northern latitudes. Land regions have warmed faster than the oceans. . . ." (IPCC, 2007, p. 2). Scientific evidence on Canada's Arctic shows a 4-degree increase in temperatures in the western Arctic between 1953 and 2003 (Simpson, Jaccard, and Rivers, 2007, p. 4). At first blush, particularly for a northern country, a certain amount of warming might be welcome, and indeed some of the effects of warming (on Canadian agriculture, for example, or our tourism industry) might actually be beneficial. Part of the policy narrative therefore is to show how, in the aggregate, global warming will lead to catastrophe. Al Gore's warnings, in his book and film, are particularly evocative on the range and scale of effects that will follow unless climate change is stopped and reversed. For example, rising temperatures will force glaciers to recede and ocean levels to increase. Gore (2006) argued that within a decade, there would be no snows on Mount Kilimanjaro in Tanzania; within fifteen years the glaciers in Glacier National Park would be gone; within fifty years the Himalayan glaciers, which produce drinking water for 40 percent of the world's population, would be severely compromised. Persistent and recurring heat waves. Rising ocean temperatures. Storms, hurricanes, and typhoons. Melting icecaps and tundra. Infestations of beetles that decimate North American forests. Disappearing species. The spread of diseases like West Nile virus well outside their normal range. And perhaps most apocalyptically, the melting or break-up of Greenland and its sinking into the sea. In the book, Gore ends this list of horrors with policy prescriptions (and some attacks on the Bush administration), and what are now considered fairly standard personal steps such as installing better insulation, using energy-saving light bulbs, and buying more fuel efficient cars.

Despite a sea change in public opinion—partly induced by Al Gore's efforts—climate change remains a fiendishly difficult policy issue for several reasons. First, the "climate" is a common property resource—no one owns the air or the ozone, and pollution produced in one place can drift to others as a negative externality (i.e., the producer does not necessarily face the cost or impact of the pollution). Second, while climate change has accelerated in the past decades, and while there are dramatic examples of its impact such as Hurricane Katrina, it still is occurring relatively slowly—or at least slowly relative to most election cycles. Third, the science behind understanding climate change remains complicated, despite an international consensus reflected in the reports of the IPCC. Fourth, tackling climate change through reducing carbon emissions probably means slowing economic growth, which is difficult enough for developed countries, but particularly difficult for developing countries such as China and India. Fifth, for all these reasons, the only real solution to climate change is a global one, requiring international agreement from both developed and developing countries. Finally, in addition to requiring global efforts, dealing with climate change also relies on individual efforts, from buying more energy efficient appliances to reducing consumption, but people are often reluctant to comply in the short-term, even if their long-term interests are better served through this behaviour.

Given these factors, it is not surprising that public policy on climate change has been, at best, uneven. For one thing, even if there is agreement that the key to dealing with climate change is controlling emissions, there are different mixes of policy instruments to tackle the problem: improved "green" technology, carbon taxes, regulated limits to industrial emissions, pollution trading systems, energy conservation, subsidies, or carbon capture. A second problem is that the sheer scope and impact of climate change policy inevitably gives it a highly political charge. Any realistic attempt to reduce emissions will have different regional and sectoral effects, pitting Alberta's energy industry against central Canada's manufacturing sector. The potential impact on business means that industrial and resource lobbies have been active in resisting government intervention. The new public fixation on climate change, paradoxically, has induced political parties to try to outbid each other in promising to meet the now emblematic "Kyoto" targets.

By any objective standard, those targets were unrealistic to begin with. In the 1997 negotiations on the protocol, the Chrétien government decided that it needed to adopt domestic targets that were "better" than those proposed by the United States. Canada went into the negotiations with a federal-provincial agreement to reduce emissions to 1990 levels by 2008–12. This alone would have been challenging, since emissions had increased by 13 percent between 1990 and 1997 (Simpson, Jaccard, Rivers, 2007, p. 35). On the eve of the negotiations, apparently with little or no analysis to gauge what the effects might be, Ottawa unilaterally announced that its new position would be to reduce emissions in 2008–2012 by 3 percent *below* 1990 levels. In the heat of negotiations, when the Americans increased their targets, Canada was forced, again without much consideration of the policy implications or of implementation, to increase its target to 6 percent *below* 1990 levels. Canada finally ratified the treaty in 2002, in the teeth of provincial and business opposition, as well as the withdrawal of the United States and Australia, and the non-participation of China and India. Various climate change policies were announced in the wake of Kyoto, even while Canada's emissions in 2005 had grown to be 25 percent higher than they had been in 1990.

The federal Conservative government had placed a low priority on environmental policy in the 2006 election campaign, but quickly realized that climate change was a potential wedge issue that might be used against it by the eco-friendly Dion Liberals. In April 2007, the government released a study showing that it would be impossible to meet Canada's Kyoto targets without incurring a severe recession, and it announced a new set of targets and policies to deal with the issue. The new target was a reduction in emissions by 2020 to 20 percent below 2006 levels, with 50 to 70 percent reductions by 2050. Since Canada had already missed its Kyoto targets by a wide margin at this point, the new targets actually were a dilution of the country's original, if unrealistic, goals under Kyoto. The policy instruments the government proposed were somewhat more robust that previous attempts at exhortation and subsidies: there would be regulated caps on large industrial emitters, new standards for automobiles and trucks, a cap-and-trade system for carbon, and a plan for carbon capture (Government of Canada, 2006). In response, the federal Liberals released their own plan on June 19, 2008 to introduce a national carbon tax in the amount of over $15 billion over four years, offset by a "green shift" in personal and corporate income taxes in the same amount. The tax would apply to all carbon emissions (except gas at the pump) and would also include the country's 700 or so "large emitters." The party was clearly nailing its colours to the mast, hoping that its carbon tax plan would create a cross-party coalition and outflank the Conservatives. It was a bold, and ultimately unsuccessful move (the Liberals lost the 2008 election), but underscored how important the environment had become as a policy issue in Canada.

The importance of dealing with climate change has assumed an almost universal consensus, and no government can appear to ignore it. The policy battleground will not be over the nature of the problem any longer, as it was two decades ago, but on how best to realistically deal with it in a context of skyrocketing fuel costs. New (for Canada) policy tools such as cap-and-trade systems and carbon taxes are now on the table, and the issue can be expected to retain its prominence and visibility in the next few years, perhaps even rivaling health care as a Canadian policy preoccupation.

HEALTH CARE

There is perhaps no issue more central to most Canadians than health care. It regularly tops the polls as a matter of public concern, and is a key issue in almost every provincial and federal election. But it is an issue like no other. In the last weeks of the 2004 federal election campaign, for example, Liberal attack ads targeted the Conservatives over value issues such as same-sex marriage and gun control, but essentially reduced its entire campaign pitch to hospital waiting lists and allegations that the Conservatives would privatize health care. For their part, all three major opposition parties (including the Conservatives) pledged to protect and extend health care. Over the five-week campaign, health care was elevated to more than just a key social policy; it was made emblematic of Canadian values, and by implication, anyone who did not support the current configuration of services was somehow "un-Canadian." This line of argument was first developed in the Romanow Commission on health care, which argued that public health care was not merely a service, but a distinguishing characteristic of Canada, a "sacred trust":

> In their discussions with me, Canadians have been clear that they still strongly support the core values on which our health care system is premised—equity, fairness and solidarity. These values are tied to their understanding of citizenship. Canadians consider equal and timely access to medically necessary health care services on the basis of need as a right of citizenship, not a privilege of status or wealth. Building from these values, Canadians have come to view their health care system as a national program, delivered locally but structured on intergovernmental collaboration and a mutual understanding of values. They want and expect their governments to work together to ensure that the policies and programs that define medicare remain true to these values. (Commission on the Future of Health Care in Canada, 2002, p. xvi)

Health care promises to be the Canadian public policy issue for the foreseeable future for several reasons. Perhaps the most pressing is its sheer cost. It is approaching 50 percent of most provincial budgets, and has been increasing at rates of about 8 percent a year. This was the reason behind the Ontario government's 2004 decision to introduce highly unpopular health premiums—unless something was done to either generate more money for the system or contain it, there would be only one item in the provincial budget. It has also been costly for the federal government. The Health Accord signed by Prime Minister Chrétien and the provincial premiers in 2003 promised to pump almost $39 billion more into the system over five years. Despite that pledge, the Martin government promised another $10 billion over two years to fix health care "for a generation" and deal with waiting lists. The federal Conservatives fought the 2006 election campaign on a promise of "patient wait times guarantees." In April 2007 the Prime Minister announced that all provinces and territories had agreed to establish Patient Wait Times Guarantees by 2010 (Office of Prime Minister, April 4, 2007). Some $600 million would be put into a Trust to help fund the initiative, which guarantees "timely access to health care in at least one of the following priority areas, either cancer care, hip and knee replacement, cardiac care, diagnostic imaging, cataract surgeries, or primary care. These areas have been selected by each province and territory based on their priorities, capacity and different starting points" (ibid.). The guarantee was itself driven by the Supreme Court's decision in *Chaouilli v. Quebec (Attorney General)* in June 2005, a decision that upheld private health insurance in cases where wait times for procedures were inordinately long (*Chaouilli*, 2005).

Governments are dealing with a system that is getting increasingly expensive. These costs are driven by an ageing population (the more elderly tend to draw more health resources) and increasingly effective but expensive technology. As the population ages, it can be expected that health costs will continue to increase. This is a "slow" crisis—very different from the ones discussed in Chapter 8—that builds and builds, generates constant public anxiety, and for which there does not appear to be any easy solution. *Chaouilli* at least opened a small discussion on the role of the private sector in health services, but each of the provinces has adopted a different mix and different strategies, even while assiduously avoiding any implication that the system is anything but completely public (Boychuck, 2007).

To some extent Canadians, and their leaders, have painted themselves into a corner on this policy issue by elevating its public character to almost religious significance. For example, it is no accident that a key recommendation of the Romanow Commission was a Canada Health "Covenant." Canada is virtually alone in the developed world in outlawing some version of a parallel private system of health care, usually covered by private insurance (*Chaouilli* applies only in Quebec). Ironically, despite the rhetoric, substantial portions of the system are "private" in the sense that they are for-profit but reimbursed or paid for by public funds. Hospitals are the most visible, and completely public (in the sense that they are run on a nonprofit basis, and services are free to patients and covered through provincial payments) elements of the system, but even they contract out ancillary services (e.g., laundry) to private firms. Virtually all physicians in Canada are effectively small businesses, since doctors work for themselves and not the state; their services are simply reimbursed on a fee-for-service basis. Services such as laboratory testing, X-rays, and medical imaging are increasingly performed by private firms, again which are reimbursed with public funds. Most famously, abortion clinics, like those owned by Henry Morgentaler, are private, as are some MRI clinics. In short, the Canadian system is actually a blend of public and private, and there is nothing in the Canada Health Act or the Constitution that forbids private provision, as long as it is covered by public funds.

Despite this reality, the overwhelming "idea in good currency" in Canada is that the system is almost entirely public, and that any element of private provision would undermine its foundations. The Romanow Commission offered forty-seven recommendations, most of which were geared to higher spending across the system: new services like home care; specific needs like rural and Aboriginal communities; and better coordination, information sharing, and performance measurement. These are laudable, and if ever implemented will both expand the system and make it more transparent and accountable. But a significant range of options that would still preserve a public system while allowing more flexibility for private purposes is off the policy table.

The Romanow Commission argued that Canadians could have an enhanced health care system if they were prepared to pay for it, and also argued that they could pay for it. Maybe. But the sheer cost of increasing health care services in competition with other public policy priorities like cities, security, defence, and infrastructure promises to make health care a controversial issue for years to come. The additional health resources channeled from Ottawa to the provinces under the last three governments have reduced the pressure somewhat, but governments like British Columbia openly mused about possibly relying more on the private sector, even while saying that this would not violate the Canada Health Act (Boychuk, 2007, p. 175).

SECURITY IN A THREATENING GLOBAL ENVIRONMENT

Governments have a basic responsibility to protect their societies from external threat; put more positively, they have an obligation to maintain and protect the security of their citizens. The new twist on the security agenda comes from the new types of threats that exist in the contemporary world, particularly since 9/11. Security can be now seen in two related dimensions: **human security** and terrorism. Since the mid-1990s Canada's foreign policy has emphasized the changing nature of human security in a globalized world, and indeed the concept of human security has become a centrepiece of Canada's actions abroad:

> Canada's human security policies are based on the premise that the safety of individuals should be at the heart of international efforts to promote peace and security. . . . The emphasis that the government of Canada has brought to the international strengthening of democracy since the April 2006 Speech from the Throne also reflects a belief that individuals should be the centrepiece of international efforts to build peace and security. In the long run, states are more stable when they provide citizens a degree of influence over decisions that affect their lives. (Department of Foreign Affairs and International Trade, 2008)

To some degree, the concept of human security is a partisan one, congenial to a Liberal government and pushed hard by a Minister of Foreign Affairs and with a strong humanitarian bent in the mid-1990s. But other governments have been forced to face similar realizations that something important has changed in the way that we conceive security in a new global context. The EU had to deal with the eruption of ethnic conflicts in the former Yugoslavia mere hours from its borders. The same ethnic conflicts have generated massive movements of people throughout Eurasia. The AIDS epidemic in Africa is threatening to swamp all current aid and development programs in the region by Western states. Environmental disasters and species extinction threaten populations in both the countries in which they occur and countries close in location and in trade. The Canadian government's response to these threats in the late 1990s was the concept of human security and "soft power." That rhetoric has been overshadowed by the current government's strong military commitment to Afghanistan, but this is not in contradiction to an international human security policy that seeks the following objectives: support democratic transitions through elaborating a citizen-focused approach to democracy building; the legal and physical protection of civilians; building capacity for multilateral and regional human rights organizations; dealing with children in armed conflict; strengthening the normative consensus of the responsibility to protect; pushing forward on corporate social responsibility; addressing gender issues.

Ethics, Accountability, and Good Governance

We mentioned earlier that the dominant tradition in policy studies has been instrumentalist, a focus on means and ends. Interestingly, discussions have turned increasingly to considerations of values and ethics in the public sector as a means to support good governance. This is not entirely new of course, with codes of ethics having been promoted by various professional associations of public servants for some years. But as we have argued throughout this book, there are some new pressures that have concentrated attention on this field, pressures that began building as early as the early 1980s and blossomed in the last decade (Kernaghan, 1996). One is the decreasing trust and faith in government among Canadian citizens. Barely 60 percent of eligible voters cast a ballot in the 2004 and 2006 federal elections. A way of addressing that is to ensure that public servants—either making or implementing policy—conduct themselves to the highest standards. Another pressure has been the effects of downsizing on morale. Encouraging public servants to cleave to strong values has been a way to forestall public sector workers' cynicism and bitterness. Finally, the emphasis on entrepreneurship, innovation, and flexibility in public sector organizations has meant less detailed oversight of the work done by public servants, fewer rules and minute procedures, and a greater focus on outcomes and performance—witness the HRDC and Groupaction scandals. These led directly to the Federal Accountability Act, the Harper government's signature piece of legislation that dramatically raised the bar on ethics and probity in government. In fact, the combination of instruments used in the Accountability Act, from whistleblowers' legislation, audit committees, accounting officers, new Parliamentary watchdogs and commissioners, and a strong emphasis on codes of ethics has severely dampened enthusiasm for flexibility and innovation within the federal public service.

The modern focus on ethics, accountability, and good governance started in 1995, when the Clerk of the Privy Council appointed nine Deputy Ministers Task Forces to deal with issues that would arise through the Program Review exercise. One of those task forces was dedicated to public sector values and ethics, reflecting the concern about ethics expressed in the Auditor General's 1995 annual report (Auditor General 1995, Chap. 1). The task force's report, entitled *A Strong Foundation* (Canadian Centre for Management Development, 2000) highlighted some of the new pressures on the public service that were creating the need to refocus on values and ethics:

> Many public servants were shocked, and their faith in public service values was shaken, both by the *fact* of downsizing—that it was done at all—and by the way it was done. Many public servants believe that an implicit employment contract and the commitment to security of tenure were breached by personnel reductions, and by the way they were carried out. Explicit union contracts were overridden by legislation. Disrespect for public servants was read into many announcements or statements that seemed to make them scapegoats, implying they were unproductive, bureaucratic and a major reason for the problems of

the debt and public distrust of government. Some downsizing processes were perceived as punitive, secretive, and capricious, in an environment where the main purpose was to cut, and there was little interest in enforcing rules or due process to protect people. Ruthlessness, some public servants believe, was permitted, or even rewarded at certain times. To them, it appears that power counted for more than values and ethics, and a focus on short-term results crowded out concern for public policy purposes and values. (Canadian Centre for Management Development, 2000, p. 32)

Many public servants are trying to cope with issues of increasing complexity, issues moving at increasing velocity that allow them less and less time for action. They are under pressure to downsize, reorganize, and, at the same time, increase performance with reduced resources. The demands of ministers and citizens are growing, as are those of employees. There are also growing (and welcome) demands from the centre of government to participate in corporate and horizontal activities. (Canadian Centre for Management Development, 2000, p. 72)

The Task Force concluded that public service values can be clustered in four families or categories: democratic values, professional values, ethical values, and people values. Democratic values are the foundation for all the rest and refer to "helping ministers, under law and the Constitution, to serve the public interest." They hinge on the concept of accountability within a parliamentary regime, on providing "fearless advice" to ministers and faithfully carrying out their decisions under the law and the Constitution. Professional values are closely related and include "excellence, professional competence, continuous improvement, merit, effectiveness, economy, frankness, objectivity and impartiality in advice, speaking truth to power, balancing complexity, and fidelity to the public trust" (Canadian Centre for Management Development, 2000, pp. 67–68). They also entail some "new" values such as innovation, creativity, client service, partnership, and networking. Ethical values include "integrity, honesty, impartiality, taking responsibility and being accountable, probity, prudence, fairness, equity, objectivity, disinterestedness, selflessness, trustworthiness, discretion, respect for law and due process, and the careful stewardship of public resources" (Canadian Centre for Management Development, 2000, p. 69). Finally, people values is a category that touches on how we relate to others and includes such things as courage, trust, integrity, reasonableness, and decency. The Tait report laid the foundation for the federal government's June 2003 Values and Ethics Code; it relied on the same categorization of values and also dealt with conflict of interest issues (Office of Public Service Values and Ethics, 2003).

In addressing ethical issues related to changes in the nature of the public sector, Canada is of course dealing with a more general problem. The OECD flagged precisely the same set of concerns:

> Public servants operate in a changing world. The nameless, faceless public servant is becoming a relic of the past. Greater transparency in government operations, through public access to official information, when coupled with an increasingly zealous media, and well organised interest groups, means that public servants today work in a virtual "fishbowl." Their actions are more visible and publicised as are their mistakes and misdemeanours. Moreover, they face pressures from increased public expectations about the quality of public services and their capacities to deliver them. This pressure is driven partly by governments' own attempts to publicly state standards to be achieved (through Citizen's Charters for example). If these standards are not met, the result is public dissatisfaction.
>
> Public management reform itself has changed the internal environment in which public servants operate. In some countries individual government departments now enjoy substantial autonomy. This has led to concerns that systems of "professional socialisation," that is, the inculcation of public service values across the public sector, are breaking down as departments define their own "corporate culture," standards and ways of operating. This breakdown is compounded by more recruitment from the private sector. The old style coherent public service culture or ethos may be disappearing. In any case, traditional public service values may need to be amended as countries move away from an emphasis on strict compliance with rules and procedures, towards considerations such as "efficiency and effectiveness," "value for money," "service to the citizen," and "equal opportunities." For example, is it unethical to waste taxpayers' money or give bad service? (Organisation for Economic Co-operation and Development, 2000)

Like the Canadian Task Force, the OECD recognizes the limitations of rules-based enforcement and the importance of overlapping institutional frameworks, organizational culture, and individual practice. In its work with member countries to deal with the problems of public sector ethics and corruption, the OECD uses the concept of an "ethics infrastructure," which is reproduced in detail in Box 9.1 on page 420.

Much like the Accountability Act itself, the focus has remained on ethics but has been broadened quite considerably to deal with a wider range of issues concerning probity in the public sector. For example, the

BOX 9.1   OECD ELEMENTS OF AN ETHICS INFRASTRUCTURE

The following eight key elements comprise a sound Ethics Infrastructure:

POLITICAL COMMITMENT AND ETHICAL LEADERSHIP

In the absence of sustained political commitment to ethical behaviour in the administration, efforts to encourage such behaviour will be in vain. Attempts to improve public sector ethics in OECD countries have been sponsored at the highest political levels, such as the approval of comprehensive anti-corruption strategies and programme requested by the President in Mexico and the Republic of Korea, or the Government Programme to Promote Transparency and Fight Against Corruption adopted by the Government of Hungary in 2003. Other actions, such as the integrity measures sponsored by the Minister of the Interior in the Netherlands in 1995 or the ten inquiries of the Committee on Standards in Public Life since it was set up in 1994 by the Prime Minister in the United Kingdom, have demonstrated strong political support. Furthermore, political leaders also serve as important role models. This is also true for senior public officials who should set a positive example for other employees.

WORKABLE CODES OF CONDUCT

Codes of conduct play a vital role in stating the expected standards of behaviour, particularly in OECD countries that have reduced the rules applying to public servants and have adopted more "managerial" styles of public management. Some countries (e.g. New Zealand, the United Kingdom) chose a broad public service code of conduct from which individual agencies design a purpose-built code to reflect their particular objectives and mission. In other countries (e.g. Netherlands, Norway), codes are all agency-based. The ethical issues confronting an employee of a defence ministry might vary significantly from those facing social security officials. Criticisms of codes include being too specific or too general, unworkable, unused, unknown or merely that simplistic statements of rules are not the ideal medium for answering complicated ethical dilemmas faced by public servants.

PROFESSIONAL SOCIALISATION MECHANISMS

However, the content of the codes of conduct or even legal provisions remains simply words on paper, if it is not adequately communicated and inculcated. Socialisation mechanisms are the processes by which public servants learn and adopt ethical norms, standards of conduct, and public service values. Training—both induction and ongoing—is an essential element to raise ethics awareness and develop skills capable of solving ethical dilemmas. Ethics, for example, now constitutes an integral part of the initial training of future managers in Belgium, whereas all senior private sector entrants to the civil service in the United Kingdom focus on ethics issues in their mandatory induction training. In the same way, training on vulnerable areas can help public servants solve ethical dilemmas by defining practices for managing organisational and strategic risks proactively.

SUPPORTIVE PUBLIC SERVICE CONDITIONS

The high standards of ethical conduct expected of public officials are one side of the coin. The other side is a "package" which provides decent working and living conditions for the "servants of the public". This "package" consists of such basic elements as sufficient job security, prospect of possible promotion and career, fair remuneration or social appreciation. Fair and impartial human resources management policies could ensure that the selection and promotion processes in the public sector would be based on general professional requirements, and that other factors such as, for example direct political interventions, would be minimised. If public servants are feeling underpaid, overworked and insecure, then they are less likely to embrace initiatives to improve performance including in the ethical domain.

ETHICS CO-ORDINATING BODY

These take various forms—parliamentary committees, central government agencies, or specially created bodies—and assume various functions: "watchdog" including investigation, such as France's permanent anti-corruption investigation commission, Korea Independent Commission Against Corruption, or the New South Wales Independent Commission Against Corruption in Australia; "general promoter" of public sector ethics, a role performed by the Department of Employers Affairs in Norway and the New Zealand State Services Commission; "counsellor and advisor", such as the United States Office of Government Ethics and the Canadian Ethics

BOX 9.1 (continued)

Commissioner that also plays the role of "watchdog"; or "permanent ethics workshop" like the Committee on Standards in Public Life in the United Kingdom. The existence of a co-ordinating body should not, however, be construed as absolving departments and managers of the responsibility for ensuring ethical conduct within their jurisdictions.

EFFECTIVE LEGAL FRAMEWORK

The legal framework is the "teeth" of the overall ethics infrastructure. Laws and regulations define the basic standards of behaviour for public servants and enforce them through systems of investigation and prosecution. In reviewing its legal framework, a country must check that existing criminal codes and civil service laws, conflict-of-interest statutes and other regulations which apply to public servants are clear and consistent. A prominent effort is the implementation of the National Public Service Ethics Law in Japan, the country's first such legislation (passed in August 1999 and taking effect in April 2000). This law basically bans public servants from receiving gifts and/or entertainment from private companies under their jurisdiction. Furthermore, senior officials in the central government will be required to report gifts or entertainment worth more than 5 000 yens, with some in higher positions required to report their stock and income transactions as well. In Central Europe, Poland adopted a law requiring all public officials to declare their financial assets, property and business capital, whereas Hungary introduced in 2001 a wide-range property declaration system for civil servants and adopted in 2003 a specific act on ensuring transparency of public expenses.

EFFICIENT ACCOUNTABILITY AND CONTROL MECHANISMS

Accountability and control mechanisms encourage ethical behaviour by making unethical actions hard to accomplish and easy to detect. Accountability mechanisms set guidelines for government activities, for checking that results have been achieved, and for checking that due process has been observed. They include internal administrative procedures (requirements that activities or requests be recorded in writing), comprehensive processes such as audits and evaluations of an agency's performance, or new forms of procedures such as whistle-blowing (which can encourage public servants to expose wrongdoing committed by others or to say no when asked to do something inappropriate). They might also be external to the public service: for example, oversight mechanisms such as legislative or parliamentary committees.

ACTIVE CIVIL SOCIETY

Ethics is everybody's responsibility, including that of an assertive media, which through its probing reporting helps to raise awareness among citizens and act as watchdog over the actions of public officials. Freedom of information laws, now present in 28 out of 30 OECD countries (most recently adopted in Mexico in 2002 and Switzerland in 2004) can institutionalise and support public awareness and responsiveness.

SOURCE: Organisation of Economic Development and Cooperation (2005). *Public Sector Integrity: A Framework for Assessment.* Annex I.A1. Paris: OECD.

OECD moved from ethics per se to developing standards on anti-corruption, bribery, transparency around lobbying, integrity in public procurement, and conflict of interest (Organisation for Economic Cooperation and Development, 2007). The Accountability Act also contains similar provisions on lobbying and procurement, values and ethics, public integrity and transparency and disclosure. This is broadly consistent with the argument made in Chapter 5 that in recent years there has been a rediscovery of the special and demanding qualities of the public sector and the public service. Values and ethics were a key theme of the 1990s and into the early 2000s, but as private as well as public sector scandals appeared to multiply, as demands continued to grow on government, and as a series of events from terrorist attacks to public safety to epidemics and safe drinking water dominated the headlines, a new respect and appreciation for the public sector and good governance began to emerge. As we argued, not without some caution and some skepticism, but the mood by 2006 was quite different from what it had been a decade before. With the new appreciation of the importance of good governance came an appreciation of the need to ensure that every aspect of behaviour in the public sector had to meet the highest standards. For example, Canadian law has recognized that the standards for conflict of interest for public servants are stricter than those for persons in the private sector:

> In setting a high standard for both apparent and actual government integrity, the Courts distinguish this from the standard that applies outside government. "[G]iven the heavy trust and

responsibility taken on by the holding of a public office or employ, it is appropriate that government officials are correspondingly held to codes of conduct which, for an ordinary person, would be quite severe". The expectation that public servants recognize and observe this is stated by the Supreme Court in *Fraser* in the following way: "A person entering the public service or one already employed there must know, or at least be deemed to know, that employment in the public service involves acceptance of certain restraints".

This distinction between working in the public sector and in the private sector was addressed by the Federal Court of Appeal (*Threader*). Here, the public servant who had been disciplined on the ground of an apparent conflict of interest argued that the appearance of a conflict of interest cannot, in law, support disciplinary action. The argument was based on private sector law, under which "only an actual conflict of interest supports dismissal for cause". The Court emphatically rejected this argument, underlining the higher standards expected of the public service. (Canada Public Service Agency, 2008)

Benchmarking the Policy Process

It is difficult to develop standards for "good policy" in terms of specific programs and instruments. As we argued earlier in the book, there is usually agreement about broad objectives such as reducing poverty or crime but often wide disagreements about the problem situation and the right way to tackle those perceived problems. But there is growing agreement on one thing: effective and responsive policies (however defined) are not likely to arise from flawed policy processes. An effective policy process is no guarantee of quality outputs and outcomes, but it helps. Rethinking and reforming the policy process has emerged in recent years as a complement to more general organizational redesign and reform in the public sector, as well as the new emphasis on good governance discussed in Chapter 1. It has several distinct aspects, however. One is the sense that if governments downsize and partner, and do fewer things directly themselves, there will be greater emphasis on their capacity to develop policy objectives and monitor outcomes. As we noted in Chapter 1, the emphasis on policy capacity is also linked to a sense that the pressures on societies and governments today are increasing and are more intense. Rapid, and rational, response is increasingly important, and well-designed policy frameworks provide a filter and a foundation for concerted action. Another aspect has been the wider public sector reform project itself—in some countries like New Zealand, as we pointed out in Chapter 5, there was a more radical separation of policy advice functions from central administration than has been characteristic of Canada, but the elevation of the policy function proceeded apace in many countries after 2000. Accordingly, there is greater need for benchmarking the policy development function to ensure that it meets recognized standards.

By policy development function, we mean the process of determining and elaborating policy issues or problems, articulating solutions, making recommendations, and calibrating that process with other important ones in government such as the wider priority setting process and expenditure management. We do not include the process of actual decisionmaking and choice of options, which is primarily political and takes place through a host of governmental institutions, from cabinet to legislature. Nor do we include actual implementation or evaluation of selected options. Obviously these are crucial phases in making public policy but entail different sets of standards and techniques. Implementation is a management function and involves administrative skill in combining resources and personnel in the right amounts at the right time to achieve the desired policy or programmatic outcome. Evaluation, by the same token, is normally undertaken within a fairly well-defined framework with relatively clear operational standards (see Chapter 7). Policy development is the "front end" of these processes, though of course it also entails consultations and communications about policy issues from time to time. An effective policy process in the largest sense of the term will be effective at all these stages—policy development (the analysis of the problem and development of options and recommendations), implementation (putting into effect the chosen option and elaborating on its programmatic elements), and evaluation (assessing efficiency and effectiveness). But implementation and evaluation take the option as given, the choice made. Our concern here is to address the first, crucial phase of policy development and ask if there are benchmarks of standards of practice that might improve the way it is conducted.

There are three immediate problems with posing the issue this way. First, as this book has stressed repeatedly, policy development is a mix of craft and science. A good deal of what goes into problem recognition and definition is subjective and not necessarily guided by well-known techniques (indeed, the same point applies even in apparently technical arenas such as cost-benefit evaluation). By definition, something that is craft-based is difficult to improve through better technique. Second, of necessity, policy development touches on some highly politically sensitive issues. It involves "speaking truth to power," and in that sense it may seem that truth will be sacrificed to power, that politics and political orientations are the most important part of developing policy advice. It is obviously true that public servants developing policy advice for a government of one political stripe will offer different advice in some respects to a government of a completely different political stripe. However, that is not the end of the story. Many problems are simply "there" as an empirical reality—the ageing of the population or globalization. From some perspectives these may not be problems, but they do encapsulate forces that no government can really ignore, however it might want to interpret those forces. As well, as we noted in Chapter 3, problem definition does rely on hard research, and this should not be ideologically driven. And finally, while governments and politicians may have strong ideological orientations, that does not mean that they can simply dream up policy options based on these orientations. There is a still a good deal of analytical work that has to go into the mix.

The third problem is that policy development is only in part a process that takes place inside government and between officials and their political masters; it also involves citizens, interest groups, the media, and a host of other actors. It has a wider political/social dimension and embraces the governance system more widely.

These are valid objections and issues, but the fact remains that a major responsibility for governments is to develop policy, and this function is performed in large part in central agencies and departments staffed by professional public servants. Governments have not been blind to the importance of improving the policy development function—we saw various instances throughout the previous chapters where nationally and internationally there have been calls for improved governance and, as part of that, improved policy development and implementation. In the mid-1990s, the governments of Australia and New Zealand, for example, routinely assessed and evaluated the policy development function through "policy management reviews" (Uhr and Mackay, 1996). In April 2000, the Canadian federal government released a report on the law-making process that made explicit reference to improving the process of policy development and advice (Government of Canada, 2000). The report argued, for example, that policymaking could be improved by "challenging the traditional choice of instrument for effecting change; setting clear, objective outcomes and reporting on their results; putting greater emphasis on a balanced analysis; planning policy development better; and finding the most appropriate ways to engage and consult the public." New Zealand has continued to emphasize the policy function among its operational agencies (Chapman and Duncan, 2007), and the Canadian Treasury Board has also underlined the importance of evidence-based analysis in submissions coming from departments (Treasury Board of Canada, 2007).

As we noted in Chapter 1, these early efforts have been magnified in recent years in a growing international interest in good governance, on the assumption that governance is key to economic development and poverty reduction. A recent OECD study noted that in the last fifteen years there has been "a veritable explosion in interest in the quality of "governance" in the developing world," accompanied by "equally explosive growth in the use of quantitative governance *indicators . . .*" (Arndt and Oman, 2006, p. 13, emphasis in original). The UNDP notes: "There is an increasing demand from developing country governments, civil society organisations and donor agencies to measure different aspects of democracy, human rights and governance. This demand has resulted in a tremendous growth in indicator sources, which are used to measure the performance of governments, the quality of public institutions, as well as people's perceptions of various aspects of governance" (UNDP, n.d.). There are various drivers for this phenomenon, the most recent being the adoption of the Millennium Development Goals (MDGs), with requirements of specific indicators of recipient government performance. The MDGs are supported through *Global Monitoring Reports,* which include reviews of governance (Levy, 2007). The World Bank Institute estimated in 2006 that there were some 140 user-accessible sets of governance indicators, in turn made up of thousands of individual indicators. The more visible ones are well-known: Transparency International's Corruption Perceptions Index (CPI), Freedom House's "Freedom in the World," the World Bank's Country Policy and Institutions Assessments (CPIAs), the International Country Risk Guide (ICRG), and the World Bank Institute's "KKZ" indicators. One of the interesting things about these indicators is that they contain strong and often quite explicit judgments about what constitutes good governance and good policymaking, and many of them even rank countries either in international league tables or at least in broad categories of "better" or "worse."

One of the most widely cited governance indicators comes from the World Bank Institute, and is produced by Daniel Kaufmann, Aart Kray, and Massimo Mastruzzi (originally, the third author was Pablo Zoido-Lobatón—hence the reference to the "KKZ" indicators). It aggregates hundreds of perception based indicators produced by over 30 organizations into six dimensions of governance: (1) voice and accountability, (2) political stability, (3) government effectiveness, (4) regulatory quality, (5) rule of law, and (6) control of corruption. "Government effectiveness," for example, is defined by the authors as "measuring the quality of public services, the quality of the civil service and the degree of its independence from political pressures, the quality of policy formulation and implementation, and the credibility of the government's commitment to such policies" (Kaufmann, Kray, Mastruzzi, 2007, p. 3). Consulting dozens of data sources (primarily surveys), and selecting questions from those surveys that cast light on each dimension, KKZ then aggregates these to a single indicator. For example, government effectiveness concretely reflects questions about government stability, the quality of e-government, infrastructure, schools, satisfaction

BOX 9.2   CIVIL SERVICE MANAGEMENT ACTIONABLE INDICATORS

OBJECTIVE	INDICATOR
Competition in recruitment and selection	Percentage of civil service (CS) vacancies filled through advertised, competitive procedures
Turnover unrelated to changes in political leadership	Quarterly CS turnover rates plotted against changes in political leadership
Effective performance evaluation practices	Percentage of CS staff for whom annual performance evaluations were completed
	Percentage of CS performance evaluations falling in each rating category

SOURCE: B. Levy (2007). *Governance reform: Bridging monitoring and action.* Washington, D.C.: The World Bank, Box 2.3.

with highways and other services. Most crucially, it also reflects measures on the "quality of bureaucracy" with questions about competence, public service vulnerability to political pressure, excessive red tape. Levy (2007, p. 44) provides another example from a World Bank project in several countries to yield actionable and non-subjective indicators to monitor civil service reform. Note that these indicators are for objectives that are presumed to be positive and beneficial for governance (see Box 9.2).

As Levy (p. 42) notes, "In the early 1980s and early 1990s, a first generation of administrative reform focused principally on scaling back the bloated apparatus of government. In the 1990s, attention shifted toward improving administrative capability. Some consensus has been generated on the characteristics of an effective public administration. . . . [one of which is] Well-functioning mechanisms for policy coordination that ensure policy consistency across departmental boundaries and facilitate clear decisions on policy and spending priorities."

Our approach to good governance is guided by the conviction that policy development, despite its messiness, does have some identifiable stages or phases, principally moving through problem identification, analysis of issues, development of options, and finally recommendations based both on analysis and other input in the process. As well, we have to acknowledge the balance of craft and skill that defines policy development work. A crucial issue then is how to enhance craft, how to build in mechanisms that will improve a process that resists easy categorization or measurement, despite recent attempts at developing more precise indicators. And finally, we need to acknowledge that policy work is part of a larger democratic conversation and that it should reflect strong democratic values as well as contribute to them. In these terms then, we can suggest several benchmarks that, while they will not guarantee good policy design, will certainly contribute to it:

Training of policy development staff: This should not be occasional but continuous. Policy development staff have to know what the policy process is about, the different elements of policy design and implementation and evaluation, and various techniques for both the development of policy ideas and communication. They should have a solid grounding in policy analysis and administration.

Well-organized information and research resources: Having information, being able to access it quickly, and organizing it well, is a basic requirement of good policy work. As we noted earlier in this book, there are huge new developments in social networking technology that are enabling much better pooling of and access to information.

A balance of scanning and service orientations: Good policy work not only requires immediate and effective responses to demands from political masters but also demands the scanning of the political and social environment to see what is coming up in the near to medium term. Policy work needs to be tactical as well as strategic.

Horizontal and integrated: The policy function is a whole-of-government process, mapping out broad, consistent priorities and linking them to spending priorities. As policy problems become more complex and multi-dimensional, there needs to be better horizontal policy coordination across departments, pooling knowledge and sharing perspectives.

Rigour and honesty: Policy development, as we noted above, is at the intersection of political necessity and analytical research. Policy analysts should keep that balance in mind and be wary of sacrificing professional standards and rigour for political purposes. The concepts of "speaking truth to power" and offering "fearless advice" capture this quality.

Transparency and consultation: Confidentiality is often unavoidable as policy problems and options are being debated and defined. To the greatest extent possible, however, policy development work should hear from all sides, consult widely both within and outside government, and put out as much information as possible for public discussion, debate, and review. This builds on the wisdom of crowds, the capacity of many independent and dispersed minds with diverse information resources to arrive at surprisingly good judgments.

Develop a good challenge function: Further to the previous point, the policy development process should be designed in such a way as to incorporate challenge and debate and testing—this is a key ingredient for ventilating policy ideas, avoiding group think, exposing unacknowledged errors, and for working through limitations and unexpected design flaws.

Policymaking is nothing less than developing public responses, primarily through government but in close cooperation with citizens and other organizations in the private sector and civil society to public problems. Doing it well matters for lots of reasons, not least because the quality of the responses affects our everyday lives as well as the texture of our democracy. In the end, governance matters, and effective public policy is a crucial ingredient of good governance.

KEY TERMS

governance—the process of governing or steering complex systems in cooperation with a variety of other actors

human security—a broader definition of international security that goes beyond geo-political and military considerations to consider threats to humanity and ordinary citizens such as environmental degradation, international crime, and child labour

instrumentalism—a philosophical orientation that tries to make a sharp distinction between means and ends

FURTHER READINGS

Commission on the Future of Health Care in Canada. (2002). *Building on values: The future of health care in Canada*. Retrieved April 1, 2008, from http://www.hc-sc.gc.ca/english/care/romanow/hcc0023.html

Levy, B. (2007). *Governance reform: Bridging monitoring and action*. Washington, D.C.: The World Bank.

Peters, B. G. (2001). *The future of governing*. 2nd. Ed. Lawrence: University of Kansas.

Throne Speeches, Policy Documents and Reports (Privy Council) (Canada) Retrieved April 1, 2008, from http://www.pco-bcp.gc.ca/list-liste.asp?lang=eng&Page=search&txtSearch=speech+from+the+throne&rdoSearch=0&txtFrom=&txtTo=&chkAllCategories=%2F&cmdSearch=Search

REFERENCES

Arndt, C. and Oman, C. (2006). *Uses and abuses of governance indicators*. Paris: OECD, Development Centre Studies.

Auditor General of Canada. (1995). *Annual report, 1995*. Retrieved March 31, 2008, from http://www.oag-bvg.gc.ca/domino/reports.nsf/html/95menu_e.html

Boychuck, G. W. (2007). Patience! . . . Wait time guarantees and conservative health care policy. In G. B. Doern (Ed.), *How Ottawa spends, 2007–2008: The Harper Conservatives—Climate of change* (pp. 161–79). Montreal and Kingston: McGill-Queen's University Press.

Canada Public Service Agency. (2008). *Apparent conflict of interest*. Office of Public Service Values and Ethics. Retrieved on March 31, 2008, from http://www.psagency-agencefp.gc.ca/veo-bve/publications/aci-cia_e.asp

Canadian Centre for Management Development. (2000). *A strong foundation: Report of the task force on public service values and ethics*. [CCMD is now the Canada School of Public Service.] Retrieved April 1, 2008, from http://www.csps-efpc.gc.ca/Research/publications/html/p91/1_e.html

Chaouilli v. Quebec (Attorney General). (2005). 1 S. C, R. 791, 2005 SCC 35. Retrieved on March 31, 2008, from http://scc.lexum.umontreal.ca/en/2005/2005scc35/2005scc35.html

Chapman, J., and Duncan, G. (2007). Is there now a new 'New Zealand Model'? *Public Management Review*, 9 (1), pp. 1–25.

Commission on the Future of Health Care in Canada. (2002). *Building on values: The future of health care in Canada*. Retrieved April 1, 2008, from http://www.hc-sc.gc.ca/english/care/romanow/hcc0023.html

Department of Foreign Affairs and International Trade (Canada). (2008). *Glyn Berry program by thematic focus: Democratic transitions*. Retrieved March 31, 2008, from http://geo.international.gc.ca/cip-pic/cip-pic/gbpbythematicfocus-en.aspx

Doern, G. B. (1994). *The road to better public services: Progress and constraints in five Canadian federal agencies.* Montreal: Institute for Research on Public Policy.

Gore, Al (2006). *An inconvenient truth: The planetary emergency of global warming and what we can do about it.* Emmaus, PA: Rodale.

Government of Canada. (2006). *Canada's fourth national report on climate change: Actions to meet commitments under the United Nations Framework Convention on Climate Change.* Retrieved on June 17, 2006 from http://www.ec.gc.ca/climate/4th_Report_on_CC_e.pdf

Government of Canada (Privy Council Office). (2000). *Report on lawmaking and governance: A summary of discussions held by the deputy ministers' challenge team on law-making and governance.* Retrieved April 1, 2008, from http://www.tbs-sct.gc.ca/ri-qr/ra-ar/default.asp@language=e&page=publications&sub=reportonlawmakingandgove.htm

Gow, J. I. (1995, Winter). Frauds and victims: Some difficulties in applying the notion of service to the clientele in the public sector. *Canadian Public Administration*, 38, 557–77.

Howe, P., and Northrup, D. (2000). *Strengthening Canadian democracy: The views of Canadians.* Montreal: Institute for Research on Public Policy.

IPCC (Intergovernmental Panel on Climate Change). (2007). *Climate change 2007: Synthesis report. Summary for Policymakers.* Retrieved on June 16, 2008, from http://www.ipcc.ch/pdf/assessment-report/ar4/syr/ar4_syr_spm.pdf

Kaufmann, D., Kray, A., and Mastruzzi, M. (2007). *Governance matters V: Aggregate and individual government indicators, 1996–2006.* World Bank Policy Research Working Paper 4280. Washington, D.C.: The World Bank.

Kernaghan, K. (1996). *The ethics era in Canadian public administration.* Ottawa: Canadian Centre for Management Development, Research Paper no. 19. Ottawa: Supply and Services Canada.

Levy, B. (2007). *Governance reform: Bridging monitoring and action.* Washington, D.C.: The World Bank.

Mintzberg, H. (1996, May–June). Managing government, governing management. *Harvard Business Review*, pp. 75–83.

Office of the Prime Minister (Canada). (April 4, 2007). *Canada's new government announces patient wait times guarantees.* Retrieved on March 31, 2008, from http://pm.gc.ca/eng/media.asp?id=1611

Office of Public Service Values and Ethics. (2003). Values and ethics code for the public service. Retrieved April 1, 2008, from http://www.psagency-agencefp.gc.ca/veo-bve/index_e.asp

Organisation for Economic Co-operation and Development. (2000). *Pressures affecting public service ethics and conduct.* Paris: OECD.

Organisation for Economic Co-operation and Development. (2007). *OECD guidelines for managing conflict of interest in the public service; Report on implementation.* Retrieved on March 31, 2008, from http://www.oecd.org/dataoecd/18/35/39691164.pdf

Peters, B. G. (2006). *American public policy,* 7th ed. Washington: CQ Press.

Rhodes, R. A. W. (1997). *Understanding governance: Policy networks, governance, reflexivity, and accountability.* Buckingham, UK: Open University Press.

Rhodes, R. A. W. (2007). Understanding governance: Ten years on. *Organization Studies* 28 (8), 1243–64.

Simpson, J., Jaccard, M., and Rivers, N. (2007). *Hot air: Meeting Canada's climate change challenge.* Toronto: McClelland and Stewart.

Treasury Board of Canada (2007). *Management accountability framework assessment—Round V. "Policy and Programs."* Retrieved April 1, 2008, from http://www.tbs-sct.gc.ca/maf-crg/indicators-indicateurs/2007/policies-politiques/policies-politiques_e.asp

Uhr, J., and Mackay, K. (Eds.) (1996). *Evaluating policy advice learning from Commonwealth Experience.* Canberra: Federalism Research Centre, The Australian National University, and Commonwealth Department of Finance.

UNDP (n.d.). *Governance indicators: A user's guide,* 2nd ed. New York: UNDP.

Credits

p. 50: World Trade Organization (2007). *International Trade Statistics 2007.* Chart I.3, p. 2. Retrieved Feb. 2, 2007, from http://www.wto.org/english/res_e/statis_e/its2007_e/its2007_e.pdf.

p. 51: Adapted from Statistics Canada, *Provincial Economic Accounts, 2006 Preliminary Estimates,* Catalogue no. 13-213-PPB, April 2007, pages 324 to 326.

pp. 58–59: Fair World Fair, G8 2007—THERE ARE ALTERNATIVES! www.g8-alternative-summit.org/en/media/Call_1.pdf.

pp. 62–65: Ben Lockwood, Michela Redoano, (2005), *The CSGR Globalisation Index: An Introductory Guide,* Centre for the Study of Globalisation and Regionalisation Working Paper 155/04.

p. 83: K. Kernaghan, *The Post-Bureaucratic Organization and Public Service Values,* March 2000. International Institute of Administrative Studies, 2000, published by Sage Publications Ltd. Reprinted by permission of Copyright Clearance Center.

p. 85: White House (United States) (2007). *The President's Management Agenda: The Scorecard of December 31, 2007.* Retrieved February 15, 2008, from http://www.whitehouse.gov/results/agenda/FY08Q1-SCORECARD.pdf.

p. 91: Treasury Board of Canada Secretariat. *Management Accountability Framework.* © Her majesty the Queen in Right of Canada represented by the President of the Treasury Board, 2003.

pp. 116–117: Dunn, W.N. (2004). *Public Policy Analysis: An Introduction,* 3rd ed. (Englewood Cliffs, NJ: Prentice Hall), Chap. 3.

pp. 118–119: Adapted and amended from Rochefort and Cobb. (1994). "Problem definition: An emerging perspective". In D.A. Rochefort and R.W. Cobb (Eds.), *The politics of problem definition: Shaping the policy agenda* (pp. 1–31). Lawrence: University Press of Kansas.

pp. 149–152: Salamon, Lester M. (Ed.). (2002). *The tools of government: A guide to the new governance.* Oxford: Oxford University Press. By permission of Oxford University Press, Inc.

pp. 175–176: *Report of the Auditor General of Canada – September 2003,* Office of the Auditor General of Canada. Reproduced with the permission of the Minister of Public Works and Government Services, 2008.

p. 181: Excerpted from *What Are Technical Barriers to Trade?* World Trade Organization, http://www.wto.org/english/tratop_e/tbt_e/tbt_e.htm.

p. 184: © Her Majesty The Queen in Right of Canada, Environment Canada, 2008.

p. 209: Sabatier and Mazmanian. (1981). The implementation of public policy: A framework of analysis. In D.A. Mazmanian and P.A. Sabatier (Eds.), *Effective Policy Implementation* (p. 7). Lexington, MA: Lexington Books.

p. 219: *Results for Canadians: A management framework for the Government of Canada* (2000), Treasury Board of Canada. Reprinted with permission of the Government of Canada.

pp. 222–223: Cabinet Office (United Kingdom). (2008). *New standard raises the bar for public services.* Retrieved March 10, 2008, from http://www.cabinetoffice.gov.uk/newsroom/news_releases/2008/080310_new_standard.aspx.

p. 225: I. Joumard et al. *Enhancing the effectiveness of public spending: Experience in OECD countries* (2004). Retrieved March 16, 2008, from http://ideas.repec.org/p/oec/ecoaaa/380-en.html.

p. 229: IPAC. *Innovative Management Award—Themes.* Retrieved March 16, 2008, from http://www.ipac.ca/Award_InnovativeManagementThemes.

pp. 231–232: Denhardt, R.B., and Denhardt, J.V. (2003). *The New Public Service: Serving, Not Steering.* Armonk, N.Y.: M.E. Sharpe.

pp. 232–233: Privy Council Office (Canada). (2008a). *The Public Service of Canada: Too many misperceptions.* Remarks by Kevin Lynch, Clerk of the Privy Council, February 18, 2008.

Retrieved February 26, 2008, from http://www.pco-bcp.gc.ca/index.asp?lang=eng&page=clerkgreffier&sub=clerksspeeches&doc=20080218_e.htm.

pp. 235–236: Government of Canada, *Values and Ethics Code for the Public Service.* 2003. Retrieved March 17, 2008, from http://www.tbs-sct.gc.ca/pubs_pol/hrpubs/TB_851/vec-cve1_e.asp#_Toc46202803.

p. 237: From the report *Citizens First 4*, Exhibit 3.1, p. 18 (2005). Published with permission from the Institute for Citizen-Centred Service and the Institute of Public Administration.

p. 266: Pross, A.P. (1995). Pressure groups: Talking chameleons. In M.S. Whittington and G. Williams (Eds.), *Canadian Politics in the 1990s* (p. 267). Toronto: Nelson Canada.

p. 268: Lindquist, E.A. (1992). Public managers and policy communities: Learning to meet new challenges. *Canadian Public Administration, 35, 135.*

p. 269: Pal, L. (1992). *Public Policy Analysis: An Introduction,* 2nd ed. Toronto: Nelson, p. 112.

p. 272: Sabatier (1993). Policy change over a decade or more. In P. A. Sabatier and H. Jenkins-Smith (Eds.). *Policy Change and Learning: An advocacy coalition approach.* Boulder, CO: Westview, p. 18. See also Sabatier and Jenkins-Smith (1999).

p. 282: Government of Canada. (2007). *Cabinet directive on streamlining regulation.* Retrieved on March 22, 2008, from http://www.regulation.gc.ca/directive/directive-eng.pdf.

pp. 286–287: Commission on the Future of Health Care in Canada. (2002). *Building on values: The future of health care in Canada,* pp. 271–72.

pp. 289–290: Source: http://www.tc.gc.ca/majorissues/APGCI/governance.htm, Transport Canada in July 2007. Reproduced with the permission of the Minister of Public Works and Government Services Canada, 2008.

pp. 290–291: Canadian Council for Public-Private Partnerships. (2008). *Definitions.* Retrieved on March 24, 2008, from http://www.pppcouncil.ca/aboutPPP_definition.asp.

p. 307: Curristine, T. (2005). Program information in the budget process: Results of the OECD 2005 Questionnaire. *OECD Journal on Budgeting, 5(2),* pp. 87–132. Retrieved March 20, 2008, from http://www.oecd.org/dataoecd/13/2/37714836.pdf.

p. 309: American Evaluation Society Guiding Principles for Evaluators, 2008. Retrieved March 20, 2008, from http://www.eval.org/Publications/GuidingPrinciples.asp.

pp. 319–321: Gyarmati, D., de Raaf, S., Nicholson,C., Palameta, B., Hui, T., and MacInnis, M. *Improving Skills, Networks, and Livelihoods Through Community-Based Work: Three-year impacts of the community employment innovation project* (2007a and 2007b). Reprinted with permission of Social Research and Demonstration Corporation.

pp. 362–363: Treasury Board of Canada. (2001a). *Risk management policy.* Retrieved March 31, 2008, from http://www.tbs-sct.gc.ca/pubs_pol/dcgpubs/RiskManagement/riskmanagpol1_e.asp#_Toc457619040.

p. 365: Treasury Board of Canada. (2001b). *Integrated risk management framework.* Retrieved March 31, 2008, from http://www.tbs-sct.gc.ca/pubs_pol/dcgpubs/RiskManagement/rmf-cgr_e.asp.

p. 368: Canadian Centre for Management Development. (2004). *Crisis and Emergency Management: A guide for managers of the public service of Canada.* Table 2 at p. 9. Retrieved April 2, 2008, from http://www.csps-efpc.gc.ca/Research/publications/pdfs/crisis_e.pdf.

pp. 376–379: CBC News (August 24, 2006). *Mad Cow in Canada: The science and the story.* Retrieved March 29, 2008, from http://www.cbc.ca/news/background/madcow/.

pp. 384–388: Public Safety Canada (2007). *Currently Listed Entities.* Retrieved March 30, 2008, from http://www.publicsafety.gc.ca/prg/ns/le/cle-eng.aspx.

p. 419: Organisation for Economic Co-operation and Development. (2000). *Pressures affecting public service ethics and conduct.* Paris: OECD.

pp. 420–423: Organisation of Economic Development and Cooperation (2005). *Public Sector Integrity: A Framework for Assessment.* Annex I.A1. Paris: OECD.

p. 428: B. Levy (2007). *Governance reform: Bridging monitoring and action.* Washington, D.C.: The World Bank, Box 2.3.

Index

Structural approach to network
analysis, 267
Study circles, 284, 295
Subgovernment, 261, 265, 274, 278, 295
Subprime mortgage crisis, 53–54,
129,190
Subsidy, 148, 196
Summative evaluation, 306, 342
Sunk costs, 330, 344
Surpluses (1998–2008), 171–73
Supreme Court of Canada, 2, 78, 108
Surowiecki, J., 25
Sustainability, 326
Sutherland, S. L., 27, 332, 333, 334
Synectics, 116–17, 139

T
Tait Report, 3, 418
Tasers, 113
Task Force on Values and Ethics, 234
Taxation, 148, 177–80
Tax cuts, 174–75, 178
Taxes, 4, 144, 153, 196
Tax expenditure, 196
Tax-Free Savings Account (TFSA), 161
Tax revenues, 177
Taylor, C., 74
Technical Barriers to Trade Agreement
(TBT), 181
Technology, 129, 405. *See also*
Information and communications
technology (ICT)
policy networks and, 275, 276–77
regulation, effects on, 182
Telecommunications and information
revolution, 62–63
Tellier, Paul, 92, 217
Terrorism
international, 129. *See also*
National security
September 11, 2001 attack, 49, 84,
352, 362, 367, 389
Thaler, R. H., and Sunstein, C. R., 192
Thatcher, Margaret, 80, 256
Think tanks, 340, 344
Thomas, P., 26. 293
Thomas, T., 283
Threat events, *see also* Emergencies,
policymaking for
factors in, 353–54
increasing common, 354
Thurow, L. C., 52
Tipping point, 398

Toner, G., 4
Trade liberalization, 56, 98, 180–81
Transfer payments
cuts to, 172, 173
policy on, (2008), 177
Transnational corporations (TNCs),
52–53, 98
Transnational networks, 276
Transparency, 196
decisionmaking and, 186
Transparency International (TI), 34
Transport Canada, 219
Treasury Board (Canada), 12, 219, 220,
221, 426
Action Plan (2008), 177
Getting Government Right, 88–89,
218–19
Government On-Line initiative, 89,
187, 220
management accountability
framework, 91
mandated program evaluation
(1977), 333–34
Results for Canadians, 89,
219–20, 336
True, J. L., Jones, B. D., and Baumgartner,
F. R., 125
Truman, D., 261
Turning the Corner (Canada), 179
Types of evaluation, 308–31

U
U.S.–Canada Power System Outage
Taskforce, 2004, 355
Uhr, J., and Mackay, K., 426
Union of International
Associations, 69
United Kingdom
Charter Mark program, 84–87,
95, 167
Citizen's Charter, 84, 86, 95
joined-up government, 226–27
Next Steps program (1980s-1990s),
84–86, 97, 222
Office of Public Services Reform
(2002), 222
Service First Program, 222–23
social services delivery (2002), 87
United Nations (UN), 17–18, 113, 275
Charter, 64
Human Rights Committee, 76
Universal Declaration of Human
Rights, 19, 64

United States
    Department of Homeland Security
        (DHS), 381–82
    deregulation, 185
    *Innovations in American
        Government,* 228–30
    vouchers, 161
User charges, 163, 178, 196

V

Values, 219
    ethics, and, public service code for,
        235–36
    importance in public policy, 6
    postmaterialist, 190–91, 263, 294
    in public sector, 231, 235–36, 417–18
    renewed emphasis on, 233–36
Values and Ethics Code for the Public
    Service, 3, 418
Van Waarden, F., 270
Vannijnatten, D. L., and MacDonald, D., 5
Vedung, E., 1 58, 152, 155, 158
Vedung, E., and van der Doelen,
    F. C. J., 157
Vertical consistency of policies, 12–13, 38
Violent crime legislation (2008), 8–9
Vogel, D., 60
Vogel, D., and Kagan, R., 60
Voluntary codes, 153, 167, 196
Voter turnout, reduced, 77–78, 282–83
Vouchers, 161, 196

W

Walker, J., 274
Walker, R. B. J., 274
Walker, S., 71
Warrant, 122
Weaver, R. K. and Rockman,
    B. A., 262
Webb, K., 189
Weiss, A., and Woodhouse, E., 24
Weiss, C. H., 25, 311, 316, 323
Western Standard, The,
    75, 77
White House Office of Faith-based and
    Community Initiatives, 82
Wholey, J. S., 308, 310
Wildavsky, A., 15
Wilks, S., and Doern, G. B., 185
Williams, A. D., 240
Williams, J., and Goose, S., 277
Williams, M., 58
Winter, S., 212
World Bank, 33, 49
World Bank Institute, 427
World Health Organization (WHO),
    112, 113
World Trade Organization (WTO), 49,
    57, 181
World view, clash of, 58–60

Y

Young, I., 73